Marx, Critical Theory, and Religion

Studies in Critical Social Sciences Book Series

The Studies in Critical Social Sciences book series, through the publication of original manuscripts and edited volumes, offers insights into the current reality by exploring the content and consequence of power relationships under capitalism, by considering the spaces of opposition and resistance to these changes, and by articulating capitalism with other systems of power and domination—for example race, gender, culture—that have been defining our new age.

Haymarket Books is pleased to be working with Brill Academic Publishers (http://www.brill.nl) to republish the Studies in Critical Social Sciences book series in paperback editions. Titles in this series include:

Culture, Power, and History: Studies in Critical Sociology
Edited by Stephen Pfohl, Aimee Van Wagenen, Patricia Arend, Abigail Brooks, and Denise Leckenby

Dialectic of Solidarity: Labor, Antisemitism, and the Frankfurt School
Mark P. Worrell

The Future of Religion: Toward a Reconciled Society
Edited by Michael R. Ott

Globalization and the Environment
Edited by Andrew Jorgenson and Edward Kick

Hybrid Identities: Theoretical and Empirical Examinations
Edited by Keri E. Iyall Smith and Patricia Leavy

Imperialism, Neoliberalism, and Social Struggles in Latin America
Edited by Richard A. Dello Buono and José Bell Lara

Liberal Modernity and Its Adversaries: Freedom, Liberalism, and Anti-Liberalism in the Twenty-first Century
Milan Zafirovski

Marx, Critical Theory, and Religion: A Critique of Rational Choice
Edited by Warren S. Goldstein

Marx's Scientific Dialectics: A Methodological Treatise for a New Century
Paul Paolucci

Race and Ethnicity: Across Time, Space, and Discipline
Rodney D. Coates

Transforming Globalization: Challenges and Opportunities in the Post 9/11 Era
Edited by Bruce Podobnik and Thomas Reifer

Marx, Critical Theory, and Religion

A Critique of Rational Choice

Edited by Warren S. Goldstein

Haymarket Books
Chicago, Illinois

First published in 2006 by Brill Academic Publishers, The Netherlands

Published in paperback in 2009 by
Haymarket Books
P.O. Box 180165
Chicago, IL 60618
773-583-7884
www.haymarketbooks.org

ISBN: 978-1-608460-41-0

Trade distribution:
In the U.S., Consortium Book Sales, www.cbsd.com
In the UK, Turnaround Publisher Services, www.turnaround-psl.com
In Australia, Palgrave Macmillan, www.palgravemacmillan.com.au
In all other countries, Publishers Group Worldwide, www.pgw.com

Cover design by Ragina Johnson.

This book was published with the generous support of the Wallace Global Fund.

Printed in the United States on recycled paper containing 100 percent post-consumer waste, in accordance with the guidelines of the Green Press Initiative, www.greenpressinitiative.org.

10 9 8 7 6 5 4 3 2 1

Library of Congress Cataloging-in-Publication Data is available.

To Vicki, Benjamin, and Rachel

Contents

Acknowledgements

I would like to thank all the people who have made this book possible. First, I would like to thank David Fasenfest, editor of *Critical Sociology* and Series Editor for the Studies in Critical Social Science for Brill. David is the one who first proposed a special issue for Critical Sociology (31/1–2) on Religion and Marxism and, later, that it be transformed into an edited volume. I would like to thank Lauren Langman who showed up to my roundtable presentation on Walter Benjamin and Ernst Bloch at the American Sociological Association Meeting in Miami Beach, FL in 1993, while I was a doctoral candidate. Together, David and Lauren, with their ongoing support, have been my surrogate mentors.

I would like to thank the authors in this book, all of whom submitted multiple revisions of their articles. They are Rudi Siebert, Lauren Langman, Anne Rawls, Mike Ott, Chris Brittain, Ken MacKendrick, Andrew McKinnon, George Lundskow, Will Roberts, Bonnie Wright, David Gay and Anna Campbell Buck.

I would like to thank Lesley Kenny, a PhD student at the University of Toronto, who did a splendid job copyediting all of the articles in this book, and Michael Bachmann, an outstanding PhD student in the Department of Sociology at the University of Central Florida, who had the arduous task of combining all of the bibliographies.

I would like to thank all of my colleagues in the Department of Sociology (and Anthropology) at the University of Central Florida. They have been friendly and open minded toward my critical theory, with all its associations.

I would like to thank my comrades from the New School, with whom I have had an ongoing friendship since our days of alternating between being scholars and activists in the streets of Manhattan during the days of the first Persian Gulf War. In particular, I thank comrades Joel Stillerman, Perry Chang, Jan Lin and Harry Dahms.

I would like to thank my mother, Muriel Goldstein, who not only made my career as a sociologist possible, but with whom I share a common political understanding.

Finally, I would like to thank my family, to whom this book is dedicated. My wife, Vicki Spetter, and children Benjamin and Rachel Spetter-Goldstein, have had to live with a husband/father trying to get tenure at a research university. They give my life meaning that makes the stresses of my career in contrast seem insignificant.

Gravestone of Max and Maidon Horkheimer, Jewish Cemetery, Bern, Switzerland, photograph by Gianni Pauciello.

Warren S. Goldstein

Introduction: Marx, Critical Theory, and Religion: A Critique of Rational Choice

The Sociology of Religion has had several frameworks guiding its analysis including functionalism, interpretive sociology, phenomenology, symbolic interactionism and now rational choice theory. Marxism has tended to ignore religion, assuming that it would eventually disappear even though Marxism itself retained theological elements. This collection of essays brings together a group of scholars who use frameworks provided by Marx and Critical Theory to analyze religion. Our goal is to establish a critical theory of religion within the sociology of religion, as an alternative to rational choice. In doing so, it engages in a critique of the positivism, uncritical praise of the market (neoconservativism) and one-dimensional conception of rationality of the rational choice theory of religion.

This edited volume comes out of a special issue of the journal *Critical Sociology* (Volume 31:1–2, 2005) on Religion and Marxism. All of the authors were asked to revise their articles for the edited volume making them fit more into the framework of a critical theory of religion as an alternative to rational choice. Some of the authors revised their articles, a few submitted entirely new articles, and a few new authors signed on.

The critical theory of religion has the promise of providing an alternative to mainstream approaches in sociology of religion. The goal of this edited volume is to make the case for a critical theory of religion – a paradigm in opposition to the market-driven neoconservative paradigm of rational choice.

The first generation of the Frankfurt School had the relationship to religion as its subtext. This was the result of the work of Walter Benjamin (1968) who became increasingly interested in the contradictory relationship between historical materialism and theology. In the *Dialectic of Enlightenment* (1991), Horkheimer and Adorno have a dialectic between myth and enlightenment, faith and reason, and reason and understanding, where Enlightenment becomes a new myth. In *Negative Dialectics* (1973), Adorno attempted to purge the dialectic of its theological elements. In contrast, Horkheimer, in his later years, became increasingly interested in religion.

The critical theory of religion, taking Habermas (1984/1987) as its model, is highly integrative of other theoretical perspectives in sociology and is able to selectively incorporate elements of these competing paradigms within it. Rather than being value free, the critical theory of religion sides with the forces of Enlightenment and modernity against the rear guard of traditionalism and fundamentalism. It takes the Frankfurt analysis of the authoritarian personality and applies it to clerico-fascism (Protestant and Islamic Fundamentalism).

The methodology of the critical theory of religion is the use of critique as a form of self-correction. In doing so, it engages in a critique of itself, either by becoming self consciously aware of the theological elements within it, or purging itself of them, thereby moving more in a social scientific direction.

The critical theory of religion is not just a conflict approach but more specifically analyzes religion from a dialectical perspective. It looks at the relationship between religious differences and class differences. It views the ideological divide between denominations in a religiously pluralist society as an expression of class, cultural and ethnic differences. It sees a dialectical interplay between ideology (religion) and material interests (economics). Religious conflict occurs along multiple lines, some of which are the ideological expression of regional, ethnic or cultural conflict (which themselves often have a class/economic base).

At the heart of a critical theory of religion is a dialectical theory of secularization. Rather than seeing secularization occurring in a unilinear process, a critical theory of religion sees secularization and, more specifically, religious rationalization, as occurring in a dialectical manner. It views the ongoing conflict between fundamentalism and modernity as part of this dialectic.

This edited volume is divided into three parts. The first two articles, by Andrew McKinnon and Will Roberts, look at Marx's views on religion. The second set of articles, by Rudolf Siebert, Michael Ott, Christopher Brittain and Kenneth MacKendrick, all examine aspects of critical theory in relationship to religion. The final set of articles, by Warren Goldstein, George Lundskow, Bonnie Wright and Anne Rawls, Lauren Langman, and David Gay, Warren Goldstein and Anna Campbell Buck are attempts to take the critical theory of religion and apply it to religion.

The first two articles (McKinnon and Roberts) are a reexamination of some of Marx's writings, which are relevant to religion. Andrew McKinnon examines Marx's well known and misinterpreted quotation that, "religion is the opium of the people." McKinnon discusses it in the historical context of the mid 19th century, when it was written. Whereas today the text is read literally and opium is perceived as an illicit narcotic, McKinnon argues that the passage needs to be understood in its historical context with all its complexity. At the end of his essay, McKinnon argues that Marxism needs to move away from its reified conception of religion as exemplified by the misinterpretation of the opium quotation. He attempts to set the direction for a Marxist sociology of religion arguing that religion needs to be understood dialectically.

The second article, by William Clare Roberts, focuses on Marx's use of Dante's *Divine Comedy* in his critique of political economy. Roberts focuses on the parallels between Marx's critique of political economy and Dante's trip through purgatory and hell. He draws our attention to Marx's 1859 Preface to the Critique of Political Economy in which Marx quotes from Dante's *Divine Comedy* the inscription on the gates of hell, "Abandon all hope, ye who enter here." Roberts raises the question of why Marx, at the beginning of his critique of capitalism, posts the warning sign that you are now about to enter hell. Is Marx's critique of capitalism a trip through purgatory and hell? Roberts also points out that this sign is misleading, that Dante, with Virgil as his guide, was able to escape hell. So, must we abandon all hope or is capitalism also something, which we, with Marx as our guide, can escape?

The second set of articles (Siebert, Ott, Brittain, MacKendrick) are theoretical articles which fit into the framework of a critical theory of religion. These articles are concerned with those writings by theorists associated with the Frankfurt School in which issues pertaining to religion play a role.

We are honored to have Rudolf J. Siebert contribute to this edited volume. Rudi Siebert is the founder of a critical theory of religion and coined this term. He has been developing it for the last forty years. In the essay that he contributed to this volume, Siebert sets his eyes on sociology of religion. He explains how a critical theory of religion has a dialectical understanding of the relationship between the religious and the secular but also engages in a critique of the positivism used by rational choice theory and the clerico-fascism which it legitimizes.

In Siebert's article, he reveals that Max Horkheimer, the most influential director of the Institute for Social Research (the Frankfurt School), had the passage "In you Eternal One, alone I trust" (Psalm 91:2) inscribed on his gravestone in Bern, Switzerland (for photograph, see page x). Horkheimer wrote an essay on Psalm 91 five years before his death. Michael Ott, who did his dissertation under Rudi Siebert, has beautifully translated this essay for this edited volume. The paradox is that Horkheimer, as a founder of critical theory, which is neo-Marxist, in his later life returned to Jewish theology without giving up the Marxism. Horkheimer comes to advocate trust in the eternal one as a way to deal with the conditions of oppression, injustice and suffering here on earth. Siebert and Ott explain that the imageless nameless totally other, articulated by Horkheimer, is the theological inversion or negation for what is and thus serves as the basis for the critique.

Michael Ott, in his article for this book, takes rational choice theory of religion head on. Ott sees rational choice theory's positivistic market-based approach to religion as a legitimation of the larger capitalist economic system to which it belongs. The rise of rational choice theory coincides with the rise of the Christian right. He offers as an alternative to this a critical theory of religion, which dialectically retains the prophetic messianic roots of Judeo-Christianity.

Christopher Brittain continues the critique of rational choice from the perspective of critical theory. He uses a scene from the film *A Beautiful Mind* which is about John Nash, one of the developers of game theory (which is associated with rational choice). He points out the limitations of the one-dimensional type of rationality of rational choice and juxtaposes it with the multidimensional types of rationality articulated by Max Weber and the Frankfurt School. Brittain explains how rational choice theory, which is market-based and uses the term supply-side to describe itself, has elective affinities with neoconservativism. He proposes critical theory's interdisciplinary approach to religion as providing a less reductionist explanation.

Kenneth MacKendrick delves into thanatology (death studies) from the perspective of a critical theory of religion. Basing his framework on Tony Walter (thanatology), he argues that there are three ideal typical attitudes toward death: traditional, modern and neo-modern (the last of which is comprised of late modern and postmodern). Whereas traditional attitudes to death are rooted in the community, in the modern attitude there is a rationalization of death in which death becomes institutionalized. Postmodern attitudes toward death, which are paradoxical, are a reaction toward modern ones. The disenchantment of death creates the need for reenchantment. MacKendrick takes the work of Jürgen Habermas and superimposes it over this schema. The linguistification of the sacred represents a move toward postmetaphysical thinking. Being more true to the idea of critical theory than even Habermas himself, MacKendrick synthesizes postmodernism within critical theory.

The last five articles (Goldstein, Lundskow, Wright and Rawls, Langman, and Gay, Goldstein and Campbell) are applications of the critical theory of religion. In my own article, working off a framework provided by Max Weber, Karl Kautsky and Ernst Bloch, I apply a conflict approach to biblical history. What I find is not only class-based conflicts but conflicts between elites and with other nations. These conflicts were part of a dialectic whose tensions caused ancient Jewish society to be dynamic. In this analysis, I maintain a critical distance from the biblical text.

In George Lundskow's article, he continues the critique of rational choice by focusing on Rodney Stark's *Rise of Christianity*. Lundskow questions the validity of taking a cost-benefit analysis within the context of a religious market and applying it to the Roman Empire. In its place, he offers a critical theory of religion which looks at religion in relationship to class structure. Especially after the adoption of Christianity by the Roman Empire, religion was only a matter of choice for the elites; for many others, it was imposed upon them and despite this, other religious traditions (i.e., Paganism and Judaism) endured.

Bonnie Wright and Anne Warfield Rawls engaged in ethnographic research focusing on the practices of two Assemblies of God churches in Detroit, Michigan. Basing their argument upon Marx, Durkheim, Mills, Goffman and Garfinkel, they establish that there is a dialectical relationship between belief and practice. While religious beliefs are based on practices, once they arise they are used to regulate them. In the congregations they studied, they found that public practices like speaking in tongues must be preapproved by the pastor to be perceived as legitimate. Inappropriate and unapproved messages are perceived of as illegitimate (not of God) and negatively sanctioned.

In "From the Caliphate to the *Shaheedim*: Toward A Critical Theory of Islam," Lauren Langman uses the framework of critical theory of the Frankfurt School to engage in an analysis of Islamic Fundamentalism. Like the Frankfurt School, he integrates concepts from Marx, Nietzsche, Freud and Weber in his analysis of Political Islam or Islamism. Like Weber, who attempted to explain why the process of rationalization (i.e., the development of capitalism) did not occur outside the West (the Occident), Langman asks this specifically in relation to the Islamic world. One of the answers that he provides is that a process of differentiation (separation of church and state) did not occur in Islam. This is particularly true in the area of law where Sharia (Islamic law) has been adopted by the state. One of the Frankfurt School's central concerns was the rise of Fascism made possible by the authoritarian personality. Langman illuminates the similarities between the clerico-fascism of Islamic fundamentalism and classical fascism. Islamism appeals to those who have been alienated and uprooted by the processes of modernization. It arises from feelings of powerlessness and is the result of a ressentiment toward the West. It idealizes a Golden Age from the past and projects it into the future. In his conclusion, Langman points out that Islamism is not a rational choice. The only way for Islamic societies to escape the economic conditions which give rise to Islamism is through societal rationalization.

In an article coauthored by David Gay, myself, and Anna Campbell, entitled "Operationalizing the Critical Theory of Religion," we take some of the central ideas of a critical theory of religion articulated by Karl Marx, Max Weber and Sigmund Freud and operationalize them using data from the GSS (General Social Survey). We are particularly interested in the relationship between trauma and religiosity. Consistent with rational choice theory, we do find that people with higher church attendance report lower levels of trauma. Nevertheless, we look at this relationship differently. Because there is a two-way dialectical relationship between trauma and religion (religion arises in response to trauma and helps to alleviate it), the data set is insufficient to establish this relationship. We encourage others to set up nonrecursive models, which could be used to establish this reciprocal dialectical relationship.

A critical theory of religion provides new directions for research in the sociology of religion. We invite other to join us.

Orlando, FL
January 2006

Part I: Marx

Andrew M. McKinnon[1]

Opium as Dialectics of Religion: Metaphor, Expression and Protest

This is the premise of a Marxian analysis of religion: "Religion . . . is the opium of the people". But what does it mean to equate religion with opium? For most twenty-first century readers, opium means something quite simple and obvious, and the comparison between the two terms seems perfectly literal. Opium is a drug that kills pain, distorts reality, and an artificial source of solace to which some poor souls can become addicted; so also religion.

Friedrich Nietzsche argues that the 'true' or literal meaning of a word is one "to which one has become accustomed due to frequent use . . . a metaphor . . . whose metaphorical nature has been forgotten" (1995:72). Through the "interminable repetition" of the phrase in Marxian analyses of religion (O'Toole 1984:68), "opium of the people" has lost its metaphorical sense. Even when readers of "Towards a Critique of Hegel's Philosophy of Right: Introduction" encounter the text as a dialectical analysis of religion, their understanding is governed – and loses its dialectical force – by a literal and presentist reading of this central metaphor.

[1] I am grateful for the responses to the first published version of this paper, and for those who have continued to push my thinking on the questions and challenges posed by Marx on religion. In particular, thanks to Y. Michal Bodemann, Roger O'Toole, William Clare Roberts, Thomas Kemple and Warren Goldstein.

In what is quite possibly the greatest work of Marxist literary theory, Frederic Jameson argues that

> . . . texts come before us as the always-already-read; we apprehend [them] through sedimented layers of previous interpretations, or – if the text is brand-new – through the sedimented reading habits and categories developed by those inherited interpretive traditions. (Jameson 1981:9)

Few texts come before us more always-already-read than the beginning pages of "Towards a Critique". In order to re-read Marx's analysis of religion in this text, we need first of all to disrupt the truth of our received literal understandings of "opium of the people", and dig through the sedimented layers that have accumulated since 1843. While this will not provide us with the "True" meaning of the text, if we fail to do so, our reading of the text will inevitably become yet another ritual repetition, reinforcing the received reading of the text, further repressing the metaphor and ironing out the dialectics of the text. This received reading turns Marx into a minor disciple of Feuerbach, and provides a gently politicized account of the latter's view of religion.

I will begin rethinking this seminal text first by destabilizing our understanding of opium; looking briefly at Europe in the nineteenth century, I will propose several different – and contradictory – senses of "opium" in the middle of that century. This will give us the space to re-think the larger text in which the metaphor occurs, to encounter the text dialectically, including the dialectical metaphor that is the heart and spirit of Marx's analysis of religion.

Opium and the People of the nineteenth century

In Europe, at the beginning of the nineteenth century, opium was largely an *unquestioned good*. Such was its importance as a medicine that in the first years of the nineteenth century, people would have understood "opium of the people" as something we could translate into twentieth century idiom as "penicillin of the people". By the end of the nineteenth century, however, its medical uses had largely been supplanted by other medicines, and medical and moral puritans effectively demonized opium. It is between these two periods that Marx penned opium as his metaphor for religion. In 1843, it is an ambiguous, multidimensional and contradictory metaphor, expressing both the earlier and later understandings of the fruit of the poppy.

"Opium at present is in great esteem, and is one of the most valuable of all the simple medicines": thus the first edition of the *Encyclopedia Britannica* (Smellie 1771) expresses the late 18th and early nineteenth century attitudes and beliefs about opium. Small doses are medically useful. Moderate doses can make a person somewhat intoxicated, "bold and above the fear of danger; for which reason the Turks always take it when going into battle" (1771). In 1820s England, there were somewhere between 16,000 and 26,000 completely unregulated opium sellers (Berridge and Edwards 1980:25). Because it was relatively inexpensive and used for such a wide range of ailments, every British home had laudanum in the cupboard (Butel 1995:37); its use was so common that, as one writer suggests, "[o]pium itself was 'the opiate of the people'" (ibid.). Opium "use in the early decades of the century was quite normal . . . it was not . . . a 'problem'" (Berridge and Edwards 1980:37). The concept of addiction had not even been formulated.

Between the 1830s and 1850s, opposition to opium-use grew, particularly from the newly formed 'temperance' and 'public health' movements. The problem was expounded as concern over longevity and baby doping but also over 'luxurious', or as we would now say "recreational use". Government inquiries followed, the most famous of which was Edwin Chadwick's (1842) *Report on the Sanitary Condition of the Labouring Population* (Berridge and Edwards 1980:77). The physicians and their allies in the temperance movements conjured 'opium poisoning' (which had long been recognized as *possible* with 'very immoderate doses') into an epidemic. Despite this nascent censure, opium continued to be widely accepted, and as late as the 1860s, up to 20% of *all* medicines sold in England were opium based (ibid.).

In the last quarter of the nineteenth century, the movements against the opium trade, and intemperance, and for public health, joined forces with the medical inebriety experts. With the constitution of a new knowledge-régime (Foucault 1978:109–33) came the concept of 'opium addiction', a truth with both a medical and a moral component (Berridge and Edwards 1980). Not only did Parliament grant control over opium-use to the physicians and pharmacists, but in 1891 it also called a halt to the 'morally indefensible' opium trade, even if the official opium trade would last another two decades, until the international treaties of 1907 (Butel 1995:376–403).

What then, could "opium" have meant in 1843, for Marx and for his readers? Metaphors draw a comparison between two things, in order to provide a new way of looking at one or both of them. They are unstable, fluid, and polysemic – and an unavoidable dimension of Marx's writing (Kemple 1995). More than one meaning can be compressed into a metaphor, and these meanings change over time. This prevents us, at the very outset, from describing the singular meaning of any metaphor. I suggest here several connotations of "opium" that would have been relevant in Europe in the middle of the nineteenth century:[2] opium was a medicine (albeit one with significant, newly discovered 'problems'); it was a source of enormous profit (which also provoked protest and rebellion); finally, it was a source of 'utopian' visions. Here I will sketch out these meanings of opium in the mid-nineteenth century, and forgo elaborating their theoretical import until later.

Medicine, not recreational use, was the most common use for opium in the first half of the nineteenth century, and opium was a medicine of utmost significance. Physicians and surgeons prescribed opium to their patients, while working-class people (who rarely encountered a doctor) administered the drug to themselves (Berridge and Edwards 1980:28). Opium was an important pain reliever, but was also used for *curing* diseases. We routinely distinguish between these two aspects of a medicine; nobody in the middle part of the century would have made such a firm distinction. It was prescribed for 'fatigue and depression', sleeplessness, rheumatism, 'women's ailments', fevers, diabetes (ibid. 31), and was regarded as an extremely useful styptic. Opium was used as a treatment for all matter of bronchial infections, including pneumonia, bronchitis and tuberculosis (67). The most important use for opium was as a treatment for diarrhea, dysentery, and cholera; during the European cholera epidemics of 1831–32 and again in 1849–53 its use was 'virtually unchallenged' as *the only effective* treatment for this deadly disease (Berridge and Edwards 1980:67).

That opium was an important medicine was a given for Marx. As a means of coping with *his* various illnesses, Marx himself used opium. Along with other "medicines" such as creosote and arsenic, regular opium use became

[2] My focus in the following historical passages will be on Britain. Britain is important for a number of reasons. First, our understanding of opium comes from later moments in the history of opium there (the movement to ban opium emerged there). Secondly, throughout the nineteenth century, Britain played a central role in the production and distribution of opium on a global scale. It was also an important producer of Opium meanings, consumed throughout the rest of the continent (Butel 1995). Perhaps as a result, there is more solid historical research on opium use and meanings in the British context. Finally, when Marx and Engels discuss opium, most of their discussions deal with the English context.

more important as a means for ridding himself of the carbuncles which caused him so much suffering in later life (McLellan 1973:337; Regnault 1933).

While Opium was an important medicine in mid nineteenth century Europe, it was not a medicine without its 'social problems'. Two of these stand out in particular. The first is a concern with the purity of the opium in the marketplace and in household medicine cupboards. The second was the concern over 'baby doping'.

Adulterated opium was a common concern throughout much of the nineteenth century, since it lead to very irregular doses, and highly adulterated opium would not be effective (Berridge and Edwards 1980:87–93). In a footnote of *Capital: Volume 1*, Marx writes:

> From the reports of last Parliamentary Commission on adulteration of means of subsistence, it will be seen that the adulteration even of medicines is the rule, not the exception in England. E.g., the examination of 34 specimens of opium purchased at many different chemists in London showed that 31 were adulterated with poppy heads, wheat flour, gum, clay, sand, &c. Several did not contain an atom of morphia. (1967:601)

The location of the text, in the midst of a section on the poor dietary condition of the working class, is important. Given the tendency in capitalist society to cut every possible corner in pursuit of profit, petit bourgeois merchants were cheating sick people out of medicine that they badly needed.

In the nineteenth century, opium-based medicines were commonly used for children, and there were many brands marketed specifically for children's use. A very partial list of those sold in England includes Godfrey's Cordial, Dalby's Carminitive, Daffy's Elixir, Atkinsons's Infants Preservative, Mrs. Winslow's Soothing Syrop, Slowe's Infants Preservative and Street's Infant Quietness (Berridge and Edwards 1980:98–99). The name of the last of these, Street's Infant Quietness suggests one of the common uses for opium-based elixirs. In Volume 1 of *Capital*, Marx writes that

> . . . the high death rates are, apart from local causes, principally due to the employment of mothers away from their homes, and to the neglect and maltreatment, consequent on their absence, such as, among others, insufficient nourishment, unsuitable food, and dosing with opiates. (Marx 1967:398)

While this passage draws primarily on a government report from 1861, Engels wrote about infant-doping in *The Condition of the Working Classes in England* (1845) and it had begun to be seen as a social problem beginning in the 1830s

(Berridge and Edwards 1980:97–105). Unlike many of the liberal reformers, Marx and Engels don't blame 'bad mothers' or the ignorance of the working class for infant doping. First, the declining standard of living among the working classes made it necessary for women to work in the factories, leaving their infants at home, or in the care of a babysitter. These working class babysitters were reputed to use opium-based cordials to keep the many children in their care quiet (Marx and Engels 1975a, vol. 4:399, 402–3,437). Secondly, while Marx was concerned about the adulteration of opium for the sake of profit, he and Engels also argued that profit-driven pharmacists promoted the inappropriate use of opiates for children – once again for the sake of profit.

In addition to the important uses and abuses of opium as medicine in the nineteenth century, opium had wider economic, political and cultural significance. Opium was an extremely important commodity, particularly for the British Empire, as well as a cause for the two Opium Wars. Finally, it had an important relation to cultural and intellectual life – especially as exemplified through the lives and work of the Romantic poets.

For the British Empire, for example, trading opium was a very lucrative venture, generating a seventh of the British-Indian government's total revenue. So crucial were these trading arrangements that the British army fought two Opium Wars against the Chinese government in order to defend them. The first war broke out in 1839 and ended with the treaty of Nanking in 1842, the year before Marx penned his 'opium of the people' epithet. A second war was fought between 1856 and 1860; however, many people (including Marx) had anticipated it several years earlier. Marx's (and Engels') writings on the opium trade and opium wars during the 1850s, all of which appeared in the *New York Daily Tribune*, were concerned primarily with 'opium' as an instance of economic imperialism.

The British-Chinese conflict was regularly called the 'Opium War' throughout Europe, as well as in Marx's and Engels' writings (Marx and Engels 1975a, vol. 12:93, vol. 15:282,354, vol. 16:14); even to say "opium" in the year after the end of the first Opium War is to conjure-up images of massive social conflict. In 1853, Marx went so far as to argue that the increasing use of opium in China was the primary cause of an emerging anti-imperialist war. The irony was not lost on Marx when he wrote that "the occasion of this outbreak is unquestionably been afforded by the English canon forcing upon China that soporific drug called opium" (1975 vol. 12:93). Opium is not only a trope for conflict, but it implied certain oppositional groups, and a certain oppositional rhetoric about the trade. In China, Marx notes that opium use and trade were legally a 'heresy' (Marx and Engels 1975a vol. 16:19), the implication being that opium use was opposed on religious grounds, as was the trade itself in England.

Opium also had its recreational users. Like ether for William James, hashish for Walter Benjamin and Ernst Bloch, and LSD in the Sixties, opium provided a glimpse of "another reality" for mid-nineteenth century intellectuals, artists and poets. The meanings associated with these visions circulated so commonly in the nineteenth century that they would have been difficult to ignore. Especially prominent were the visions of the English Romantics who were also heavy opium users: De Quincey, Coleridge, Shelley, and Byron. The 'opium-eating' habits of the first two were particularly well known, and while Marx discusses in many places De Quincey's economic writing, De Quincey was best known throughout Europe as the author of an autobiographical book, *Confessions of an English Opium Eater* (1821).

Particularly striking about this opium-inspired poetry is its visions of 'no-places' that are at the same time 'good-places', reflecting St. Thomas More's constructed etymology of 'Utopia' (Goux 1990). M. H. Abrams, in his important study of the opium poets, writes: "This fantastic land is not the fleeting shadow of an ordinary dream, but is a reality nearly as vivid as actual experience" (1971:5). Admittedly, the visions of the "opium romantics" are often enigmatic, and are only in part visions of a 'good place'. Coleridge's 'Kubla Khan' contains images of destruction, chaos, and war, and some of De Quincey's visions, especially in part II of *The Confessions* (1956:291–332) are positively haunting. They remain undeveloped, or *as yet* incomplete utopian visions (Bloch 1964).

Opium had a complex history in the nineteenth century, and yet when we, early twenty-first century readers, encounter "opium of the people", we read it in a straightforward, literal, (and uniformly negative) manner that is alien to Marx's time. In other words, we read opium as people who have learned to think about opium in a world after the puritanical prohibitions against opium use have become naturalized. By drawing a parallel between religion and opium, Marx alludes to all of the mid-nineteenth century connotations that opium would have had for his readers. Any reading of "Towards a Critique" must deal with the complexity and ambivalence of this metaphor.

Towards a Reading of Marx's Critique of Right: Introduction

Having destabilized the "truth" of our established understanding of religion as opium, or at least having put it into question, we can now turn to take a closer look at "Towards a Critique". In order to grasp Marx's text dialectically, it is easier to work backwards, that is, to start with the reflections on the dialectics of the proletariat; only then can we really deal with the beginning of the text, where we encounter the dialectics of religion.

The primary theoretical contribution of "Towards a Critique" concerns not religion, but the role of the proletariat in the dialectical overcoming of the current state of society. After surveying the "present" state of Prussia (1843), Marx asks: "So where is the real possibility of German emancipation?" His answer?

> We answer: in the formation of a class with radical chains, a class in civil society that is not a class of civil society, of a social group that is the dissolution [*Auflösung*] of all social groups, of a sphere that has a universal character because of its universal sufferings and lays claim to no particular right, because it is the object of no particular injustice but of injustice in general . . . It is . . . a sphere that cannot emancipate itself without emancipating itself from all other spheres of society and thereby emancipating these other spheres themselves. In a word, it is the complete loss of humanity and thus can only recover itself by a complete redemption of humanity. This dissolution of society, as a particular class, is the proletariat.
>
> . . . When the proletariat declares the dissolution of the hitherto existing world order, it merely declares the secret of its own existence, since it is in fact the dissolution of this order. When it demands the negation of private property, it is only laying down as a principle for society what society has laid down as a principle for the proletariat, what has already been incorporated in itself without its consent as the negative result of society. (Marx 1977a:72–73)

Marx's dialectical method is enormously complex, and cannot simply be reduced to the schema developed by British Hegelians at the turn of the century, and sometimes incorporated into Marxist writings: it is not simply "thesis, antithesis and synthesis". This schema, especially when applied to Marx, usually covers more than it reveals. The passage just quoted helps us come to grips with two of the senses active in Marx's writings, and these will be helpful to us in understanding the religion passages.

While Marx never explicitly refers to *The Phenomenology of Spirit* (Hegel 1994), here we find an account of the dialectics of Proletarian and Bourgeois that is strikingly reminiscent of Hegel's story of the Master and Slave (1994: §189–196).[3] Marx argues that it is only because of its universal exploitation, the universal suffering of the proletariat, that this is the group that embodies the potential to transform itself, and with it, the whole set of social relations that make up "this society". By transforming society, it transforms itself, and while it transforms society, it transforms itself. For Marx, these are not separable from one another. In short, dialectical logic points, not to the stasis of being, but rather to *becoming*, through overcoming contradictions: it is only because of the universal chains that universal emancipation becomes possible.

When the proletariat demands "the negation of private property" (Marx 1977a:73), it declares the secret of its own existence, both as the essence of this society, and of the new communist society. The proletariat dialectically overcomes its status as propertyless through the abolition of private property, thereby abolishing the proletariat itself, and making propertylessness into something very different. A class without private property is in seed form the same as, and yet totally different from, a society without property. *Aufheben* is the key dialectical term for both Hegel and Marx. For Marx it indicates the way "in which negation and preservation (affirmation) are brought together" ([1844] 2002:87). While Engels cannot usually be trusted for his interpretation of Marx's dialectic, he nonetheless provides a useful gloss on *Aufhebung* as a philosophical term. He suggests that it means "'Overcome and Preserved'; overcome as regards form, and preserved as real content" (Engels [1877] 1969:166). Denys Turner (1991) suggests that the contradiction between form and content are crucial to the problem of religion in Marx. For this reason, Engels' formulation is helpful for making sense of one way that *Aufhebung* operates in this text, even if it cannot be taken as the *only* means by which overcome and preserved can be related, even in this text.[4]

---

[3] Why Marx would not engage with *The Phenomenology* is quite strange, given that it is clearly the most 'materialist' of all of the great philosophers' writings. In terms of allusion, however, the figures of Master and Slave seem to keep recurring throughout "Towards a Critique". It could be argued that "Towards a Critique" rallies the young Hegel (of the *Phenomenology*) against the old Hegel (of the *Philosophy of Right*). Such an argument, however, is well beyond the scope or concerns of this paper.

[4] Engels tended towards understanding the dialectic in a distinctly scientistic manner, formulating the logic of dialectics in terms of rigid principles not unlike that of

In the conclusion to "Towards a Critique" (Marx 1977a:73), Marx points to a similar dialectical relationship between philosophy and the proletariat. Philosophy finds in the proletariat its material weapons, and the proletariat finds its intellectual weapons in philosophy. He continues: "Philosophy cannot realize itself without transcending [*Aufhebung*] the proletariat, and the proletariat cannot transcend [*aufheben*] itself without realizing philosophy."

The dialectical relations of the proletariat to society and to philosophy helps us to begin unraveling the logic of Marx's thinking on religion, and to see how he dialectically overcomes the work of Feuerbach. Marx begins "Towards a Critique" with an introductory sentence, "the criticism of religion is essentially complete, and the criticism of religion is the presupposition of all criticism", followed by a two-paragraph summary of Feuerbach's analysis of religion. While this is usually read as part of Marx's analysis, Feuerbach could have written most of the material here himself (*The Essence of Christianity* (1957), *Philosophy of the Future* (1972)). Marx's only addition comes where he begins to critique Feuerbach for his abstract conception of religion: "[Religion for Feuerbach] is the imaginary realization of the human essence, because the human essence possesses no true reality. Thus, the struggle against religion is indirectly the struggle against the world whose spiritual aroma is religion" (1977a:63). The struggle demands that we be concrete; our struggle is with "this state, this society" not with the Essence of Man.

Most readers of Marx, sensitive to his indebtedness to Feuerbach, and his early participation in the *Doctorklub*, unwittingly end up treating "Towards a Critique" as a minor contribution to the Left-Hegelian critiques of religion (Rojo 1988), a mere supplement to Feuerbach's work. While Marx certainly is indebted to Feuerbach's writing, this text is an *Aufhebung* of the latter's writings. Feuerbach developed a "theological" critique of religion, but Marx is here moving beyond Feuerbach's "abstract" conception of religion, to one that focuses on "this state, this society" which produces religion – rather than seeing the "superman" in the sky as a reflection of Man's essence, since "the human essence has no reality". In other words, Marx takes issue with Feurbach's abstract essence of man as much as with his abstract "essence of religion", which in Feuerbach are conceptually inseparable. As Marx writes in his

---

the British Hegelians and their schema of thesis-antithesis-synthesis. Despite my reservations about Engels' use of dialectics in general, I am nonetheless convinced that *this* formulation is helpful for helping us grasp the logic of *this* text.

"Theses on Feuerbach": "Feuerbach resolves the religious essence into the human essence. But the human essence is no abstraction inherent in each single individual. In its reality it is the ensemble of the social relations" (Marx 1977b:157). I will return to this point later, arguing that to treat religion as an essential or reified category is to violate the terms and the spirit of Marx's concrete analysis. "Marxian" analyses of religion that analyze the "essence" of religion (rather than concrete social relations) have far more in common with Feuerbach than with Marx.

For Marx, the criticism of religion, although essentially finished (1977a:62), is not an end in itself, but rather a means (1977a:62). Marx's concern is to take the latest developments of Hegelian philosophy, and turn them into praxis-oriented critique of the social world, one rooted in the "*categorical imperative* to overthrow all relations in which man is a debased, enslaved, forsaken, despicable being" (1977a:69). Thus, *Towards a Critique* is not primarily a "philosophical" text. The point of the text is not that "Man makes religion, religion does not make man" – this was Feuerbach's thesis and his claim to fame – but rather to overcome the situation in which human beings are enchained (Thesis 11, *etcetera*). The philosophical point is here but a premise or an "assumption" (*Voraussetzung*) from which Marx proceeds.

Marx's own analysis begins in the fourth paragraph:

> Religious suffering is at the same time an *expression* [*Ausdruck*] of real suffering and a *protest against* real suffering. Religion is the sigh of the oppressed creature, the heart of a heartless world, and the spirit of a spiritless situation. It is the *opium* of the people.
>
> The [*Aufhebung*] of religion as the illusory happiness of the people is the demand for their real happiness. The demand to give up the illusions of their condition is a demand to give up a condition that requires illusion. The criticism of religion is therefore the germ of the criticism of the valley of tears whose halo is religion.
>
> Criticism has plucked the imaginary flowers from the chains not so that man may throw away the chains without any imagination or comfort, but so that he may throw away the chains and pluck living flowers. The criticism of religion disillusions man so that he may think, act, and fashion his own reality as a disillusioned man come to his sense; so that he may revolve around himself as his real sun. Religion is only the illusory sun which revolves around man as long as he does not revolve around himself. (Marx 1977a:64; translation emended from Marx 1976 as noted, emphasis original)

These passages begin with an essentially dialectical logic. Religious suffering is both "expression of" and "protest against", both of which Marx highlights by underlining. He further underlines their "simultaneity, when he writes that they are expressed *in einem* and repeats another time *und in einem*"; together they comprise a single moment, and an indivisible whole (Rojo 1988:214). Sergio Rojo writes,

> The characteristic of the definition which Marx gives to the two terms "expression of real suffering and protest and against real suffering" constitutes a dialectical relation, an unstable equilibrium, which mutually influence each other, even if, historically, one aspect has prevailed over the other. (1988:210; my translation)

Unlike in Feuerbach's analysis, religion is not an "abstract" expression of the human essence. Rather, expanding on the "expression", Marx highlights the social dimension by writing that religion is the spirit and heart of a spiritless, heartless social situation, where religion is a sigh that bears witness to oppression.

Marx's underlining (*expression, protest, opium*), suggests that "opium" is the dialectical culmination of the movement from *expression*-and-*protest* to *opium*. Opium, then, is the moment of *aufheben* "in which negation and preservation (affirmation) are brought together" ([1844] 2002:87). The "traditional" readings of religion as "opium of the people" neglect the context and dialectical movement, in which opium, as a condensed signifier, brings together both expression and protest in one moment. Opium is already a metaphor; Marx's use of it in this context highlights these multiple significations of the term, and forces us to look at them dialectically: opium/religion as expression *and* protest.

In the nineteenth century opium expressed the immiserization of the people. Opium use increased with declining conditions for the working class: more health problems, and the outbreaks of epidemics such as cholera. As Engels, for example, pointed out in *The Condition of the English Working Class* (1845), declining health was directly related to the ravages of capitalist relations. Opium thus 'expressed' in an indirect way the ravages of capitalism on the health and well being of the population, but most particularly the workers. Similarly, the "dosing" of children with opium, expressed the miserable lot of working class children, due to their parents' prolonged and ever increasing hours of labor outside the home (Marx and Engels 1975a, vol. 4:399, 402–3,437).

Ausdruck means "expression", something ex-pressed, squeezed-out. As an important commodity, opium was pressed out of poppies, but it was also the product of labor squeezed out of peasant workers, and sold at great profit by European capitalists. Marx recognized that religion was increasingly becoming a commodity, rupturing its traditional imbeddedness in Feudal relations, and becoming thoroughly imbedded, not just as an element of the cultural "superstructure", but also as a commodity, sold on an open market (see, most (in)famously, "On the Jewish Question" (1977c)). Religion today, even more than in Marx's day is both expressed as a commodity, and expresses the topsy-turvy relations of capitalist society. As Theodor Adorno puts it:

> Religion is on sale, as it were. It is cheaply marketed in order to provide one more so-called irrational stimulus among many others by which the members of a calculating society are calculatingly made to forget the calculation under which they suffer. (1992:294)

Religion in this aspect is not "superstructure" (insofar as this is a useful term), but part and parcel of economic production and exchange. It is this distinctive character of religion in capitalist social formations that makes the tools of neo-classical economics of some utility in comprehending the social logic of religion. By neglecting, however, to situate their analysis in a broader conception of capitalism per se – that is, by failing to understand religious or economic markets as socio-historical phenomena, the rational choice theorists miss the big picture entirely.

This expression also leads to protest and conflict, something sorely neglected in most Marxian understandings of religion. The Opium trade with China (enforced by canons) occasioned protest, first among the Evangelicals and Quakers in Britain, and also became the source of two major wars between China and Great Britain, the first of which had only recently ended in 1843. It bears repeating that Marx himself articulated this as a dialectical relation when he wrote, "the occasion of this outbreak has unquestionably been afforded by the English cannon forcing upon China that soporific drug called opium" (Marx and Engels 1975a vol. 12:93). If we attend only to the "soporific" effects of religion, we miss an important part of the picture, the allusion to the potential for religion to induce conflict, robbing the text of its dialectical thrust.

If opium was an important medicine, the social forms into which it was inserted – capitalism in the broadest sense – characterized by baby doping, shameless profiteering and warmongering, were, and continue to be, oppressive, situations with neither heart nor spirit. I quoted Engels earlier, when he defines *Aufheben* as "'Overcome and Preserved'; overcome as regards form, and preserved as real content" (Engels [1877] 1969:166). It is the form of relations in which opium is embedded, the contradiction between form and content, which must be overcome.

"Religion is the sigh of the oppressed creature, the heart of a heartless world, and the spirit of a spiritless situation" (Marx 1977a:64). The object of Marx's critique is not the sigh (though this is a product of the situation), heart, or spirit. The Left-Hegelians's theological critiques attempt to deal with this "content", with religion *an sich* in abstraction from its social forms; Marx's critique, by contrast, is thoroughly *in situ*; it is "this state, this society" which are the object of his critique. The content in this dialectical phrase is in fact preserved, at least in seed form.

For Marx, religion is to be *aufheben*, not simply "abolished". Most of the English language versions of "Towards a Critique" translate *aufheben* in a theoretically preconceived fashion. When Marx calls for the *aufheben* of philosophy, or the proletariat, the translators use words that indicate a positive overcoming, for example, "transcend", or "supercede". When Marx calls for the *aufheben* of religion, there is a marked tendency for translators to choose "abolish" (Marx 1963,1975, 1977a, 1983). This is a legitimate choice of words for a translator, but as readers, unless we see *aufheben*, and recognize the dialectical thought beneath the translation, we are quite likely to miss Marx's dialectical argument.

> The [*Aufhebung*] of religion as the illusory happiness of the people is the demand for their real happiness. The demand to give up the illusions of their condition is a demand to give up a condition that requires illusion. The criticism of religion is therefore the germ of the criticism of the valley of tears whose halo is religion. (Marx 1977a:64)

It may be, as the argument usually goes, that this illusory happiness forestalls the motivation for emancipation. But following in the wake of the opium metaphor, we need to think of these illusions as "utopian" openings, visions of another world, "an ordinary dream, but [nonetheless] a reality nearly as vivid as actual experience" (Abrams 1971:5). Engels gave the idea of "Utopia" a bad name, most famously in his *Socialism: Utopian and Scientific* ([1880] 1954), but he had long held such a view, and it was a position to which Marx moved in the late 1840s. Nonetheless, in *Towards a Critique*, Marx still uses "utopian dream" in a positive sense, as parallel to the "radical revolution" and in contrast to the "merely political revolution" of the bourgeoisie (Marx 1977a:71).[5]

If, as Marx suggests, religion offers a picture of an imaginary world, its dialectical overcoming is by no means simply the world in its actuality, an actuality of suffering, domination, oppression and brutality. It is imagination in fact that cracks open the merely existent world and offers other possibilities. In the "Economic and Philosophical Manuscripts" (1844) Marx suggests, in fact, that it is this capacity for imagination and creative production that gives human beings their unique species being. Even in his later thinking (*Capital* vol. 1), Marx suggests "... what distinguishes the worst architect from the best of bees is this, that the architect raises his structure in imagination before he erects it in reality" (1967:178). Max Horkheimer once wrote about precisely this dimension of religion-as-utopia:

> The concept of God was for a long time the place where the idea was kept alive that there are other norms besides those to which nature and society give expression in their operation ... Religion is the record of the wishes, desires and accusations of countless generations. (1995:129)

While it is true that in Marx's text, religion is an "illusory happiness", there is still a kernel of happiness there, happiness in promised form. The history of religion records the "wishes, desires and accusations" of oppressed human beings. When they are not *sui generis* dreams, these visions of another reality are designed as the promise of a blissful hereafter for obedient slaves. Do they not, nonetheless, in their vision of another reality, also open up new possibilities for imagining 'real happiness'? To create this 'real happiness' is to "break the chains and pluck the living flower" (1977a:64), which, given the context, is clearly an opium poppy!

---

[5] This may not be immediately apparent, since we are so habituated to reading Marx's later diatribes against the utopian socialists, especially those he encountered in France (St. Simon, etc). The structure of Marx's sentence assumes this equivalence: radical revolution = universal emancipation = utopian dream; partial [revolution] = political revolution = pillars still standing. Universal emancipation, the utopian dream requires that the pillars of society be torn down and rebuilt from the ground up. The anti-utopian orthodoxy in Orthodox Marxism, I would argue, ultimately stems from Engels' proclivity for scientism. Those who want to distance themselves from this positivistic stream of Marxism need to re-examine the negative disposition towards utopias that springs from such scientism. Ernst Bloch (1964) clearly promises to be a good guide and starting point for this re-examination.

In *The Political Unconscious* (1981), Frederic Jameson argues that if Marxist analysis is to escape a narrow and unconvincing instrumentalism (or functionalism) in its study of culture, it must not only continue to exercise a negative (unmasking) hermeneutic, but also recover a positive (or utopian) hermeneutic. It must come to recognize the interplay between the ideological and the utopian in all cultural forms, including religion. Writing of the media in mass culture, Jameson argues that

> . . . a process of compensatory exchange must be involved . . . in which the henceforth manipulated viewer is offered specific gratifications in return for his or her consent to passivity. In other words, if the ideological function of mass culture is understood as a process whereby otherwise dangerous and protopolitical impulses are 'managed' and defused, rechanneled and offered spurious objects, then some preliminary step must also be theorized in which these same impulses – the raw material upon which the process works – are initially awakened within the very text that seeks to still them. (Jameson 1981:287)

According to Jameson, the Marxist critic must look for both the ideological and utopian dimension of any cultural form, since in an alienated situation, they cannot be separated. Marx's demand, then, becomes to actualize the utopian kernel that is the spirit of a spiritless situation, to achieve a dialectical overcoming, whereby the promised happiness becomes an actualized or, as Marx puts it, a "real happiness".

If we take Marx's call for the *aufheben* of religion seriously, this means reading the metaphor, and hence religion, with all of its contradictions. Opium, as a medicine, was not a "bad" thing (Marx never thought to criticize the fruit of the poppy itself, and used it himself when the need arose); but it was often used (form) for the dubious purposes of baby doping and was a "good" sold for considerable profit by shameless profiteers. It was a "soporific" which awakened serious conflict, both within Britain and abroad. It has the capacity to "distort reality" (the ubiquitous "pie in the sky"), but also to offer an imaginary counterpoint to the actuality of domination and oppression (Brittain 2005, Siebert 2005). The driving force of Marx's critique of religion is his insistence on the "categorical imperative" – a very Lutheran notion, deriving from Kant – to "overthrow all circumstances in which man is humiliated, enslaved, abandoned, and despised . . ." (1977a:69). This imperative itself may be rooted in the very religious traditions that Marx critiques, providing an ongoing impetus to negative critique (Siebert 2005), but there is nothing unusual about this in Marx's thinking. On the contrary, all dialectical thinking insists on, and consists of, the reflexivity of critique critiquing itself (Karakayali 2004).

Beyond Religion as an Abstract Category[6]

As I have argued, Marx's critique of Hegel's *Rechtsphilosophie* is an *aufhebung* of Feuerbach, rather than a mere repetition of the latter's a/theology. First, Marx moves the question of religion away from a/theology and decisively makes it a political and economic problem. Second, Feuerbach's critique of religion is abstract, whereas Marx insists on the necessity of being concrete – an adequate analysis of religion can only address "this state, this society", which is why his analysis in that text is concerned almost exclusively with the situation in Prussia in the 1840s.

If there is one lesson to be learned from the endless debates about an adequate definition of religion, it is that religion is not a singular thing with a singular set of dimensions or effects, and is hence extraordinarily resistant to conceptual definition (cf. Spiro 1966; J. Smith 1998; Lambert 1991; McKinnon 2002). In effect, contrary to Feuerbach, there is no *Essence of Religion* (1967). It has become a reified category (an essence) through historical, political, and cultural processes, and scholars who continue to treat it as such fail to live up to the Marxian imperative: "Always Historicize!" (cf. Jameson 1981). In *The Meaning and End of Religion* Wilfred Cantwell Smith (1978 [1962]) historicizes religion and demonstrates precisely why religion has proven impossible to define adequately. Smith's history of the concept demonstrates that "religion" (not only as phenomena, but also as a concept) is a social construction.

Most languages historically had no word that corresponds with our concept "religion", and the equivalent terms in contemporary non-European languages have been imported from the West. Even in Europe, for most of its history the word "religion" (*religio*) meant something very different than it does today. Smith argues that in early Latin texts, *religio* had to do with specific cultic rites and piety, rather than with a "name for a system of ideas and beliefs" (1978:40). This is for the most part the sense in which it is used even in the history of the West up to the seventeenth century. Smith argues that even at the time of the Reformation, *religio* and its derivatives in the European

[6] This section draws on my essay on the definition debates in sociology of religion and in religious studies, proposing a social constructionist account of the category "religion" (McKinnon 2002).

vulgata still meant "piety" or "worship". The idea that religion "names a system of ideas and beliefs" emerges for the first time in the Enlightenment (1978:40). In pamphlet after pamphlet, tract after tract, this new idea was driven home, either by polemicists or by apologists of particular traditions. Initially, "religion" was something that someone else had, whereas the critic had "faith", "piety", or, in the case of the *Lumières*, "rational thought". Slowly, however, people began to refer to their own faith as "religion" as they began to defend "true religion" (as a coherent system of beliefs and practices) against the critics of "religion".

After the seventeenth century, there were several new developments in the understanding of "religion" in the West. First was the use of the word "religions" (plural) to denote phenomena that were different, but somehow equivalent. Missions, particularly Catholic missions, and the encounter with and construction of "other religions" in trade and proselytizing, led for the first time to the concept of the "world religions" (cf. Jonathan Z. Smith 1998). The second was the use of "religion" as a generic "essence". Feuerbach himself is particularly important in this story, since he was the first to argue that "religion" in the generic sense was a single thing with a single essence (1957 [1854], 1969 [1846]).

In modernity, religion has become a reified category (now exported from the West around the globe) through political, economic, and juridical means (cf. Haan 2005). Marx presumes this reified concept and treats religion as a singular phenomenon (Feuerbach, after all, provides his "premise"). However, in thinking religion dialectically, and by demanding that critical analysis be concrete, he points beyond Feuerbach's rigidly reified (and thoroughly a/theological) understanding of religion.

Unfortunately, most Marxian understandings of religion are content with a reified – and thoroughly Feuerbachian – understanding of religion. Where religion is not treated as merely epiphenomenal, it has still become a reified category, with a singular (or at least primary) function. In this respect, traditional Marxian analyses of religion shares much more with Parsonian functionalism (with a touch of Voltaire) than it does with Marx, even if it expresses its rubric differently: religion functions to maintain the pattern of (an unjust) social order (by making the working class quiescent with pie-in-the-sky promises). This kind of analysis becomes a slightly more political version of Feuerbach's analysis, rather than a distinctly Marxian one. In treating religion as a reified category, it turns a blind eye to the multiplicity of phenomena that we call religion: regardless of what instance we're talking about, they are all non-contradictory moments, and all have basically the same effect. Thus, the Melanesian cargo-cults, Ultra-Montanist Catholicism, Reconstructionist Judaism, Fundamentalist Islam, the Levelers and Diggers, Liberation Theology, the Puritans, and Theravada Buddhism are all seen – 'in the last instance' – as the same thing (religion) having the same effects (social control with a view to quiescence). Such an account is not only abstract, but it lacks sensitivity to contradictions – attentiveness to which is the hallmark of any authentically Marxian thinking.

Given Marx's emphasis on concrete and dialectical thinking, we can not legitimately make his concrete analyses of religion in a particular time and place (particular forms of Protestantism, Catholicism and Judaism in nineteenth century Germany and England) and make abstract universal theories that would apply to every "religious" phenomena. As a "type" of social object, there is nothing in the genus "religion" that requires special treatment; as particular phenomena, in particular times and places, however, each needs to be accounted for in all of its particularities, contradictions, and social effects.

Given that the category "religion" is a modern social-construction, we cannot hope to produce a – let alone *the* – Marxian theory of religion that will apply trans-historically and cross-culturally. Marx's analysis in "Towards a Critique" does offer us useful tools with which to begin analysis of, not just "religion", but also culture as a whole. It calls for attentiveness to the oppressive and the emancipatory, the ideological and the utopian, within each social moment. It requires attentiveness not only to heart and spirit, but also to the concrete heartless and spiritless situation in which heart and spirit are expressed. Religion as culture "reflects" those situations, but it also plays a role in constituting those heartless, spiritless situations; at the same time, it points beyond them to other possibilities. Such is the dialectics of religion for those who want to follow in the spirit of Marx.

William Clare Roberts

The Origin of Political Economy and the Descent of Marx

> And, putting his hand on mine
> with a cheerful glance from which I drew strength,
> he introduced me into the secret things.
>
> Dante,
> *Inferno*, 3.19–21

This essay offers a novel reading of Marx's project in *Capital*. First, I want to dislodge the standard reading, which sees in *Capital* simply a continuation of the modern techno-scientific project, an attempt to reveal the truth about capitalism which will allow us to finally control the economy. Marx does construct a science of capital, I argue, but not for the sake of knowing how capitalism works. Rather (and this is my second thesis), Marx leads his readers through a presentation of the idea of capital in order to work a poetic transformation on them. I will argue that Marx based *Capital*, in part, on Dante's *Inferno*, and that Marx's goal is similar to Dante's, a conversion of the reader by means of a trial. Finally, I will discuss the nature of this converted subjectivity. Together, I hope these arguments will convincingly portray a Marx quite other from the one we're used to.

Of course, I am hardly the first to claim to present a "new Marx." It seems, however, that these periodic efforts to rediscover Marx, to find a "Marx beyond Marx," must proceed under the assumption that there is no point looking for that "beyond" in *Capital*. The "1844 Manuscripts,"[1] *The German Ideology*,[2] and the *Grundrisse*[3] have functioned, since their addition to Marx's published corpus, as bases for elaborating an "unknown" Marx, one who challenges "Marxist orthodoxy" (however that orthodoxy may be conceived). Marx's journalism and polemics are evidence of a Marx engaged in concrete and uncertain political and rhetorical struggles, rather than dogmatic system-building.[4] The unpublished drafts and marginal notes reveal a Marx whose approach to political economy is at once more nuanced and more visionary than Marxist economics is supposed to be.[5] But *Capital* itself is ceded as the natural homeland of orthodoxy. It is the old, bad Marx, the one that everyone knows, and with whom nothing new can be done. As Terrell Carver summarizes the popular wisdom, "amongst those works thought to be boringly literal in their scientificity, it would be hard to find one more widely derided than Marx's Capital" (1998:9).[6]

I think the pigeonholing of *Capital* follows in the train of certain uncritical notions of Marx's intellectual career: the "mature" Marx, according to the common wisdom, set aside philosophy and pamphleteering and became a social scientist, retreating to the British Museum Reading Room to discover the truth of capitalism. *Capital* is supposed to be the fruit of this essentially scholarly labor, a monumental (even if monumentally flawed) attempt to outline a new science of society and to offer a firm foundation for a rational class struggle. Whether a particular commentator defends or derides Marx's science matters less than that defender and derider alike conceive of Marx's

---

[1] The 1844 Manuscripts have spawned: David McLellan (1970), Takahisa Oishi (2001), and the entire range of Marxist Humanism.

[2] The more famous first part of *The German Ideology* supports the whole sub-genre on "historical materialism," and its second part has provided ammunition for those who develop a picture of Marx the politician, as opposed to the economist and philosopher. See, e.g., Mark Reinhardt (1997).

[3] See: Carol C. Gould (1978), Thomas M. Kemple (1995), Richard Marsden (1999), Antonio Negri (1991), and Moishe Postone (1993) (for starters).

[4] See, e.g.: Terrell Carver (1998), Martin Harries (2000), and Reinhardt (1997).

[5] See: Michael Heinrich (1996), Leszek Nowak (1980), and, most explicitly, James D. White (1994).

[6] Carver's work stands out in this regard, in that he actually begins the process of reading *Capital* differently. There is also a growing body of new scholarship on Marx's approach to economics in *Capital*. I would highlight the work of Chris Arthur (1986, 2004), Patrick Murray (1988, 2000a, 2000b), and the volumes of essays edited by Moseley (1993) and Moseley and Campbell (1997). These are welcome and important works. To date, however, this research remains the province of a small number of specialists, and has had very little if any impact on the wider world of social, economic, and political theory.

effort along the same lines: Marx wanted to reveal, in *Capital*, the inner workings of capitalism, thereby arming revolutionaries with firm knowledge of the enemy. *Capital* stands or falls as a work of *theory*; if Marx's theory is a *critical* theory, this is because, having brought its readers to understand capitalism, it allows them to judge capitalism to be somehow faulty.

In this paper, I will challenge these common notions of Marx's project in *Capital* by recasting Marx's relationship to science in general, and to political economy in particular. The standard reading of *Capital* cannot make any sense of numerous details of the text. Taking these textual details seriously, as I will try to show, produces a radically unorthodox redescription of Marx's undertaking. I will begin with what I take to be the cornerstone of the common wisdom, namely a certain reading of the 1859 Preface to *A Contribution to the Critique of Political Economy*. In the first two sections of this paper, I will attack this cornerstone by placing Marx's famous comments within the textual and political context from which they are usually abstracted. This will orient the reading of *Capital* that will follow in the next three sections. This reading will show that, for Marx, a science of capitalism cannot possibly ground our revolutionary action, but is rather a trial that teaches us the limits of science as theory, and of knowledge as such.

I. At the Entrance to Science

The common wisdom regarding Marx's turn to science has so much cogency because it seems to be the plain meaning of Marx's 1859 Preface, the prologue to his first attempt at writing *Capital*. So many commentators agree on the basic outline of the story because it is the story Marx himself tells. Therefore, if I am to succeed at reformulating Marx's encounter with science, I must first wrestle with Marx's own presentation of that encounter.

The 1859 Preface is composed of what he calls a "sketch of the course of [his] studies," an intellectual autobiography that traces his trajectory from editor of the *Rheinische Zeitung* to surveyor of bourgeois political economy. Marx portrays this development as a movement from ignorance to knowledge. While engaged in journalism, he claims, he had run up against "so-called material interests" involuntarily, and, he claims further, much to his embarrassment. He says he resisted the first pushes of those around him toward French socialism and communism, out of a principled unwillingness to botch the job. Only after his researches in Paris did he come to see that "the anatomy of bourgeois society is to be sought in political economy." Only in London was he able to pursue his research systematically (1970:20).

It is remarkable how central this short text has become to our efforts to know where Marx stands. Whether or not it is cited explicitly, the autobiographical narrative of the 1859 Preface is the cornerstone of the edifice of Marxology, "an obstacle to developing an alternative to traditional Marxism" (Marsden 1999:91). This centrality, moreover, rests upon the unexamined assumption that, in the Preface, Marx is "really" or "honestly" telling us "what he's up to." Rather than following the actual workings of his texts, as soon as Marx says, "This is what I have been doing," we happily take him at his word, and then read his other works on the basis of the intention he plainly and conveniently revealed to us in 1859. Here, we seem to think, we have gotten behind all the difficulties of textuality, and are exposed directly to Marx's self-consciousness. The hermeneutics of suspicion is suspended in the face of Marx's simple declaration.

What Marx declares is that he is an unbiased scientific investigator. The 1859 Preface, he writes, "should merely demonstrate that my views, however one may judge them, and however little they agree with the interested prejudices of the ruling classes, are the result of conscientious and lengthy research" (1970:23). The point of the Preface is to portray Marx as a serious scholar, and thereby to foreclose the accusation of political partisanship. This strategy gives the whole preface what Terrell Carver calls "a curiously depoliticized form" (Marx 1996:xiv), which is only reinforced by Marx's *other* preface to the critique of political economy, the one to the first edition of *Capital*, where Marx analogizes his work to that of the physicist, the molecular biologist, and the natural historian (1976:90, 92). The one-two punch of these prefaces seems to make it impossible not to read *Capital* as "boringly literal" in its scientificity.

There is, however, a detail in each preface, consistently overlooked by Marxologists of every stripe, that puts a question mark after Marx's self-presentation and, thus, after the standard readings of *Capital*. Both prefaces end with citations from Dante. The final sentence of the 1859 Preface, directly following Marx's *apologia*, incorporates a quotation from the *Inferno*; "But at the entrance to science, as at the entrance to Hell, this demand must be registered: 'Here one must abandon every suspicion; every cowardice must die here'" (1970:23). Similarly, the final lines of the *Capital* preface contain a slightly doctored citation of *Purgatory*; "Every opinion based on scientific criticism I welcome. As to the prejudices of so-called public opinion, to which I have never made concessions, now as before the maxim of the great Florentine is mine: 'Follow your own course, and let the people talk'" (1976:93). (Dante's line runs, "Come after me, and let the people talk" (Pur. 5.13).)

To my knowledge, no one has made anything of these citations, despite their critical placement in the unfolding of Marx's science. Why is Marx twice drawn to Dante's poem at the very same moment – the *final* words before entering into his critique of political economy? What can account for the apparent need to turn to Dante immediately before investigating the commodity? Is it not remarkable that Marx closes both published prefaces to his life-long scientific project with references to the greatest poet of Christianity?[7]

I want to pause over these citations, and take them seriously for once. In 1859, Marx compares the entrance into science to the entrance into Hell. My hypothesis is that Marx thereby situates his critique of political economy as the heir to the Western tradition of the *katabasis*, the "educational" descent into the underworld. If this hypothesis is correct, then science is not, for Marx, the destination, but something that must be overcome. With these citations, he casts his readers as pilgrims – joining, among others, Orpheus, Odysseus, Theseus, Heracles, Dionysus, Socrates, Aeneus, Jesus Christ, Saint Paul, and Dante himself – who must be guided on a round-trip to a place no one wants to visit and from which no one expects to return.

Marx's citation links his project to a very particular lineage within the history of the *katabasis*. Dante's Hell is an elaborate reworking of the Hades from Virgil's *Aeneid*, which, in turn, draws heavily from the Land of the Dead in Homer's *Odyssey*. Examining this direct citational lineage reveals a tendential pattern that fosters expectations of Marx's own descent. With every reiteration, the passages of the Homer-Virgil-Dante line transform and empower the pilgrim to a greater degree. Odysseus returns from the Land of the Dead knowing his fate, foretold by Teiresius. This knowledge does not, however, alter his course in any obvious way. Odysseus is immutable, and so is the world; he had to await Plato to give him a chance at a new life as a private man. Aeneus also learns his fate in Hades, but this fate is the future of his productivity, extending through his offspring to the creation of the Roman

[7] Richard Marsden notes the 1859 citation, but, quite inexplicably, decides that "by quoting Dante in conclusion, Marx cloaks himself in the legitimacy of science" (1999:107).

Empire. It is not something befalling him from beyond, but something he will make. Dante's journey, in turn, radicalizes Aeneus' education by inwardizing it as "a descent in humility, a death of the self," as John Freccero has called it (1986:4). Dante's descent makes him into a new person, readying him for the labor of Purgatory. At the beginning of the poem, he is damned, unable to climb toward the light. Were Beatrice not to intervene, he would be consigned eternally to Hell. Because of her intervention, however, he must only go *temporarily* to Hell. Unlike Odysseus or Aeneus, Dante has a salvific conversion experience; his *katabasis* changes his fate by changing his soul.

This inward transformation is not, for all that, a repudiation of the worldly effects of the *Aeneid*. Before entering Hell, Dante compares himself to Aeneus and Paul, the acknowledged precedents for his descent, and questions his presence in such illustrious company. He refers to "the high effect that was to come" from Aeneus; "Through this journey that you [Virgil] claim for him, he understood things that were the cause of his victory and of the papal mantle" (2.17–18, 25–27). He then says of Paul: "Later the chosen vessel went there, to bring back strengthening for that faith which is the principle of the way of salvation" (2.28–30). Aeneus' *katabasis* prepared him to give birth to Rome. Paul's *katabasis* led to the transformation of Aeneus' Roman Empire into a Holy one. The *katabasis* is a sign of election, a propaedutic for playing a world-historical role. Dante sees this and protests: "I am not Aeneus, I am not Paul" (2.32).

Despite this display of modesty, Dante, through his descent, is actually establishing himself as a *new* Aeneus, a *new* Paul. The protest of the pilgrim might be honest, but for the fact that the pilgrim is also the poet, who already knows the pilgrim is strong enough to succeed, since he is writing the poem from the perspective of the completed journey. We must conclude that Dante's self-effacement is insincere; the poet is writing himself into history as the third of a glorious imperial triumvirate. Aeneus founded an empire on earth. Paul founded an empire of the heart. Dante's trip, he himself implies, inaugurates a third empire. When one reflects, as well, that Dante is the first great poet to write in the vernacular, that he (in *De Monarchia*) calls for a global political order on the basis of humanity's oneness, and that he reveals to all readers "the secret things" of Christianity (Inf. 3.21), one can justifiably conclude that the empire Dante claims to inaugurate is modernity itself.

Thus, Dante's *katabasis* gives rise not only to a metamorphosis of his own soul, but also to an immense new power. Aeneus' generative powers were revealed to him in Hades, but it is not at all clear that they were bestowed upon him *by* his descent. Dante, however, could not produce his poem without undergoing the journey it relates. The proof of the descent's productivity is that we know about the descent in the first place.

That Marx cites Dante's *katabasis* in 1859, therefore, mouthing Virgil's reassurance to the pilgrim, suggests to me that Marx is engaged in an analogous project. Certainly Marx had a great interest in the Florentine poet. Citations from Dante begin cropping up in Marx's writings from the 1850s, and continue throughout the rest of his life. Karl Liebknecht, who was close to Marx throughout the '50s, testifies that Marx declaimed aloud from *The Divine Comedy*, and that he taught himself Italian by reading Dante and Machiavelli.[8] Dante also heads a list of Marx's favorite poets – also including Aeschylus, Shakespeare, and Goethe – in an undated "confession" in his hand found in his daughter Jenny's album.[9] I think Marx's love of Dante – like his love of Shakespeare, Cervantes, and Balzac – speaks to his understanding of his own endeavor, and can fruitfully illuminate that endeavor if we only pay it some honest attention.

I will use the remainder of this essay to build upon this hypothesis by outlining Marx's descent into political economy. I will first examine the relationship Marx establishes between himself and his readers in the two prefaces; this, I hope, will go some distance toward explaining why Marx tells the story he does in the 1859 Preface. I will then, in section three, turn to Marx's approach to political economy. Examining *Capital* itself, as well as the *Contribution*, I will show that Marx does not, as is usually assumed, identify his project with political economy, but indicates a sharp and necessary separation between the two. With this preparatory work out of the way, I will substantiate, in section four, the parallels between *Capital* and Dante's *Inferno* by reference to textual and structural details, before drawing some conclusions, in section five, about the role of science in Marx's efforts to overcome modernity.

---

[8] The first published citation I know of is in his column for the *New York Daily Tribune*, 4 April 1853. There is also a cluster of citations from '59 and '60 – from the *NYDT*, *Herr Vogt*, and the *Contribution* – and another cluster from the first volume of *Capital* (Prawer 1976: especially 208, 239–40, 261–264, 338–9, 383–4, and 419–421). Finally, there is a page of excerpts from Karl Lüdwig Kannegießer's German translation, *Die göttliche Komödie dem Dante Alighieri*, in one of Marx's notebooks from 1859 or 1860 (IISG: B 93, S. 19), all from *Inferno*. These excerpts form the basis of the citations in *Herr Vogt*.

[9] Another version of the "confession," from the spring of 1865, does not include Dante (Marx and Engels 1956 vol. 42:569, 674n620).

2. Marx as Guide

Both preface citations were originally Virgil's words to Dante. In repeating them, I suggest, Marx casts himself as a Virgilian guide to his readers. Therefore, we must first investigate Virgil's role as a guide. Marx's 1859 citation comes from Canto III of *Inferno*. Virgil has brought Dante to the gates of Hell, which bear this inscription:

> Through me the way into the grieving city,
> through me the way into eternal sorrow,
> through me the way among the lost people.
> Justice moved my high maker;
> divine power made me,
> highest wisdom, and primal love.
> Before me were no things created
> except eternal ones, and I endure eternal.
> Abandon every hope, you who enter. (Inf. 3.1–9)

Dante reacts the way one just sentenced to death might react; he is stunned, and can only mutter; "their sense is hard for me." Virgil, "like one alert," responds with the words Marx quotes; "Here one must abandon every suspicion; every cowardice must die here." Then he smiles, takes Dante's hand, and leads him into Hell.

Virgil's response is initially unsatisfying, in that it does not explicate the inscription, as the pilgrim requests. The inscription instructs travelers to abandon all *hope*; Virgil tells Dante to abandon only his suspicion. The words on the gate *inspire* fear, yet Virgil demands that Dante put his cowardice to death. As hermeneutics, Virgil's response fails miserably. Nonetheless, the poet explicitly tells us Virgil is alert – the Italian is *accorta*, which connotes more than sense perception, and could also be rendered as "shrewd" in order to stress the many levels of Virgil's awareness – so the guide must have some other aim than explication. Dante has already indicated this aim. When Beatrice descended to limbo to recruit Virgil, she made special reference to Virgil's "ornamented" and "virtuous speech" (2.67, 2.113). The response at the gate is an early and prominent example of this speech; what fails as hermeneutics succeeds as rhetoric. Virgil does not explain the gate's sense because he does not need to do so in order to accomplish his goal of strengthening Dante and moving him along. He redirects Dante's attention away from the inscription and back to himself as guide, drawing upon his charge's trust and admiration. Virgil implies that the only possible reasons the pilgrim would not enter Hell would be mistrust of his "master and author" – something we know Dante could not admit – or cowardice. This classic rhetorical strategy – "What? Are you chicken?" – is still used to high effect on school-yards everywhere.

It is also used by Marx in the 1859 Preface, though he faces obstacles Virgil did not. First, the average reader in Germany didn't know him from Adam. As a journalist and polemicist, he was known in socialist and democratic circles, but he was hardly a household name. Virgil can use the pilgrim's avowed adoration to his advantage. When Virgil says, "Trust me," Dante does. If Marx's audience were to stop at the threshold and say, "I'm not sure . . .," what trust could Marx possibly draw upon to lure them on? Second, those readers who do know his previous work – mostly the *Manifesto* – are less devotees who will follow Marx anywhere than wary, embattled radicals suffering through a long hangover from 1848. This new dispatch from the expatriate Marx would be noted, but perhaps with skepticism. Finally, the readers who probably know Marx best, and to whose reactions he must attend before all others, are the Prussian censors. Nearly two generations have passed since A. M. Prinz indicated the effects of censorship upon Marx's presentation in the 1859 Preface, reminding us that "censorship had produced the art of reading between the lines and thus induced authors to practice the art of writing between the lines" (1969:439).

It seems to me that Marx attempted to placate the censors, encourage the supporters, and establish himself as a trustworthy guide, all in the space of a few pages. His statements about his own past are ambiguous, open to double readings (Marsden 1999:107). His conclusions are couched in utterly impersonal terms, and revolution is depicted as an abstract social process, in no way suggesting violent struggle. The only conflict mentioned is between "the social forces of production and the relations of production" (Marx 1970:21). It is a great irony of Marxology that so much orthodox and academic Marxism takes as its absolute touchstone a characterization of Marx's project deliberately written to allay fears of revolution, to seem absolutely unthreatening, and to be completely acceptable to Prussian censors in a time of reaction.

Yet, securing his critique's arrival at its audience is only the first hurdle for Marx's Preface. The primary task remains enlisting the readers' trust. Here Marx exploits the fact that most of his audience doesn't know him from Adam, or from Adam Smith. Since moderns trust no one so much as they trust a scientist, it is no surprise that Marx dons the mantle of the scholar, highlighting his lengthy research, carried on under the most disagreeable circumstances. Expelled from France and Belgium because of his fearless inquiries (wisely, he doesn't mention Germany), continuously set upon by necessity, Marx has finally arrived. His "whole material lies before" him, and he is prepared to guide his reader – who, if they "want to follow," "must decide to climb from the singular to the general" (1970:19) – the decision is theirs. When Marx comes to the end of his self-portrait, he is finally in a position to make a demand. He has established the basis on which he can be trusted – as a scientist and fearless seeker of truth – and he has cast himself as the sort of brave soul who can challenge others to be brave. Science is not for everyone. It is for the fearless few. Marx asks his readers to elect themselves fearless enough to enter science with him.

This tactic is redeployed and further developed in the *Capital* preface. Marx alters the Virgilian command he cites. Virgil rebukes Dante; "Follow me and let the people talk." Marx says only, "Follow your own course and let the people talk," and not as a command, but as a simple report of his own motto. This alteration follows from the difference between Virgil's personal relationship to Dante and Marx's impersonal relationship to his readers. Marx cannot possibly draw upon any personal authority; to flatly command his readers to follow him would get him nowhere. Yet, his feigned solitude and indifference is belied by his efforts, frequently attested, to popularize *Capital* as much as possible. Marx wants his audience to follow him, but he also knows his audience. If he claims to be following his own course, then those who follow him can tell themselves the same thing. He has hit upon a rhetorical device that could only work in modernity: "Be an individual – like me." Only self-election will suffice.

3. Getting Past the Inscription

If rhetorical analysis shows that Marx tries to provoke his readers into trusting and following him, we must now ask: How does Marx approach political economy such that he can make this attempt? Why does Marx think he can guide us into political economy? And why do we need a guide in the first place? What is at question here is Marx's entire conception of science: what it is, what value it has, and how a revolutionary must engage with it. To reiterate, the common wisdom would claim that science breaks through ideology to reveal the real inner workings of society, and that the revolutionary must understand these real inner workings in order effectively to overthrow capitalism, in the same way that a mechanic must understand the inner workings of a car in order to fix one. But, on this understanding, we do not need a trustworthy *guide* to prod us along, but a *teacher*, who will simply explain things as clearly as possible. All the drama seems superfluous, if not obscurantist. And, indeed, Marx has been accused of both superfluous dramatics and obscurantism. If we are taking the dramatics seriously, however, then we must ask what they might mean, on their own terms.

To get our bearings, let's return to Virgil. I've mentioned that Dante describes him as "alert." To what is he alert? By definition, a guide must know something a pilgrim cannot. The point of the pilgrimage is for the pilgrim to come to see what she does not yet see, but the guide sees from the very beginning, namely, the end of the pilgrimage. Virgil does not explicate the gate's inscription because he knows what Dante cannot yet know, and what the gate does not tell: the way out of Hell. After all, Virgil's reassurances are completely at odds with the inscription and its apocalyptic ending, "Abandon every hope, you who enter." Dante's fear and suspicion are *warranted* by that inscription. No pilgrim would willingly enter Hell after reading and understanding the sense of these words, for they depict Hell as having no exit. Indeed, this impression persists in the pilgrim right up to the moment he leaves Hell. With Dante on his back, Virgil is climbing down Satan's flank; when he reaches the very center of the cosmos, he turns 180 degrees and begins to climb up into the cave beneath Purgatory. Dante thinks Virgil is climbing back into Hell, and he is confused when they emerge to find Satan's feet protruding helplessly into the cavern (Inf. 34.38–90). Dante cannot understand this reversal and exit as he is experiencing it, much less foresee such an experience at the beginning of his journey.

In fact, however, the gate's depiction of Hell as a hopeless eternity was a lie before Dante ever encountered it. Virgil recounts Christ's harrowing of Hell, when "[he] led forth from here the shade of our first parent, [. . .] and many others, and he made them blessed." Virgil does not, and cannot, rule out a repeat performance. Moreover, Dante has already admitted that Aeneus and Paul – two mortal humans – have gone down and returned safely (Inf. 2.13–30). But if people have passed through Hell, then its fearsome admonition seems less like fate, and more like braggadocio. Hell *wants* those who enter to have no hope, but, given these past exceptions, it might not get its wish. Indeed, it is precisely this empirical warrant for hope that compels Hell so vehemently to demand that hope be abandoned. Hell cannot be filled with hopeful souls and remain Hell. If hope is reasonable – and the slimmest odds are reasonable over eternity – then Hell *must* scare that hope out of its denizens. Hell can be Hell only by successfully interpellating its denizens as hopeless. If Hell were *really* hopeless, it would not need to say so. It could welcome entrants mutely to their doom.

Hell's gate lies, therefore, but it is a performative lie. The inscription seeks to construct an existence that is not real, and cannot be real, but can asymptotically approximate reality only through the lie that it is already real. Virgil seeks to disrupt this performance with his demand that Dante abandon his suspicions and put his cowardice to death. Virgil's response does not take Dante through the inscription, but bypasses it without probing its meaning. Virgil is aware of Hell's limit from the very first, for it is only in view of such a limit that his demand that Dante abandon his cowardice and suspicion is at all reasonable.

It is the same with Marx. Political economy performs the same interpellation as does Hell.[10] Bourgeois economics depicts itself as opening up the realm imposed on us by necessity and scarcity. It claims to establish justice in this world of necessity by showing how the market provides the most fitting distribution of goods. Above all, it claims its truths are timeless. Thus, Ricardo expects that ancient hunters and fishers calculated labor times, and Smith imagines that the impulse to "truck and barter" holds sway everywhere and at all times. The laws of the bourgeois world are the laws of all history; this is just how things are. According to what economics claims for itself, then, the notion of passing through its world to some other, post-economic world is as fantastical as the idea that one could travel through Hell and come out the other side. "Abandon every hope, you who enter."

Mirroring Hell's braggadocio, however, political economy is actually trying to produce the situation it claims to describe as already the case. Marx asks us to ignore this façade. He doesn't immediately counter it, or parse its intricacies; he simply begins his descent into political economy by putting the proclamations of eternity off to one side. In both the *Contribution* and *Capital*, the first sentences after the Dante citations direct our attention very specifically to "bourgeois wealth" and "the wealth of societies in which the

[10] I am indebted to Hasana Sharp for first drawing my attention to this parallel.

capitalist mode of production rules," respectively (1970:27; 1976:125). In the face of science's claim to eternity, Marx has simply pointed off the other direction. He does not pretend to examine something timeless; contrarily, he continuously directs us towards the limited scope of his investigation.[11] Just as at the gate of Hell, at the gate of science we must confront the moment of decision: either we abandon all hope, or we turn aside from science's claim to portray things as they always have been and ever will be.

Marx can redirect us from this apparent eternity because he sees political economy's limit, and is thus able to lead us to that limit. According to Marx, Ricardo is the "finisher of political economy" (1970:61).[12] Political economy is defined as a science by "the determination of exchange-value by labor-time," and Ricardo works up this determination into its "purest" formulation (1970:61). Thus, Marx writes that "with [Ricardo's] contribution the bourgeois science of political economy had reached the limits beyond which it could not pass" (1976:96). Marx himself, in his presentation of the commodity, begins with Ricardo's formulation, as virtually all commentators note. What follows from this beginning, however, is rarely grasped. Harry Cleaver has rightly criticized the tendency to read Marx's *critique* of political economy as essentially a *correction* of political economy, "either as fulfilling its promise or as having corrected its errors" (2000:32).[13] The truth is there is nothing to fulfill or to correct. Political economy is done, finished, closed; Marx says this explicitly. Therefore, when he begins with the commodity, the exchange-value of which is determined by socially abstract labor-time, he begins with the boundary marker of political economy before his eyes. He has this limit in view because the whole task of his critique is to guide us to

[11] This plain statement has been continuously misunderstood, ever since Engels' unfortunately concluded that, in the first two sections of *Capital*, Marx is investigating some heretofore unknown form of society called "simple commodity production," lying somewhere in the past. Even more confusing are the claims made by Philip J. Kain, that "the 'commodity', with which *Capital* begins, is in fact a transhistorical category" (1986:63). It is unclear what Kain means by "transhistorical," since it can hardly be maintained that commodities have always existed. Perhaps, instead, he means only that no matter when commodities exist, they will be as Marx describes them. But this is a trivial claim, since the same can be said of anything whatsoever; it is what it is as long as it remains what it is.

[12] Jon Elster agrees with Paul Samuelson that Marx is "basically 'a minor post-Ricardian'" (1985:513). Since this judgment is confined to Marx as an economist, Marx would certainly agree; *all* economists after Ricardo are *necessarily* minor post-Ricardians, in Marx's estimation.

[13] Compare Althusser's discussion (Althusser and Balibar 1970:18–30).

an encounter with this limit, to the point where we can cross over this limit and leave political economy behind.

4. The Anatomy of Hell

Having accepted Marx as our guide into political economy, the "anatomy" of bourgeois society (1970:20), we can finally ask what Marx discloses of this anatomy. What is the structure of capital, and how does the text of *Capital* proceed through that structure? Of course, the structure of *Capital* has been endlessly debated; I do not hope to provide an exhaustive exposition. I take as a starting point that Marx approaches capital as a systematic whole, an internally differentiated totality, akin to Aristotle's approach to natural things, or Hegel's approach to Spirit (Reuten 2000). However, I will show that the structure of this totality, as Marx presents it in *Capital*, bears a striking resemblance to the structure of Dante's Hell. This is not as outlandish as it may sound. Marx and Dante both bear the influence of Aristotle, and this common ontological lineage goes some way toward shaping their works, aside from any direct influence. Nonetheless, given Marx's intense interest in Dante during the drafting of *Capital*, I also suspect the latter.[14]

In Dante's cosmology, Hell descends to the center of the earth. When Lucifer turned against God, he was cast down to the lowest place, as far from God as one can be. This corresponds to Satan's absolute materiality. Dante and Virgil descend, therefore, from the airy shades of limbo and the windblown lovers of the circle of lust, through water, mud, and fire, to the very bodily Malebolge and the entombed and frozen sinners in Cocytus. They also encounter sins in the order of their increasing severity. Incontinence, going beyond the bounds of natural desire, is a lesser representation of violence, which is the denial of the natural order itself. Fraud, in turn, is that of which violence is the image, for fraud transgresses the ontological distinction between appearance and reality, which founds the natural ordering itself. But fraud is a mere representation of a sin more fundamental yet, treachery; traitors act directly against the foundation of their own being. The purest and most originary instance of this treason is Satan's act of turning away from his creator at the very moment of his creation. This archaic sin establishes the possibility

[14] I have argued elsewhere (Roberts 2003) that Marx modeled *The Eighteenth Brumaire* on the play-within-a-play in *Hamlet*, and I think it is worth looking for such literary patterns in other of Marx's works.

of all others, and sinks Satan to the deepest point of Hell, where he gnaws on the sinners whose deeds bear the greatest verisimilitude to his own: Brutus, Cassius, and Judas.

Capital reproduces this narrative structure. It replicates the descent into materiality, from the abstractions of the value-forms to the "blood and dirt" of primitive accumulation (1976:926). Each stage of this descent is dependent upon the stage that comes after it, giving *Capital* the form of an excavation. The major divisions, moreover, are distinguished by logics reminiscent of incontinence, violence, fraud, and treason that constitute the architecture of Dante's Hell.[15]

Dante's *Inferno*	Marx's *Capital* [& *Contribution*]		
Hell's gate	Preface		[1859 Preface]
Circles of Incontinence	Pt. 1: Commodities & Money		[*Contribution*]
The gates of Dis	Pt. 2: The Transformation of Money into Capital		
Circles of Violence	Pt. 3: The Production of Absolute Surplus Value	Pt. 4: The Production of Relative Surplus Value	
Circle of Fraud (Malebolge)			
	Pts. 5 & 6: Summing up & Wages		
Circle of Treason (Cocytus)	Pt. 7: The Accumulation of Capital		
Encounter with Lucifer	Pt. 8: The So-Called Original Accumulation		
Exit from Hell	Ch. 33: The Modern Theory of Colonization		

I do not know whether this isomorphism was intentional, but as Marx himself maintained vis-à-vis Hegel's accommodations to the Prussian state, what matters is not the "exoteric consciousness" of the writer, but the inner movement

[15] Marx even reworked the chapter divisions of *Capital* in such a way that they mimic those of the *Inferno*. Beginning with the French edition, and carrying over into the English edition, *Capital* is divided into a preface and 33 chapters. The *Inferno* has 34 cantos, the first of which is a preface to the whole *Comedy*.

of the work itself (Marx and Engels 1975 vol. 1:84). In its inner workings, *Capital* constitutes an *Inferno* for the capitalist era. Fully substantiating this claim requires an extended, point-by-point analysis; however, the major structural relationships – schematized in Figure 1 – can be narrated fairly succinctly.

Beginning at the beginning, just as the outer circles of Dante's Hell house the sins of incontinence – desire beyond the proper measure – so too the first major part of *Capital*, which recapitulates the *Contribution*, treats the market, a place of boundless desire. Bourgeois wealth is first encountered as "a monstrous collection of commodities" (1976:125). These commodities enter into exchange, where they give birth to new desires and new commodities. The desires treated cease to be human desires, and come to be the desires of the commodities themselves. Marx discusses the flirtation of the coat with the linen (1976:139–44), and the willingness of a commodity "to exchange not only soul, but body, with each and every other commodity, be it more repulsive than Maritornes herself" (1976:179). The limitlessness of this readiness for exchange transforms the commodities' desire for one another into their desire for money, for "commodities are in love with money" (1976:202). Thus does the incontinence of exchange spread and intensify; "the lust for gold awakens" (1976:229).

In both *Inferno* and *Capital*, it is difficult to move beyond this realm of incontinent desire. Dante and Virgil must confront the devils and furies at the gates of Dis, where Aeneus turned aside. Dante must descend further than his predecessor. Likewise, Marx must transgress a boundary here, leading us deeper than the political economists ever went. The marketplace, that "noisy sphere where everything takes place on the surface, and in full view of everyone" (1976:279), cannot account for the growth of capital. The market seemed to be limitless, but circulation is always limited externally by consumption and formally by the exchange of equals. Circulation cannot generate the "more" that exhibits itself in all of these commodities. Beyond the market, Marx must lead us into the realm of capitalist production.

In Dante, the violence punished in the second division, the outer circles of Dis, is the denial or perversion of the divine order of generation. The epitome of this violence against natural generation is the figure of the usurer, the last sinner encountered at this level, who makes money grow unnaturally (Inf. 17.34–75). The problem of usury confronts Marx as capital; money has become perversely productive. Marx cites Aristotle's paradigmatic critique of money-making, which also underlies Dante's treatment of usury (1976:253n6,

267). But Marx transforms the traditional problematic, for he does not treat usury as its own final term, but inscribes it within capital. No longer is usury an inexplicable or unholy breeding of money; instead it is revealed to be a derivative form of the "tanning" of the workers.

Marx is slow to reveal this. He plays out the theme of the productivity of capital until "the voice of the worker" pipes up in his discussion of the working day (1976:342), and it returns once again in the first chapters of Part Four, when Marx begins to discuss relative surplus value. The productivity of capital is not unreal for Marx. The subsumption of labor actually does render capital productive. The monstrous (*ungeheuere*) collection of commodities that greeted our eyes at the entrance to political economy has become the animated monster (*beseeltes Ungeheuer*) (1976:302). The problem of incontinence – the going beyond measure of bourgeois wealth – has been found to conceal within it, as a more fundamental moment, a measureless and measure-destroying productivity.

In both *Inferno* and *Capital*, this confrontation with monstrous productivity leads the pilgrim to fraud. The usurers provide Dante the transition from the circles of violence to the circles of fraud; the two-pronged examination of the subsumption of labor allows Marx to reveal that capital's productivity rests upon the capitalist's fraudulent extraction of surplus-labor.[16] Exploitation is mentioned for the first time only in Chapter Nine, and it is only then that Marx begins to use the language of "tricks, artifices, temptations, threats and falsifications" to characterize capital (1976:337). Precisely where Dante enters into the greatest detail – crossing the circle of fraud takes thirteen cantos – Marx begins the fine-grained historical treatment of the struggle between the working class and capital, the details of which occupy the long middle of *Capital*.

As in Dante's Hell, each level of Marx's critique is conditioned by the levels that come after it. There could be no monstrous collection of commodities without the animated monster of capital, and no capital without the fraudulent exploitation of the workers' labor-power. But what underlies the possibility of exploitation? In order to buy labor-power on the market, I must already have accumulated some capital; I must have a surplus on hand, over and above what I need for my life, with which I can purchase the means and

[16] There is, therefore, a doubling back in Marx's descent; Part Three descends from violence into fraud, and then Part Four retraces this same movement.

materials of production, and hire workers to do the producing. Capital seems to always presuppose itself. Therefore, Marx writes; "From our current standpoint it [. . .] seems likely that the capitalist, once upon a time, became possessed of money by some form of original accumulation that took place independently of the unpaid labor of other people, and that this was therefore how he was able to frequent the market as a buyer of labor-power" (1976:714). Whence this original accumulation of capital? "'From [the capitalist's] own labor and that of his forefathers,' is the unanimous answer of the spokesmen of political economy" (1976:728). The original accumulation must derive from some original labor.

From this, the assumption of political economy, Marx shows that even the simple reproduction of this original capital fund, to say nothing of the actual accumulation of further capital, transforms the entirety of the original fund into "value appropriated without an equivalent, the unpaid labor of others" (1976:715). Thus, even if all capital was born of an immaculate conception, it must, in the course of its own reproduction and propagation become completely and utterly the product of exploitation: "When a person consumes the whole of his property, by taking upon himself debts equal to the value of that property, it is clear that his property represents nothing but the sum total of his debts. And so it is with the capitalist" (1976:715).

The capitalist owes his entire wealth, his whole substance, to the workers. The fraud inherent in capital's exploitation, therefore, in the course of reproduction and accumulation, comes to be treacherous fraud, in precisely Dante's sense of breaking a special bond. Capital *is* the growth of capital, but it can only accumulate by defrauding its sole benefactors, its "parents." The more fully capital develops, the more massive its debt, and the greater its treason. This treason is nowhere more clearly manifested than in capital's apocalyptic wastefulness. Capital does not merely steal from the workers; it undermines the very sources of its productivity, squandering the earth and the workers from which it draws its strength. Capital is a traitor to its kin, a fratricide and a matricide, rightly placed in Cocytus alongside Cain.

We have now descended, in both the *Inferno* and *Capital*, to the deepest level. But now that we have reached the ground floor, we must ask: 1) Upon what does this ground rest? and 2) How do we get out of this place? Marx and Virgil have both promised us that they can lead us out from these inverted worlds, so where is the exit?

Dante's *katabasis*, if it is to be successful, must lead him to confront his own sins, but also to grapple with the *arkhē* of those sins, Satan himself. In Aristotelian terms, Satan is the *pros hen* of infernal cosmology, that one toward which everything else gestures. But when Virgil and Dante reach this *arkhē*, they have also reached the ladder out of Hell, climbing "down" his flank to the center of the world, where they turn and climb up to exit from his realm (Inf. 34.70–93). Only then does Satan appear as he truly is, an upside-down king of an upside-down realm. Only through grappling with this inverted foundation of Hell can Dante and Virgil turn right-side up again, and escape from the world of no hope.

Marx's critique of political economy also contains this dynamic of radical confrontation and reversal. As we've seen, Ricardo's formulation of the labor theory of value marks the limit of political economy as a science. But Ricardo's formulation marks the end of political economy precisely because it also supplies political economy with its foundation. All of political economy is a premonition of, or reference to, the labor theory of value in its purity.[17] But the labor theory of value refers most directly to labor that has undergone a process of social abstraction. Labor that is really subsumed under capital most truly creates value (Murray 2000a). Therefore, it is a mistake to imagine that the labor theory of value only matters for the opening section of *Capital*. The development of capital from its simplest appearance to its constitution as the self-reproducing form of society (Parts 1–7) is also the progression through more and more adequate expressions of the labor theory of value. At the end of this progression, we encounter the foundation of political economy in its purest form; labor as it appears here can only produce capital.

And yet, there still remains an entire Part Eight ahead of us, which does not seem to continue either the historical or logical progression established by everything prior to it (see, e.g., Murray 2002:161). Instead, Marx presents us with "the so-called primitive accumulation," a historical tour stretching back as far as the Fourteenth Century. There is no wonder that numerous commentators have found Part Eight to be tacked on, an addition that in no way furthers the argument (Arthur and White 2001:130). If *Capital* ended here, however, Marx would have led us into the heart of capital only to leave us there. Capital would be a self-creating, self-sustaining, self-reproducing

---

[17] As Marx writes, "the historical course of all sciences leads first through a mass of crusades and diversions to its actual point of departure. Science, unlike other architects, builds not only castles in the air, but may construct separate habitable stories of the building before laying the foundation stone" (1970:57).

system, with no way out except the eventual collapse of the biosphere. But this would be the case only if capital were indeed able to found itself, if the foundation of its logic – labor that posits capital – were also its historic foundation. Luckily, this is not so. The foundation of political economy rests upon a historical foundation it does not comprehend.[18] Political economy as a science expresses the logic of capital, but this logic was itself born into the world and given some power over the world by a very specific set of circumstances. Descending through this logic, Marx has led us to the point where the logic betrays its a-logical condition. Only through contact with this condition can the *katabasis* come to an end.

This condition, the origin of both political economy and of the capitalism it reflects, is the forceful rending of the peasant from the land, "the expropriation of the agricultural producer," and in these events "the knights of industry" "played no part whatsoever." Capitalists did not create capitalism, and certainly not through their own labor. "The dissolution of [feudalism] set free the elements of [capitalism]" (1976:875–6). The deterioration of feudal power in England, brought on by the growth of cities, on the one hand, left most of the land in the hands of free peasants, and, on the other, made money into "the power of all powers" (1976:879). This provided the old feudal lords with the incentive to drive the peasants off the land, in order that it might provide sheep for the wool market in Flanders. The expropriation of the peasants, in turn, created workers who *must* posit exchange-value, workers who cannot work for themselves, but must sell their labor-power and create value for another. It is the creation of these free workers that makes political economy possible, for it is this labor force that founds the possibility of the abstractions with which economics deals. It is this violent "abstraction" of the workers from the land and tools by which they could sustain themselves that makes possible scientific abstractions like labor-power, exchange-value, and capital. These conceptual abstractions, in their interrelations, compose the Hell of political economy, but they cannot account for

[18] Compare this to Alfred Schmidt's discussion of Marx's systematic presentation of capitalism: "Certainly an immanent presentation of the system has its limits, for when carried out rigorously, it immediately refers back 'toward a past lying behind this system.' Conversely – and here Marx goes beyond Hegel – the analysis leads 'to the point at which the suspension of the present form of production relations gives signs of its becoming – foreshadowing of the future'" (1981a:31–2). My argument maintains that it is only because Marx brings us up to the first limit that he is also able to point us toward the second.

themselves. Political economy, when followed into its inner sanctum, must give up its secret: property is founded on theft, order on violence, "the exclusive realm of Freedom, Equality, Property and Bentham" on "the expropriation of the mass of the people by a few usurpers" (1976:280, 930).

In his *coup de grace*, Marx shows us how political economy itself confesses these inversions. The final chapter, "The Modern Theory of Colonization," seems superfluous, coming, as it does, after Marx forecasts the expropriation of the expropriators. But it is in this chapter that Marx wrings from political economy's own mouth – in the person of E. G. Wakefield – the admission, not only of the fact of expropriation, but of the continued necessity of expropriation wherever conditions are such that people can easily establish themselves as self-subsisting. Reading Wakefield's advice on how to prevent colonists from obtaining any property from their labor, one finds oneself in the same state as Dante: "I raised my eyes, thinking to see Lucifer as I had left him, and I saw that he extended his legs upward; and if I labored in thought then, let the gross people ponder it who do not see what point it is that I had passed" (Inf. 34.88–93).

5. From Critique to Revolution

The tendency of my presentation, thus far, has been to insist upon a strong separation between political economy as a science and the actual workings of capitalism, since Marx's critique descends through the former, rather than offering a "better description" of the latter. Nonetheless, by the time we reach the so-called primitive accumulation, it has become much harder to hold the science of political economy separate from the world of capitalism. Political economy's ideal premise – the labor theory of value and property – has been exchanged for its actual premise – original expropriation – but this is *also* the historical premise of capitalism itself. Science and the world seem to have merged in this point of origination. Because it leads us to confront this double origin, *Capital* takes on a double existence; it is a critique of political economy, but it is also a critique of "actually existing" capitalism.[19]

[19] Compare Reuten (2000: 140): "Marx had a double object: critique of the economy, and critique of the economists (in the German '*Kritik der politischen Ökonomie*, it is even clearer that the object is two-fold)." Despite this formulation, Reuten, in the very same article, complains about precisely this duality; "Within a general systematic dialectical structure, we find a number of deficient transitions as well as many historical excurses that are not accounted for as such and that seem to replace systematic

Or is it? Certainly it leads us to *confront* actually existing capitalism, but does this confrontation constitute a critique? What would it mean to criticize capitalism? The critique of political economy takes the form of a descent through its concepts and proclamations to the point where the science deconstructs itself, overturning its own premises. But capitalism is not a system of concepts and pronouncements; it is a form of society. How does one descend through a social form? Can one do so in a book? I think the answer is "No." Critique *just is katabasis*. We cannot descend through capitalism in a book anymore than we can grow up by reading about child development. The critique of capitalism must take place in the medium of capitalism, that is, in life, in society, in productive activity. In other words, the "critique of capitalism" is – and, if we are to avoid a gross category mistake, can only be – revolution. In *Capital*, Marx leads us to the overturning of political economy, the overturning of the idea of capitalism. But nothing short of overturning capitalism will overturn capitalism.

Yet, the critical project and the revolutionary project cannot be strangers to one another. Certainly Marx's activity suggests that he thought his critique of political economy and the revolutionary overturning of capitalism were intimate partners. I will attempt, in the space remaining, to specify this relationship. This does not mean we will be leaving Dante behind. I already suggested that the transformation and empowerment of the pilgrim is the point of Dante's *katabasis* as much as of Marx's. But, whereas I have so far marked similarities in form or appearance between the *Inferno* and Marx's critique – Marx and Virgil offer similar rhetorics, and command similar knowledges; Hell and political economy make similar threatening promises, and present similar structures – I must now trace the movement of the workings of these texts. Or, to be more precise, I must trace the play between appearances and workings in both texts. I don't think Dante and Marx want to work the same transformation on us, but the moments of the drama are similar enough to be mutually illuminating.

Taking our cues again from John Freccero, Dante faced a very peculiar poetic dilemma writing the *Inferno*: to depict in words a place that seemingly precludes the possibility of meaning. Within the Christian semiotics of spirit

---

argument as such" (152n53). In a similar vein, Michael Heinrich writes; "In Marx's work we can find a superposition of two discourses: on the one hand, we have the breach with the theoretical field of classical political economy; on the other, he remains inside that field in many aspects. The superposition of such discourses produces quite a number of problems and unresolved ambivalences" (1996:465n).

and letter, God is the ultimate signified, the spirit that animates every letter. Hell, being the furthest removed from God of any part of creation, is a place of hopelessness precisely because the signifiers there have been cut off from their signified, they no longer communicate with the God that is the sole source of their meaning. If the cosmos, according to Thomistic neo-Aristotelianism, is a set of love letters God has written to himself, then Hell is the dead letter office, the elaborate storage center for missives that can be neither delivered to their addressee nor returned to their sender (which are the same in this case). Depicting such a realm in words that operate according to the normal rules of signification seems to contradict precisely the hellishness of Hell. Thus, Dante's dilemma: how can his poem possibly convey Hell, when the very conveyance of meaning is antithetical to Hell?

Dante's solution, according to Freccero, is to mimic in his poetry the very coagulation of meaning that is Hell. He does this by means of ironic literalization, the substitution of something bodily for anything spiritual. Such literalization is ironic in Schlegel's sense of *parekbasis*; it steps aside from the signified in order to signify the signifier itself. It "turns words into icons, souls into bodies [,] the spirit into the letter, [and] rhetorical figures into things" (Freccero 1986:106). We've already seen this conflation of signifier and signified in Dante's plea that the sense of the gate's inscription is as hard (*duro*) as the stone in which the letters are inscribed, but the prime example of this ironic materialization is the fact that sinners spend eternity engaged in precisely what they chose and pursued on earth. As Freccero writes, "If the bodies in hell are really souls, then it follows that their physical attitudes, contortions and punishments are really *spiritual* attitudes and states of mind, sins made manifest in the form of physical punishment. It is therefore correct to say the punishments *are* the sins; sin bears the same relationship to punishment as the souls in hell bear to their fictive bodies" (1986:106f).[20] The *Inferno* is the Hell of language, where what is meant is always meant at a remove, where every sign is a sign of a sign, where the channels by which a signifier normally signifies are multiplied into a labyrinth.

Given the double character of Marx's critique, it seems that *Capital*, too, steps aside from the signified (capitalism) to address, instead, its signifier

[20] Thus, the philosophers in limbo are condemned to philosophize forever, to love wisdom from afar without ever becoming *sophoi*; the lustful are buffeted about in Hell by the same love they chose to be buffeted by in life; the gluttonous, who lived like pigs, eternally rut about in the mud; etc.

(political economy). Furthermore, according to Marx, this signifier is characterized by reification, in much the same way that Hell constitutes a clotting of the normal circulation of providential meaning within creation. Within political economy, relations are "hidden by a thingly veil" (1970:34). This is necessary, claims Marx, for – turning a Hegelianism to very un-Hegelian purposes – "Reflection only begins *post festum*":

> The forms which stamp products as commodities and which are therefore the preliminary requirements for the circulation of commodities, already possess the fixed quality of natural forms of social life before man seeks to give an account, not of their historical character, for in his eyes they are immutable, but of their content and meaning. Consequently, it was solely the analysis of the prices of commodities which led to the determination of the magnitude of value, and solely the common expression of all commodities in money which led to the establishment of their character as values. It is however precisely this finished form of the world of commodities – the money form – which conceals the social character of private labor and the social relations between the individual workers, by making those relations appear as relations between material objects, instead of revealing them plainly. (1976:168–9)

That Minerva only flies at dusk means science only encounters things it takes for dead. These corpses it inters within itself as its categories. In the same way that Hell seals off its inhabitants from vivifying contact with God, locking their souls in bodily death, so too does political economy preserve social relations in a state of reification, severed from the historical forces that created them, maintain them, and will transform them anew. By addressing his critique to these reified categories, Marx ironically doubles political economy's own characteristic method, speaking not of his actual, historical and material concern, but rather of its icon, giving us only signs of signs.[21] As irony, Marx's critique presents readers with commodities, money, capital, and labor, "personifications of economic relations" (1976:179), speaking and dancing, falling in love and going to market, bleeding and sucking blood. But these "characters" are only stand-ins, symbols, not the *actual* objects of his

[21] Marx's irony has been suggested before by John Seery (1990), Robert Paul Wolff (1988), and Dominick LaCapra (1983), all for slightly different reasons. Only Wolff has attempted to extend an ironic reading into *Capital* itself, but even he sees this irony as appropriate only to the sphere of circulation.

concern. Claiming that Marx's critique of political economy is ironic amounts to claiming that his text's effectiveness, the way it works, is not to be found in his explicit discussions, but lies in silence elsewhere, though this elsewhere is the elsewhere of the words themselves, their own silence. We must now turn explicitly, first, to those words, and then, finally, to their silence.

Political economy is an excellent phenomenology of the modern world; as such, it is only the systematic re-presentation of the forms and language in which that world presents itself.[22] The categories of political economy "are forms of thought which are socially valid," as Marx puts it (1976:169). That the world of political economy is, for Marx, one of phenomena is quite explicit from the very first lines of both the *Contribution* and *Capital*; the monstrous collection of commodities is how the wealth of bourgeois society appears (*erscheint*). Moreover, this mode of appearing of modern relations of production is also the *logos* of its appearance. Thus, "the manner of speaking of the English economists" amounts to "commodities speak[ing] through the mouth of the economist" (1976:177). Marx remains insistent, right up to the end of the book, that the political economists are the mouths through which capitalism speaks (e.g., 1976:932). Capitalism is a mode of life that, like religion, gives rise to *Vorstellungen* (presentations, imaginings, ideas) that are themselves actual (*wirklich*), that do work (*wirken*). Political economy is the systematization of these presentations.

But this social validity of political economy's phenomenology is the danger that Marx seeks to overcome in *Capital*. As in the *Inferno*, the danger of Hell lies precisely in its spectacular character. As Dante writes in *Purgatorio*, the sensuous soul can become fixated:

> [. . .] when we hear or see something
> that holds the soul strongly turned to it,
> time passes, and we do not notice its passage. (Pur. 4.7–9)

---

[22] Terrell Carver is right, I think, when he claims that, in *Capital*, Marx "was primarily interested in the language employed ordinarily within capitalist and commodity-producing societies." I begin to diverge from him when he continues; "*Capital* is an analytic work, proceeding from that ordinary language, through a critique of the 'science' of political economy which purported to explain it, ascending ultimately to a realm in which conceptual relationships, deemed 'logical' or 'conceptual', can be traced out" (1998:27). Obviously, I think the directionality of Marx's movement is slightly different than does Carver, and I am trying to show that the ordinary language of capitalism, the science of political economy, and the realm of conceptual relations are all one.

Hell has the power to turn the soul toward it; if it succeeds, that soul does not notice the passage of time, even unto eternity. This is the danger Dante confronts at the gates of Dis, the inner citadel of Hell. The gates are closed and barred by devils, and, while they wait, Virgil and Dante are accosted by the Furies, who threaten that Medusa is coming. Virgil responds dramatically; he orders Dante to turn and close his eyes, "for if the Gorgon appears and you should see her, there would never be any going back up." Not waiting for Dante to act, Virgil grabs him, turns him around, and covers his eyes with both of their pairs of hands. Medusa never appears, however; instead, Dante opens his eyes to see an angel arriving to open the gates, and the duo proceeds downward (Inf. 9.34–63).

Freccero (1986:126) believes this threat of petrification is central to the whole *Inferno*. Hell threatens the interloper with petrifying appearances that, if seen, prevent all escape. Medusa, if she were to appear, would be the condensed manifestation of Hell's paralyzing frightfulness; she is Hell's attempt to make good on the gate's threat of eternity. But this attempt necessarily remains only an attempt. The Gorgon – like the gate's inscription – is a damnation that is never actually present. The petrifying face never shows itself, but always only threatens from the immanent future. The Gorgon may represent the threat of corporeality, but it is Dante's very corporeality – the fact that he is a living body, whose sight can be blocked by his motion and by the opaque materiality of his hands – that preserves him from that threat.

But isn't the threat of the Gorgon precisely the threat we sense in Marx's presentation of the phenomenology of capital? And isn't it this threat that keeps the rediscoverers of Marx from breaking the seal on *Capital*? Don't we fear that, after all, the logic of capital is an iron cage? The greatest danger of paralysis seems to confront us at the very place I cast above as Marx's own entry into Dis, the transition from the market to the abode of production. It is here where those Marx characterized as the vulgar economists were frozen, unable to see in labor-power anything but one more commodity. Here, too, most of Twentieth Century economics has languished, fixated on the equilibrium of the market. The phenomenology of capitalism is extremely persuasive, but if we are persuaded by it, then we must also conclude that capitalism will never end. Indeed, we would not even notice that it *is ending* all around us as we stand paralyzed.

In Marx, as in Dante, it is materiality itself that will preserve us against this paralysis threatened by the appearance of reified relations of production.

There is an admonition that runs throughout Marx's corpus: don't judge an individual, a class, an era, or a social formation by what it says or thinks about itself; judge it by what it does.[23] As much as the phenomena of capitalism may *say* to us, Marx is not primarily concerned with this saying, with this way capitalism sets itself forth in speech. There is a level of *Wirklichkeit* or happening that exceeds the science of political economy. Marx's aim in escorting us through this science is to open us to the trace of this materiality. The appearance of bourgeois wealth threatens to paralyze common action with fear and suspicion. But, just as Dante's body can always preserve him from the paralyzing appearance – which is threatened but never actually presents itself – so also, as long as we are embodied social beings, it is never quite too late for us to avert our eyes, to look away from the always impending capitalist fantasia towards the coming force of transformation within ourselves. This is the empowering transformation promised by the *katabasis* through political economy. Our Virgil holds out to his readers this prospect of founding a fourth empire – to succeed the Roman, Catholic, and Modern Empires – the counter-empire of materiality, of revolution, of the multitude.

Concluding Unscientific Postscript

In this essay, I hope to have accomplished three tasks. First, I hope, through my re-reading of the 1859 Preface, to have driven a wedge between Marx's critique of political economy and what Terrell Carver aptly summed up as the "boringly literal" approaches that assimilate these texts to a modern project of techno-scientific knowing. Certainly, Marx puts on the mask of the economist, but there is good reason to be suspicious of this mask. Second – and giving some content to the first point – I hope to have made an admittedly provocative, but also serious and textually grounded case for an alternative reading, according to which Marx plays Virgil, leading his readers on a tour of the dead concepts of political economy in order, in the end, to set us free from the paralyzing mystique of science. I don't imagine that this reading is uncontroversial, but I think the textual evidence I have cited cannot be ignored, and that my reading of that evidence is plausible.

[23] See, e.g., Marx's dissertation (Marx and Engels 1975a vol. 1:84); *The Holy Family* (1975 vol. 4:37); *The German Ideology* (1975 vol. 5:62); and *A Contribution to the Critique of Political Economy* (1970:21).

More importantly – and this brings me to my third task – I think my outline of a reading is *productive*. There is important work being done by Chris Arthur, Patrick Murray, Geert Reuten, and others (to which I referred in the introduction), work which seeks to reconstruct Marx's presentation of the science of political economy in accordance with the Aristotelian-Hegelian conception of science. According to this Aristotelian-Hegelian lineage, science is not the discovery, through abstraction, of predictive laws, as in the dominant empiricist tradition, but rather the systematic presentation of the imminent logic of a world of phenomena. I absolutely agree that Marx is a son of this classical lineage, but I would add that he is an unruly son. Marx's text does not merely present a science, but critiques that science by leading the reader through and beyond it. Science, for Marx, is a trial, not a foundation. Unlike Aristotle and Hegel, Marx proceeds in his work from the irreducible difference between the effective forces and processes that make our world and the logic of appearances to which those forces give rise. The latter is the realm of science, while the former is the realm of history and of revolution. We will make ourselves citizens of this realm of revolution only by showing ourselves strong enough to overcome the realm of science.

Part II: Critical Theory

Rudolf J. Siebert

Toward a Dialectical Sociology of Religion: A Critique of Positivism and Clerico-Fascism

It is the goal of this essay to trace and explore Max Horkheimer's and Theodor W. Adorno's and other critical theorists' attempts at a dialectical sociology of religion. This is an integral part of their critical theory of society, particularly the longing for the fundamentally nameless and imageless entirely Other than what is the case in nature and history, and the often cruel evolutionary laws governing them (Horkheimer 1996:62–67; Adorno 1997:85–87). This critical theory of religion was developed in opposition to positivism and neo-positivism as the merely quantifying and mathematizing philosophy of what is immediately given and at hand, and of what is the case, and of the facts and data, and to fascism, including national socialism, and to neo-fascism as extreme forms of an often racially grounded nationalism, which believes in nothing else than the aristocratic principle of nature: that is, the unbridled and blind natural forces and the power of the predator over the prey, or of the winner over the loser (Adorno 1970; 1979; Marcuse 1966; Hitler 1943:64–65; Taylor 1986; Kogon 1979:24; 1965; Weber 1979; Mosse 1975; Paassen and Wise 1934; Dubiel 1994; Siebert 1987).

A. From Judaism to Enlightenment

The main purpose of Hegel's philosophy of religion had been the reconciliation of the modern antagonism between the religious and the secular, between faith and reason, between revelation and enlightenment (Hegel 1986m; 1986n). This is still the purpose of the Left Hegelian critical theory of society, insofar as it is concerned with faith and knowledge (Habermas 2001).

Faith and Knowledge

This is so, because Hegel's idealistic reconciliation between the sacred and the profane had succeeded as little as that of Goethe or Beethoven (Hegel 1986n). Of course, the materialistic critical theory of society is not able to reconcile the modern antagonism between the religious and the secular (Siebert 2001; 2002). But it tries at least to keep open this dialectic between the sacred and the profane, and to prevent under all circumstances that it is closed prematurely either fundamentalistically or scientistically and positivistically. It is the purpose of this essay to clarify and to develop further a new critical theory of religion, and to develop an open dialectic between the religious and the secular. The goal of this essay is indeed to develop further a critical theory of religion, which would have its foundation in the theological dimension of the original critical theory of society – its negative, inverse, cipher or semblance theology – but would also go beyond it (Horkheimer 1985a; Habermas 1991; 2001; Siebert 2001; 2002). The essay also aims at the clarification of the fact that the longing for the imageless and nameless totally Other than history – what Hegel had called in his philosophy of history the slaughter-bench, or the holocaust altar, or the Golgatha, or the skull hill of nature and world –, was indeed not only the manifest fundamental motivation of the critical theory of society of the first generation of critical theorists, but remained that also – at least latently – for the second and third and fourth generations (Hegel 1986k; Adorno 2001; Todenhöfer 2003). This longing for the entirely Other has so far prevented the critical theorists of society from falling victim to dull positivism, into which the great bourgeois enlightenment, and sometimes even the Marxian and Freudian enlightenment, have degenerated, and beyond that from regressing back into mythology (Adorno 1970; 1966; Horkheimer and Adorno 1969; Marx 1972:18–20, 1964:43–44; 1961; 1953; Feuerbach 1957; Freud 1964; 1962; Jones 1961; Horkheimer 1985a; Benjamin 1978; Lonitz 1994; Adorno and Kogon 1958). This longing for the totally Other alone guarantees that the critical theory of society, or the new dialectical theory of religion, will not turn into an uncritical one. The longing for the entirely Other is the critical theorist's definition of religion. It is the expression and the basis of religion. It is also the concrete supersession of all the God-hypostases present in the still living as well as in the dead world religions in terms of what Ernst Bloch has called humanism as religion in inheritance (Hegel 1986m; 1986n; Bloch 1985). The longing for the totally Other is indeed the basis and the motivation of the critical theory of society as well as of the dialectical theory of religion to be developed out of it, and remains necessary for their survival under the enormous identity – and conformity – pressure of a more and more globalizing late capitalist society (Horkheimer 1985a; Adorno 1979:354–372, 578–587; Siebert 2001; 2002). The insatiable longing for the totally Other can even carry and strengthen a religious faith – Jewish, Christian, or Islamic, etc. – which is no mere putting off toward a Beyond, but which is a basis for protest and resistance against unjust conditions in present globalized late capitalist society: critical religion (Adorno 1979; Küng 1994:904–905).

Redemptive Quest

The longing and the hope for the fundamentally imageless and nameless totally Other as a redemptive quest for the rescue of the hopeless is – as the main motive of the critical theory of society as well as of the dialectical theory of religion to be developed out of it – to be inversed and translated into a post-Enlightenment era that has seen Auschwitz and Treblinka, Hiroshima and Nagasaki, Vietnam, Yugoslavia, Afghanistan and Iraq (Horkheimer 1985a; Siebert 2001; 2002). This essay is concerned with the development of a critical theory of religion in a post-religious and post-metaphysical, as well as post-enlightenment world, which has lost not only its religious eschatologies, but also its secular political utopias, and is thus characterized by positivism as the – as Adorno put it – metaphysics of what is the case, and by the consequent universal despair, which may be more or less conscious (Adorno 1993; 1998; 1970). The new dialectical theory of religion is informed by a vision of alternative Future III – the right or reconciled society, beyond the present antagonistic civil society, which is not as it ought to be, measured by its own cultural closure values, and which daily contradicts its own most noble institutions and aspirations (Horkheimer 1985a; 1970; Fromm 1973;

Habermas 2001; 1991; 1998; 1990). The critical theory of religion aims at the mitigation at least, of the fast approaching global alternative Future I – the totally administered, bureaucratized, computerized, roboticized signal – society; and at the resistance against the still possible and probable arrival of global alternative Future II – the more and more militarized society possibly involved in what Samuel Huntington, a student of Carl Schmitt and an advisor to the Pentagon, has called the clash of religiously based civilizations, which could easily climax not only into conventional local wars or civil wars, but even into a third world war using nuclear, biological and chemical weapons of mass destruction, and into the consequent ecological catastrophes; and the critical theory of religion aims at the passionate promotion of alternative Future III – a society, in which personal autonomy and universal, i.e., anamnestic, present and proleptic solidarity would be reconciled (Hegel 1986k; 1986j; 1986c; Marx 1961; Horkheimer 1985a; Adorno 1998; 2000; Tucker 1978; Flechtheim 1962; 1966; 1971; 1985; Flechtheim, Lohmann and Martin 2003; Bloch 1970a; 1970b; 1971; Habermas 1987; Kogon 1967; Küng 1994; 1991). Unfortunately, while alternative Futures I and II are not desirable, they are, nevertheless, very possible and probable, and while alternative Future III is very desirable, it is, under the present neo-conservative and neo-liberal conditions of advanced capitalist society, less possible and probable. The longing for alternative Future III – a society characterized by the solidarity of one human being with another without loss of his or her autonomy, is not the same as, but rather the necessary concretization, presupposition for, and consequence of, the hope for the totally Other than the slaughterhouse of nature and history, in which almost everybody is programmed to eat everybody for the purpose of self-preservation and self-maintenance (Siebert 2001; 2002). The longing for the entirely Other transcends not only all personal longings for another human being but also the collective historical longings: e.g., the traditional European longing for India, or for Greece, or for Rome, or for America, or for the Slavic world (Hegel 1986k). Theology cannot, and must not, be reduced to anthropology.

Negative Theology

While for Hegel the finite was the other of the Infinite, for the critical theorists the Infinite was the other of the finite: the totally Other of the finite world as nature and history as gigantic sacrificial altar (Hegel 1986n). Like Marx before, the critical theorists turned Hegel upside down once more and put him on his feet, on which, to a large extent, he stood already anyway. Thus, what Horkheimer and Adorno called the totally Other is what once in the great world religions and world philosophies had been called the God or Gods, Eternity, Heaven, Beauty, Infinite, Transcendence, Being, Idea, Absolute, Unconditional, Absolute Spirit (Horkheimer 1985a). The great Protestant theologian, Paul Tillich, friend of Horkheimer, Adorno, and Fromm, had spoken of the Ultimate Reality. Talcott Parsons, the father of American structural-functionalism, the great positivistic competitor of the critical theory of society, took over Tillich's theological notion (O'Dea 1966; Parsons 1965; 1964). Parsons opened up his system of human condition, and particularly his human action system, embracing culture, society, personality and behavioral organism, upward through culture, i.e., ideas, values, symbols, techniques, toward the Ultimate Reality, and downward through the human behavioral organism toward nature. Horkheimer discovered that Hegel did not only have a very well developed positive theology, but also a negative one, which reached, of course, far back to the Second and Third Commandment of the Mosaic Law, i.e., the prohibition against making images of the Absolute or naming it or conceptualizing it and thus disclosing its nature, qualities and attributes (Solomon 1996).

Inverse Cipher Theology

Likewise, on the Island of Ibiza in the early 1930s, Adorno and Walter Benjamin developed, out of Hegel's positive and negative theology, an other, or an inverse, or a cipher theology, particularly in response to Franz Kafka's work (Witte 1985:104; Adorno 1970; Scholem 1989). This new inverse cipher theology allows some religious and theological contents to migrate from the depth of the mythos into the secular discourse of the expert-cultures of psychology, sociology, anthropology, philosophy, etc., and through it into communicative and even political praxis, in order thus to stem the always new waves of rebarbarization of Western civilization. Benjamin's and Adorno's inverse theology is still at work in Habermas's theory of communicative action, under the auspices of his methodological atheism (Habermas 1990; 1991). Habermas admittedly takes the Second and Third Commandment of the Mosaic law and the inverse theology so radically seriously, that – unlike his teacher Adorno – he never even mentions the concept of the totally Other, in spite of the fact that he knows very well its origins not only in Hegel, but also in Kant and Sören Kierkegaard (Küng 1990:70–71). Methodological atheism simply means the formal exclusion of theological or metaphysical presuppositions (Hegel 1986k:19–29).

Agnosticism and Atheism

For the critical theorists, the totally other is indeed unknowable in its entirety. In this sense they are – following Kant – agnostics (Küng 1990; 1978). In the critical-theoretical perspective, the entirely Other does not reveal itself in the traditional sense. At best, traces of the totally Other may be discovered in terms of – what Adorno has called – micrology: in the smallest, not yet socially preformed, most detailed ciphers of nature or society (Adorno 1980:7–12). Horkheimer practiced such micrology in his aphoristic notes under the title *Dusk* and Adorno in his *Minima Moralia* dedicated and devoted to his eight years older friend and teacher Horkheimer (Adorno 1980). There had been a methodological atheism at work in the critical theory of society long before Habermas – the most outstanding member of the second generation of critical theorists – re-invented and used the name (Habermas 1991). It is true that once, even Horkheimer and Adorno broke the Third Commandment of the Mosaic Decalogue: the former named the totally Other perfect justice and the latter called it unconditional love. But these instances have remained the exceptions to the rule of agnosticism or methodological atheism. Thus, in Habermas's secular view, we may not even get a glimpse of a tip of the Absolute, or the totally Other in itself (Theunissen 1983; Habermas 1988). The same must, of course, also be true of the description of the entirely Other in this essay. But while we can not determine the entirely Other, we can nevertheless certainly describe the longing, or the hope for the Infinite, which has motivated four generations of critical theorists: the longing that the finitude of the finite may not be the last word of history; the hope that the murderer may not triumph over the innocent victim, at least not ultimately. We can also describe in this essay more concretely what negative, or inverse theology, or agnosticism, or methodological atheism is. All this can be done best ex contrario: that means against the background of Hegel's dialectical philosophy as well as against the positivism and the fascism which followed it (Hegel 1986:a–o).

Theology as Theodicy

The critical theory is no less a theodicy than Hegel's historical idealism, or Marx's historical materialism, or Sigmund Freud's psychoanalytical philosophy (Hegel 1986k:28,540; 1986m:88; 1986p:497; 1986q:248,455; Marx 1964:43–44; 1972:18–20,142; 1961; 1953; Freud 1964; Jones 1961; Horkheimer 1985a). The critical theory embraces in itself not only a theodicy in the sense of Max Weber (Weber 1963; Horkheimer 1970:37). According to Weber, a theodicy was every theoretical effort to explain the suffering on this earth. In the Weberian sense, the teaching of Marx, Schopenhauer, Nietzsche, or Freud can be called a theodicy (Horkheimer 1985a; 1985b; 1970:37). Beyond that, the critical theory of society is a theodicy also in the original sense of the word, which Hegel still used: a justification of God in opposition to the injustice, the evil dominating in his world (Hegel 1986k; 1986m:88; 1986p:497; 1986q). As little as the critical theorists could talk about false consciousness or ideology critique without careful recourse to Hegel, so little could they speak about theology as theodicy without reference to him (Benjamin 1978:682). After Auschwitz and all the horror and terror this name stands for, the Jewish critical theorists had – inspired by Hegel – to remind the Christian theologians of the 20th century again, that their theology had been originally a theodicy, and that they had forgotten their own origin, and that it was time for them to remember it again (Oelmüller 1990; Neuhaus 1993; Schuster & Boschert-Kimmig 1993; Metz 1995; Greinacher 1986; Sölle 1989). Of course, in the critical-theoretical perspective, after Auschwitz and Birkenau, Dresden, Hiroshima and Nagasaki, Hegel's instrumental theodicy seems not to be plausible or acceptable any longer: God instrumentalizing the slaughterbench of nature and history as sacrificial altar for the purpose of the achievement of the realm of Divine and human freedom – the freedom of all. Hegel's gravestone in the socialist Dorotheen Cemetery in Berlin still represents the holocaust altar of the first and second Temple in Jerusalem. Up to the present, 174 years after his death, Jewish friends put little pebbles on Hegel's gravestone. Certainly, in this sense, for the critical theorists, Hegel's philosophical system has indeed broken down once and for all in so far as it had been a last gigantic theodicy attempt. Only, to be sure, most precious fragments remain. The critical theory of society is an eschatological theodicy in so far as it insists that what Hegel had called most realistically the slaughterbench, or holocaust altar, or Golgatha, or Skull hill of nature and history will at least ultimately not prevail. The critical theory is not protology, but eschatology.

It is not orientated toward the beginning, but rather toward the end: the last things rather than the first things.

The Concept of Infinity

The critical theory is a theodicy also in the sense of Horkheimer's book *Eclipse of Reason* of 1947. Here Horkheimer stated that without the thought of truth and thereby of that which guaranteed it, the Infinite, the Absolute, the totally Other, there was no knowledge of its opposite, the abandonment of the human beings, for the sake of which the true philosophy had to be critical and pessimistic (Horkheimer 1985b). Without this thought of truth and what guaranteed it, the Unconditional, there was not even sorrow, without which there was no happiness. While Horkheimer never mentioned Adorno's and Benjamin's negative, inverse, cipher or semblance theology, he nevertheless practiced it continually as theodicy: which again was possible only because the theodicy had been present in the inverse theology from its very start as well (Adorno 1970a; Lonitz 1994; Horkheimer 1970; 1985a).

Absolute Truth

The critical theory is a theodicy in so far as it remembers the martyrs of our time (Horkheimer 1947; 1985a; Siebert 1993). In the perspective of Horkheimer, the real individuals of our time were the martyrs who have gone through infernos of suffering and degradation in their resistance to conquest and oppression: not the inflated personalities of popular culture, the conventional dignitaries. These unsung heroes consciously exposed their existence as individuals to the terrorist annihilation that others undergo unconsciously through the social process in antagonistic civil society (Horkheimer 1985a). For Horkheimer, the task of philosophy was to translate what the martyrs had done into a language that would be heard, even though their finite voices had been silenced by the fascist tyranny. As philosophy fulfills this task it turns into theodicy.

Semblance of Otherness

Horkheimer received the notion of the longing for the totally Other from Adorno, who was the better Hegelian, not vice versa (Horkheimer 1985b). Thus, it is not amazing that the theological dimension in the critical theory of society reached its climax in Adorno's (1973) conclusive work, *Negative*

Dialectics. Toward the end of this extraordinary book, which embraces the main accomplishment of his whole philosophical life work, Adorno speaks about the great Anselm of Canterbury's specifically Christian ontological proof for the existence of God: that God is the highest Notion or Idea, which a greater one can not be conceived, and which therefore must contain being or existence, since otherwise a greater one could be thought of: ergo God exists (Anselm 1962; Adorno 1973:402–405). According to Adorno, Hegel had tried, in opposition to Kant, to determinately negate, i.e., not only to criticize, but also to resurrect dialectically, and thus to preserve, and to elevate, and to fulfill Anselm's ontological argument for the existence of God (Anselm 1962; Hegel 1986n). In Adorno's view, Hegel failed in his attempt to restore the ontological proof (Adorno 2003:402–405). Adorno, rather, sides with the monk Gaunilon and with Kant against Anselm of Canterbury and Hegel: he denies the identity of the Notion, or the Idea, and being, and stresses their non-identity, and thus negates Anselm's proof once more, but still not merely abstractly, but rather determinately and concretely (Anselm 1962; Hegel 1986n). In Adorno's perspective, in Hegel's consistent resolution of non-identity into pure identity, the notion becomes the guarantor of the non-conceptual. According to Adorno, Transcendence, captured by the immanence of the human spirit, was supposedly at the same time turned into the totality of the human spirit and thus abolished altogether. Here Feuerbach's projection theory is of course presupposed.

Radical Objectivity

Adorno was truly and honestly convinced, that his negative dialectic with its emphasize on non-identity preserved and protected better the radical objectivity of the Absolute, or the totally Other, than Hegel's positive dialectic with its emphasize on identity and its consequent pantheistic tendencies, which of course Hegel had always denied (Hegel 1986a:347; Adorno 2003:402–405). Adorno observed that, after Hegel, the more Transcendence crumbled under the pressure of the bourgeois, Marxian and Freudian enlightenment movements, both in the world and in the human mind, the more arcane it would become, thus concentrating in an outermost point above all mediations. In this sense, so Adorno argued, the anti-historical Barthian theology of downright Otherness has its historical index. For Adorno, the question of theology and metaphysics was sharpened into the question of whether this utter tenuousness, abstractness, and indefiniteness of the Absolute was the last, already lost, defensive position of theology and metaphysics, or whether theology and metaphysics survived only in the meanest and shabbiest refuse of the phenomenal world, the so finite and transitory ciphers; whether a state of consummate insignificance will let it restore reason to the autocratic human reason that performed its office without resistance or reflection (Adorno 2003:402–405; Habermas 1988:278–279). In Adorno's view, theology and metaphysics could possibly survive in the micrology of the smallest, shabbiest, meanest detail or cipher of reality. While this micrology is certainly far removed from any post-ontological proof for the existence of God, it is, nevertheless, almost a Judeo-Christian idea: to see the resemblance of the entirely Other in the oppressed, exploited, tortured, hanged, shot, gassed, crucified, hopeless innocent victims of, what the otherwise optimistic Hegel and his opponent, the father of metaphysical pessimism, Schopenhauer, had identified as, the slaughterbench, or the holocaust altar of world-history (Hegel 1986k; 1986n; Adorno 2003:402–405; Oelmüller 1990; Neuhaus 1993; Schuster & Boschert-Kimmig 1993; Metz 1995; Greinacher 1986; Sölle 1989). Hegel had also spoken of the little flowers, or the foul existences, on which the powerful were stepping all the time (Hegel 1986k). While Hegel took suffering into the dialectical notion, for the critical theorists, the extreme suffering of the 20th century exploded and shattered the dialectical notion altogether: the result was the negative dialectics (Hegel 1986f; 1986n; Adorno 2003). While Adorno stressed the non-identity between even the highest notion and the smallest existence, micrology could at least still discover a semblance of the former in the latter (Adorno 1973:402–405). Such semblance of the totally Other in the smallest existential detail of nature, personal biography, family, civil society, political state and history is not entirely without consolation. Motivated by their longing for the entirely Other, or as Fromm put it, by the X-experience of a humanistic religiosity, the critical theorists did not only allow semantic and semiotic materials and potentialities to migrate from Judaism, Christianity, Buddhism and other world religions into the modern bourgeois, Marxian and Freudian enlightenment movements, but they also made the attempt to rescue them from positivism and fascism, and thus to renew the barbarously threatened spirit of the West (Fromm 1992; 1981; 2001; 1990; 1970b; 1970a; 1999; 1980; 1969; Habermas 2002; Mendieta 2005). That, precisely, they considered to be their mission.

B. Anti-Positivism

According to Adorno, the thesis of positivism from Auguste Comte to Max Weber, Emile Durkheim, the Vienna School, Carl Popper, Talcott Parsons and Niklas Luhmann and the cognitivists was, that even a theology or metaphysics that had escaped to profanity was, nevertheless, void (Adorno 1973:402–405; Adorno 2003; 1970a; Marcuse 1966). In Adorno's view, contemporary positivists sacrificed even the idea of truth on the account of which positivism had been initiated in the first place. They were satisfied with the simple correctness of statements concerning facts.

Transcendence

Adorno's micrology did not decapitate thought, it turned into an other, negative, inverse cipher or semblance theology, engaged in what his friend Benjamin had called anamnestic solidarity with the innocent victims (Habermas 1986:53–54). In the perspective of a dialectical theory of religion, Adorno's and Benjamin's inverse cipher theology, which allows semantic potentials to migrate from the depth of the mythos into the secular social-scientific discourse, can indeed mediate between monotheism on one hand and radical enlightenment on the other (Habermas 1990; 1982). While we cannot at this point in history reconcile the deep contradiction between faith and knowledge, revelation and autonomous reason, and must express it honestly and truthfully, we can at least point already the direction out of it in terms of an open dialectic, which avoids either a fundamentalist or a scientistic-positivistic closure (Habermas 2001:9–31).

Reliability and Usefulness

According to Horkheimer, modern positivism or empiricism was the worldview, which lived essentially from the forgetfulness of two moments (Siebert 1987). Both elements were related to the spiritual or cultural world. First of all, the representatives of empiricism or positivism asserted most readily that the generalizing conclusions, analogies, presumptions and probabilities, which were drawn from the refined investigations through social and individual objects concerning man and society, and the methods of which have been taken from the natural sciences, were in themselves in no way reliable. The studies aimed only at a limited circle of facts and a limited time and space, to which they related themselves. If, however, that was the case, so the anti-elitist Horkheimer argued, then any good observer and clever and sensible human being had at least as much right concerning his or her imagination, intuition, or speculation as the social researcher's conjectures. In Horkheimer's view, to the contrary the professional researcher was in danger, not to see the forest for the trees: not to identify the universal tendencies in the individual and historical collective life over its particular formations, facts and figures. Secondly, the empiricists were used to admit that feelings did not manifest any differences in reference to the truth. The positivists asserted that it was epistemologically equivalent if an individual reacted to an event with comfort or with uneasiness and discontent. Both were likewise facts. However, the positivists liked to recommend their view and opinion as the cleanest one, the most decent and proper one, and the most useful one for the general welfare of civil society. They pretended to stand in closest connection with the progress of humanity in the present industrial or late capitalist society (Adorno 1979).

Totalitarianism

According to Horkheimer, toward the end of the 1950s the positivists liked to point toward the masses, which had only recently been grasped by the totalitarian intoxication and the following of national socialism and fascism as examples for the consequences of religious, metaphysical and other kinds of erroneous teachings and heresies. A positivist stood in the residuals of Auschwitz and blamed Hegel's notion of the absolute Spirit for the Shoa. Only doing so, so Horkheimer explained, the positivists abstracted from the fact, that the fascist tyrants themselves, e.g., the people's enlightener Dr. Joseph Goebbels, who put into motion the masses on behalf of the likewise soberly thinking capitalist magnates and oligarchs, e.g., the master club in Düsseldorf, including Krupp and Thyssen, etc., and many foreign industrialists, like Henry Ford, and bankers who consented with Hitler and who traded with fascist Germany, behaved philosophically correctly and perfectly in terms of the positivistic doctrine, which is still valid and dominant in European and American universities even today, in 2005, now under continually economizing neo-conservative or neo-liberal auspices (Taylor 1983; Adorno 1979; Higham 1983; Baldwin 2001). In case Adolf Hitler and his propaganda minister had won the war, they could not have been scolded in the light of any positivistically conceived form of instrumental or functional rationality (Horkheimer and Adorno 1969; Adorno 1997). In Horkheimer's view, the positivists did not know the facts of the true insight and the right action in the emphatic sense. The positivists did not know that the hate against a decent person and the deep respect toward a base and mean individual were not only in the face of social morality, but also, before the truth, wrong impulses and feelings. They were not only ideologically blameworthy, but they were as a matter of fact, objectively factually wrong experiences and reactions, no matter if they achieved a purpose or not. From the standpoint of positivism, no moral politics could be derived. In a purely positive scientific, or scientistic perspective, hate was, in spite of all social-functional differentiation, not worse than love. For positivism there was no logically cogent justification, reasoning or argumentation for why somebody should not hate, if doing so brought him social advantages: Jews in fascist Germany, or African Americans in the old or new Confederacy. The positivist can say in the sense of George Orwell or Aldous Huxley that war is as good or as bad as peace; freedom is as good or as bad as slavery and oppression; truth is as good or as bad as lies (Adorno 1997:97–122). Orwellian lies about weapons of mass destruction lead to the second Iraq war. What Dachau, Gulago, Guantanamo Bay, Abu Ghraib, etc., have in common in spite of all differences, is the fact that they are all barbarous expressions of a positivistic trend toward alternative Future I – the entirely administered society, and alternative Future II – the totally militarized society aiming at total war. The tortured victims could care less if their pain, if their torturers were motivated by black, red or brown fascism, neoconservatives, or neo-liberalism.

Heaven and Hell

Horkheimer argued that the positivists still depended on heaven and hell. They allied themselves with religion. Even the most positivistically orientated universities in Europe and America still have chapels and chaplains and religion or theology departments. Even the SS employed Christian chaplains during World War II and carried belts saying: God with us! As Herbert Marcuse discovered already in the 1950s and 1960s, the academic promotion of religion fell only too often in line with the predominant positivistic trend in antagonistic civil society (Marcuse 1962:65–66). The positivistic-scientistic attitude was unable to liberate the repressed and transfigured critical and revolutionary content of religion (Marcuse 1962:65–66). In some positivistic sociology departments, religion is considered to be good, i.e., eufunctional, for the survival of civil society, but it is untrue. No genuine religious person could possibly accept such compromise. In Marcuse's view, where religion still preserved the uncompromised, critical and revolutionary aspirations for peace and happiness, its so-called illusions would still have a higher truth value than the positivistic sciences, which for so long have worked for their elimination (Freud 1961; Marcuse 1962:65–66).

Mythology and Metaphysics

If people in secularized civil or socialistic society, so Horkheimer argued, would overall be still more genuinely inclined toward religion, the positivists would probably not have less scruples to recommend the renunciation of mythology, than Francois de Voltaire, together with Jean-Jacques Rousseau, the fathers of deism, for whom it seemed still to be indispensable for the canaille – the proletariat. The struggle of the positivists was directed against the critical theory of society, which, contrary to the presently dominant ruling class in antagonistic civil society, has for its immanent precondition the idea of alternative Future III – the more adequate, humane, more right, truer, more proper condition of the reconciled society, in which the deep contradictions of present civil society would be overcome (Horkheimer 1985a). According to Horkheimer, as the positivists did only want to grant validity to the facts and data, they banished the difference between the right and the wrong intention out of the dimension of reason, and left it to the status quo of civil society alone, to determine the tasks and the ways, how it was to be judged. It was the mythology and metaphysics of the positivists to elevate the status quo of civil society to the one and all, the only thing, besides which one should not have any other gods. The positivists violated in their mythology and metaphysics the second and third commandment of the Mosaic Decalogue: the prohibition against making images of the Absolute and naming it. The positivists committed idolatry. Of course, Weber had already noticed that modern civil society and its iron cage of capitalism were as polytheistic as the Greek or Roman societies, just less poetical and more prosaic in their conception of their gods or fundamental natural and social forces: capital instead of Pluto, commerce instead of Mercury, pill-love instead of Venus or Aphrodite, war instead of Mars, restless oceans instead of Poseidon, etc. (Habermas 1981).

Functionaries

According to Horkheimer, through the way in which the positivists determined what was to be called science, they designated the scientist as mere functionary of the already dominant operation and bustle of antagonistic civil society. That was the reason, for Horkheimer, why the neopositivism was, in the 1950s, and still is today in 2005, the identity card, the cipher, the code name, the pass word, the mark and the characteristic of the reliable intellectual elite, which gets all the grants and academic honors and promotions. According to Ludwig von Friedeburg, a former director of the Frankfurt Institute for Social Research, the great and most creative, but also very critical Adorno, never received any real academic award: the more critical the less awards and maybe the more police files. The enthusiasm for Martin Heidegger's fascist philosophy, even his metaphysics of death, fits excellently into this picture (Adorno 2000). This was so because Heidegger's separation of philosophy and positive science tended in the direction, that the latter, as positivism wanted it, had to content itself with the facts and data alone. Furthermore, this was so, because the Heideggerian craftsman- or tradesman-like philosophy pretended, that in this division of labor between philosophy and positive science the former could plough the field of Being as soberly, as the professors in the latter, the different realms of beings. Through the way in which positivists determine what is to be called a real science, they take the natural sciences as their prototype rather than the social sciences, or the humanities.

Eastern Europe

For Horkheimer, both positivism and Heidegger's fundamental ontology were one in principle. Horkheimer predicted that both the positivists and the fundamental ontologists would come the more to an understanding with the former socialist powers and rulers in Eastern Europe, the more the people over there would have to eat (Marcuse 1961). Indeed, Heidegger's student, Hans Georg Gadamer, was already in the 1950s as close to the Soviet cultural attaches as to the cultural ministries of the German Federal Republic (Gadamer and Habermas 1979; Habermas 1987; 1976). Since Stalin had come into power, it had always been obvious, natural and self-evident for the rulers in Eastern Europe that the idea of change could not be allowed to be inherent in thought. Inside the Eastern-European Republics the defeated and overcome people had to practice negation in the dialectics, the critique, always on themselves. Outside the Eastern European republics negation in the dialectics was valid only in the interest of expansion. The so-called dialectical materialism in Eastern Europe only glorified its own state. This dialectical materialism was the more domineering, the worse the domestic situation became. In the 1950s this dialectical materialism was almost already called realism. The critical theorists spoke about red fascism. In Eastern Europe the word positivism was taboo only because of Lenin's main book on *Materialism and Emperio-Criticism* (Horkheimer 1990). According to Horkheimer, for Moscow as well as for New York, it was valid that the thought could not oppose to what existed, a totally Other. In the critical theory's longing for the totally Other, which separates it most sharply and deeply from all forms of positivism, the faith in the God of all three Abrahamic religions is concretely superseded: i.e., not only criticized, demythologized and de-anthropomorphized, but also preserved, elevated and fulfilled (Küng 1991; 1994; 2004).

Positive Religion

In spite of the fact that, for Horkheimer, secular positivism was utterly being opposed to genuine religion and theology, he observed, nevertheless, like the young Hegel had done before, how Christianity became positive and even positivistic: in the transition from Jesus of Nazareth and the early Jesuanic movements of the Primordial Christian Apocalyptic Paradigm to the Old Church Hellenistic Constellation, and to the Medieval Roman Catholic Model, and to the Reformation-Protestant Paradigm (Hegel 1986; Bloch and Reif 1978; Küng 1994). That happened as Christianity developed its cognitive, normative and expressive aspects and objectivated its interpretation of reality and its orientation of action. There is not only a secular, but also a religious and theological positivism. According to Horkheimer, the Jew Jesus of Nazareth died for all human beings. He could not keep himself back for himself, miserly and meanly. He belonged to all that suffered. However, so Horkheimer argued, the Greek and Roman Church fathers made of Jesus' suffering and death a positive religion. Rabbi Jesus announced the immediate arrival of the Kingdom of heaven, and all that came in the long run was the Church.

Spiritual Energies

Horkheimer had to admit, that if this transformation of Jesus' life and suffering into a positive religion had not happened, he would probably have been forgotten. His followers would have wasted and squandered themselves. They would have gone down in darkness. Also, religious positivism has its survival value. Instead of forgetfulness, there came into being the positive religion, the Church as a successful organization, which has lasted through twenty centuries and which has also been rich in educational results. Without such religious positivism, nothing would have remained. The good and bad deeds and institutions of Christianity would not have been registered in any history book. Of course, even in a positive religion good people can waste and squander themselves and can be forgotten.

C. Beyond the Religious and the Secular

After Auschwitz and Treblinka, Hiroshima and Nagasaki and all the horror and terror of the slaughterbench of the 20th century, which these names indicate, the critical theorists could not share any longer with Hegel the Jewish, Christian, and Islamic prophetic presupposition, that Divine Providence, Plan, Purpose, Law and Judgment govern the world as nature and history (Hegel 1986k). Thus, the critical theorists also found it impossible to share with Hegel the Greek-Anaxagorian metaphysical presupposition, that Reason governs the world. Jerusalem and Athens were equally criticized, not to speak of Rome: the three seedbed societies of the Western civilization.

Traces of the Religious

In this sense, the critical theory of society is definitely post-religious and post-metaphysical (Habermas 1990; 1988). But the critical theorists still discover, in terms of Adorno's micrology, traces or ciphers of the religious and the metaphysical in the smallest detail of the life world. In this sense, the critical theorists move on the modern continuum between the religious extreme, represented, e.g., by Gershom Scholem's mystical theology or by Theodor Haecker's theology of history on one hand, and the secular extreme, represented, e.g., by Bertolt Brecht's historical materialism and epical or dialectical theater, on the other (Hegel 1986m; Scholem 1957; 1977; 1973; Horkheimer 1988c; Brecht 1961). Being post-religious and post-metaphysical, the critical theorists, nevertheless, do not fall victim to the dominant positivism in its many forms, by the dull conformity with which they are horrified (Adorno 1970; 2003). Such positivism sometimes even creeps into the otherwise most critical poetry of Brecht (Adorno 1970a; Benjamin 1978). Then critical theorists do not only move beyond the religious and the metaphysical, but also beyond the secular, as for example, expressed in positivism and fascism, toward alternative Future III: a post-modern and post-secular society, in which faith and knowledge would be reconciled in a post-secular reconstructed form, as well as personal autonomy and universal solidarity (Adorno 1997b; 1973; Habermas 2001; 1990).

Radical Enlightenment and Critical Religion

It is against the Hegelian background and prototype that this essay explores the fundamental motive and motivation of Horkheimer's and Adorno's critical theory of society, which were no longer constituted by faith in the Kingdom of Heaven, Eternity, or Beauty, as it had been present in the old world-religions and world-philosophies, but rather by the longing and the hope for the totally Other than nature, civil society, political state, or world-history, which transcends the religious as well as the secular: beyond the dialectic of religion toward critical religion, which penetrates the depth of the theodicy – the theological glowing fire, and beyond the dialectic of enlightenment toward radical enlightenment, which goes to the roots of humanity (Horkheimer 1996; Adorno 1970; 1973; Benjamin 1977). The radicalization of theology leads into a humanistically reconstructed historical materialism. The radicalization of historical materialism leads into theology and theodicy. At the roots of the class struggle lies the longing for the totally Other as perfect justice and unconditional love. To be sure, concerning the deep and still further widening and globalizing modern dichotomy between the religious and the secular, revelation and autonomous reason, mythology and enlightenment, the critical theorists have stood decisively on the side of radical enlightenment (Hegel 1986m; Horkheimer and Adorno 1969; Adorno and Kogon 1958; Adorno 1997; Habermas 1990). As this had been true for the first generation of the critical theorists – Horkheimer, Adorno and Benjamin – thus this is still true today for the second and third and even fourth generation. For Horkheimer, the process of enlightenment was marked out in the first thought a human being conceived of (Horkheimer 1996a). According to Horkheimer, of this same process of enlightenment Hegel had said in his *Phenomenology of the Spirit* that if it had once started, it was irresistible (Hegel 1986c; Horkheimer 1996a). It is the purpose of this essay to follow the critical theorists as they, as radical enlighteners, and as being at the same time motivated by their longing for the totally Other, tried to mitigate at least alternative Future I –

the totally administered society, to resist alternative Future II – the militaristic society, and to promote in theory and praxis alternative Future III – the right society, inside the wrong one – the extremely antagonistic late capitalist society (Adorno 1997d; Flechtheim 1985).

The Notion of Dialectic

According to Horkheimer and Adorno, with the notion of dialectic or determinate negation, Hegel had emphasized an element which differentiated genuine enlightenment from its positivistic and pragmatistic decay (Hegel 1986c; 1986e; Adorno 1997a). However, according to the critical theorists, as Hegel supposedly made finally known the result of the whole process of the determinate negation – the totality in system and history – after all into the Absolute, he violated the second and third commandment of the Mosaic Law – the prohibition against making images or naming the Unconditional – as well as their secularization, i.e., Kant's taboo against any excursion of the intellect into the realm of the Intelligible, or the Thing-in-itself, or God, Immortality and Freedom, and thus fell himself victim to the dialectic of enlightenment as Marx, Nietzsche and Freud did after him (Kant 1965; Hegel 1986n; Horkheimer and Adorno 1969; Horkheimer 1985a; 1990). As the critical theorists determinately negated Hegel's philosophy, they preserved its dialectical form – the process of determinate negation – but uncoupled the latter from the former's idealistic totality in system and history – and in the strictest obedience to the radicalized second and third commandment of the Decalogue and to Kant's prohibition against any penetration of the realm of the Intelligible, considered its result to be unknown. Thus they rescued themselves from the dialectic of enlightenment: departing from Hegel they engaged in an open dialectic, or a determinate negativity (Horkheimer 1985a; Habermas 1987).

Theology and Agnosticism

In Horkheimer's and Adorno's notion of the longing for the entirely Other – sometimes characterized as non-reified Transcendence, or the Infinite, or the Absolute, or the Truth, or Perfect Justice, or standpoint of Redemption and Messianic Light, or Unconditional Love, or simply the Theological – met and were united with each other, Jewish negative and inverse theology, on the one hand, and Kantian philosophical agnosticism, on the other (Kant 1965; Horkheimer 1970; 1985a; Adorno 1970a; 1980). For the critical theorists, in the face of radical evil in the most murderous 20th century, the religious dogma of an all-powerful and all-benevolent God had become almost unbelievable. However, in the critical theorists' perspective, the longing for the totally Other could still be concretized, expressed and preserved through commitment to ethical norms and the celebration of cultic or liturgical events in the context of the old world-religions (Hegel 1986m; 1986n; Fromm 1976). It was certainly continually newly re-ignited through the never-ending theodicy-events and -experiences: tsunamis, hurricanes, earthquakes, and always-new wars, etc. As a matter of fact, according to the critical theorists, the world-religions could possibly continue to exist and survive for some time, if they were willing and able to transform their dogmatic interpretations of reality and orientations of action into such longing and hope for the totally Other as the source of unconditional meaning, ethical validity claims, and possible if not theoretical, then at least practical theodicy solutions (Horkheimer 1970; Habermas 1991). In any case, for Horkheimer and Adorno the reference to the totally Other was no utopianism (Horkheimer 1996). In the critical theorists' perspective, without an object in the theological sense the very notion of theory became meaningless, archaic and obsolete. An atheistic-communistic theory was a contradiction in adjecto: the pure contemplation of something, which did no longer exist. Thus today Habermas can speak of a *post-secular society*: one which has become aware that religion does not disappear so fast as bourgeois, Marxist and Freudian enlighteners had once expected (Habermas 2001).

The Other Dimension

To be sure, the critical theory of society claims to be thoroughly scientific, and participates fully in the argumentative discourse between the positive natural and social sciences (Schmidt and Altwicker 1986; Habermas 1971). However, it remains, nevertheless, deeply rooted in philosophy and even in theology (Schmidt and Altwicker 1986; Küng 1981). While the Hegelian philosophy had for its other dimension the absolute Spirit, and the Parsonian structural-functionalism had for its highest sphere the Ultimate Reality, the leading critical theorists, Horkheimer and Adorno, had for their highest longing and hope the totally Other (Hegel 1986j; Parsons 1964; Horkheimer 1970). While according to Hegel the finite realms of nature, subjective and objective spirit had been the other of the Infinite, for Horkheimer and Adorno the

Infinite was the entirely Other of man and society and history. It is precisely through its determinate negation, or turning upside down, or turning inside out, or concrete inversion that the critical theorists – like Marx had done before – preserved in their social theory the Hegelian philosophy: even some of its positive theology in the form of their other, or negative, or inverse cipher and semblance theology (Marx 1961; Hegel 1986e; Horkheimer 1985a; Adorno 1970a). While Hegel's and Marx's philosophy and Horkheimer's and Adorno's critical theory of society were radical, in the sense of penetrating to the very roots of things, i.e., to the originally theological dialectical notion, the structural functionalists stay, like all other positivists, consciously, intentionally and purposively at the surface of social reality, using entirely subjective concepts, and are thus continually engaged in the harmonization of the fundamental contradictions of civil society and, thereby, in its stabilization and normalization, no matter how unjust its conditions may be (Hegel 1986f, 1986g; Horkheimer 1985a).

Structure of Thoughts

While the Frankfurt School's critical theory of society is admittedly unsystematic, it is nevertheless a very methodological and rather organized body of ideas, or structure of thoughts and categories, or connection of knowledge related to alternative Future III – the truth of human society (Horkheimer 1988a; 1988b; 1988c; Löwenthal 1989; Arato and Gebhardt 1982; Jay 1981). While contrary to all forms of positivism, the critical theory of society transcends facticity in terms of relational notions, for example, the antagonistic totality of civil society, it is nevertheless derived from the study of a large number of psychological, social and cultural facts and data, relating particularly to traditional and modern civil society: the relational essence of society as exchange or commodity society, which overshoots facticity, is nevertheless real only in its particular data (Adorno 1993; Schmidt 1981). The critical theory of society is not only the result of the study of psychological, social and cultural phenomena, but it is also to some extent the result of the exercise of the dialectical method and imagination: of radical negative dialectics (Adorno 1997a). It includes in itself the knowledge of several social sciences, particularly psychology and sociology, and artistic, religious and philosophical forms, derived from such study of facts and from such dialectical method and imagination.

From Idealistic to Materialistic Dialectic

Already in 1942, Horkheimer had stated in American exile, that if one thought through precisely Hegel's teaching, that the originally theological notion was the interior of the thing itself, then its execution, the idealistic dialectic, became materialistic all by itself (Horkheimer 1985a). The critical theorists were engaged in such inverse theology no less than Hegel or Marx before. It is in its materialistic form that the religious text is inverted and negated, but also preserved, elevated and fulfilled. As late as May 2, 1968, a year before his death, Adorno taught in his 4th Lecture on the *Introduction to Sociology* at the University of Frankfurt, that the decisive difference between a dialectical and a positivistic teaching about society was, that the former, the critical theory, referred to the objectivity of the notion, which lay in the thing itself, while the latter, the positivistic sociology, denied the process or removed it at least into the background and posited the formation of the concept exclusively into the looking, watching, considering, contemplating, meditating, examining, observing, ordering and concluding subject (Adorno 1970, 1993; Popper 1961, 1967; Zerin 1998).

Dialectical Sociology

Adorno stated in his 5th Lecture of his *Introduction to Sociology*, that the notion of society could not be reduced either to the sum of individuals or to a social reality in and for itself, e.g., according to the image of an organism (Adorno 1993). For Adorno, the notion of society was a kind of interaction between the individuals and a social objectivity, which made itself independent in opposition to them. It was a dialectical interaction between individual and collective. In Adorno's view that precisely was the macrocosmic, or better still, macro-sociological model for the critical theorists' dialectical conception of society: their dialectical sociology. To be sure, sociology had to be thought of dialectically, because here the notion of mediation of the two opposite categories – the individual on one hand and the society on the other – was intrinsic in both of them. That, precisely, constituted for Adorno the pressing and urging reason for the development of a dialectical consideration of society: a dialectical sociology.

Critical Theory of Religion

The critical theory of religion was an integral part of the critical theory of society (Adorno and Kogon 1958). In their dialectical theory of society, Horkheimer and Adorno were interested in religion in so far as it was situated in the antagonistic totality of civil society and at the same time transcended it: that being the case, it went nevertheless non-positivistically beyond that which was the case. While the Lutheran Hegel had comprehended Christianity not only as the religion of becoming and freedom, but also as the absolute religion, and as such as the end of the history of religions, the Jewish critical theorists considered it to be a most advanced, but nevertheless only relative, positive world-religion situated among other relative, positive world-religions: like magic or fetishism, Taoism, Hinduism, Buddhism, Sikhism, Shintoism, Zoroastrianism, the Greek and Roman Religion, Judaism, or Islam (Hegel 1986c; 1986m; Adorno and Kogon 1958). While Hegel had found the absolute goal of the history of religions in Christianity as the absolute religion of freedom, the critical theorists foresaw and promoted the determinate negation, i.e., inversion of its and all other religions' semantic and semiotic materials and potentials into their own secular critical theory of society. And, beyond that, into the likewise profane general discourse of expert cultures, and through them into emancipatory communicative and political action in the antagonistic totality of globalizing late capitalist society toward alternative Future III – the free, solidary, reconciled, redeemed, shortly, the right society (Hegel 1986c; 1986n; Adorno 1970a; 1997d; Horkheimer 1988b; Habermas 1990).

Prima Philosophia

Adorno and his eleven years older teacher, colleague and friend, Benjamin, had formulated for the first time their notion of an inverse cipher theology on the Island of Ibiza in 1932/1933 (Adorno 1970a; Witte 1985). On November 6, 1934, Adorno wrote from Merton College, Oxford, to Benjamin, that he saw in his *Arcades Project* truly that piece of prima philosophia, which was given to the critical theorists as a task to be realized (Lonitz 1994; Benjamin 1983). It seemed to be necessary to Adorno, that Benjamin would energize most forcefully precisely the most distant motives of his Arcades Project: that of the always the same and that of hell. In Hebrew, hell or Gehenna was the name for a continually burning rubbish dump near Jerusalem as well as for a valley in which the Cananites had sacrificed their children to their gods.

According to Adorno, at the same time Benjamin was to represent and expose the notion of the dialectical image in full lucidity. Nobody knew better than Adorno that every sentence in Benjamin's *Passagen Werk* had to be loaded with political dynamite. But, so Adorno argued, the deeper the dynamite was carried into the depths, the more it would tear and sweep things away. Adorno wanted to act as advocate for Benjamin's own intentions against a tyranny, which had only to be called by its name in order to disappear: the despotism of Brecht's all too abstract Marxist atheism. Of course, the prima philosophia – i.e., concern with the first things – suggested by Adorno, was rather an *ultima philosophia*, i.e., concern with the last things – or an eschatological theodicy, which aimed in theory and praxis at the end of the Hegelian, as well as of the Brechtian, and any other form of positivism: ultimately at the end of the hellish slaughterbench, Golgatha, and holocaust altar of nature and world-history: Shalom – It shall be well! (Adorno 1997e).

Hell and The Golden Age

Adorno referred back to the language of Benjamin's glorious first design of the Arcade Work, which had still been very theological (Benjamin 1978, 1983). Here Benjamin had stated, that if the dialectical image was nothing else than the mode of conception of the fetish character of the commodity in the collective consciousness of civil society, then admittedly the Saint-Zionistic conception of the world of commodities as utopia may reveal itself, but not its reverse side, namely, the dialectical image of the bourgeois society of the 19th century as hell (Benjamin 1978, 1977). However, in Adorno's view, only this dialectical image of modern capitalist society as hell would be able to put the dialectical image of the Golden Age into the right place and position. Thus, to Adorno, Benjamin's liquidation of the task of the category of hell in his new design of the Arcades Project and particularly of the ingenious quotation concerning the gambler, seemed not only a loss of splendor, but also of dialectical correctness. Adorno did not want to deny at all the relevance of the immanence of consciousness for the bourgeois society of the 19th century. But, according to Adorno, out of this immanence of consciousness could not be gained the notion of the dialectical image. It was rather so, that the immanence of consciousness was itself, as interior, the dialectical image for the civil society of the 19th century, as alienation. Here Adorno had to insist on the continuing validity of the second chapter of his book on Kierkegaard (Adorno 1997c; Benjamin 1978). According to Adorno's book, the dialectical image was not to be put into the consciousness. To the contrary, through the dialectical construction the dream would have to be externalized and the immanence of consciousness would itself have to be understood as a constellation of the social reality. It would have to be understood, so to speak, as the astronomical phase, in which hell travels through humanity. Only, so it appeared to Adorno, the star-map of such travel would be able to open up the view on history as the primordial history of the 19th, and the 20th, and – we may add – the 21st centuries.

The Oldest and the Newest

Adorno wanted to formulate this same objection against Benjamin's new design of his Arcade Project once more, but from the extremely opposite point (Benjamin 1978, 1983, 1977). According to Adorno, Benjamin had constructed in his new design, in the sense of the immanent conception of the dialectical image, the relationship of the oldest and the newest, which had already had a central position in the first design, as one of the utopian relationship to alternative Future III – the classless society (Marx 1961; Benjamin 1978). Thereby, so Adorno argued, the archaic became a complementary added thing instead of being the "newest" itself. Thus, it was de-dialecticized. At the same time, so Adorno criticized, Benjamin dated – likewise undialectically – the classless image back into the mythos, where it had come from in the first place as theological semantic and semiotic potential, instead of making it here truly transparent as hell-phantasmagoria. Thus, it appeared to Adorno, that the category, under which the archaic arose in modernity, was much less the Golden Age than the catastrophe. That, precisely, was for Adorno the catastrophe, that things went on in antagonistic civil society as they did – namely in the direction of alternative Future I and II. According to Adorno, the most recent past represented itself always as if it had been annihilated through catastrophes.

Disenchantment

If, so Adorno argued in his famous Hornberg letter, the disenchantment of the dialectical image as dream, as Benjamin used it in the second design of his Arcades Project, psychologized it, then it fell precisely thereby victim to the magic and spell of the bourgeois psychology (Benjamin 1985; 1978). Adorno asked, who was the subject of the dream? He answered himself by saying that, in the 19th century certainly, only the individual could be the subject of the dream. However, so Adorno argued, out of the individual's dreams neither the fetish character of the commodity nor the monuments could be read immediately as reproductions. Therefore, so Adorno criticized, Benjamin had brought in the collective consciousness. Adorno was afraid that in the present conception of the collective consciousness or unconsciousness as it appeared in the second design of the Arcade Project, it could hardly be differentiated from that of Carl G. Jung, who had been a fascist, but who had, unlike Martin Heidegger, Carl Schmitt, or Mircea Eliade, given up fascism after World War II (Jung 1933, 1990, 1958; Benjamin 1978). In Adorno's view, the collective consciousness or unconsciousness was open to critique from both sides. It could be criticized from the perspective of the social process as it hypostatized archaic images, where dialectical ones were produced through the commodity character, just not in an archaic collective ego, but in the alienated bourgeois individuals (Adorno 1993; Benjamin 1978). In Adorno's perspective, it was the task of the critical theorists to polarize and to dissolve dialectically this consciousness in terms of society and individual, and not to galvanize it as pictorial or figurative correlate of the commodity character. According to Adorno, that in the dreaming collective there remained no differences for the social classes, spoke clearly enough and should be a warning.

Mythical Thinking

According to Adorno, the mythical-archaic category of the Golden Age had fateful consequences also for the commodity category (Marx 1961; Benjamin 1978). For Adorno, that was decisive, particularly in a social sense. If, so Adorno argued, in the dialectical image of the Golden Age the decisive ambiguity, namely that in relationship to hell, was suppressed, then, instead, the commodity became as the substance of the bourgeois age, hell as such, and it was negated in a way which indeed may let it appear as truth, the immediacy of the primordial condition. Thus, in Adorno's view, the disenchantment of the dialectical image lead right away into a broken mythical thinking and, as Jung before, so here Klages announced himself as danger. For Adorno, nowhere did Benjamin's second design of the Arcades Project bring with it more remedies than at this place. Here would be the central place for the teaching about the collector, who liberated the things from the curse to be useful in civil society. Here belonged, if Adorno understood it rightly, Haussmann, whose class-consciousness initiated precisely through the completion of the commodity character in the Hegelian self-consciousness the explosion and blasting of the phantasmagoria.

The Restitution of Theology

Here Adorno tried to sum up in a daring grasp the bow of his critique so far carried out in his Hornberg letter (Benjamin 1978, 1983; Lonitz 1994). According to Adorno, this grasp had to close itself around the extremes of the bow: theology on one hand and historical materialism on the other (Benjamin 1978, 1977). For Adorno, as well as for Benjamin, that could not be otherwise. According to Adorno, a restitution of theology, or better still a radicalization of the dialectic into the theological glowing fire, would at the same time have to be an extreme sharpening of the social-dialectical, and even the economical motive. In Adorno's view, the theology to be restituted was the other one, which he shared with Benjamin: the negative, inverse, cipher or semblance theology. In his Passage Work, Benjamin had compared this inverse theology, which he shared with Adorno, with something so profane as a blotting paper (Benjamin 1985; Lonitz 1994). Later on, in his *Minima Moralia*, Adorno would compare the inverse cipher theology with a mirror (Adorno 1980). According to Adorno, the fully developed negativity or contradictoriness of civil society, once taken completely into view, would shoot together into the mirror-script of its very opposite: alternative Future III – the redeemed society (Hegel 1986g; Adorno 1980). Sometimes, Adorno and Benjamin compared their inverse cipher theology with a jacket, which was to be turned inside out (Adorno 1970a). According to Adorno and Benjamin, theology was to be rescued, if at all, not as Gerhard Scholem, or Siegfried Kracauer, or Karl Barth, or Paul Tillich, or Theodor Haecker, or other philosophers, theologians or social scientists wanted to do it, namely in linear and romantic and positive terms, but rather dialectically, in the form of their negative as well as inverse theology of the totally Other, the entirely Non-Identical, the absolutely New, which theology would contain in itself historical materialism as its political instrument (Horkheimer 1985a; Lonitz 1994; Benjamin 1977; Horkheimer 1988a; Kracauer 1995).

D. Anti-Fascism

In the early 1940s, Adorno concentrated some of his social research on the psychological technique of the Protestant minister and clerico-fascist Martin

Luther Thomas' radio addresses (Adorno 1997). Thomas was the Protestant counterpart to the clerico-fascist Catholic radio priest of Detroit, Father Charles E. Coughlin, a friend of Henry Ford, and both were friends of Dr. Joseph Goebbels and Adolf Hitler (Hitler 1943:639; Taylor 1983:6; Baldwin 2001).

Christian Crusade

Both clerico-fascist religious as well as political radio agitators, Thomas and Coughlin, were the American intellectually and theologically smaller, light-weight versions of the German intellectually and theologically greater heavy-weight, Carl Schmitt, Hitler's main jurist and political theologian. Both followed, purposely or automatically, the Hitlerian wave technique (Hitler 1943; Adorno 1997:40). Both were always cautious enough to keep open the road for retreat and could even counterbalance their anti-Semitic statements by appeals to gentiles and Jews alike (Adorno 1997:40; Baldwin 2001). As a whole, the speeches of both clerico-fascists may show a certain crescendo in violence and aggressiveness, due to the increasing scope of their Christian crusade against Jews and Bolshevists. This crescendo, however, was interrupted, whenever they met any difficulties with public agencies. By and large Thomas' and Coughlin's radio speeches belonged to the realm of indirect semi-hidden, fascist and anti-Semitic propaganda. Most of their techniques could be traced back to their endeavor to excite hatred and violence without committing themselves. Both clerico-fascist orators fed upon the general bias of commonsense connected with a particular phenomenon and expanded it by subsuming it under high-sounding categories, such as the forces of evil, the Pharisees, or the Battle of Armageddon. Both agitators replaced argumentation by the technique termed the name-calling device (Adorno 1997). This device was grounded not only in the weakness of the fascist reasoning. That was, from the viewpoint of its profiteers, reasonable enough. It was, rather, based upon a cynical contempt for the audience's capacity or incapacity to think. Hitler expressed this contempt overtly. Thomas and Coughlin reckoned with an audience who was too weak to maintain a continuous process of making deductions. The people were supposed to live intellectually from moment to moment and to react to isolated, logically unconnected statements, rather than to any consistent structure of thought. The people knew what they wanted and what not, but they could not detach themselves from their own immediate and atomistic, individualistic reactions. It was one of the main devices or tricks of Thomas and Coughlin to dignify this atomistic thinking of the masses as a kind of intellectual process. By producing in their speeches the vagueness of a thinking process confined to mere associations, Thomas and Coughlin provided a good intellectual conscience for those people who could not think. They cunningly substituted a paranoic scheme concerning Jews, Bolshevists, terrorists, etc., for a rational process. According to Adorno, Thomas was thoroughly acquainted with the Hitler techniques through his affiliations with Detheradge, Henry Allen, and Mrs. Fry (Adorno 1997). Thomas knew everything about the manipulation of his own ego for propagandist purposes and had skillfully adapted the Hitlerian technique of revelation and confession to the American scene of the 1930s and to the emotional needs of the group to which he addressed himself: the middle-aged and elderly, lower-middle-class people with a strong fundamentalist or sectarian religious background. In the perspective of the critical theory of religion, all these techniques, devices and tricks of the 1930s and 1940s are far from being over, but continue to be used today in American religious as well as secular mass media, e.g., in Pat Robertson's program or in Fox News, except that now not only communists, but also Muslims are identified and demonized as the arch-enemies of the American way of life.

Religion as a Racket

For Horkheimer and Adorno, rackets ruled civil, industrial or late capitalist society (Hegel 1986g; Adorno 1979). According to Adorno, the clerico-fascist Thomas' racket was religion (Adorno 1997:85–86). For Thomas, religion provided the characteristic color of his speeches. Religion gave Thomas the trademark, by which he could be distinguished from his religious and secular competitors. As Protestant minister, Thomas could appear as an expert promoting the specific interests of a particular group. The basic idea of Thomas' whole framework was to appeal to people of orthodox and even bigoted religious leanings, mainly Protestant fundamentalists, and to transform their religious zeal into conservative political partisanship and subservience: from religious to political fundamentalism. For Adorno, it was this transformation rather than the more or less obsolescent religious doctrines of Thomas from the Protestant-Evangelical Paradigm of the Reformation, which made it worthwhile to consider his theological manipulations (Küng 1994; Adorno 1997:85–86). Adorno remembered that, in the Germany of the 1930s, religion had played but a minor role in fascist propaganda (Adorno 1997:85–86; Adorno 1997:85–86; Stone and Wiever 1998; Siebert 1993; Matheson 1981). At any rate, Adorno had to admit that the whole Nazi tradition was bound up with a certain tradition of monistic free thinking, which in many respects was actually hostile to Christianity (Adorno 1997:85). The American fascist propaganda, which Adorno observed as a refugee in American exile, showed a very strong affinity to certain religious movements (Adorno 1979).

The Secularization of Christian Motives

According to Adorno, the pragmatic value of a socio-psychological survey of some of the more specific characteristic aspects of Thomas's theology lay, above all, in the possibility of making clear the background of his psychological technique (Adorno 1997). Many of Thomas' devices, techniques and tricks consisted of the secularization of religious stimuli, which he expected still to operate within his listeners. In Adorno's view, without this associational theological background and the considerable weight of traditional religious authority still carried with it, Thomas' whole propagandistic set up would probably not have been half as effective as it proved to be in the America of the 1930s and 1940s and even later on. It was, therefore, imperative for Adorno to deal explicitly with the theological elements of the fascist propaganda of Thomas and of Coughlin and their ilk. In the perspective of the critical theory of religion, this remains true up to the present – 2006. And probably beyond, as neo-labs, and neo-cons, and theo-cons continue to secularize religious motives for entirely profane economic and political purposes, which may even utterly contradict the content of the former. To the contrary, the critical theory of religion recommends obedience to human nature and to the goal of alternative Future III – a hopeful, humane, liberation-society, and to be disobedient to all sorts of blasphemous and idolatrous propaganda devices, techniques and tricks, which prepare the masses in antagonistic civil society for and lead them to alternative Future I – the totally one-dimensional and technocratic society, and beyond that to alternative Future II – the entirely militarized society initiating one illegal war after the other (Adorno 1997; Fromm 1981; 1968; Marcuse 1966; 1995; 1970; 1980). According to Fox News of December 2005, we find ourselves already in the Third World War predicted by Samuel Huntington as the result of the clash of civilizations, preferably Christian and Islamic. Precisely, therefore, that disobedience to conformism and a critical stand on the common non-sense in the counter-revolutionary civil society, characterized merely by sporadic revolts, remains the main objective of the critical theory of religion.

Anti-Religious Purposes

According to Adorno, the fascist propaganda in the America of the 1930s and 1940s, by secularizing Christian motives, perverted a great many of them blasphemously into their very opposite (Adorno 1997e). Adorno was mainly concerned with precisely this process of the fascist perversion of Christianity and religion in general. Adorno tried to bring out the contradiction between the religious stimuli applied by Thomas or by Coughlin or any other clerico-fascist, and their ultimate aims. Their true purposes were not only profane, but also outright anti-religious. In Adorno's view, Thomas, the shrewd mass-psychologist, knew very well why he talked religion: he had to reckon with the existence of religious feelings within his audience. If the groups, so Adorno argued, which he specifically addressed, were shown unambiguously that his aims plainly contradicted the Christian ideals which he professed to uphold, these religious feelings might express themselves in the opposite direction, just as they did in Germany after the Nazis had shown their hand: e.g., in the Confessing Church and its Barmen Declaration (Furfey 1966). Nothing hurts and damages Christianity, and religion in general, more in a secular world, than such neo-conservative or neo-liberal perversion of its fundamental motives, as e.g., collected in the so-called Sermon on the Mount (Furfey 1966). Hitler had always called himself the most conservative of all revolutionaries (Rauschning 1940; Stoddard 1940; Machtan 2001; Haffner 2001; Kershaw 2001; Rosenbaum 1999). This notion of conservative revolutionary, or, better still, counter-revolutionary, had been older than Hitler and survived him up into the present American political scene.

Totalitarianism

According to Adorno, the use of religion for fascist purposes and the perversion of religion into an instrument of hate-propaganda, through providing the principle appeal, the trademark of Thomas, was by no means a unique phenomenon (Adorno 1997:86–87). Adorno knew of innumerable spiritual trends within the American and European civil society of the 1930s and 1940s, which pointed towards the establishment of alternative Future I – some sort of a totalitarian society and state and regime (Adorno 1997; Kohn 1961; Marcuse 1964; Stone and Weaver 1998; Baldwin 2001; Goldhagen 2002; Furfey 1966; Paassen and Wise 1934; Brenner 1983; 2002; Flechtheim 1971; Kertzer 2001; Valentin 1936; Rissmann 2001). For Adorno, there could be little doubt, that every shade of pre-fascist ideology – understood critically as false consciousness, as masking of racial, national, or class interests, as untruth – be it religion or free-thinking, nationalism or pacifism, elite theories or folk ideologies, would be swallowed up by the totalitarian trend and stream toward alternative Future I, which was little troubled by philosophical or religious inconsistencies. According to Adorno, fascist rationality consisted in the establishment of an omnipotent power system rather than in the enforcement of any philosophy or theology. Thus, Adorno warned, the importance of the dogmatic content of the religious medium should not be overrated. However, for Adorno it was worth studying, how such a concrete medium as religion, apparently quite separate from fascist doctrine, was, nevertheless, transformed to fit totalitarian purposes. Adorno was sure that fascism could not possibly succeed on its way to alternative Future I without creeping into all the different and divergent forms of life in antagonistic civil society.

Crystal Night

What Adorno had to say about Thomas concerning anti-Semitism was true for Father Coughlin as well, who had once been a priest here in Kalamazoo, Michigan, where this essay is written (Adorno 1997). According to the opinion of the radio-priest Coughlin, later of Detroit, the harsh historical lessons of the Crystal Night, in consequence of the assassination of a German official by a young Jew in Paris, were inevitable (Baldwin 2001). When in the afternoon before the Crystal Night I, as an eleven year old boy and member of the Catholic Youth movement, came out of the central swimming pool of Frankfurt a. M., I saw close by the huge old Frankfurt synagogue burning (Siebert 1995). There were firefighters around, but they did not fight the fire coming out of the doors and windows of the synagogue, but only protected the swimming pool and the neighboring buildings. After having walked to Frankfurt's main street, the Zeil, I found it empty, except that commodities flew out of the many Jewish stores, including broken and shattered crystal lamps, which gave the horrible day and night their name. In the evening, I heard on the radio, that thousands of Jewish men had been put into prison. Next day, I heard both priests of my Sta. Familia Parish, Father Georg W. Rudophi and Father Hermann Schlachter, condemn the horrible events of the previous night (Siebert 1993, 1995). Not so Father Coughlin of Detroit! A few days after the Crystal Night, on Sunday afternoon, 3.00 pm, November 20, 1938, Father Coughlin entitled his weekly broadcast sermon: Persecution –

Jewish and Christian (Baldwin 2001). As Coughlin – following the wave device – raised his rich baritone voice, he reminded his audience of more than three million listeners, that since the time of Christ, Jewish persecution only followed after Christians had been persecuted first by the Jews: the Ecclesia by the Synagogue. Coughlin continued to say that students of history recognized that Nazism was only a defense mechanism against communism. Seen from this historical-logical perspective, so Coughlin argued, the atonement fine levied by Hermann Goering paled in significance, when measured against the forty billion dollars worth of Christian property appropriated by the Lenins and the Trotzkys, the Zinovieffs and the Kameneffs, the Liotvinoffs and the Lapinskys: by the atheistic Jews and gentiles. His voice permeated with sarcasm, Coughlin concluded:

> By all means, let us have the courage to compound our sympathy, not only from the tears of Jews, but also from the blood of the Christians.

For Coughlin, the Crystal Night was not an irrational release of pent-up hates, but it was, rather, justified by past events (Warren 1996; Schornick 1996; Baldwin 2001).

Anti-Liberalism

Today – in 2006 – religious-fundamentalist anti-liberalism masks the political neo-conservativism or neo-liberalism. Likewise, according to Adorno, religious authority functioned psychologically as a substitute for the political authoritarianism to come on the way to alternative Futures I and II. In Adorno's view, within the framework of general anti-liberalism, however, Thomas drew upon Protestant orthodoxy – in particular Southern fundamentalism – as well as upon evangelism and revivalism, while Coughlin depended on Catholic orthodoxy. In November 2004, anti-liberal Catholics and Evangelicals gave the war-President his electoral victory. In the meantime they have concluded a formal alliance. In Adorno's view, this orthodox theological attitude was furthered by the fact that these trends had many likenesses, since both were positive in contrast to enlightened religion, i.e., the so called modernism in Europe or Americanism in the USA: religious positivism. According to Adorno, Thomas's nondiscriminatory attitude and his neutralization of religious teachings went so far, however, that he did not make the slightest objection to blatant contradictions between the religious trends, which he exploited. Thomas sometimes posed as a defender of the Church. He appeared to identify himself with certain denominations. He rallied his crusaders with the battle cry "The Church is in danger!" But sometimes Thomas professed extreme religious subjectivism, and went so far as to state that the time of denominations was over. He seemed to look toward some future religious Integration, to be consummated by alternative Future I – a totalitarian state.

Religious and Political Sects

Adorno considered it to be possible, that the vestiges of religious authority, and love, and feelings, on which Thomas relied, were due to the essentially sectarian character of religion in America, in contrast to the established Churches in Germany, which were more or less state institutions: the Roman Catholic, Lutheran and United Churches. American sects, so Adorno argued, were closer to the individual's personal beliefs, emotions and traditional particularities. Therefore, they had a stronger hold over the individual than they did in Germany. According to Adorno, the organizational hold of the sect over the family, where the authoritarian personality was shaped, and its appeal to tradition, was much stronger than in Germany, where at least the Protestant Church had been reduced for centuries to a kind of social function (Adorno 1997; Küng 1994). For Adorno, the fascist agitator had to reckon with the presence of sectarian substance within the individual, secularized though the form may be; a fascist agitator could not simply oppose this sectarian substance. He had to try to lead it into the channels of his own secular political purposes. However, Adorno estimated this was not too difficult. This was so, because some of the more radical sects had developed within their womb certain traces of repressiveness and even – under the name of apocalyptic trends – destructiveness (Adorno 1997; Fromm 1973; Marcuse 1984; 1970; 1995). Thus, they showed a more real affinity to fascism, than the big European denominations ever did. Moreover, so Adorno argued, the nucleus of all fascist movements was always somewhat like a sect: with all the features of intolerance, exclusiveness, and particularism. For Adorno, this deep-rooted similarity between the political and the religious sect, upon which fascist propaganda in the USA fed, pointed in the direction of alternative Futures I and II (Adorno 1979; 1997).

Positivism, Fascism, Neo-Conservativism

Like a flash of lightening Reverend Pat Robertson's recent statement concerning the assassination of the head of a foreign, sovereign state made visible the otherwise often hidden connections between positivism and neo-positivism, neo-conservativism and neo-liberalism, and fascism and neo-fascism, particularly clerico-fascism. On Monday, August 22, 2005, the Christian fundamentalist preacher, politician and broadcaster Pat Robertson, called, in the old tradition of fascist radio and television evangelists since Martin Luther Thomas and Charles Coughlin, for the assassination of Venezuelan President Hugo Chavez (J. Levine and D. Walsh, August 24, 2005/Source: www.wsws.org). Robertson issued his Mafia-like appeal for the US Government to take out Chavez, on his television show, "The 700 Club". Robertson broadcasted it to over one million viewers on his own Christian Broadcast Network and Disney's BC Family Network. After a ten-minute news clip aimed at portraying Chavez's Venezuela as a major threat to the United States, Robertson proceeded to make the case for assassination:

> He [Chavez] has destroyed the Venezuelan economy, and he's going to make that a launching pad for communist infiltration and Muslim extremism all over the continent. You know, I don't know about this doctrine of assassination, but if he thinks we're trying to assassinate him, I think that we really ought to go ahead and do it. It's a whole lot cheaper than starting a war . . . and I don't think any oil shipments will stop. This man is a terrific danger, and this is in our sphere of influence. Without question, this is a dangerous enemy to our south, controlling a huge pool of oil that could hurt us very badly. We have the ability to take him out, and I think the time has come that we exercise that ability. We don't need another $200 billion war to get rid of one, you know, strong-arm dictator. It's a whole lot easier to have some of the covert operatives do the job and then get it over with.

Robertson is not simply a crackpot. He was a candidate for the Republican presidential nomination in 1988 and is still a major force within the Republican Party. Robertson and his ilk on the fundamentalist Right, like James Dobson of Focus on the Family and Tony Perkins of the Family Research Council, hold *de facto* veto power over the Bush administration's policy decisions, such as which individual to nominate for the Supreme Court.

Denunciation

The Venezuelan Government denounced Robertson's comments, describing them as terrorist. Venezuelan Vice President, Jose Vicente Rangel, told a news conference in Caracas:

> It's the height of hypocrisy for the US to continue talking about the war against terrorism when at the same time you have someone making obvious terrorist declarations in the heart of the country. This type of statement justifies the Venezuelan Government's worry about preserving the life of its president . . . President Bush said yesterday that his government rejects all forms of terrorism. The reaction of the US to this presumably religious man will put to the test US rhetoric.

Chavez told reporters before boarding an airplane in Havana, where he met with Cuban President Fidel Castro, "I don't know who that person is. I don't care what he said. I prefer to talk about life, about the things we've been working on." Castro, standing beside Chavez, commented, "I think only God can punish crimes of such magnitude." In June, Chavez asserted that the Venezuelan government had a lot of evidence, not just rumors, that there are people (referring to the United States) who think the only solution is to kill Hugo Chavez.

Such an action by the US military or intelligence apparatus would certainly violate an assassination ban instituted by President Gerald Ford in 1976, not to speak of international law. Since Chavez was first elected in 1998, Washington has repeatedly sought to undermine and topple his government. A mass outpouring of popular support allowed the Venezuelan President to survive a US-backed coup attempt in 2002. After numerous attempts to unseat him through a presidential referendum, a vote was held in August 2004, with Chavez winning a landslide victory that was certified by international inspectors, including former US President Jimmy Carter. According to polls, Chavez's popularity has soared in recent months, buoyed in part by a rally in the price of oil that has allowed him to increase government spending. The percentage of Venezuelans saying they back Chavez rose to 71.2 percent in May, 2005, from 67 percent in April, according to the latest poll by Caracas-based pollster Datanalisis. Washington is hostile to the Left-wing government of Chavez because it has become an obstacle to the drive to privatize Venezuela's considerable oil resources as a step towards their takeover by American-based energy conglomerates. In spite of the assassination and war threats, President Chavez is delivering cheap oil to the poor classes along the American Atlantic coast during the present harsh winter conditions and the consequent high oil prices. In the meantime, Robertson has begun to threaten even Christians in the USA with hell fire, if they do not support creationism or intelligent design against evolutionism. And this, in a year in which the tsunami in the Indian

Ocean, Hurricanes in the American South, and earthquakes in Pakistan have killed tens of thousands of human beings and have shown the intelligence of the design to be rather problematic: theodicy!

Premonition

Robertson has, nevertheless, at least a premonition, that ultimately not Islam, with its emphasis on usury, but socialism, with its stress on value theory, use-value, exchange-value and, particularly, surplus-value, remains the most dangerous opponent for the American and global bourgeoisie, and that he may thus very well concentrate, like all fascists and liberals before him, on the enemy image of communism, while the enemy image of Islam is still of greatest actuality. However, the best way for Robertson to compete with both communism and Islam, would be, of course, to act for once as what he pretends to be, a genuine Christian, and as such to follow the Mosaic Decalogue and the Sermon on the Mount, which both prohibit killing and murder, and thus assassination and war, and not as a clerico-fascist. If Robertson was a true Christian, the well-paid television evangelist would be driven not by American nationalism and bourgeois class consciousness and interest, but rather by a Jesuanic longing for the totally Other: what Jesus called during his trial before the mass murderer, the Roman Governor, Pontius Pilate, his kingdom:

> Mine is not a kingdom of this world; if my kingdom were of this world, my men would have fought to prevent my being surrendered to the Jews. But my kingdom is not of this kind.

Jesus' kingdom was entirely other than at that time the State of Israel or the Roman Empire, or today the American Empire: and neither murder, assassinations, nor wars would take place in it any longer. From the 1930s to the present, the Right wing Radio- and later Television Evangelists, have not lead people to Jesus' completely other kingdom, but rather to alternative Future I – the totally administered society and to alternative Future II – the totally militarized society, engaging in one war or civil war after the other. They have prepared fascism in the name of anti-fascism, and anti-communism, and now anti-Islam.

Critical or Uncritical Nationalism?

The Roman Catholic Priest and President of the Institute for the Study of Religion and Liberty in Grand Rapids, Michigan, Robert Sirico, counseled

Reverend Pat Robertson and all the other Evangelicals, to rethink nationalism {The *Detroit News*, September 3, 2005; Levesque and Siptroth 2005}. The function of the Grand Rapids Institute is to reconcile Catholicism and neoliberalism and capitalism. Catholics and Evangelicals had substantially contributed to the re-election of President Bush Junior in November 2004, after he had already, as Governor of Texas, executed – after 10 minutes of consideration for each case – 150 prisoners, against Catholic teaching and Papal interventions, and after he had initiated two wars, which had been characterized as being unjust on the basis of the Sermon on the Mount and the Augustinian Seven Point Just War Theory, not only by Pope John Paul II, but also by members of the World Council of Churches, and which, by that time, had cost already the lives of over 1000 American soldiers and close to 100,000 Iranian civilians. After the Presidential election, Catholics and Evangelicals concluded even a closer, more formal alliance, in order to continue their nationalistic political cooperation during the federal elections of the future: my country, right or wrong! Sirico, the Catholic, of course, hates the socialists Chavez and Castro as much as the Evangelical Robertson does, in spite of the fifth commandment of Jesus' Sermon on the Mount, which demands not only the love of the neighbor, but also the love of the enemy, in imitation of God and also of the Nazarene himself. Sirico agrees with Robertson's goal, that Chavez and, of course, also Castro, and the Chinese communists, and all other socialists, must be removed from power, no matter if they have been voted in democratically or not, or if they have strong popular support or not. Sirico differs from Robertson only concerning the means: before assassination and war as last resort, persuasion, example, economical and political pressures, etc. Critical rather than uncritical nationalism! Shortly before the Robertson scandal, Father Sirico gave a sermon at the St. Thomas Moore Student Parish in Kalamazoo, Michigan. First he read with his Coughlin-like baritone voice from the Sermon on the Mount concerning God and money:

> No one can be the slave of two masters: he will either hate the first and love the second, or treat the first with respect and the second with scorn. You cannot be the slave both of God and money.

Then Father Sirico explained for 20 minutes, and proved how the students could nevertheless love and respect both God and capital. Most students were grateful for this accommodation of Christianity to the globalizing late capitalist society, on which their livelihood will depend. Sirico and Robertson share this affirmative religion and this conformity, to the point of betrayal. To the contrary, the critical theory of religion emphasizes critical, prophetic religion in antagonistic civil society.

E. Perfect Justice

According to Horkheimer's programmatic 1935 essay, "Thoughts on Religion," in spite of all positivism and fascism, the productive kind of criticism of the status quo, which had found its expression once in earlier times in the form of a religious belief in a heavenly Judge and a Last Judgment, becomes a struggle for more rational forms of societal life (Horkheimer 1988b; Habermas 1986). But just, so Horkheimer argued, as reason after Kant, could not avoid falling back into shattered, but nonetheless recurring illusions, so too, ever since the transition from religious longing for God to conscious social praxis, there continued to exist another illusion, which could be exposed but not entirely banished: it was the image of perfect justice.

No Compensation

From its very start in the Frankfurt Institute for Social Research, the critical theory was a new form of historical materialism, which integrated into itself most intensively and extensively Freudian psychoanalysis (Horkheimer 1988b; Fromm 1992; 1980; Marcuse 1962). Horkheimer and the other critical theorists concretely negated, i.e., criticized, the works of both Marx and Freud, because they had fallen victim to the dialectic of enlightenment, but also rescued them and preserved them and elevated them and fulfilled them in their own critical theory of individual, family, civil society, political state and culture (Horkheimer 1985a; 1988b; Horkheimer and Adorno 1969). Thus, for Horkheimer, the urge to transcend the merely conceptual and impotent revolts against the reality of traditional and modern antagonistic civil society was part of man, as he had been molded by his history. What, according to Horkheimer, distinguished the progressive type of man from the retrogressive one, was not the refusal of the idea of perfect justice, but rather the knowledge of the limits set to its fulfillment. Erich Fromm – likewise combining Marx and Freud – had from the very start of the critical theory in the Frankfurt Institute for Social Research spoken of the revolutionary or democratic and the authoritarian or fascist personality type (Horkheimer 1988b).

The Authoritarian State

Only once, as mentioned before, did Horkheimer break the third commandment of the Mosaic Decalogue, and the Kantian prohibition against all wandering into the intelligible dimension of the Thing-in-itself – God, freedom and immortality – and the Hegelian determinate negation, and named the totally Other perfect justice. Otherwise, the absolute justice was a projection of the human mind, and the entirely Other – while existing – was nevertheless completely unknown (Horkheimer 1988b). Of course, even the Hebrew Psalmist had deviated from the third commandment of the Mosaic Law, taken radically, when, in Psalm 91 he gave God four names in the first two verses: Elyon, Shaddai, Yahweh and Elohim. Horkheimer's mother used to pray Psalm 91, in Stuttgart, under fascist oppression. Horkheimer's parents let the first verse of Psalm 91 be put on their gravestone in the Jewish Cemetery of Bern, Switzerland, where they had lived in exile for some time from fascist Germany. Horkheimer had the second verse of Psalm 91 inscribed on his gravestone in the same cemetery: "In you, Eternal One, alone I trust." Obviously, the Psalmist, who wrote Psalm 91, relaxed somewhat the third commandment of the Mosaic Ten Words. Certainly, the critical theorists had radicalized the second and the third Commandment of the Decalogue to the extent that they practically considered the use of any name for the Absolute, or the totally Other, to be forbidden. Thus they had to pay for it with some compromises: be it that Horkheimer called the totally Other perfect justice, or that he allowed one of the four names of God in Psalm 91, Elohim, to be put on his gravestone, or that Adorno named the absolutely Non-Identical unconditional love (Horkheimer 1988b).

Action instead of Patience

According to Horkheimer, it was a vain hope that contemporary debates in the Church would or could make religion once again the vital reality, it had been in its beginning (Horkheimer 1985a). Horkheimer was sure that good will, solidarity with wretchedness and the struggle for alternative Future III, a better world order, had now thrown off their religious garb once and for all. The attitude of today's martyrs was no longer patience, but action. The martyrs' goal was no longer their own immortality in the afterlife, but rather the happiness of the human beings, who would come after them, and for whom they knew, how to die. According to Horkheimer, good will, the solidarity with the innocent victims of history, and human progress, and the struggle for alternative Future III had migrated from Judaism and Christianity and Islam into secular historical materialism and humanism and their praxis (Benjamin 1977; Horkheimer 1988b). Religious contents had been inverted into a secular theory and praxis: e.g., the critical theory and action.

From Religious to Secular Discipleship

As a matter of fact, Benjamin, as well as Adorno, was deeply engaged in that secular, but nevertheless true discipleship, the prototype of which was still in the context of salvation history, the Jewish *Imitatio Dei* and the Christian *Imitatio Christi*, the task of which was the spreading of the image of perfect justice and unconditional love, and which would not bring power or respect or awards or rewards in antagonistic civil society and in its political state, and which in the 20th century was accompanied by a growing awareness of its own vanity in the face of the fast arriving alternative Future I – the totally reified, bureaucratized signal society (Hertz 1956; Benjamin 1977; Bolz and Reijen 1996; Witte 1985; Scheible 1989; Steinert 1989; Flechtheim 1971). The more critical Benjamin or Adorno became during the 20th century, the less academic awards, grants, or titles they received from German, or American, or French, or any other civil society and state, and the larger their police files became. Certainly, Benjamin's academic career was full of disappointments and sufferings and he was finally driven into suicide by German, French and Spanish fascism. Only decades after his death did he receive a monument in Port Bou. Also, Adorno was most vulnerable and suffered much and never found much recognition by American or European universities and states, and was hated much by fascists, neo-fascists, and neoconservatives in Europe and America. Only decades after his death, in 1969, a street was named after Adorno in his home town of Frankfurt a. M. How could Ludwig von Friedeburg, when he told me about Adorno's suffering in the great critical scholar's former office in the Frankfurt Institute for Social Research, expect anything else? Von Friedeburg's father had been a high officer in the German navy during World War I and II. After von Friedeburg's father had co-signed the armistice in Eisenhower's headquarter in Reims, he took his own life, because he could not endure Germany's defeat a second time. In the last months of World War II, von Friedeburg himself brought singlehandedly and heroically a German u-boat from a French to a German harbor. After the return of Horkheimer and Adorno to Frankfurt in the late 1940s and early 1950s, and after having become their student, von Friedeburg converted from the traditional German nationalism and militarism of his parents and ancestors to the critical theory of society. Not for nothing Horkheimer often compared, in the last years of his life, particularly during the third student movement, the critical theorists with the Jewish initiators of Christianity, who had likewise been misunderstood and had suffered much. In any case, the critique of late capitalist society out of the longing and the hope for the totally Other obviously has its high price. Discipleship – religious or secular – is costly.

God-Hypostases

For the critical theorists, in this longing for the entirely Other as perfect justice or as unconditional love, the God-hypostases of the past world-religions and philosophies were concretely superseded (Hegel 1986m). The notion of the totally Other not only negated critically, but also preserved, elevated, and fulfilled not only the notion of the Infinite or Infinity, but also that of the Thing-in-itself, the Absolute, the Unconditional, the Ultimate Reality, the Transcendent, the Truth, the Eternity, the Beauty, the Summum Bonum, the Divine, the Idea, Reason, Providence, Wisdom, Infinite Power, shortly, the Theological, in terms of the absolutely Non-Identical or New, which does not only transcend the traditional world religions, dead or alive, but also the secular modernity, which has tried to neutralize or liquidate them (Hegel 1986k; Horkheimer 1970). In this sense, the critical theory is truly post-modern. While in 1970 Horkheimer could no longer remember exactly who had used the notion of the totally Other first, he or Adorno, in 1971, two years before his death, Horkheimer was certain that it stemmed from Adorno and not from himself. In any case, precisely that notion of the totally Other was the very content of the negative and inverse cipher theology which Benjamin and Adorno had initiated explicitly on the Island of Ibiza and which Horkheimer accepted implicitly (Adorno 1970a). It does not really matter who first formed the notion of the inverse theology, Adorno or Benjamin, or who articulated first the concept of the longing for the totally Other, Horkheimer or Adorno. It is important only that all three critical theorists shared explicitly or implicitly the notion of the inverse theology of the entirely Other and that it permeated their different versions of the critical theory of society, and that it motivated them to reach beyond the modern dichotomy between the religious and the secular.

Productive Forces

In his essay "Thoughts on Religion," Horkheimer was of the firm conviction that human kind was in the process of losing religion as it moved through history (Horkheimer 1988b). But that loss, so Horkheimer was certain, left its mark behind. According to Horkheimer, part of the drives and desires, which religious belief had preserved and kept alive, were detached from the inhibiting religious form and became productive forces in the social practice toward alternative Future III – the realm of the freedom of All rather than only the freedom of the One or the Few (Adorno 2001; Hegel 1986k). In this process, so Horkheimer argued, even the immoderation characteristic of shattered religious illusions acquired a positive form, and was truly transformed. In Horkheimer's critical-theoretical perspective, in a really free mind the concept of Infinity – which entered world history only through the Jewish and Christian and Islamic prophets – was preserved in an awareness of the finality of human life, and of the inalterable aloneness of human beings (Horkheimer 1988b; Adorno 1998). The notion of Infinity kept modern civil society from indulging in a feeble-minded optimism: in an inflation of its own scientific and technological knowledge into a new religion. Obviously, Horkheimer did not only want to allow the image of perfect justice, but also the notion of the Infinite, to migrate from Judaism and Christianity and Islam into the secular critical theory of society in the form of a negative, inverse cipher or semblance theology, and through it into a political praxis, which could successfully resist the always new waves of rebarbarization, and prepare the way to alternative Future III – a post-modern society, in which the reconciliation of the religious and the secular could be accomplished on the secular side, and in which the reconciliation of personal autonomy and of universal solidarity could be achieved on the side of solidarity, and – in Brecht's and Habermas's words – a friendly and helpful living together could be made possible (Horkheimer 1988b; Adorno 1970a; Horkheimer 1970; Brecht 1961). This inverse theology was also a negative one in so far as the Infinite could not be imagined or named: in the last analysis, not even as perfect justice or unconditional love (Horkheimer 1985a). Later on, Horkheimer and Adorno spoke instead of the concept of Infinity rather of the notion of the totally Other: or better still, of the longing or of the hope for the entirely Other, or even just of the fear, that such Otherness may exist as little as the religious notions of Heaven, Eternity, or Beauty had done before (Horkheimer 1970; Habermas 1991).

Messianic Redemption

Adorno stated at the end of his book *Minima Moralia* of 1951, which he dedicated as a sign of gratitude and as a promise to his friend Horkheimer, and which dealt with the damaged life people lived in globalizing late capitalist society, that philosophy, as it alone could still be done responsibly in the face of the universal despair, would be the attempt to consider all things in such a way, as they represented themselves from the standpoint of Messianic redemption: i.e., from the standpoint of the totally Other (Benjamin 1977; Adorno 1980). Adorno was convinced that knowledge had no light other than that which was shining from the redemption on the antagonistic world. Everything else exhausted itself in reconstruction, and thus remained a piece of positivistic technique. According to Adorno, perspectives would have to be established, in which the world would transfer itself, and alienate and distance itself from itself, and would reveal its tears, antagonisms and abysses in a similar way, as some day it shall lie prostrate and needy and distorted in the Messianic light of Judgment Day and its perfect justice. Such perspectives had to be gained without arbitrariness and force: completely out of being in touch micrologically with the natural and social objects themselves. For Adorno, that alone was what counted for genuine human thinking, and living, and acting.

The Messiah

According to Adorno, to establish such perspectives was, on the one hand, a most simple procedure, because the condition of the antagonistic totality of late civil society called for and demanded, irrefutably, such kind of knowledge (Adorno 1980). Furthermore, the completed contradictoriness and negativity of late bourgeois society, once taken fully into view, shut together into the mirror-script of its opposite: alternative Future III – the right, the free, and reconciled society (Hegel 1986g; Adorno 1980). However, for Adorno, the establishment of those perspectives was also the completely impossible, because it presupposed a standpoint which was removed from the spell, the magic circle, of existence: even if it was only a tiny little bit (Steinert 1989; Schweppenhäuser 1996; Adorno 1980). The more passionately, so Adorno argued, the thought sealed itself off from its being conditioned for the sake of the Unconditional, the totally Other, the more unconsciously and thereby the more fatefully it fell victim to the antagonistic world. The thought had even still to comprehend its own impossibility for the sake of its possibility. In relation to the demand, which was thereby directed toward thought, the question concerning the reality or the unreality of the Messianic redemption, the appearance or non-appearance of the Messiah, was itself almost a matter of indifference: almost, not completely (Adorno 1980; Benjamin 1977). Once, for the old Jews, every second in time had been the small gate, through which the Messiah could enter (Benjamin 1977; Adorno 1980:333–334). The Messiah would interrupt the sameness and the identity pressure of the horrible historical continuum of force and counterforce, crime and punishment, guilt and atonement, reformation and counterreformation, revolution and counterrevolution. The Messiah would break the law of the talion: the law of retaliation. The Jewish mystics already thought that men had to do the work of redemption all by themselves. If the Messiah would still come, he would only have to put his signature underneath it.

Remembrance

The secular enlighteners went further and thought that, if the Messiah would not have to do more than merely putting his signature underneath the redemptive work done already by men, then they may very well do the whole thing without the Messiah. But then there occurred the dialectic of enlightenment, and the moral catastrophe of fascist anti-Semitism, and the fraud of mass culture in civil society, as described most ingeniously by Horkheimer and Adorno: the more rationalization, the more irrationality, and the more integration the more disintegration (Horkheimer and Adorno 1969; Benjamin 1978). Enlightenment came to its antinomistic limits. The dialectic of enlightenment still continues in late capitalist society today in 2006. In any case, the longing and the hope for the radically non-identical Other, which drove the thought and praxis of the critical theorists as enlighteners under and against the identity principle of uncivil civil society throughout the 20th century, tolerated no reification of its Otherness and thus no forgetfulness. Certainly, the critical theorists agreed with Baal Shem Tov's motto, that "Forgetfulness leads to exile, while remembrance is the secret of redemption" (Adorno 1980). The Kabbalists had the most logical solution to the theodicy problem: the infinite God could not double himself up. He could not create another Infinite. He could only create a finite world, which is more and more in desperate need of re-membrance and redemption (Adorno 1997a; 1997c; 1980; Benjamin 1977).

The critical theory of society is the most intense secular consciousness and awareness of this need for future-orientated remembrance and redemption out of the deepest religious roots in the present transition from the modern to the postmodern paradigm or constellation of human history: the longing for the totally Other and the rescue of the hopeless (Habermas 2002; Mendieta 2005; Küng 1991; 1994; 2004).

F. Conclusion: Truth?

In 1967, six years before his death, Horkheimer stated that, without faith in God, every friendliness carried the stamp of meaninglessness (Horkheimer 1988a:369; Ott 2001). Also, without faith in God, the notion of truth had no meaning.

The Effort of Thinking

According to Horkheimer, Adorno went even further and said that, without a God, thinking was meaningless: everything else had been finished for a long time or was without interest. At that time – 1967 – Adorno was still alive and thus could have objected: but he did not. In Horkheimer's view, without faith in God, men and women fell back behind the Middle Ages, if not even behind Antiquity and what Karl Jaspers had called the axis – time: shortly, into utter barbarism. Also, for Bloch, thinking meant transcending (Horkheimer 1988a:369). In Horkheimer's view, for the positivists the notion of the truth was as much a superstition as the notion of God. But then, for Horkheimer, the question arose: why should one still make the effort to think in so far as one did not deal with purely pragmatic goals? Horkheimer's answer was: out of despair. For the positivists, there was no Other, for which the mere functioning or the usefulness for some practical purposes was no measure. An ideology like positivism, did not presuppose the notion of truth, but only the concept of harmony. All that has been true, particularly also for positivistic sociology in the tradition of Max Weber or Emil Dürkheim. In Horkheimer's perspective, it had been the error of Kant and Schopenhauer, that they concluded, unlike Hegel, with the same categories, which belonged to the world of appearances, to something beyond the phenomena.

A Better Human Life and Society

According to Horkheimer, the critical theorists wanted the Other: that meant also a life and a society, which were other and different from the horror of the present, i.e., 1967 (Horkheimer 1988a:369–370). This relationship to the Other was supposed to be concretely superseded in each of the critical theorists' reactions toward the extant antagonistic civil society. This was to happen also if the Other could not be expressed positively, but if it appeared only in the critique of that which was the case in present society and history. To the contrary, the positivists saw, without naiveté, in the Other nothing more than mere *utopia*, and in what was the case the unchangeable necessity. However, so Horkheimer criticized the positivistic attitude, precisely this reality-conforming recognition of the status quo prevented every change toward alternative Future III – a better society and a better human life. For Horkheimer, particularly the being-oriented-ness of positivism was the mortal enemy of the truth. This positivistic being-oriented-ness, mediated so many details, which were *correct*, that behind them the truth disappeared.

The Relative and the Other

In 1967, Horkheimer stated that all his feelings, considerations, impressions and experiences were obviously conditioned through his sense-organs, in Kantian terms, through his ability of apperception, and through the society, and through the closer environment, the family, the neighborhood, in which he had grown up. For Horkheimer, it was therefore senseless to dispute that all his statements were relative. However, so Horkheimer argued in Hegelian terms, when there was something relative, then there had also to exist the Other which was not relative, the Transcendent (Hegel 1986n; Horkheimer 1988a:370–371; Siebert 1987). Horkheimer had to admit that this conclusion underlay the same objections as all his other statements. This was so also because the method of Horkheimer's thinking had only relative validity. Horkheimer remembered that even Kant had broken through his own prohibition against excursions into the notion of the thing-in-itself: God, Freedom and Immortality (Horkheimer 1988a:370–371; Kielmansegg 2004:10). Recently, the possibility that the Vatican may cancel limbo for unbaptized children, a non-dogmatic medieval afterlife tradition, was another lesson that, while faith in God may not change, the things people believe about Him most certainly do (Fisher 2005). For Horkheimer, there existed something in space and time, which went beyond the relativization of our knowledge. Therefore, so Horkheimer argued, this statement, insofar as it wants to express something, which goes beyond human knowledge, was a contradiction in itself. In Horkheimer's view, relativization could mean two things: 1. That what Kant meant, when he said that all our statements are conditioned through our categories and that therefore they related only to appearances. 2. That what Marx meant, when he stated that our knowledge depended on the stage of the social development. Therefore, for Horkheimer, nothing remained except the faith, that statements, which were made by men and the validity of which were limited through historical factors and through their ability to know, must not be taken and accepted and put up with as ultimate ones. Maybe, so Horkheimer admitted, this Ultimate, this totally Other, could not be formulated. But in any case, for Horkheimer this faith had as much and as little weight and conclusiveness as its opposite.

The Energy of Longing

According to Horkheimer, the notion of the *energy of longing* came originally from Hegel (Hegel 1986a; 1986c; 1986e; 1986k; 1986o; 1986q; Horkheimer 1988a). The notion meant that mere knowledge – in so far as it did not serve the domination of nature – was useless. In any case, it was not useful for the knowledge of the truth. Here for Horkheimer belonged the problem of truth versus evidence. Thus, what, for example, Walter Laqueur had written in his article *Bonn is not Weimar*, in March 1967, may all be correct (Horkheimer 1988a:405–406). But in Horkheimer's view, Laqueur's exposition was nothing else than information, superficial appearances, through which the truth was not revealed, but rather covered up.

Pragmatism

In January 1968, Horkheimer wrote, following Schopenhauer and Freud, that the intellect was purpose-conditioned (Schopenhauer 1989; Freud 1992; Horkheimer 1988a:465). On its highest level, the intellect remained purely pragmatic: i.e., in the service of the will to life, understood not only in terms of Schopenhauer or Freud, but also of Buddhism, as Religion of Inwardness and of Christianity, as Religion of Becoming and Freedom. For Horkheimer, history was a collection of materials, which one may occasionally be able to use in order to look up, how human beings have behaved in certain situations. In so far as philosophy was a science, it was likewise pragmatic. Logic and dialectic teach the correct thinking. But in Horkheimer's view, all that has nothing to do with the truth. The difference, so Horkheimer explained, between the image of the world, as it appeared, when it is seen through a work of art, e.g., Marcel Proust' s *Remembrance of Things Past* or James Joyce's *Ulysses*, on the one hand, and the image, how the scientist sees it, on the other, referred to the Other. This Other could not be defined. But it was nevertheless the presupposition of every effort concerning the truth.

The Miracle

Horkheimer wrote in February 1968, that it was easy to demonstrate, which naïve error great thinkers had committed, when they wanted to make somebody understand the miracle of all that what was happening in history (Horkheimer 1988a:469–470). Nature was full of miracles as long as its laws had not been discovered. History remained full of miracles as long as its laws were not yet completely discovered. Horkheimer, Kant and Marx were good examples: 1. Kant, the idealist, spoke of an Absolute, but at the same time forgot that this Absolute was grasped through the same categories, for the relativity of which he had furnished the proof. 2. Marx, the materialist, said that everything spiritual depended on the material. At the same time, Marx did not notice that this sentence itself fell under the same verdict. Horkheimer did not even want to mention that Marx took the realization of the bourgeois demands of *Liberte, Egalite Fraternite* literally and most seriously. Marx took these ideals as real demands, while, according to his own theory – dialectical materialism – they were nothing else than bourgeois ideology understood as false consciousness and masking of class and national interests. According to Horkheimer, the miracle of all that was happening in history had usually been understood as a process, which could in principle not be explained through laws of nature. However, for Horkheimer, laws of nature were nothing else than the resume of experiences and their abstract formulation. The natural laws grant no insight whatsoever into the *essence of things* – into the truth. What the natural laws speak about falls itself under the category of miracle. In Horkheimer's view, the longing for the totally Other, the Truth, which could not be formulated, one could explain not only idealistically, but also materialistically: e.g., as a special case of the horror *vacui*. In any case, for Horkheimer, the longing for the totally Other remained the driving motive for all thinking about the truth.

Science and Insight

Horkheimer wrote, in June 1968, that positive science was instrumental and functional (Horkheimer 1988a:487–488). Science limited itself to the ordering and registration of facts, which in principle were accessible to every *idiot*. For Horkheimer, insight was related to the truth. The truth was neither provable nor could it be defined. All depended on *what* a person was thinking, when he or she wanted to get to the truth. While for Adorno – contrary to Hegel – the social totality – the extremely contradictory modern exchange society – had been the untruth, Horkheimer still agreed with Hegel, that the whole of knowledge was the truth (Hegel 1986c:24–25; Horkheimer 1988a:487–488). Thus, for Horkheimer, what really mattered in the process of thinking was that its object had its right place in the totality of knowledge. According to Horkheimer, it differentiated human beings, if they were able to think in this sense, i.e., to have insights, or if they were merely able to order and register facts and their functional interconnections. In Horkheimer's view, positive science had no criterion, in order to differentiate between faith and superstition. For Horkheimer, insight could originate from many sources: out of tradition or theology, but also out of the unconscious, and out of the structure of the thinking of a person. Horkheimer asked himself what it meant when he said that the what of thinking had to find its right place in the whole of thinking. What, so Horkheimer asked himself, did he want to express, when he said, for example, that A and B were base and mean people? Or that the results of the positive sciences, as necessary as they may be for the life of human beings moved nevertheless like the positivistic thinking, which was related alone to these results, on a most miserable and pathetic level? However, Horkheimer also asked himself how he could know that those insights were true and not a great error. Horkheimer had to admit that there were very smart people who had been firmly convinced to possess the right insights and the truth: a truth for which they risked and often sacrificed their lives. But, according to Horkheimer, today we had nevertheless to say of these people that they had thought wrongly and that often they had fallen victim to a conscious swindle and fraud. In the perspective of the critical theory of religion, there are probably not too many scientific statements in the sacred writings of the world religions, but there are certainly some insights in them, without which the human species may not be able to survive: e.g., the fall of man, the resurrection of the flesh, or the Golden Rule and a global ethos built on it (Küng 1990).

Negative Notion of the Truth

According to Horkheimer, the critical theorists of society were able to say what was not true (Horkheimer 1988a:488; Haag 1983). Through this negative notion of the truth, the critical theorists were able to contribute to – in Kantian terms – approaching the truth. The critical theory meant an approach to the truth in so far as it could express what was not true, and thereby implicitly that there was a truth. For Horkheimer to say that something was not true, presupposed that there was something that was true, in spite of the fact that the critical theorists were not able to know it, not to speak of formulating it. If this presupposition was disputed, so Horkheimer argued, then the statement that something was not true, was meaningless. For Horkheimer, in these thought processes revealed itself the affinity of philosophy and art. It was the task of the artist to express the truth. But while the philosopher expressed the truth on the level of the notion, the artist could do this only in a notionless language, e.g., in music. Maybe, so Horkheimer argued, then truth could express itself also through religion and ethics, shortly, through *the right life.* But the truth cannot be grasped through art, religion or life in the way of the notion, as for example, Hegel tried to do in his dialectical philosophy. For Horkheimer, what was accessible to man was all relative and transitory as he himself. But, so Horkheimer insisted, in the concepts of the relative and the transitory and the finite, were contained the notions of their opposites: the Absolute, the Intransitory, the Infinite – the totally Other, the Truth.

Secularized Messianism

According to Horkheimer, Marxism had often been called secularized Messianism, and that rightly so (Horkheimer 1988a:491). Marxism, so Horkheimer explained, is grounded in the longing for the *We want to be happy on earth.* This longing was then represented as alternative Future III – the good society, in which freedom and justice were realized. The critical theory had to do with Marxism only in so far as it shared its longing for alternative Future III. However, according to Horkheimer, the critical theory of society was guided by another decisive Jewish thought: *You shall not make yourself a carved image* (Horkheimer and Adorno 1969:23–24; Horkheimer 1988a:491). Horkheimer inversed and translated this Jewish religious thought into the modern secular language: *You cannot say anything about the Absolute.* For Horkheimer, that statement was identical with the prohibition of Kant that the thought was not allowed to move into the world of the thing in itself – God, Freedom and Immortality. For Kant, God as well as Freedom and Immortality had been postulates, without which a truly human life was not possible. The finite man could not deem, decide, or adjudicate on the qualities, properties or attributes of God. For Horkheimer, the same judgment was valid for the truth. Thus, the critical theorists could speak about the truth only negatively in terms of a negative metaphysics and a negative theology.

The Fall of Man

For Horkheimer it was nevertheless thinkable that through intuition a positive piece of the truth could be experienced. An example for such intuition was what Schopenhauer had said about the myth of the Fall of man (Schopenhauer 1989; Horkheimer 1985a; Horkheimer 1988a:491). According to Horkheimer, Adorno had inversed the religious story and insight of the Fall into the secular statement: *all in the world stands under a curse*, or better still, *under a universal spell* (Adorno 1997a:239; Horkheimer 1988a:491). Adorno said about the fall of man, that whatever the individual or the group undertakes against the social totality, which is antagonistic and therefore untrue, and of which they are a part, will be infected by its evil, and that no less so than who does nothing against it, or simply conforms to it (Adorno 1997a:241).

Meaning of Life

In July 1969, Horkheimer stated self-critically in Flims, Switzerland, that the longing for the Other had probably no other meaning than the worry about and trouble with the deeds of Jupiter in the Roman Religion of Utility or with the wrath of Jehovah in the Jewish Religion of Sublimity: that is, the theodicy problem (Horkheimer 1988a:527–528; Horkheimer 1985a). For Horkheimer, the trend in globalizing late capitalist society was unequivocal: the trend toward alternative Future I – the totally administered society characterized by instrumental and functional rationality. Already in the present industrial society everything became more and more subordinated under the instrumental or functional reason. It showed itself, that through *rational* administration the productive forces were sufficient to provide all human beings on this earth with the means of consumption, which corresponded to each present level of civilization. According to Horkheimer, the removal of the old religious authorities and of the sexual taboos opened up the way for alternative Future I – a purely instrumentally and functionally administered society, in which the needs could be lived out without any further sublimation: like love, art, or friendship. In alternative Future I all that could not be justified through the functional reason, would then be considered to be meaningless: even the question concerning the meaning and truth of life. But, according to Horkheimer, in spite of this trend towards alternative Future I, one had to hold in contempt the man who resigned himself to it, and who renounced, forewent and gave up, what constituted the very humanity of man, and what differentiated him from the chimpanzee in spite of the affinity of their genomes, from which he separated 7 million years ago: the longing for the entirely Other, the Truth.

Truth and Dialectic

Horkheimer considered dialectically Friedrich Nietzsche's troubles, pains and efforts concerning the truth, and negated him not abstractly, but concretely and determinately (Horkheimer 1988a:535). As Horkheimer searched for the truth, he surrendered to the power of the dialectic as radical, but still determinate negation. For Horkheimer as well as for Adorno, there existed no concluded or finished, but only an open, dialectic. In Horkheimer's view, there also existed no dogma on the basis of which he could decide what is good and bad. But Horkheimer knew that weapons of mass destruction, e.g., poison gas, were bad for the individual as well as for humanity. However, Horkheimer also knew, that to this thesis there existed an anti-thesis: how do things stand when somebody used weapons of mass destruction in order to prevent somebody else from applying them? Horkheimer used another example, in spite of the fact that dialectic does not allow for examples: Horkheimer knew that man was a nothing in the universe. Likewise the earth was a nothing in the universe: a little ball, as Arthur Schopenhauer had said, with a little bit of mildew on it. However, so Horkheimer asked, was this *I know* to be made an ultimate statement about the Absolute? Should that be the truth? Horkheimer admitted that the statements about the nothingness of men and earth were correct. But the statements became untrue when they claimed to contain the Absolute. For Horkheimer, the statements of the great philosophers, like Schopenhauer or Nietzsche, were no dogmas which could be allowed to claim for themselves the unconditional truth. But, so Horkheimer asserted, even as dogmas, the statements of the great philosophers were still by far superior to positivism, since they pointed and referred to the Absolute –

the totally Other, the Truth – of which the positivists have not the slightest inkling.

Longing for Light

In January 1970, Horkheimer reflected on his own biography (Horkheimer 1988a:536). At the time, Horkheimer had already lost his beloved wife Maidon and his great friend Adorno and had himself been diagnosed with prostate cancer and heart disease. Horkheimer had to confess, that in his biography the motive of longing was present already in his earliest youth (Horkheimer 1988d; 1988a:536). It was first the longing *for light*, for love and friendship, for a meaning of life. According to Horkheimer, in the course of years this first longing concretized itself further. It became the longing for alternative Future III – a good society as the presupposition for the realization of a meaningful life of all people. Later on followed the insight that the socialistic societies of Eastern Europe, which under Stalin had sometimes even degenerated into red fascism, could not achieve this goal of alternative Future III – the reconciled society, but rather moved toward alternative Future I – the entirely administered world. That led Horkheimer to the confession to liberalism in Western Europe and America, which in its socially modified form still allowed for an intellectual, mental and spiritual life. But in the face of the permanent crisis of liberalism, neoconservativism and neoliberalism and of the bad infinity of antagonistic civil society, Horkheimer's longing became, finally, one for the totally Other, as opposed to the horror and terror of nature and history, for the Truth: which final longing nevertheless preserved, elevated and fulfilled in itself its earlier, less concrete forms, in which it had after all been present already from the poetical and religious beginning of the critical theory of society: longing as transcending from inside into this life and beyond (Horkheimer 1988d; 1987b; Habermas 1991; Ott 2001).

Max Horkheimer

Psalm 91[1]

1] "You who sit under the shelter of the Most High and remain under the shadow of the Almighty,

2] who say to the Lord: My confidence and my fortress, my God in whom I hope.

3] Because he saves you from the trap of the hunter and from the deadly pestilence.

4] He will cover you with his wings, and your confidence will be under his wings. His truth is a shelter and a shield

5] so that you do not have to be frightened by the horror of the night, of the arrows that fly in the day,

6] of the pestilence that prowls in the darkness, of the epidemic which stalks at noon.

7] If a thousand fall to your side and ten thousand to your right, this nevertheless will not befall you.

8] To your delight, you will look at and see with your eyes how the godless will be repaid.

9] Because the Lord is your certainty; the highest One is your refuge.

10] No evil will befall you and no trouble will come near your tent.

[1] Max Horkheimer 1985. Psalm 91 in Max Horkheimer, Gesammelte Schriften, Band 7: Vorträge und Aufzeichnungen 1949–1973, [Tr. Michael R. Ott], Frankfurt am Main: Fischer Taschenbuch Verlag, 207–212.

11] Because the Lord has ordered his angels over you to protect you on all your paths,
12] that they will carry you on their hands so that you will not strike your foot on a stone.
13] On lions and vipers you will walk and tread on young lions and serpents.
14] 'He who longs for me, I will help; he who knows my name, for that reason I will protect.
15] He who calls me, I will listen to him; I am with him in distress; I will deliver him and bring him to honor.
16] I will satisfy him with long life and will show him my salvation.'

I have not been asked to determine precisely the historical-philological meaning of individual passages, idioms, and words of Psalm 91, of which I want to speak. The translations of Jews, Christians, and of theologians and other scientists differ. I quote from the text, which seems appropriate to me. The first verse is engraved on the grave of my parents: "Who lives in the shelter of the Most High is in the safety of the shadow of the Almighty." My mother loved that Psalm; I am not able even today to separate it from my remembrance of the gleam in her eyes whenever she spoke it. It was the expression of her certainty of a divine homeland in the face of the misery and the horror in reality. "My refuge and my fortress, my God, in whom I trust" states the second verse. Such confidence prevailed throughout her life in spite of a full consciousness of the disaster on the European horizon.

Fear lurks in everyone. The one who always asserts to not know fear is mentally damaged or a fool. As other negative emotions can be overcome, such struggle is indebted to the Psalm. The distinction of anxiety and fear, in Ontology's grandly presented teaching on Being, may lead to the definition of empirical research in which a confidence in godly help is irrelevant. Jewish thinking, as it is my tradition, neither confronted the accidental with an existing fear, nor luck and misfortune in this life with a future in the world to come. Longing for safety in the midst of daily dangers, in the presence of shame and ruin and chaos, is the thought of an immanent God. "You do not need to be afraid of the terror of the night, or of the arrow that flies by day, or of the plague that moves in the darkness, or of the epidemic that devastates at Noon. Because your confidence is the Lord, the Highest One you have made your refuge."

Progressive youths know the psychological-sociological mechanisms from which this confidence can be explained. Furthermore, it is well-known why the name of God served again and again as the pretext for injustice, for massive failures and mass murder. *"Deus vult* – God wills it!" was the justification of the blood-thirstiness during the conquests of the Middle Ages as it was during the crimes of the Inquisition. However, this does not reflect on the fact that its own love for the truth, its contempt of manipulation by unscrupulous cliques, finally even that faith owes itself to that which it denounces. Still through bitter disdain, with which it disavows its own realization, it unconsciously recognizes a homesickness that cannot refrain from the thought of paradise. The despair is not annulled by a consoling confession but only by the transformation of the impulse into rebellion. The contrast of a mistaken earnest devotion to the unknown Highest is in any case not so crass as is the new policy of conformity that today, as is well known in this post-war period, ignores the horror that has dominated history.

If true rebellion against the bad ever included the idea of the Other, the Right, so trust in the Eternal includes the thought of going under. As already said, that which belongs to the idea of divine shelter on earth is also that of the ruin of those who are protected, of constantly vigilant envy, of malice and betrayal, of the threat of absolute disaster. The Eternal means refuge and where refuge is required, danger lurks. The offence, which is rightly expressed in the human way of thinking in the Psalm as well as in many other places in the Bible, produces out of itself the praise of God's goodness and omnipotence. Who trust and long for God will be set free. "The one who calls to me, to him I will listen," proclaims God of the End. "I am with him in distress, pulling him out and bringing him to honor." The downfall of innumerable ones count as the "reward of the godless." Those who rely on the Eternal One, will share in God's help. The horrible history should thereby become a just state of being. Were the victims of Pharaoh and the Roman Caesars up to those of Hitler, Stalin and Mao more wicked than their inhuman executioners? Was it by Grace that their going under is to be regarded? Should the terror that happens in the world every day and every hour, both openly and secretively, should this horrible injustice be called well-deserved punishment? As a contradiction to common sense, the plausible, I know only powerlessness as an explanation in the midst of the terrible existence; the insanity of another reality that compensates by renouncing all of one's own competence through the flight into a trust in that which is totally Other, to that which is good despite everything.

The Jews, who had sang the Psalms through the millennium, knew that all too often they themselves were counted as sacrifices to the swords of barbarians, to the torture chambers, to the funeral pile. However, rather than renounce the love, exuberance, and praise of God, who will finally rescue the just of all nations, they calculated their own dead, their own people, individual as well as the collective, among those who had been punished justly. The unperturbed by these difficulties were relieved, it seems to me, that in Judaism the teaching of the individual soul did not develop the meaning that it has in Christianity. When it states in the Psalm, "you make the Highest your refuge. He has commanded his angel to protect you on all your ways," this concerns the protection of all as well as the individual. Throughout the dispersion, the entire, united people had meaning through their praxis of the divine Commandments, not just from time to time or as just a past historical moment, but as one people until the end of time. The idea of a life after death means first of all not the hereafter but the bond with the nation, which has its prehistory in the Bible, and which has crassly been distorted by modern nationalism. By conforming to the Torah, life is provided to the individual, who spends his days, months and years in obedience to the law. The individual thereby becomes so united with the others in spite of differences, that after his own death he continues to exist through their practice of tradition, the love of family and of the faithful ancestry in the expectation that it will once become good in the world. To bear witness to and stand up for this is the meaning of belonging to the chosen people, which determines the conviction of the martyrs. Not unlike the figure of Jesus in Christianity, so Judaism is responsible for the redemption of the whole world. To combine Judaism's teaching of the Messianic kingdom with that of the gospels, of the society in relation to the autonomous individual soul, so that the destiny of the subject at the same time means the realization of righteousness on the earth, seems to me to be the theology that the culture of the West today has given up.

Like always, the historical verses to be explained are, for many, those they have sung, those they proclaimed; a perception of history so contrary to reason, whose existence runs so contrary to and is so far removed from illusion and untruth, that it is just like science. Hegel called the Psalms "classical examples of genuine sublimity set forth for all time as a pattern in which what man has before himself in his religious idea of God is expressed brilliantly with the most powerful elevation of soul. Nothing in the world may lay claim to independence, for everything is and subsists only by God's might and is only there in order, in praise of this might, to serve him and to express its own unsubstantial nullity."[2] Hegel continues "we have to marvel at the force of the elevation of the mind which abandons everything in order to declare the exclusive power of God." There is no longer such confidence in reason being moral and human, as it had once been called in the early bourgeois era. Immanuel Kant still had the notion of duty, of moral commandments as moments of practical reason; that they are in-born in all humanity. Since it is immanent in human beings, Kant postulated the idea of the autonomous individual as well as of the just God out of the demand to treat one's neighbor never merely as a means but also always as end. Whoever considers this demand as necessary and true cannot reject the trust that is announced in Psalm 91 as mere arbitrariness. Such unchangeable certainty once belonged to today's deeply threatened civilization no less than did such certainty belong to the 18th century enlightenment's recognition of that highly problematic Kantian imperative, which existed without faith in God. Being different from the categorical principles that are ascribed to reason, the thought of refuge as it expresses itself in Psalm 91 awakens not merely obedience but the love for that which is other than the world and which gives meaning to life and the suffering in it. Despite everything. "May God's wings cover you, under God's wings may you hide, shield and wall is God's faithfulness."

In modern theology, one may think of the unforgettable Paul Tillich who attempted to mitigate the crass opposition in the biblical teaching, Christian as well as Jewish, of the antagonism between the Goodness of God and the unjust, malevolent horror in reality. Divine help, redemption, should not be taken literally but symbolically. Not to speak of the logical problematic of the notion of symbol in such connections, its seems to me decisive that the Psalms witness a need, a devotion to the good, which itself is truly not symbolical. Precisely, this devotion which is formed in the texts has forever cooperated in the unfolding of childlike experiences. However, the adult who has not preserved and also superceded his own childhood is not a true grown up. He has resigned. Otherwise he could not remain unconditionally in the thought that the world of terror should remain as it is. Rather, he flees to the utopia of the Psalms, according to which one's own judgment about right and wrong is not the last one. There the Lord says: "Because he longs after me, thus I

---

[2] Vorlesungen über die Ästhetik, Erster Band, in: Jubiläumsausgabe, Stuttgart 1927, Bd. 12. S. 499. [English Text: Hegel, G. W. F. Hegel's Aesthetics: Lectures on Fine Art. Volume 1, (Tr. T. M. Knox), Oxford: Clarendon Press, 1975, 375].

liberate him." After what has happened in the present, to say the words "I liberate him" can only be understood as not being a bad contradiction if, as the Jews believe, at the end of history the Messiah arises and leads the just from all nations to Zion, and if the individual feels one with such promise and tries to serve it and trusts it. If a father raises his child in this thought and if a mother looks at the child in expectation, the child could serve that infinite happiness and may even experience it. Also, if the parents themselves have died, the child can continue to experience the love and is able to radiate it again, which in the emphatic sense makes human beings human.

Michael R. Ott

The Notion of the Totally "Other" and its Consequence in the Critical Theory of Religion and the Rational Choice Theory of Religion

A New Paradigm?

As proclaimed by its own proponents, Rational Choice Theory is expressive of a "new paradigm" in the field of the sociology of religion (Warner 1993; Stark 1997a). In the face of such an assertion, however, questions need to be asked, such as "what" is this paradigm? *"Cui bono?"* – For whose benefit or interest does this paradigm serve? Finally, is this really a "new" paradigm for the sociological study of religion? In the first part of this essay, I briefly will address these questions. It is my contention that there is nothing new about this paradigm at all. To put it metaphorically, this appeal to a new paradigm is simply the stirring up and re-serving of the same old stew of the past, only now in a new theoretical form (Hegel 1967b:2). The substance of Rational Choice Theory is little else than the contemporary reformulation and thus legitimization of the early liberal bourgeois paradigm of the *"solus ipse:"* the isolated, monadic individual/Ego whose theoretical being and practical actions are served by a self-serving, instrumental, strategic rationality and praxis over and against a reified "objective" natural and social world. This is the paradigmatic basis of positivistic natural and social science as well as what is known today as "neo-liberalism." The supposed new paradigm of the entire Rational Choice Theory itself, but particularly in its application to the sociological study of religion, proves the old cynical adage that:

> All things are wearisome; more than one can express . . . What has been is what will be, and what has been done is what will be done; there is nothing new under the Sun. (Ecclesiastes 1:8–9)

Instrumental Reason and Action

Modern instrumental rationality and its resulting praxis, as the dominant form and content of what is today called "reason," came into being through the natural sciences, whose mode of operation was based on mathematics and mechanics. Such instrumental rationality is based on a subject-object dualism, where the independent subject is confronted by objects that need to be empirically analyzed for the purpose not only of understanding them but more importantly for controlling and manipulating them according to the subject's interest. The isolated, monadic individual set over and against reified objects in nature and society became the positivistic paradigm of the Modern age of the bourgeoisie, its science and the development of civil society. The professed father of modern philosophy, René Descartes (1958:118), gave expression to this extreme emphasis and thus collapse of the individual into him/herself in the well known Latin dictum: "*Cogito, ergo sum*" – "I think, therefore I am." One's being was no longer seen to be an expression of, or dependent on, the "other" – be it divine, human, or natural. Humanity was now abstractly understood to be autonomous from any controlling or unknown "other" through one's own almost self-originating and self-sufficient thought and the resulting experience of the objectified world. The isolated, compartmentalized "ego" over and against the rest of the natural and socio-political world seen as object became the theoretical cornerstone for the creation of the modern Western world. This is the case in both its liberating, progressive cultural ideals (as in the realization that the life of each individual is of the utmost value and importance as expressed in the bourgeoisie's formal laws and rights of independence: life, liberty and happiness) as well as the socio-economic development of social class domination, colonialism and imperialism.

Such an over-emphasis on the subject-object paradigm of instrumental rationality produces an instrumental action that objectifies, compartmentalizes, and functionalizes not only nature but also other human beings according to the interests of those who have the power to control and manipulate the other. Individuals are no longer seen as subjects or "ends" in and for themselves but now only as "means", objects or "human resources" to be used for the realization of another's purpose. Sociologically expressed, others have meaning only in how they – as individuals, a social class, or a nation – can be used to help realize the interests and goals of those who have the power and wealth to enforce their will. There is no longer any sense of "community" ("*Gemeinschaft*" – finding one's autonomy in solidarity or covenant with others) but only a sense of utilitarian proximity to the other that is conditioned by space and time and strategic purpose – "*Gesellschaft.*"

In modern civil society, such an instrumental, strategic and autarchic rationality and praxis, expressive of the interests of the real social "subject", i.e., the capitalist class, have become the dominant system imperative for the functioning of a class driven social totality. The "masses" who populate the other classes of this society are socialized into, and have to learn quickly, how to "play the game" in the context of their class position for the purpose and possibility of their own survival. Such "game playing" by the masses should not be called "action" or "praxis." The very notion of action or praxis implies and requires a "subject," who has the autonomy and power to give expression to itself willfully through such activity. Obviously, given the historical and ever-increasing class inequality in modern civil society, such willful and "owned" action belongs to the social domain of the capitalist class. The activity of the masses is systematically reduced to the operant conditioning of behaviorism, through which the masses learn the benefits of adopting the acceptable "behavior" of social conformity by imitating the instrumentally rational actions of their masters. The social parameters set by capitalism and its paradigm of domination in the form of the professed isolated subject/class require all those within these parameters to conform themselves to the same self-centered way of life as the social norm for the sake of their own survival.

"Methodological Individualism"[1]

It is this very same positivistic, bourgeois, or more contemporarily named "neo-liberal" paradigm of the *solus ipse* that produces the harmless sounding

[1] Although it was his student, Joseph Schumpeter, who created the phrase "methodische Individualismus", it was Max Weber who developed the theoretical meaning of the phrase in his *Economy and Society*, ed. Guenther Roth and Claus Wittich, Berkeley:

"methodological individualism" of the rational choice theory, and its leveling of all forms of reason and praxis to a strategic "cost-benefit" formula. According to this notion, people act rationally through weighing the costs and benefits of their potential and possible actions, and then choosing the action that maximizes their benefit *at the least cost to themselves.* In this theory, there is no sociological or humanistic recognition of the resulting increased cost, burden, sacrifice or suffering that others have to bear due to such a self-centered, "bargain" approach to life, reason, society and history.

As acknowledged by its own proponents, this formalistic reduction of reason and human behavior to individual choice is rooted in and expressive of the microeconomics of the capitalist production system, with its *homo economicus* (economic man, i.e., the bourgeois) serving as the model of rational action. Although the purported focus of this theory is on the rational action of the individual subject, in critical, sociological terms, it is the capitalist class that is privileged to be the so-called "rational" subject of this theory and its social system, who accrues to itself the massive benefits produced by the existing social totality while the other social classes, particularly the working class, bear the crushing weight of the resulting social and personal costs. The truth of this statement is born out everyday as the antagonistic divide between the capitalist class and the rest of the social class continues to widen. This class antagonism, which the Rational Choice Theory in general and its theory of religion in particular expresses, was graphically depicted in an article entitled *"Gesellschaft der Eigentümer? Wohlstandsverteilung in den USA (2001)"* ["Society of Owners? Wealth Distribution in the USA (2001)"] (Fischermann 2004). This graph, which was produced by Edward N. Wolff of the Levy Economics Institute, reveals that the top 1% of the US population possessed 33% of the society's wealth in 2001, and that the next 4% owned 36% of the socially produced wealth. Sixty-nine percent of the society's wealth was owned and controlled by 5% of the population, which make up the capitalist class. At the same time, however, there were 18% of the US population who possessed nothing of this wealth whatsoever.

University of California Press, 1968, p. 13f. This notion of methodological individualism became a fundamental principle of free market capitalism developed by the Austrian School of Economics and Friedrich August von Hayek, whose writings are appealed to as foundational in the development of contemporary neo-liberalism. See, Friedrich August von Hayek 'Scientism and the study of society', *Economica* 9, 267–291 & 10, 34–63 & 11, 27–39; (1942/44). Reproduced in *The Counter-Revolution of Science*, The Free Press, 1952.

Such capitalist class dominance of civil society in the service of its own interests also is the essence of the neo-liberal/neo-conservative theory and praxis that has gained dominance in the social totality of the United States and in many Western European countries. It is the driving rationale behind the globalization of transnational corporate interests, which is increasingly called a continuation of Western "imperialism" (Radice 2005; Harvey 2003; Cox, 2002; Halliday 2002; Sutcliffe 2002; Wood 2002; Petras & Veltmeyer 2005, 2001). This exploitive capitalist system, steered in the interests of ever-increasing wealth and power for the capitalist class, is in the process of colonizing the life-world of the inter-subjective formation of the human psyche as well as of the social realm of culture on a global scale. According to proponents of Rational Choice Theory, this instrumental and strategically conceived rationality and praxis of the *solus ipse* has now been audaciously imputed to be the dominate dynamic and purpose behind the socio-historical development of religion, primarily that of Christianity (Sharot 2002; Stark 1996).

Religion as Commodity

The developed critique of this truly "sacrilegious" (Stark 1996:4) distortion of the meaning and purpose of religion in general, and of the prophetic, emancipatory, eschatological religions of Judaism and Christianity in particular, which attempts to bring them into conformity with this positivistic theory, goes beyond the scope of this article. Yet, it must be said that the advocates of Rational Choice Theory extraneously and thereby artificially apply this bourgeois paradigm of the isolated subject and the resulting positivistic method of a self-serving, strategic, if not authoritarian rationality, with which individuals seek to maximize the benefits of their decisions and actions over and against cost, to their sociological study of religion. This so-called paradigm does not grow out of the political-theological substance, morality or hope of religion itself, particularly that of the prophetic religions of Judaism and Christianity. From a dialectical materialistic perspective, Rational Choice's micro-sociological and economic theory is derived from and ideologically functions to legitimate the "macro" system and structures of the capitalist production and reproduction process and its civil society. In this theory, the notion of the self-centered and self-serving bourgeois as the paradigm of human nature, values and action are used to explain and implicitly justify the social functioning of capitalist markets and their various "economies"

(Spickard 1998). Within this framework, religion is treated as merely one of the many "economies" functioning within capitalist civil society. From this "religious economies" perspective, religion is nothing but a "commodity" that is produced, packaged and sold by churches or "firms" – as they are called in this theory – to religious consumers. It is quite obvious that this theory merely takes the early liberal and now neo-liberal capitalistic principles of a market economy and applies them in "cookie-cutter" fashion to religion as a mere constitutive institution of the established society. The Rational Choice Theory of religion proceeds quite dogmatically and in a simplified manner to apply its generalized paradigm of detached bourgeois subjectivity and the resulting utilitarian methodology of an instrumental rationality and praxis to its sociological construction of religion.

The Rational Choice Theory of religion is not concerned with religion's essential wrestling with, and expression of, the meaning and critical theodicy questions of "why" life or society is as it is. As such, this theory is not concerned with religion giving voice to the cries and longings of suffering humanity for liberation, redemption and the creation of a more humane and just future society. Even with Rodney Stark's attempt to justify this Theory's reading of Christianity by proof-texting utilitarian statements in the Bible as being substantive, this theory's focus is positivistically on the *techné* of *how* religion accommodates and functions within a reified, capitalist status quo. This is not only a corruption of the emancipatory, prophetic and Messianic hope expressed as essential to the biblical proclamation, which is foundational for the critical and eschatological praxis of the church for social change; this is also a not-so-subtle extension of a bourgeois Christianity as a cultural expression of the dominant neo-liberal doctrine in the United States to the rest of the world religions. To paraphrase Max Horkheimer (1993:12) from his opening address upon becoming the Director of the Institute for Social Research in Frankfurt, Germany, the positivistic paring down of religion to conform to a pre-determined capitalist paradigm is not only badly understanding religion, it is also bad social science and falls under the suspicion of being ideology, i.e., false consciousness. This domination of the solipsistic bourgeois paradigm in the religious conceptual realm is tragically the expression of its actual, concrete domination in the class antagonism of civil society and its globalization.

The Abstract Negation of the "Other"

Although a broader and historical focus can be found in the later work of Rodney Stark (2001), the Rational Choice Theory of religion has limited its analysis of religion essentially to the development of Christianity in the United States. From this myopic, undifferentiated, and I would say, dogmatically positivistic analysis of a particular religion (Christianity) within an obvious ethnocentric and dominant class-specific representation of a particular social totality (the United States), this theory admittedly seeks to universalize the application of its findings to all religion. The methodological parallels between this and the U.S. led expansion of neo-liberal policy into third world or "peripheral" countries, all in the altruistic name of globalizing "democracy," "freedom," "free trade," etc., is no accident. Both express the authoritarian application of the bourgeois paradigm of the particular subject who abstractly negates the distinctiveness of all socio-historical "others," not even to mention the totally "Other," through an instrumental rationality and praxis that serves the "subject's" own interests by creating the objective natural and social world in its own image. As Horkheimer and Adorno (1972) have shown, the marginalization and denial, if not the destruction, of any and all "others" is the essential task of the bourgeois Enlightenment and its positivistic science. The resulting creation and systematically developed sociological and psychological "identity principle" of such scientific enlightenment, however, is nothing other than a modern form of mythology, fear, and continued hierarchy of class domination.

Traditional and Critical Theory

In a 1937 article in which he compared what he called "traditional" or positivistic social theory to the critical theory of society, Horkheimer (1972:239) expressed the extreme problematic of attempting to turn the critical theory into a sociology. The critical theory of society and religion is a multi-discipline, dialectical theory that cannot be reduced to one of its research disciplines nor to the traditional, positivistic methodology of bourgeois social science. Thus, the difference between sociology and the critical theory of society is the same fundamental difference that exists between the Rational Choice Theory of religion and the Critical Theory of religion. Respectively, it is the privileging difference between form and content, quantity and quality, "Being" and "Becoming," dogmatism and radicalism, *stasis* and *metanoia*, the capitalist class and the working, or better stated, "under" class, civil/bourgeois religion and a determinately negated prophetic/Messianic/Eschatological religion. Unlike positivistic thought, which analytically compartmentalizes and separates these categories from each other, dialectical logic and theory grasp the inherent inter-relational dynamic of these supposed antithetical pairs.

In the early 20th century, the French Priest, Fr. Alfred Loisey, is purported to have said, "Jesus came proclaiming the kingdom of God and all that came was the church." This truism pictures the difference between these two theories of religion. Rational Choice Theory of religion admittedly is concerned only with the functioning of the institutional church or "firm" (Stark 1996) according to the market theory of the given capitalist controlled civil society. Conversely, the Critical Theory of society and religion is founded upon, and is expressive of, suffering humanity's longing for that which is totally "Other" than the class produced exploitation of this civil society. This prophetic, Messianic and eschatological longing for the totally "Other" is translated through the Critical Theory into a secular, and thus relevant, meaningful, and revolutionary theory that seeks the determinate negation of the reified capitalist civil society and its barbarism for the creation of a better future society. The determinate negation of the religious notion of and longing for the totally "Other" into the Critical Theory itself is an essential element of this completely secular and materialist Theory's work for a more just, equitable, good, rational – in terms of both instrumental *and* communicative reason, free – in terms of both autonomy *and* solidarity, and shalom-filled future society.

Positivism

The fundamental difference between Rational Choice and the Critical Theory of religion is expressive of modernity's long contentious history of philosophical/theoretical debate as well as national and international class warfare between the advocates of positivism and dialectical thought. As Adorno has stated, "positivism [is] the myth [or metaphysics] of things as they actually are" (Horkheimer and Adorno 1972:x). In the attempt to understand and thereby control how things function in both nature and society, positivism analytically reifies and, possibly better stated, kills "things as they actually are" as they are disconnected from its historical past as well as any change towards a real future. In being dissected from its past development, the present also has no real future, other than the progress of what already is. In this, there is no future or anything new. The mythical expression of this real, historical life process of qualitative change and becoming, in terms of a differentiated experience of time, is not contained in positivistic logic or sciences. The Greek notion of *"Kyrios,"* or the mystical *"nunc stans"* or *"Jetztzeit"* (the revolutionary "now time" of something other or new) that explodes open and puts an end to the mechanical, repetitious, horrifying and deadly continuum of history under the reign of *"Chronos"* (clock time) and thereby opens history toward its possible new creation, is unthinkable, if not forbidden, in positivism. Through its reified paradigm of bourgeois subjectivity and the resulting instrumental and authoritarian rationality and praxis that is produced, Rational Choice Theory does not concern itself with the qualitative socio-historical change of the revolutionary *kyrios* time but only with advocating as rational a self-serving, utilitarian system of conformity, if not power-driven behavior, of individuals, social institutions, and nations that strengthens and further legitimates the deadly progression of what is the case. It is just this a-historical, abstract yet concretely exploitive system of a capitalist social totality that the advocates of the Rational Choice Theory of religion have extrinsically applied to the functioning and purpose [*telos*] of religious institutions within that society. Rational Choice Theory of religion is little more than another form of an ideological bourgeois civil religion, which distorts if not destroys the liberational, redemptive, hope-filled cry and longing of the oppressed, for a better future society as well as for the *kyrios* of the totally Other, which is the revolutionary content and call to action of the prophetic and Messianic religions (Judeo-Christianity) to which this Theory appeals. Rational Choice Theory instrumentally objectifies religion into being nothing more than a service-oriented institution within the capitalist civil society.

Dialectical Methodology

Unlike the positivism of Rational Choice Theory, the Critical Theory of society and religion is founded upon and is expressive of the revolutionary logic and socio-historically applied methodology of dialectics, particularly that of negative dialectics. In January 1930, Horkheimer became the third director of the Frankfurt Institute for Social Research since its beginning in 1922. It was under the directorship of Horkheimer, whom Habermas (1993b:49) called its *"spiritus rector,"* that what is now known as the critical theory of the

Frankfurt School began. In 1971, Horkheimer reflectively gave expression to his critical theory of society and religion's purpose from its very beginning. In this interview, he stated that the driving dynamic of the appeal to the totally other than this world is concretely grounded in the cries for help and justice of the innocent victims that are systemically created by the unjust, "untrue" (Adorno), exploitive and deadly structures of the existing status quo (Jay 1971:xii). This materialistic inversion of the meaning and purpose of metaphysics and theology back into the cries of suffering and oppressed humanity for liberation and a better, more happy future gave a more positive judgment to religion as a fundamental element of the entire critical theory. As Horkheimer (1973a:xii) stated, "the hope that earthly horror does not possess the last word is, to be sure, a non-scientific wish." However, it is precisely herewith this non-scientific wish for a more reconciled future society that, as Adorno (1973:207) stated, "materialism comes to agree with theology." The determinate negation of this religious "non-scientific wish" for a truly revolutionary ending of the historical continuum of the systematically produced horrors of modern capitalist society, which could open up the future for the creation of a new, more reconciled society, is the very substance and purpose of the materialistic critical theory of society and religion.

As will be developed in the later part of this essay, the critical theory of society and religion's appeal to a totally "Other" than this "untrue" world is the radically secularized expression of Judaism's prohibition of naming or imaging God, as expressed in the second and third commandment of the Decalogue. This negative or inverse theology of the critical theory is also philosophically founded on the materialistic sublimation of G. W. F. Hegel's dialectical methodology of determinate negation (Ott 2001, chapt. 5). For the critical theorists, dialectics is the consistent recognition of the non-identity between the socially created concept of a thing and the thing itself. Contrary to positivism, dialectics is "the ontology of the wrong state of things" as they actually are (Adorno 1973:11). Dialectics is the thinking against the thought of what merely is given. It shows the delusion of thought and its logical claim to universality, which thereby becomes totalitarian. As Herbert Marcuse (1960:viii) states,

> the power of negative thinking is the driving power of dialectical thought, used as a tool for analyzing the world of facts in terms of its internal inadequacy.

Unlike positivism's drive for the reduction of multiplicity (the "other") to the mathematical point of immanence, equivalence and identity, dialectics, particularly negative dialectics, "contradicts the traditional norm of adequacy" as it is "the consistent sense of nonidentity" (Marcuse 1960:5). Dialectical theory seeks "to change the direction of conceptuality, to give it a turn toward nonidentity" (Marcuse 1960:12).

The dialectical thought of the Critical Theory, therefore, does not begin with a pre-established, paradigmatic theoretical position that is then externally applied to and forced upon its object. Rather, dialectical thought is the negative process of realizing its own theoretical insufficiency in the face of reality. It is the realization that things do not fit neatly into their socially created concept or definition. Dialectical thought, in general, critically recognizes, enters into, and seeks the concrete or *determinate* socio-historical negation of the tension/contradiction between reason and reality, essence and existence, the infinite and the finite, sacred and profane, religion and secularity, the individual and the collective, etc. Unlike the dualistic methodology of modern natural and positivistic social science as expressed in Rational Choice Theory, which abstractly negates or crassly reduces this tension to a calculating stratagem of individual interest, the dialectical dynamic of determinate negation seeks a higher historical form of this tension's reconciliation beyond the mere existence of what is. The reduction, if not negation of this contradiction and the suffering it produces, is not just an issue of logic, methodology, or theory formation. Rather, the very concrete and historical goal of this dialectical method of the critical theory is the specific negation of those social systems, structures, and powers of the reified status quo that prevent the creation of a more reconciled future society.

Dialectic or critical theory gives expression to that which is "other" than what is; to that which doesn't fit into the neatly constructed concepts of the status quo's logic or social system. The critical theory of society and religion gives revolutionary articulation to the voice and longings of the innocent victims of the class exploitation, domination, and barbarism of capitalist civil society. Through negative dialectical thought and its methodology of determinate negation, the critical theory of religion gives expression in a materialistic voice to suffering humanity's religiously expressed longing for justice, redemption, happiness, God or that which is "totally Other" than what is. In the critical theory, this totally "Other" is not conceived in a metaphysical, theological, or idealistic way, which abstracts from people's experiences in the society and history. For the critical theory, being grounded in and expressive of the desperate cries of the innocent victims of the "slaughter-bench" (Hegel 1956:21) of history and society, the religious notion of the totally "Other" translated into a materialistic theory and praxis has the potential of being a socio-historical force of revolutionary social change for the creation of a better future society.

However, unlike the negative and positive dialectics of Hegel, who idealistically professed to know in advance the positive goal toward which history was moving, Horkheimer and the other critical theorists sought only the determinate negation of the existing socio-historical produced antagonisms that produce the needless suffering, horror and death of humanity and the destruction of nature. For the critical theory of society and religion, the future is open toward something new, *if at all*, only in a negative not a positive way. As stated above, the focal point of the critical theory's negative dialectical method was summarized in Adorno's dialectical inversion of Hegel's statement that "the truth is the whole" (Hegel 1967a:81). For the entire critical theory, "the whole is the untrue" (Adorno 1974:50). Such a critical statement avoids falling into the meaninglessness of absolute nihilism or becoming a metaphysical dogmatic fundamentalism or collapsing into bourgeois skepticism and positivism only by maintaining the dialectical tension with the falseness and negativity of what is by means of the humanistic notion of and longing for that which is "other" than what is; of that which is ultimately grounded in the religious notion of the totally Other than this false socio-historical totality.

Religion's Migration into Secular Form

Along with Adorno and Benjamin, Horkheimer sought to allow the still relevant and meaningful, liberating and humanistic content of religion to migrate into a modern secular form and thereby become a possible anamnestic, present and proleptic force of resistance to the development of an "iron caged," totally administered, cybernetic, dehumanizing and oppressive society. According to Horkheimer, this secular form was his critical theory of society and religion. For Horkheimer, religion – particularly the prophetic and Messianic religions of Judaism and Christianity – was not merely a pre-modern, mythological expression of the antediluvian childhood of humanity, which thereby needed to be forgotten. Neither was religion only understood to be an ideological conservative force of control and legitimization of the existing social systems of class exploitation and domination. According to Horkheimer, religion also gives expression to the radical and revolutionary critique of such social systems that produce the oppression, suffering and death of innumerable generations of innocent victims in the hope of creating a better future society. It is this inherent social critique of religion in its narrative form of human resistance and hope, which in the face of modern capitalist society's development toward a globalized totally administered society, needs to be negatively appropriated in the continuing struggle for a more just, humane, rational, free – in terms of both autonomy and solidarity, and a peaceful future society. It is in this context of the determinate negation of religion that Horkheimer's concept of the "totally Other" than this historical development toward such an administered world is understood as a fundamental dynamic of his materialist theory of society and religion.

Longing for the Totally Other

From the mid-1960s to the year of his death in 1973, Max Horkheimer gave a number of interviews in which he addressed the question of the relationship between the critical theory and religion/theology. This fundamental and critical relationship was specifically the topic of a 1970 interview in Montagnola, Switzerland that was published under the title *Die Sehnsucht nach dem ganz Anderen* [The Longing for the Totally Other] (Horkheimer, 1970). As Horkheimer (1985:431) states, the specific expression "the Other" comes from Adorno. However, this conception of the totally Other is no less a fundamental dialectical notion of Horkheimer's materialistic critical theory of religion, which was a dynamic component of his entire theory from the very beginning.

In this 1970 interview with Helmut Gumnior, Horkheimer gave expression to the dialectical materialistic meaning of his notion of the "totally Other" in response to the question of how he, as a Marxist and a revolutionary, could be concerned with or write about "the infinite One." Contrary to the accusation that Horkheimer betrayed the revolutionary purpose of the critical theory by turning back to religion – or "crawling back to the cross" as it is derogatorily stated in German – in his old age, the critical sublation of religion as a fundamental element of his entire critical theory had already been expressed in his early work (Ott 2001), and particularly in a short essay from 1935 entitled "Thoughts on Religion" (Horkheimer 1972). Echoing Marx's

(2002:171) materialistic conception of religion giving expression to real, concrete human suffering and being a protest against it, of "religion [being] the sigh of the oppressed creature, the heart of a heartless world and the soul of soulless conditions," Horkheimer stated that religion was originally the expression through which suffering humanity gave voice to their cries and longing for justice. The dangerous memory of Judaism's foundational "Exodus" experience of God identifying covenantally with, and thereby freeing, the Hebrew slaves from their exploitation and domination by their Egyptian masters to become "God's people" in the world, echoes through such materialistic analysis. True and good religion possesses different norms than those of either nature or society and thus becomes the voice of accusation against the injustice experienced in life by countless generations of innocent victims.

At the very same time that Horkheimer was writing this article on religion in exile in the United States, such cruel norms of nature were being forcibly nationalized in Nazi Germany. In *Mein Kampf*, Adolf Hitler (1971:65) named these norms of nature and the society built on it under the title of "the aristocratic principle of Nature." Hitler's lauding of this dominational and cruel principle of nature was the further developed rationalization for the barbarism of capitalist society. Hitler's "Principle" is the more modern version of Machiavelli's maxim that the "ends justify the means" and H. Spencer's social Darwinistic conception of society in terms of the survival of the fittest, which eternalizes the privilege of power and the strength of the one and/or the few over the resulting oppressed masses. With striking and extremely disturbing similarities to political and religious statements made in the U.S. today, this law of nature was understood to be the will of God for which Hitler would fight to defend against all its foes; against the *"veritable devils"* and inhuman *"monsters"* whose contrary norms and organizations would bring about the collapse of civilization and devastate the world; in other words, against those who live by other, *"unnatural"*, non-capitalistic norms, expressly Jews and Marxists (Hitler 1971:63–64).

Tabooed Principles

Already in his writings of the early 1920s Horkheimer (1978:27–28) identified this dehumanizing and authoritarian norm developing in the post-World War I German society in the form of the tabooed principles of the nation and

God, which are the culturally legitimating corollary of the more essentially tabooed and hidden capitalist system of production. In modern civil society, the State, culture and religion are subsumed into the service of protecting, developing and legitimizing the aristocratic principle of systematic class domination and exploitation in the form of the antagonistic social totality of capitalist production. During this same time, Walter Benjamin (1996:288) wrote that capitalism itself is an essentially cultic religious phenomenon"*sans rêve et sans merci*" [without dream or mercy]. Capitalism as religion is a self-contained, identity-producing cult with no dogma or theology [nothing "other" than itself], in which everything has its meaning and purpose in relationship to the antagonistic capitalist, utilitarian system of production and consumption. Already in 1921, the capitalist essence of what is today called the Rational Choice Theory of religion was identified and critiqued.

As Horkheimer (1989:78) asserted, "whoever is not willing to talk about capitalism should also keep quiet about fascism." Conversely, it should be of no surprise then that today in the mainstream academic, political, religious and media discourses nothing is ever said nor heard about the ever present possibility of Western civil society collapsing again into the authoritarian horror of fascism since the inherent antagonistic nature of capitalism remains tabooed as a topic in those very same discourses. Fascism as state capitalism is the further historical development of the cybernetic rationalization of the capitalist mode of production and the systematic reification of the extreme class antagonisms it produces, particularly when the interests of the capitalist class are severely threatened. In his "Theses on the Philosophy of History," the last work that he produced before his suicide at Portbou, Spain on September 26, 1940 as he fled Nazi Germany, Benjamin (1968:257) stated that the "state of emergency," which existed at that time due to Fascism, was not an aberration but the very systematic principle and historical development of the antagonisms of capitalist society. As he stated, this socio-historical crisis is a reality that the socially disenfranchised, exploited and oppressed know all too well. Benjamin advised that a critical notion of history as a whole, one that is expressive of this systematically created and perpetual tragedy, be developed, not only so it can be comprehended but also resisted. Although its analysis goes far beyond the scope of this essay, the barbarous reality of this "state of emergency" of capitalist society is the dominant form of what presently goes by the name of "globalization."

Ideological Function

What socio-historical role does religion, particularly the prophetic and Messianic religions of Judaism and Christianity, play in the midst of this globalizing crisis? Do these religions have anything concretely liberating, hopeful, "new," and revolutionary to offer for the redemption of humanity and the creation of a better future society? Or, are these religions merely legitimating and harmonizing functional systems within the given antagonistic social totality? Within modern capitalist civil society, there are a variety of acceptable and harmless – at least to the capitalist class system itself – ideological functions of religion as a social institution. These non-prophetic, non-Messianic, non-eschatological, harmonizing social responsibilities of religion arise from the antagonistic bourgeois system's imperative for increased pattern maintenance and legitimization. As the system's class, race, gender, age, regional, national and international antagonisms become more extreme as they are now in U.S. society, the system's need for ideological religious legitimization increases as well. It is not by happenstance that the Rational Choice Theory of religion was and continues to be developed as paradigmatic in the field of the sociology of religion during the same time as the increasing socio-political influence of the so-called "Christian/Evangelical Right" in U.S. society. Both are symptomatic civil religious responses to the increasing crisis of capitalist society.

Such responses can be heard not only from political and military leaders, TV evangelists, and media personalities but also from the pulpits and policies of many mainline churches. The socially critical, prophetic, Messianic and eschatological substance of the Judeo-Christian religion, which is nominalistically mouthed and appealed to for consolation in the midst of the increasing social antagonisms, is corrupted to now overtly legitimate the antagonisms of capitalist society by abstractly glossing over them through such nationalistic notions of equating the will of God with the action/policies of the nation. As expressed by the political theologian Johann Baptist Metz (1980, chapt. 3) another facet of such "civil" or "bourgeois religion" is the escapist diversion of people's attention from any religious concern for or critical knowledge of the social inequalities, which translates into not loving one's neighbor, through the privatization of religion into a mystical, spiritual relationship between the individual and God. This bourgeois privatization of religion has reactionary social manifestations and consequences, however, through the formation of "evangelical" or fundamentalistic churches, who either moralistically continue religion's supposed withdrawal from any involvement in society or, conversely, become politically active to redeem society from its narrowly conceived moral errs through its return to biblical teachings. In all of these religious responses, however, the socio-economic causes of civil society's antagonisms and the horror they produce are never addressed but continue to remain hidden behind an ideological veil of class interests and power. This critique applies equally to the Rational Choice Theory of religion, which equates the bourgeois, social Darwinistic principle of capitalist market economy with the substance of all religions, especially that of Christianity. As Benjamin stated, this social Darwinistic, aristocratic principle of nature is not to be understood as only the extreme, barbaric norm of fascism. This authoritarian principle is the norm of capitalism itself and of its religious forms of legitimization.

Horkheimer and the other critical theorists had a completely different understanding of the meaning and purpose of religion from that of either its traditional or bourgeois interpretation. The critical theory of religion is expressive of the liberational substance of religion that is rooted in the suffering, cries and longing of the oppressed and "non-identical" (Adorno 1973) for that which is socially and historically other than what is in the socio-historical form of a more reconciled future society as well as for that which is "totally Other."

Revolution

The development of the critical theory of society and religion is a revolutionary expression of both resistance and hope against the continuing historical and now global expansion of the crisis of capitalist society. It was because of the increasing post-World War I danger of the development of this aristocratic principle in the form of National Socialism that led Horkheimer to the study of Marx and the advocacy of the need for a Marxist revolution as the means by which the totalitarianism from the right could be defeated. As Horkheimer (1989:94) stated,

> Disrespect for anything mortal that puffs itself up as a god is the religion of those who cannot resist devoting their life to the preparation of something better, even in the Europe of the Iron Heel.

However, unlike Marx, Horkheimer already knew that the *subject* of this revolution would not be the proletariat. The needed consciousness of their exploitation and oppression, which was to produce the solidarity of the proletariat as a revolutionary force, was becoming systematically dulled by the incremental improvement of their material well-being without the need of a revolution. The working class did not and still does not have the solidarity of class-consciousness nor even the awareness of its continued, systematic exploitation, which could produce the resolve to be such a revolutionary force.

Solidarity Through Compassion

By means of the determinate negation of Marx's theory with that of the brutally honest and pessimistic philosophy of Arthur Schopenhauer, Horkheimer attempted to critically identify a universal form of human solidarity that could not be overcome by the capitalist system of production. This solidarity is established through the consciousness that all human beings are finite and will die. According to Schopenhauer, such consciousness of universal suffering and death of all living things can create compassion and empathy for the other. Such compassion can thereby overcome the "will to life," which is the ontological cause of all suffering as well as happiness in the world. However, Horkheimer (1978:38–39) also determinately negated Schopenhauer's metaphysics of compassion with Marx's class analysis, as he stated that not everyone suffers and dies in the same way in a capitalist class society. Barring the immediacy of tragic and accidental death, the circumstances surrounding the death of a millionaire are different than the death of a worker. A millionaire dies with the knowledge that his family and friends will be secure, whereas the poor die with the added weight of fear, anger, if not guilt, at the conditions of those that are left to grieve. For such consciousness of death and compassion to be a liberating force of social change it must also become a consciousness of this social class antagonism. The suffering, pain and even death of a decent human being is directly connected with the social quality of that person's love, longing, and life struggle for a new, non-antagonistic society (Horkheimer 1978:207–208). It is this critical, social consciousness of a shared finitude, suffering, and death that has the potential of breaking down the socially produced solipsistic, monadic isolation and alienation of people from themselves, each other, and ultimately the products of their own labor in bourgeois society. Through the shared experience of suffering produced by the antagonistic society in which people live, people can break out of their isolated, compartmentalized selves and enter into solidarity with others in the attempt to overcome the causes of human suffering. The consciousness of shared suffering and the solidarity that it can produce is the catalyst for what Horkheimer (1970:56) called the "original human interest" to create a better, more reconciled future society.

According to Horkheimer, the secret motivation of Marxist thought was this "compassion" for the innocent victims of the capitalist class antagonisms. Marxism's compassion is generally not acknowledged because it can become subjectively privatized and turned into a substitute, e.g., charity, instead of the class conscious, concrete revolutionary praxis for a more just, merciful, rational, good, free and reconciled future society. It is from this consciousness of shared suffering and the finitude of all worldly things that the radicalized religious notion of the Infinite One or totally Other is understood and expressed by Horkheimer.

Absolute Abandonment

The notion of the totally Other thereby preserves the harsh reality of humanity's unalterable abandonment and prevents the creation of any social power or form of knowledge from being made into a new theistic, bourgeois civil religion of consolation or salvation. Such a religion – and its theoretical development as in the Rational Choice Theory of religion – has the capability of not only distracting humanity from the truth of its ultimate aloneness, a distraction which thereby eviscerates even the possibility of such human solidarity as a power of social change, but also functions socially to legitimate if not anoint the systematically produced social antagonisms that further create the fragmentation, isolation, suffering and horror of humanity.

As Horkheimer repeatedly states throughout his writings, humanity has no knowledge of God, whose existence, thereby, cannot be proven. Not even the consciousness of humanity's abandonment in finitude can be used in a reverse manner to prove the existence of God. Quite the contrary, the experience and knowledge of human suffering makes the belief in Christianity's theodicy of an all-loving and almighty God most unbelievable. All that can be brought about by such a consciousness of the natural and socio-historical negativity is a longing for such a totally Other than what is that can thereby become a revolutionary motivation in both theory and praxis for the creation of a more reconciled future society. The consciousness or knowledge of the abandonment of humanity is possible only with the thought and hope of such an Infinite One that transcends the horror of this world. This notion of the totally Other and that which becomes "other" or "non-identical" to the identity or equivalence producing power of bourgeois society becomes an unrelenting *"provocation"* to *"the rhythm of the iron system"* – the absolute power of antagonistic, capitalist social totality (Horkheimer & Adorno 1972:120, 183).

Second and Third Commandment

However, this notion of the longing for the totally Other cannot be made into a proof of God's existence. There is and can be no absolute certainty of the existence of a God, for if there were, then the knowledge of humanity's abandonment would be false. Such supposed knowledge of God thereby becomes an ideological reconciliation of the antagonism between the infinite and finite, the universal and particular, reason and reality; a legitimating theodicy for the *"Golgotha"* of history (Hegel 1967:808). As Horkheimer asserts, not only as a commandment of Judaism, which is his own religious heritage, but also as an essential principle of the critical theory, absolutely nothing can be stated about the totally Other. All that can be said, due to the thought of the Infinite One, is that this world is finite. Thus, it is in regards to this contradiction between the notion of God and the world that Horkheimer's critical theory of society and religion radicalizes the prohibitions of Judaism's Decalogue, particularly that of the second and third commandments (Exodus 20:4–7; Deuteronomy 5:8–11). It is in this radicalization of Judaism's prohibitions concerning God wherein the connection between the critical theory and Judaism lies. The second commandment of the Decalogue of Judaism prohibits humanity from making any image or likeness (an idol) of God.

> You shall not make for yourself an idol, whether in the form of anything that is in heaven above, or that is on the earth beneath, or that is in the water under the earth. You shall not bow down to them or worship them . . . (Exodus 20:4–5)

The third commandment upholds the ancient taboo of pronouncing and thus misusing the name of God, which equates with dragging the transcendent and holy infinite into the corruption of finitude; of equating truth with falsehood: "You shall not make wrongful use of the name of the Lord your God . . ." (Exodus 20:7).

According to Horkheimer, Judaism prevents any word or act that would ultimately alleviate the consciousness and despair of humanity's abandonment.

These negative commandments, i.e., "You shall not . . .," are to lead the followers of Judaism to a dynamic, socio-historical praxis expressive of the longing for the totally Other, which rejects all knowledge or guarantees of salvation as utter delusion. In this way, Israel – meaning those who wrestle with God and humanity (Genesis 32:28) – is to become the light of the nations who will come to Israel in search of wisdom and thereby change their weapons of war into implements for human well-being (Isaiah 2:2–4). The truth and justness of the image and/or name of the totally Other is thereby maintained by such negation, by its prohibition. This negativity of the totally Other, however, is not a total negation, which is equally a delusion. Such absolute negation of that which is other than what is the case of the given status quo is, as Horkheimer and Adorno called it, the metaphysics of positivism.

Radicalization of Kant's Critique of Reason

Horkheimer's critical theory is rooted negatively not only in proverbial "Jerusalem" – the religious foundation of Western Civilization, but also in "Athens" – the rational, humanistic, secular Enlightenment heritage. It is the negative dialectical synthesis of "faith" and "reason" that seeks to determinately negate both forms of human experience and thought into a dynamic critical materialism of human liberation, both subjectively and objectively. Thus, Horkheimer not only radicalizes the commandments of Judaism in regards to finite images or names of the infinite, but also radicalizes Kant's *Critique of Pure Reason*, (1929) in stating that humanity does not and cannot have any knowledge of anything that transcends human understanding based on experience and intuition. Humanity has no knowledge of anything *noumenal*, and thus does not need to bother with it. This rejection of the *noumena* of theistic religion, of metaphysics, of idealism is, however, quite different from that of positivism and bourgeois skepticism/agnosticism, which dualistically "brackets out" all questions of anything other than what is the case in human experience. However, unlike Kant (1929:29), Horkheimer does not find it "necessary to deny knowledge, in order to make room for faith" and religion in the face of the development of human reason and science. Rather, Horkheimer materialistically grounds the truth of religion not in the *noumena*, as a separate entity or sphere of being and value that can be thereby disassociated from all matters of this world, but in the cries and longings of the innocent victims of this world for a better future society and the totally Other.

Truth of Religion

For Horkheimer, the truth of real or good religion does not come as consolation to a person who is unjustly suffering and in need, but rather *is* the cry against that very concrete suffering and need not only of the individual but of the oppressed social class as well. The truth of religion, for Horkheimer therefore, is to keep alive the critical, compassionate impulse for social change, to break the dehumanizing, ideological "spell" of capitalism, which could open the future up toward the creation of a non-antagonistic society as well as toward the unknown totally Other. As Horkheimer (1978:163) states, "we have religion where life down to its every gesture is marked by this resolve." This materialistic, negative dialectical "resolve" is grounded in and expressive of the prophetic, Messianic, critical notion of the "totally Other" than this world. Horkheimer's critical theory of religion negatively and materialistically embodies both notions of the *malum physicum* – not only the terror of nature but the horror of the antagonisms of the capitalist social totality – and the *malum metaphysicum* – not Schopenhauer's ontological notion of the "will to life" but the consciousness of humanity's absolute abandonment; that human history is a socially created slaughterbench and a Golgotha for billions of innocent victims of its horror, with the dialectical, materialistic "resolve" to lessen if not negate this horror with the given technological and scientific means available to create a better future society.

Human Social Praxis

There is no other religion that has this commandment of not making any image or name of God. According to Horkheimer, this is due to the fact that the central focus of Judaism is not on the metaphysical question of God's existence but inversely on human beings becoming godly, holy, just, good in their praxis of life, both personally and socially. The central religious concern of Judaism – and I would say, of Christianity as well – e.g., Matthew 5–7, Matthew 25:31–46, Mark 8:34–38, Luke 3:4–17, Luke 4:18–19, Romans 12:1–2, James 2:14–18 – is not on what one believes to be true but on what one *does* for the sake of truth. As Horkheimer (1993:14) stated: it is this indomitable will to serve with single minded devotion this negative, dialectical materialistic notion of the truth that is the guiding principle of the entire critical theory. It is thus dialectically both important and unimportant, according to Horkheimer, whether there is a God or not. It is unimportant since nothing can be said or known about God in either terms of faith or of reason. The critical theory of society and religion is not concerned with Absolutes or knowledge of the Infinite, but rather with the socio-historical comprehension of all spiritual phenomena for the practical purpose of creating a reconciled future society. To this end, as Horkheimer (1970:60) states, the existence of the totally Other is nevertheless important because theology stands behind all genuine human action. Without the meaning and purpose of such an inverse or negative theology as a motivating power of human praxis, such activity collapses into being nothing more than mere business and stratagem.

Negative Theology

Therefore, for Horkheimer, theology is not understood in metaphysical or ontological terms as the science of the divine or knowledge of God. Rather, from the critical perspective of dialectical materialism, theology means the consciousness that the world is finite, appearance, and that it is not the absolute truth. Theology is the hope that the injustice and horror of history will not have the last word. It is the expression of the longing that the murderers may not ultimately be victorious over their innocent victims. It is this theological hope and longing that is subsumed into the materialism of the critical theory of religion as its dynamic purpose. Again, as Horkheimer stated in the mid-1920's, one of the most important functions of religion is to give oppressed and suffering humanity such a theological vehicle through which they can express their misery and their longing for its end in terms of the newness of that which is totally Other. Religion did not always distract people from the injustice of society and the world but functioned to expose such horror and enabled people to resist it. It is at this most historical materialistic concern that the critical theory comes to agree with the liberational substance of religion and theology. An example of such a theological longing is expressed in the mythical notions of the resurrection of the dead and the Last Judgment. Through these beliefs, the idea of an absolute and disinterested justice was expressed; a justice that holds everyone accountable for what they did or did not do to overcome the causes of human need and suffering. A biblical expression of this is found in the gospel of Matthew, where the verdict of inclusion in or exclusion from the community of God is based on what the *"nations"* did to alleviate the conditions and causes of the suffering of the least in society: the hungry, the thirsty, the stranger – the "other", the naked, and those imprisoned (Matthew 25:31–46).

By means of such a negative theology, which begins not with the notion of God but with the horror that is experienced in this world that brings about the necessity of a God, such religious beliefs as these can become a critically reflective and dynamic concept that could be applied as a standard to judge and thereby negate the reified class antagonism of capitalist society. According to Horkheimer, the content of such religious ideas must not be abstractly negated and thus discarded with their mythological form. Rather, the religious or mythological form of such theologically expressed ideas of human suffering and hope needs to be determinately negated so as to allow such expressions of indictment of unjust social powers the possibility of becoming critically effective and liberating in a inversely modern, secular form. Religion developed and contains, albeit in an inadequate form, the longing and the struggle for the totally Other of past generations, which needs to be negated, remembered and preserved, and furthered into a this-worldly, revolutionary theory and praxis that longs for the creation of a new and better future society and the totally Other. It is this materialist, negative theology of the totally Other in which there is a similarity between the critical theory and theology.

As Horkheimer (1985:431) stated in another interview in the early 1970's, the critical theory is founded on the thought that the Absolute, the totally Other, or God cannot be made into an object. All that can be said is that the critical theory cannot express, nor does it want to express, the belief that this present antagonistic world is identical with the totally Other. This Other is completely unknown, and it is in this negativity of the Absolute that the critical theory differentiates itself from every positive theology and religious doctrine. For the critical theory of religion, the unbelievable Christian theodicy of the existence of an all-loving, almighty God, who is providentially working God's purpose out in the horror of history should be materialistically, inversely transformed into the longing for the existence of such an Other, which will not allow the suffering and death of the innocent to be the last word of history. For the critical theory of religion, true theology expresses prophetically and Messianically the dialectical materialistic notions of justice, of the Good and Right, of liberation of the oppressed and exploited, of resistance to "grinding the face of the poor in the dirt" (Isaiah 3:15) by the powerful. These ideas must be critically differentiated from their distortion in the history of religious institutions, e.g., the church, or their positivistic sociological corruption as in the Rational Choice Theory. This is the fundamental thought of a negative theology of the totally Other to which both Horkheimer and Adorno have granted a right within their critical theory of society and religion.

Morality

For the critical theory of religion, such theology is the foundation of all morality, particularly in Western civilization. Based on this dialectical understanding of a negative theology of the totally Other, Jürgen Habermas (1993a:134) is correct in stating that the essential trait of Horkheimer's critical theory of religion is morality. The longing that the murderer will not ultimately triumph over the innocent victims is the foundation of morality in both its rational and, as stated above, "non-scientific" form. According to Horkheimer, this non-reified, non-fetishized, materialistic longing for that which is totally Other than the socially created barbarity and horror of existence was the original understanding of theology and morality in both Judaism and Christianity.

As examples of this theology and morality, Horkheimer (1985:432) looked to the Jewish and Christian martyrs – to those who have given themselves completely in the service of humanity's emancipation from all forms of exploitation and domination as they professed the totally Other. However, Horkheimer differentiates between the Jewish and Christian martyrs based on their theological motivation. The martyrs of Christianity – who resisted the power of the status quo in the hope of the totally Other – endured their torture more easily due to their belief that their suffering was only a brief stage before they personally entered paradise. Jewish martyrs, however, believe something completely different. Theirs was not the issue of a personal reward in heaven but that they would live on in the memory of the faithful. They sacrificed themselves not for personal salvation but for the welfare of the people. In Judaism, the particular subject does not play as large a role as it does in Christianity. In the Pentateuch of the Jewish scriptures, the word "you" applies to both the individual and to the whole people as subject, of which the individual is a part. The subject's identity and autonomy is bound up dialectically with the solidarity in and of the community. In Judaism, this relationship cannot be separated or differentiated clearly. Horkheimer illustrated this point through the work of one of his doctoral students who retranslated the Jewish moral law, which is also the second part of Christianity's "greatest commandment" – "You shall love your neighbor as yourself" (Leviticus

19:18; Matthew 22:39) – in terms of this Jewish collective understanding as being its original intent: "Love your neighbor, for he/the other is you" (Horkheimer 1970:63). This is the moral corollary of Judaism's theological prohibition of naming and making images of the Absolute that interests Horkheimer. Morality in theory and in praxis is found in this dialectical identification of one's autonomy and sovereignty in the love and solidarity with the fate of others, particularly "the least" of humanity. Morality is the expression of the dialectical dynamic between personal autonomy and social solidarity wherein one is truly a member of humanity. It is for the well-being and life chances of others that martyrs and enlighteners of all ages have thus sacrificed themselves.

Such a notion of morality cannot be found in the Rational Choice Theory of religion nor its solipsistic bourgeois, instrumental, strategic and positivistic rationality, in which there is no transcendence beyond self-interest and the status quo of what is. As Horkheimer asserts, in the thought of positivism, there is no compelling reason why a person should not hate rather than love the other, particularly if such an action is enjoyable or beneficial to the one acting. Morality is grounded in actions that put into praxis the longing for that which is Other than the antagonisms of the existing status quo, which empowers one to act not merely to survive or benefit in the midst of the antagonism. In the critical theory of religion, human actions are moral when they transcend the self and its concern for self-preservation for the betterment of life of the others. Here is a fundamental difference between the Critical Theory of religion and Rational Choice. Morality can not be justified in terms of positivism, which appeals only to facts, to science as a means of capitalistic production and the knowledge of the world as it is. According to the critical theory of religion, all attempts to ground morality in the theory and praxis of positivism – which is the reifying metaphysics of what is – becomes nothing but an insidious and harmonistic false consciousness.

Freedom of Will

In terms of Horkheimer's critical theory of religion, that which is good and moral in this world comes not from God but from human beings, who act freely for that which is Right – a better, more just, beautiful, kind, rational, free and peaceful world. Human beings can do good or bad due to their freedom of will. Horkheimer grounds this understanding of free will in terms of

Jewish and Christian theology, which asserts that human beings are created in God's image and thus, have free will. This religious notion of the freedom of will leads Horkheimer to what he terms the greatest teaching in both religions – the doctrine of original or hereditary sin. Following, yet determinately negating, Schopenhauer's pessimistic ontological interpretation of this teaching, Horkheimer explains the demythologized truth of this doctrine of original sin in terms of the sacrifice of the other's happiness and life chances in service of one's own interests and wants. In terms of the materialistic, negative theology of the critical theory of religion, the personal and social forms of sin, immorality, selfishness, greed, the domination of one individual, class, or nation over another, which creates the antagonisms, injustice, suffering and horror of history are all expressive of this notion of the original sin – not as an ontological given of human nature but as a matter of free will. This materialist notion of the mythological original sin is expressive of its concrete socio-historical realization through the exploitive capitalist class system of production and its ever-increasing need for cheap resources, cheap labor and greater market share, all for the maximization of profit for the capitalist power elite. It is this latter, capitalist system imperative for the maximization of profit, which also creates the horrendous suffering and chaos for entire nations, that is the propulsive engine of the dominant form of what is known as globalization. This antagonistic social and historical development of modern society has pushed the liberal principle of the autonomous subject into the social Darwinistic, survival of the fittest extreme of a monadic, privatized notion of self, which is isolated from, fearful of, in competition with and against any other. As stated above, it is this very solipsistic and immoral notion of subjectivity that is the paradigmatic principle of the Rational Choice Theory in general and of religion in particular.

The Totally Administered Society

In terms of Horkheimer's critical theory of society and religion, it is this modern, immoral, systematic and globalizing development of capitalist class antagonisms that is leading historically toward a totally administered and dehumanized future society. In a prophetic critique of Rational Choice Theory in all of its manifestations, Horkheimer stated that as long as people continue to live as isolated, monadic egos, seeking their identity and autonomy only by satisfying their own desires according to the exploitive system imperatives of capitalism, the world will remain as it is. Then, the terrifying neo-conservative pronouncement of capitalism being the "end of history" and the self-centered bourgeois being the "last man", who for the moment might have autonomy but no chance of solidarity, becomes reality (Fukuyama 1992). According to Horkheimer and many other critical social theorists, this development is "the immanent logic of history" that leads inexorably toward the totally administered, bureaucratized, instrumentalized, integrated and controlled society. In such a society, human individuality, autonomy, love, and longing for that which is other than what is will be increasingly diminished through the necessity of conforming to demands of the social cybernetic, iron cage system, from which no one can escape. In fact it is questionable to Horkheimer whether humanity even will be conscious of the loss due to the rhythm of the iron system becoming instinctual. Not only will serious and liberating theology, but aesthetics and philosophy too, whose true social function is also the criticism of what is in light of that which is other and socially realizable, will be thrown on the trash heap of history as mere expressions of humanity's childhood and forgotten. Life in the totally administered society will be boring.

Horkheimer does hold out that there may be also a positive side to the development of a totally administered society, namely that the material needs of humanity may be satisfied in this society, the administration of justice might be better served in the abolishment of world conflicts, and a consciousness of universal solidarity may also arise. I do not share Horkheimer's qualified optimism in regards to these issues, for even if these positive affects were possible, the question must be asked: at what and at whose cost were these developments made? As Benjamin (1968:256–257) stated, there isn't a historical act in, or document of, the development of civilization that isn't at the same time expressive of barbarism; that isn't developed on the labor and sacrifice of multitudes of unknown workers. The critical theory thus has a double task: to designate that which is to be changed, and to name that which is to be preserved. It has the task of showing what the price is that has to be paid for such "progress"; what the effect history or *"Wirkungsgeschichte"* is for any action. It is the task of critical theory of society and religion to rub against the grain of history's development and remember, reveal and possibly redeem the hopes of the past as history moves toward the totally administered society.

Resistance

In 1970, Horkheimer stated that we do not yet live in a totally administered society. Although the dominant social productive forces of globalizing capitalism, its increasingly administered national and international bureaucracies, and its imperialistic military might have moved the world closer to its realization, we today in the early 21st century can still say we do not yet live in a totally administered society. However, as Horkheimer and the entire critical theory of society and religion acknowledge, the historical development toward a totally administered society cannot be prevented or abstractly cancelled. The critical theory does not offer any reprieve from this historical development. It also, however, does not fall into nihilistic despair and resignation nor positivistic conformity to this trend as does Rational Choice Theory. The task of critical thought remains the remembrance, preservation, and critical furtherance in theory and praxis of human autonomy and solidarity in resistance to the historical trend that leads to the totally administered world. The urgent task remains of keeping alive the critical theological and materialistic notion of the totally Other than that which is ideologically justified as the "real" world by the theory and science of positivism and its economic, political, military and cultural system power brokers; a socially created world weighed down by the gravity of facts that has the capability of killing the human consciousness or spirit for anything other than what is. By means of the critical notion of, and thus longing for, the totally Other than what is, the possibility of revolutionary social change in a new historical direction of a better, more communicatively and aesthetically rational, less antagonistic, more humane and shalom-filled future society exists.

The Critical Theory of Religion

According to Horkheimer, religion has lost its social purpose of being an actual force for social change in today's world through its betrayal of any critical, prophetic notion of transcendence and the longing for the totally Other. Religion, particularly Christianity, has given up its prophetic and Messianic critique of existence and has been sublimated into the reified social function of ideologically legitimating the development of the capitalist society toward its totally administered fulfillment. This also is the very substance of the Rational Choice Theory of religion. In terms of the critical theory of religion, true religion is the critical consciousness and expression of humanity's finitude of suffering and death, which thus, produces the longing that this world is not the absolute end. Such religious or theological longing for the totally Other can then be put into the moral praxis of resistance against the making of anything finite into the Absolute. Religion, therefore, cannot be secularized – brought into conformity as an ideological social function of any existing social totality – without giving it up. It is thus a futile hope that the churches will ever reclaim its original negative, prophetic, Messianic and eschatological critique of longing for the totally Other and its revolutionary social praxis. According to Horkheimer, due to religion's betrayal of itself, of its critical function of negatively expressing this longing for the totally Other and its ideals of justice, truth, freedom, etc., this critical content has thrown off its religious form and has transformed itself into a secular, materialistic theory and praxis of historical struggle for a more reconciled future society. Unlike the positivistic bourgeois materialism of the Rational Choice Theory of religion, Horkheimer's critical theory of society and religion is a modern, dialectical materialistic heir of this prophetic, Messianic and eschatological labor for the creation of a more reconciled future society as the concrete expression of the longing for the totally Other.

Christopher Craig Brittain

From *A Beautiful Mind* to the Beautiful Soul: Rational Choice, Religion, and the Critical Theory of Adorno & Horkheimer

> The philosophers of the Enlightenment attacked religion in the name of reason; in the end what they killed was not the church but metaphysics and the objective concept of reason itself, the source of power of their efforts (Horkheimer 1974:17–18).

> Religion is on sale, as it were. It is cheaply marketed in order to provide one more so-called irrational stimulus among many others by which the members of a calculating society are calculatingly made to forget the calculation under which they suffer (Adorno 1992:294).

These statements by Max Horkheimer and Theodor W. Adorno illuminate the extent to which they probe the depths of Marx's claim that "the criticism of religion is the premise of all criticism" (Marx and Engels 1978:53). Marx's thesis remained at the core of the critical theory of Adorno and Horkheimer, although they were not as convinced as he was that the criticism of religion was *complete*. For even when the *a priori* assumptions of dogmatic theology are set aside, and the basis of Marx's "irreligious criticism" – that human beings make religion – is assumed, religious discourse remains a powerful social and political force in contemporary society. Furthermore, in Adorno and Horkheimer's analysis and criticism of positivism, they argue that even modernity's celebrated concept of reason remains intertwined with myth and irrational presuppositions. In their view, the confrontation between modernity and religion is anything but resolved. For Adorno suggests that, when the pursuit of scientific truth is split off from the idea of true society, the facts and logic of social science can themselves become "hypostatised" and even mythological (1976a:26–7).

Such a perspective on religion and modern society stands in rather dramatic contrast with the contemporary application of rational choice theory in the study of religion. This essay illustrates this difference through a comparison of the critical social theory of Adorno and Horkheimer with rational choice explanatory models of religious practice as developed by two different scholars: Rodney Stark and Lawrence Iannaccone. Both of these theorists display assumptions similar to those criticized by Adorno and Horkheimer in their methodological writings. The extent to which this is true will be illustrated by drawing from a popular depiction of the presuppositions of rational choice theory, in the form of a scene from the Academy Award winning film *A Beautiful Mind* (2001). This analysis will show that, rather than assisting the study of religion to escape from theological and metaphysical assumptions, rational choice theory is itself laden with problematic presuppositions. It is more a repetition of what Hegel calls the "beautiful soul" than it is the achievement of a "beautiful mind."

The Scientific Study of Religion and Rational Choice Theory

Prior to turning to rational choice theory, it is useful to place the intentions of its application to the study of religion in context. The social scientific study of religion has long been a scene of considerable methodological dispute. The discipline emerged in the nineteenth century out of theological schools and faculties, and has often been criticized for harbouring theological or metaphysical assumptions.[1] Although "religious studies" scholars generally distance themselves from confessional doctrines and commitments, they have sometimes been accused of defending essentialist and universal theories of religion, thereby seeming to suggest a trans-cultural relevance for religious experience and discourse.[2] Intertwined in these debates are the even more

[1] For a historical sketch of these issues, see: Preus 1987.

[2] For examples of prominent scholars in the field often criticized for such a posi-

far ranging disputes over social scientific methodology; such as the distinction between observer and participant knowledge, along with the question of whether human agency makes the object of the social sciences distinct from the object of the natural sciences.[3]

The advocates of rational choice theory in social scientific methodology enter into such debates with the intention of overcoming a perceived "disparity in development" that exists between natural and social science (Riker 1990:177). They do so on the basis of adopting mathematical models from economic theory and applying them to the analysis of social action. This approach is understood to bypass metaphysical assumptions about human nature and behavior, as well as holistic theories about the nature of society at the macro level, by focusing on strategic and instrumental decisions by individuals in social interaction. The perspective develops a voluntaristic theory of action, emphasizing the role of calculation and the achievement of expected outcomes in human behavior. Rational choice theory argues that intended consequences motivate human choice in social interaction, more than environmental conditioning, repetition of custom, or essential attribute.

A key element of this model emerges out of game theory, a mathematical approach to analyzing conflict and cooperation. Game theory employs general math techniques and equations to analyze situations where two people make decisions that influence each other. This perspective has been adopted particularly by economic theory, where it is employed to both explain and predict patterns of interaction between rational agents. Prior to analyzing the assumptions inherent to this approach, and how these bear upon the study of religion in particular, it is useful to illustrate the intentions behind this theoretical approach by way of referring to a popular exposition of its viewpoint.

A Beautiful Mind

The Academy Award winning film *A Beautiful Mind* (Howard 2001) is based loosely on the life of John Nash (one of the developers of game theory). In an early scene, the main character, John (a student at Princeton), is sitting in a bar with his friends, searching for both female companionship and a topic

tion, see: Eliade 1961 and Smith 1963. For the criticism of such positions, see: Wiebe 1998; McCutcheon 1997.

[3] For a summary of how these methodological debates impact upon the study of religion, see: McCutcheon 1999.

for his doctoral dissertation. When a group of women enters the room, the men begin to boast and tease each other over who has the best chance to attract the most desirable of the women (stereotypically enough, the blond). One of the men, referring to Adam Smith, states that in this competition, it is "every man for himself." Implied in this chauvinistic bravado is the sense that only one man will "win" the prize, while the others will have to be content with the "leftovers;" "those who strike out are stuck with her friends."

The situation results in an intellectual breakthrough for this fictional version of John Nash. He insists that, "Adam Smith needs revision," and explains as follows:

> If we all go for the blond, we block each other. Not a single one of us is going to get her. So then we all go for her friends, but they all give us the cold shoulder, because nobody likes to be second choice. But what if no one goes for the blond? We don't get in each other's way, and we don't insult the other girls. It's the only way to win.

The lesson the viewer is supposed to derive from this scene is that the best resolution to this competition, the most rational choice when faced with this situation, is for the group of men to coordinate their actions with each other so that their own private interests are furthered. The Nash-character determines that this insight proves that Adam Smith's conclusions about human self-interest were incorrect:

> Adam Smith said that the best result comes from everyone in the group doing what is best for himself. Right? Incomplete. Because the best result will come from everyone in the group doing what's best for himself *and* the group.

This analysis of the situation facing the men in the bar resembles what game theorists call a "coordination game." The group of individual (male) agents are situated within a static environment in which they are confronted with a choice of action. They then develop a strategy to achieve a desired end that takes into account the actions of the other agents in the room. The fictional Nash character calculates the different consequences of all possible actions, and selects that which maximizes the expected desired outcome. Unlike his rivals, however, he argues that it is more beneficial for all the men involved to strategize collectively so as to insure that they each individually achieve the desired goal (a woman).

Such a "rational" choice calculation results in what is known as a "Nash-equilibrium": the product of a game in which each player adopts a strategy that is the best reply to the actions of others. The result is a stable outcome, given that none of the players has a better strategy than his rivals. The insight derived by game theorists from such a model is that players have a mutual interest in coordinating their actions. The nature of social cooperation and interaction becomes something that one can explain as emerging from the individual choices of rational agents.[4]

This example serves to illustrate the basic presuppositions of game theory, which have a principal role in rational choice theory. There are two primary assumptions involved in this game model. The first is that a decision-maker is "rational," which is defined narrowly as meaning that the individual "makes decisions consistently in pursuit of his [*sic*] own objectives." It is presumed that each player's objective is to maximize the expected value of any reward earned in the course of the game. The second premise is that the decision-maker is "intelligent." A player is considered to be so when s/he is in possession of complete information about the game and is aware of all relevant data about the given situation. This is to say that the agent is not vulnerable to hidden factors, or deprived of information available to any competitors (Myerson 1991:1–4).

There is much to question about these presuppositions generally, but for the moment, it is instructive to apply them to the bar scene as presented in *A Beautiful Mind*. For the Nash-character's argument to work, the following assumptions must be granted:

a) the blond woman is the most desirable (all the men would usually pursue her);
b) the blond will not be interested in any of the men;
c) the other women will be interested in the men;
d) the particularity of each individual woman is largely irrelevant in terms of her desirability for the men (i.e. any woman is better than none).

The necessity of these presumptions makes a mockery of this application of game theory to the inter-personal relationships of dating. Why should one

[4] For more on equilibrium in game theory, see Myerson 1991: chapter 3. For a brief and less technical explication of coordination games, see Hollis 1994.

assume that any of these assumptions can be granted? In this example, the male participants in the game assume they know how the women will behave – based on a series of stereotypes about women that can surely be questioned (how they would respond to the attention of the men cannot be so simply predicted). The men "strategize" based upon their own (questionable) assumptions about "female behavior." Even more importantly, it is clear that the actual end of this competition is left outside the field of rationality. What is considered "rational" amounts to two limited concerns: strategic instrumental calculation, and maximizing personal gain. What is "rational" about the choice in no way involves determining which woman one might actually find compatible. Any woman, it appears in this situation, represents maximizing self-interest. As we shall see in what follows, this reductive treatment of women and interpersonal relationships is not unlike the treatment of religion at the hands of rational choice theory.

The Presuppositions of Rational Choice Theory

Although it has recently risen in prominence, the deployment of rational choice theory in the study of religion often resembles this fictional analysis of partner selection depicted in *A Beautiful Mind*, repeating many of its flaws. A brief examination of two scholars who apply rational choice principles to religion will serve to demonstrate the extent to which their interpretations of religion are based on questionable presuppositions. It is precisely such assumptions that Adorno and Horkheimer's criticism of positivism calls into question.

The applications of rational choice theory in the study of religion by Rodney Stark, as well as by Lawrence Iannaccone, are based upon the following premises about human activity:

i) human beings act rationally, weighing the costs and benefits of actions, and making choices with the intention of maximizing the benefits of their actions;
ii) the ultimate human preferences (or needs) used to assess costs and benefits do not vary much;
iii) the interaction of individual choices and actions result in a social equilibrium.[5]

[5] For a brief summary of these basic assumptions, see: Iannaccone 1997:26; also Stark & Bainbridge 1987.

In a manner similar to the way in which the assumptions made about women in the bar-scene from *A Beautiful Mind* are simplistic and reductive, these premises require numerous critical remarks. They are presuppositions asserted at the outset of theorizing; they are not proven or derived out of empirical study of social action. And yet, these assumptions subtly outline a very precise theory of human nature and rationality, which are based, as we shall see, on a not-so-subtle economic ideology.

The first premise reduces rationality to the calculation of costs and benefits. Thinking, in this view, is limited to what Max Horkheimer and Theodor Adorno call "instrumental reasoning," and it is this reductive understanding of reason that they criticize positivism for fostering. Drawing on Max Weber's distinction between value and purposive social action, their work sought to defend a broader and more nuanced understanding of rationality. As Horkheimer wrote, "When the idea of reason was conceived, it was intended to achieve more than the mere regulation of the relation between means and ends; it was regarded as the instrument for understanding the ends, for determining them" (1974:10).[6] In the presuppositions of rational choice theory, there is no place for the determination of ends; reason's sole purpose is to employ the means at hand to achieve whatever particular end is desired. Like Marx before them, the two Frankfurt School theorists consider such a divorce of thought from practice and context to be an abstract form of unthinking irrationality, which leaves the human subject vulnerable to the manipulations of ideology and impulse: "It is as if thinking itself had been reduced to the level of industrial process, subject to a close schedule – in short, made part and parcel of production" (1974:21). By confining what is taken to be rational thought to the task of purposive calculation, without submitting existing presuppositions or desired ends to self-examination, Adorno and Horkheimer argue that "instrumental thinking" becomes ideological and blind to unrecognized (and quite possibly erroneous) assumptions.

The extent to which rational choice theory reduces rationality to means-ends instrumental thinking is striking. In *Foundations of Social Theory* (1990), for example, James S. Coleman goes so far as to claim that Max Weber suggests that human beings "act purposively towards a goal, with the goal (and thus the actions) shaped by values or preferences" (p. 13). In Coleman's methodology, "nothing more than this commonsense notion of purposive action is

[6] Here the influence of Kant's distinction between *Vernunft* (Reason) and *Verstand* (Understanding) is in evidence.

necessary" to explain human behavior; and by "commonsense" purposiveness, he simply means, "the actor chooses the action which will maximize utility (p. 14). But this description is only a partial representation of Weber's understanding of reason. Weber's sociological method distinguishes between practical, theoretical, substantive, and formal types of rationality. Although he demonstrates that both practical and formal rationality involve means-ends calculations similar to what Horkheimer and Adorno later call "instrumental reason," Weber also shows that substantive and theoretical reason are distinctively different. Thus, while the logic of dissimilar actions like sacrifice or prayer might be compared to a modern business executive's calculation of efficiency and profit, substantive judgements of beauty, friendship, compassion and mutual assistance involve a very different approach to reasoning and decision-making (Kalberg 1980:1148).

A thought experiment proposed by Amartya K. Sen serves to illustrate what Weber means by such distinctions. While challenging the idea that individuals always choose and act in a way that maximizes personal gain, Sen imagines a situation in which a person is asked by a passer-by, "Where is the railway station?" When the addressee responds, "There" and then points in the direction of a post office, the questioner responds, "Would you mind posting this letter for me on the way?" Sen argues that this kind of interaction challenges rational choice assumptions about reason; for, based on their premises, we ought to assume that the person asked to deliver the letter will reply "Yes," because he calculates that this decision will allow him to open the letter on the way in order to see if it contains anything valuable (1977:332). But does such an assumption make any sense? Must one really assume that this decision will (or should) naturally be driven by narrow self-interest? Other values and commitments might surely influence the choice made by the individual – and understandably so. This choice cannot be reduced summarily to maximizing utility, but may be influenced by habit, custom, a sense of duty, emotional attachment, etc. In Weberian terms, forms of rationality are sometimes employed in decision-making that cannot be reduced to maximizing personal gain.

A rational choice theorist might try to argue that such non-maximizing choices are in fact "irrational." Weber does note that from the perspective of one type of rationality, another form of reasoning can appear to be non-rational (Kalberg 1980:1156). What Horkheimer and Adorno argue in their interpretation of Weber's treatment of rationality, however, is that it is purposive (or "instrumental) rationality that becomes "irrational" once it loses sight of the ends towards which it was initially employed. Calculating a way to attract *any* woman in a bar, regardless of whether one is compatible with her, is not necessarily rational; just as deciding *not to pursue* any of the women in the bar due to a preference based on values, taste, or other considerations is not necessarily irrational. This being the case, the assumptions made by Stark and Iannaccone regarding what constitutes a "rational choice" are shown to be extremely problematic.

While the first presupposition employed by both Stark and Iannaccone reduces rationality to the cost-benefit calculations of economic exchange, their second premise is vulnerable to issues that Adorno criticises regarding the "culture industry." As rational thought is limited to instrumental calculation, and ends become separated from means, Adorno argues that this results in the impoverishment of human preference and discernment. Aesthetic and moral concerns such as taste, individuality, ethics, and culture become susceptible to "fabricated need" (Horkheimer and Adorno 2002:109). This perspective presents two challenges to the rational choice premise that human preferences do not vary much. First, the question arises whether this assumption can be taken to be universal and constant. Given the scope of human diversity and cultures, it is difficult to accept that everyone assesses and weighs costs and benefits on exactly the same scale. Such a presumption is not unlike the suggestion that every man in the bar-scene of *A Beautiful Mind* desires the same woman, while simultaneously agreeing that any woman will suffice. Second, even if it can be shown that many human beings desire and value the same things, the concept of "fabricated need" alerts the scholar to the possibility that critical analysis will uncover that apparent similarities among human preferences are by no means "natural," but are rather the construct of concealed social forces and dynamics operating prior to individual decision. Should this be the case, it would be difficult to call such preference a rational "choice."

From the perspective of Adorno and Horkheimer, the limitations of these first two premises are rooted in the third presupposition of the rational choice theorists regarding social "equilibrium." The notion that existent society and social forms represent the stable outcomes of the different strategic actions of individual agents is challenged by Adorno's concept of the social "totality." If the study of social action concerns itself only with the interactions between human beings without attending to their "objectified form," it acts as if "everything really depended on these interpersonal relationships," and not on larger social mechanisms. "What disappears from sociology is not only the decisive element whereby social activity is able to maintain itself at all, but also knowledge of how it maintains itself, with what sacrifices, threats and also with what potentialities for good" (Adorno 2000a:142). For Adorno and Horkheimer, the social whole cannot simply be reduced to the sum of its parts.

Adorno's speculative concept of "social totality" intends to suggest a dialectical theory of society, in order to maintain a notion of "society as a thing-in-itself" (1976a:12). As such, it serves to "give a name to what secretly holds the machinery together" (1976b:68). The concept provides a way to appreciate Marx's critique of ideology in sociological method, and it prevents treating social structures and experiences as "natural" or *a priori*. Adorno argues that "positivist" empirical studies of social action fail to attend to the ways in which objective social structures shape the subjective actions of human agents. To ignore this is to ignore the mediated nature of all knowledge and experience, and the contradictions contained within human society. According to Adorno, modern society, with its ongoing disparities in distribution of wealth, access to education and health care, is irrational;

> By calling this society irrational I mean that if the purpose of society as a whole is taken to be the preservation and the unfettering of the people of which it is composed, then the way in which this society continues to be arranged runs counter to its own purpose, its *raison d'être*, its *ratio*. (2000a:133)

Thus, while rational choice theorists might observe how some individuals behave, and then apply this to their analysis of religious behavior, Adorno's critical perspective insists that such an approach represents only one element of the study of religion. A critical theory of religion includes analyzing, and perhaps even criticizing, the seemingly "rational choices" that individuals make, in order to determine the manner and extent to which their subjectivity is shaped by the larger social whole.

Religion and Rational Choice

Both Rodney Stark and Lawrence Iannaccone apply the above three presuppositions to their analysis of religion in North Atlantic societies. For Stark, the first premise of rational choice theory regarding the nature of rationality implies the assumption that human beings seek rewards and avoid costs. Thus, any "rational" choice will be guided by this preference, and his interpretation of religion emerges out of this perspective. He argues that, because some desired rewards are in limited supply, or remain beyond the capacity of certain people to achieve, individuals often substitute a "compensator" for a reward. A compensator is an explanation or proposal for an alternative manner to obtain a desired reward, often through elaborate and lengthy methods. Religion serves to provide compensators in the absence or unavailability of certain rewards, principally the longing for immortality. Stark writes, "it usually is necessary to enter into a long-term exchange relationship with the divine and with divinely inspired institutions, in order to follow the instructions" on how to achieve the desired goal over the longer term. He concludes, "churches rest upon these underlying exchange relationships" (1997a:6–7).

From this premise, Stark deduces axioms such as the idea that less powerful people will be more likely to accept compensators. He also suggests that, when a religious organization weakens its emphasis on supernaturalism and an afterlife, it inevitably weakens itself, due to a diminished ability to offer the promise of powerful compensators. This explains, he concludes, why liberal mainstream Christian churches are in decline. It is noteworthy that this analysis leads Stark to challenge rather than support the secularization thesis. Instead of expecting a general decline of interest in religion, spurred on by the spread of modernity and scientific knowledge, he argues that secularization is a self-limiting process. Although some people might abandon their religious traditions, Stark suggests that their children will likely be religious. While major religious denominations may decline, new faiths and traditions will emerge that offer more compelling and supernatural compensators (1997a:18–19). The general logic behind Stark's argumentation against secularization is that access to desired rewards will always be limited, and so compensators will continue to be required in order to pacify disappointed or frustrated desires.

Some of the language Stark employs to describe this approach to religion reveals the extent to which macroeconomic theoretical models inform the assumptions of rational choice theory. His explanatory concepts often draw from the vocabulary of economics. Religious communities are referred to as "firms." Those that "specialize" will flourish in the "religious economy." Those that fail to offer a compelling enough compensator will decline. He argues that, "Religious economies are like commercial economies in that they consist of a market of current and potential customers, a set of firms seeking to serve that market, and the religious 'product lines' offered by the various firms" (1997a:16–17). This view is employed to support his challenge to the secularization thesis: "to the degree that a religious economy is competitive and pluralistic, overall levels of religious participation will tend to be high." In other words, as the "monopoly" of mainline Christian churches declines, the emerging pluralistic and "free" religious market will result in increasing "religious" activity and exchange, as individual "religious investors" diversify what Lawrence Iannaccone calls their "religious portfolios" (1995:81). It is suggested that, in a "free market," flexible institutions will prosper.

There are numerous problems with this approach to religion, but two will be highlighted in particular: its reliance upon the concept of "compensators," and its roots in "supply-side" economic theory.

Steve Bruce argues that the notion of compensator is rather "slippery." Referring not only to something a person is willing to expend costs on, but also to a promised future reward, as well as an explanation of how that reward will be received, the concept becomes circular as the term shifts from one meaning to another (Bruce 1999:32). It is difficult to see how an explanation will necessarily substitute for an immediate reward. A compensator is, in fact, not a reward at all – only a substitution for one. Yet Stark, but also Iannacconne, often treat these deferred-rewards as concrete "products" delivered by the religious "firm." Surely a step is omitted in this analysis, however, for the religious "compensator" can only function as such when an individual is somehow convinced that what is on offer can substitute for an immediate reward. This process of how and why certain concepts or practices are able to function in this way remains largely unexamined in the theory of compensators.

Furthermore, why should the scholar of religion conclude that accepting the promise of a better life after death, in the face of a life of suffering, represents a "rational choice"? Again, it is instructive to refer to *A Beautiful Mind*. As the Nash-character sits in the bar, he might decide that he should avoid the blond woman he truly desires, and accept the "compensation" of whatever other woman accepts his attention. Conceivably, he might also be inspired by a sign on the wall that reads "good things come to those who wait." There are many possible courses of action available to him. The question is, why should a social theorist label a decision to accept the compensation of a generic "woman," or of the sentimental cliché on the wall, "rational" behavior? Why should the scholar conclude that the end result of his decision serves to satisfy the actual "reward" he desires? One might equally suggest that his shyness or insecurity is "irrational" and that it deprives him of the "reward" of a possible relationship. The reduction of human decision-making to the basic currency of this concept of "compensation" is based upon assumptions whose logic is tenuous at best.

It is also noteworthy that Stark's conceptualization of human desire is narrow and highly materialistic. His approach reveals how the behavior models developed by game theory contain subtle assumptions about human nature. The concept of compensation, for example, focuses on immediate material benefits (wealth, power, health, immortality), but displays little attention on other important, though less empirically measurable values, such as relationships, identity, meaning, etc.

This limitation is related to another weakness of the rational choice model as it is applied to the study of religion. Numerous scholars of religion problematize the tendency to define and conceive of "religion" strictly in terms of a belief system. Talal Asad, for example, insists upon a greater appreciation for the roles of ritual and performance in the formation of "religious" identities and communities. He argues that "embodied practice" forms the "precondition for varieties of religious experience" (1993:62–78). This broadening of the concept of "religion" reveals the extent to which Stark's reduction of it to a belief in heavenly rewards is simplistic and culturally limited. It also challenges the narrow scope of his conception of human desires and rewards. This neglect of the diversity found among religious communities and human desires suggests that the approach of rational choice theory is built upon ideological assumptions about society and human beings.[7] It does not attend in any significant way to examining its own methodological presuppositions, but often describes basic human motivations as if they are self-evident and "natural."

It is at the level of its core presuppositions that the rational choice model of religion is most problematic and bears the closest resemblance to the reductive treatment of relationships in *A Beautiful Mind*. As N. J. Demerath argues against rational choice theory, "the models may be elegant even if the world is not" (1995:105). Kenneth J. Arrow observes the role that presuppositions

[7] Donald P. Greenbury and Ian Shapiro observe a similar problem in the application of rational choice theory to the study of voter behavior in political science (1994).

have in such an approach, while criticizing the practice of equating rationality with maximization in economic theory: "the lesson is that the rationality hypothesis is by itself weak. To make it useful, the researcher is tempted into some strong assumptions" (1987:206). The assumptions guiding Stark and Iannaccone have begun to emerge above, and now they merit more direct comment.

It is instructive to note how the conclusions of these theorists echo the free market assumptions of contemporary neo-conservative economics. Simplifying secularization once again, Stark argues that state-funded clergy work less hard, which is why their churches are in decline (1997b:185). In other words, government civil servants are lazy, while the entrepreneur is successful; "religious professionals, *like anyone else*, do not exert themselves unless they need to do so – in the absence of eager competitors, religious organizations will be lax and inefficient" (191, emphasis added). So, it seems, Stark is comfortable asserting that *all* human beings are only motivated by threat and competition. The diversity and complexity of human behavior is swept aside by this assertion, and it is most intriguing to note the extent to which such a statement resembles the rhetoric often found in criticisms of the welfare state and Keynesian economics.

Similar assumptions can be found in the work of Lawrence Iannaccone. He credits greater "efficiency" for the strength of more doctrinally conservative and morally strict Christian churches in the United States. For Iannaccone, religion is a "commodity" produced collectively. In a voluntaristic and less rigid community, some individuals are able to benefit from the services of a church, without contributing significantly. Such "free riders" effectively "take more than they give" (1994:1183–1185). Since he assumes that time is money, Iannaccone argues that churches with higher average salaries have a shorter worship service (1995:79), and that shared-faith marriages result in a higher level of church attendance than "mixed" denominational marriages because "partners of the same religion can produce religious commodities more efficiently." Why? Because they benefit from economies of scale: "The same car drives everyone to church; there is no question as to how time and money contributions will be allocated to different religions" (1990:301). For Iannaccone, "subscribing to a religion is a bit like buying stock" (1995:81). But imaging that couples agree to practice the same religion because it saves on travel expenses is about as profound as suggesting that, if the men in the bar avoid the more attractive blond woman, they can have their pick of any other "grateful" mate.

In conclusions such as these, theory can be said to be shaping the scholar's interpretation of religion, rather than empirical data or critical analysis. For in their "supply side" approach to religion, both Stark's and Iannaccone's presuppositions parallel in rather striking ways the assumptions of contemporary neoconservative politics and economic theory. The neoconservative agenda is one that opposes state-led economic development, while encouraging deregulation and corporate initiative. It is assumed that market expansion is what drives innovation and prosperity. Government programs are said to result inevitably in inefficiency and stagnation, and it is presupposed that all human behavior is motivated solely by a concern to maximize self-interest. This being the case, governments should simply encourage private capital formation and a risk-taking entrepreneurial culture among its population. A statement by George Gilder sums up the emphasis of "supply-side" economic policy; "The so-called means of production are impotent to generate wealth and progress without creative men of production, the entrepreneurs . . . They are the heroes of economic life" (quoted in Devigne 1994:144).

In "A Supply-Side Reinterpretation of the 'Secularization' of Europe" (1994), Stark and Iannaccone propose a "theory of religious mobilization" that demonstrates once again the extent to which their approach to religion echoes these neoconservative assumptions. Their theory intends to account for lower church attendance and belief in European nations. It focuses on the behavior of religious "firms," as opposed to changing attitudes among "religious consumers." Thus, in opposition to the "secularization thesis," Stark and Iannaccone present a "supply-side" explanation for declining participation in religious organizations. It is not the result of a decline in "demand" for religion (which, they claim, remains a constant), but of problematic behavior on the part of religious "suppliers." They argue, for example, that the problem with religion in Scandinavian societies is that the churches there amount to government-sponsored monopolies (in the form of recognized national church organizations). But supply-side economic theory encourages deregulation and the development of a competitive free market, and so the rational choice approach of these two authors does likewise. The problem with religion in Scandinavia is that religious suppliers have created a rigid and inefficient market; "only a few, lazy religious firms confront the potential religious consumer." The result is "an unattractive product, badly marketed, within a highly regulated and distorted religious economy" (p. 232). Stark and Iannaccone suggest that, rather than being driven by religious entrepreneurs, the religious market is controlled by government civil servants (the clergy); and rather than offering choice, the market is closed to outside firms (p. 235).

It is beyond the scope of this paper to challenge the more general premises of supply-side economics and the neoconservative rejection of Keynesian models of the market and its relation to fiscal policy, taxation, and spending. Here one might briefly note Amartya K. Sen's caution that "economics is not concerned only with consumer behavior; nor is consumption confined to 'private goods'" (1997:330). In supply-side economic models, however, "private goods are the only one around," leaving the value of "public goods" like roads and parks – shared by all citizens without exhausting their value – beyond the scope of economic theory and analysis. Just as the neoconservative approach neglects the economic significance of public goods, Stark and Iannaccone overlook the ways in which "religious" behavior involves more than simply "servicing" the private interests of its members.

Beyond these macroeconomic issues, Stark and Iannaccone's interpretation of religious behavior in Scandinavia through the lens of "supply-side" theory results in erroneous conclusions. As Steve Bruce demonstrates, the "religious markets" of Scandinavian countries are far less regulated than they once were, and yet there has thus far been no revival of religious participation (2000:38). Breaking up the "monopoly" has not resulted in an infusion of new entrepreneurial religious "firms."[8] It is also important to note that significant differences of religious participation and belief exist among the individual Scandinavian countries, but Stark and Iannaccone's approach is unable to explain, for example, why Norwegians are more religious than Swedes, despite similarities of culture (1994:39). In response to this problem, Bruce counters the claim that religious demand is closely related to a free

[8] Much more could be said regarding the claim that lack of diversity and choice in the religious market results in lower participation. Historically, the trend in Europe was quite the opposite. In the Middle Ages and Early Modern periods, most nation states were quite closely tied to religious monopolies, and yet participation and "demand" for religion were much higher than at present. Stark and Iannaccone might account for this by arguing that the monopoly was the result of "a particular religious firm enlist[ing] the coercive powers of the state against competing firms," but this only accounts for the monopoly (p. 234). Such a response does nothing to explain why their "theory of religious mobilization" does not seem to apply to earlier historical periods.

and open supply of religious "products." He demonstrates that numerous other cultural phenomena factor into religious membership: the church's relationship to political dissent, national identity, economic prosperity, etc. The rational choice approach to religion in these countries is not informed by a detailed study of the relationship of particular religious organizations to local socio-cultural conditions. Furthermore, as Bruce adds, "most supply-side propositions are framed without reference to differences in theology or ecclesiology" (2000:42). It is difficult not to conclude, therefore, that this approach to religion is shaped according to external neoconservative presuppositions about human motivations and behavior.

Amartya K. Sen criticizes these assumptions in a manner not unlike Horkheimer and Adorno's arguments against instrumental rationality. He questions whether "it is appropriate to assume that people always . . . try to maximize personal gains" (1997:333). Citing economist L. Johansen, he challenges the idea that people will only be honest to the extent that they have economic incentives to do so; "the assumption can hardly be true in its most extreme form. No society would be viable without some norms and rules of conduct" (p. 332). For this reason, he concludes, "the *purely* economic man is indeed close to being a social moron" (p. 336).

This human behavior-equals-investment equation returns us to the rational choice reduction of religion to the theory of compensation, and to the deeper problems involved in the application of rational choice theory to the study of religion. Such an unflinching embrace of the compensatory role of religion is startling from a position informed by Marx's criticism of the ideological nature of religion as "the opium of the people" (1978:54). For Marx, the promise of consolation in the afterlife all too easily becomes reduced to decorating the chains of unjust social relations with flowers. The critical principle implied in this perspective is the argument that discourse which fails to acknowledge that it is shaped and produced by its historical context is abstract and naïve. On this point in particular, rational choice theory repeats errors that Adorno and Horkheimer criticize in their analysis of Logical Positivism. It is thus useful to return briefly to this critique.

Adorno and Horkheimer on Positivism

One of the principal goals of the early work of the Institute for Social Research in Frankfurt, under the direction of Max Horkheimer, was to challenge the agenda of the Vienna Circle of Logical Positivists in social scientific method. In a manner not unlike contemporary rational choice theorists, the Logical Positivists sought to purify philosophy and the social sciences of all perceived metaphysical elements and restructure them according to the logic of empirical science and mathematics. Thus, the members of the Circle focused on analysing the propositions and rules through which empirically meaningful statements could be formed and tested (Blumberg and Feigl 1931; Hanfling 1981).

Horkheimer vigorously criticized the reduction of knowledge to the results of the empirical sciences or formal logic. In his essay from 1937, "Traditional and Critical Theory," he argues that "traditional theory" (the perspective of the positivists) fails to acknowledge the social location of its assumptions. He locates their understanding of science in a bourgeois society dominated by techniques of industrial production, focused solely on eliminating contradictions and the technical control of nature. Horkheimer states that the context in which scientists and theorists operate is one that is saturated by cultural learning and pre-scientific knowledge. If this environment in which theories are developed remains unexplored, the empirical sciences are guilty of operating within an unexamined horizon. He insists that this limited subculture represents only one sector of social experience and perspective, so that failing to examine the unquestioned assumptions of the scientific community risks leaving scientific research vulnerable to theoretical blindness and ideological manipulation. Horkheimer argues that traditional theory fails to acknowledge that facts and theories can "be understood only in the context of real social processes" (1995b:194). Furthermore, he demonstrates that the "instrumental" reasoning of natural science represents but one form of possible knowledge. He defends a broader concept of reason; one that is concerned not only with logic and empirical observation, but also issues of practical reason and aesthetic judgement.

Horkheimer describes the reality of "the contradiction-filled form of human activity in the modern period" in the following manner:

> The collaboration of men in society is the mode of existence which reason urges upon them, and so they do apply their powers and thus confirm their own rationality. But at the same time their work and its results are alienated from them, and the whole process with all its waste of work-power and human life, and with its wars and all its wretchedness, seems to be an unchangeable force of nature, a fate beyond man's control. (1995b:204)

In a manner similar to Adorno's concept of "social totality," Horkheimer argues that these contradictions between the rational concept of society and the human experience of suffering, and between the attempt to control one's natural environment and the experience of powerlessness, are evidence of the irrationality of society and the incompleteness of scientific knowledge. This tension, he continues, demands a dialectical understanding of reason. It necessitates an appreciation for the ways in which human thought and action influence the world, but also a recognition of the fallibility of these same powers, and the fact that the world often acts upon human beings against their will. The rational intentions of human society cannot reach their full potential in an irrational society: "reason cannot become transparent to itself as long as men act as members of an organism which lacks reason" (1995b:208).

In the theories of religion developed by both Stark and Iannaccone, little attention is given to analyzing present social conditions, or how people respond to these conditions. Their approach is laden from the outset with free-market economic presuppositions that are not analyzed or proven. The Frankfurt School's critique of positivism challenges a social scientific method that relies upon such entrenched assumptions. It insists that social theory has to become more self-reflective about what shapes and informs it, but it also pushes reflection and analysis still further. For, even if the rational choice theorist's description of existing patterns of social behavior is accurate, Adorno and Horkheimer challenge the presumption that this description can be considered a complete grasp of social reality. For them, social theory cannot presume that observed patterns of behavior are "natural" or illustrative of social "laws." They remain suspicious of any approach that appears to turn observed patterns into confident explanations for behavior.

The debate for Adorno and Horkheimer is not over whether to study religion scientifically, nor is it over the appropriateness of employing empirical research, or analyzing patterns of behavior in social scientific method. As Adorno notes, "social regularities do self-evidently exist." Social science will thus seek to uncover such patterns through empirical research. What Adorno criticizes in positivism and in theories with approaches similar to that of rational choice, is that they fail to acknowledge the historicity of these social patterns – that they are produced and are subject to change; "there is, indeed, a very strong tendency to amputate the historical dimension altogether" (2000a:147–48). By this, Adorno means to say that a perspective which treats its object as a static fact, without exploring how it is socially constructed in history and remains subject to ongoing development, effectively reifies what it intends to study. The Frankfurt theorists argue that, not only does this attitude result in faulty theoretical conclusions, it also serves to canonize the *status quo*. It suggests that existing society is unalterable and is the best of all possible worlds. And so, the behavior of the men in *A Beautiful Mind* can be considered to be an accurate and universal portrait of relationships between the genders, and the observations of Stark and Iannaccone regarding some American Protestant churches can be taken as validation for the "rules" of free market economic theory, along with an explanation of different forms of "religion." By neglecting to appreciate the constructed nature of all social phenomena, such an approach "causes its object to congeal into something solid while at the same time 'momentizing' it. That which is nothing other than 'here and now' hardens and solidifies" (2000a:149).

For Adorno, subjective conceptual thought is always inadequate to its object. But, since one cannot think without concepts, "necessity compels philosophy to operate with concepts" (1995:11). And so self-critical thought proceeds, careful not to assume that its concept *is* identical to its object – a mistake that Adorno calls "identity thinking." This is what social theory does when it "congeals" historical experience. And so, even though one might acknowledge that Stark's approach to religion is certainly aware of historical changes and developments in different religions, from the perspective of Adorno, his rational choice model stops short of analyzing and explaining the social patterns he observes among religious adherents. Adorno argues that such phenomena need to be examined and explained in the context of the larger social totality – in order to determine how society is shaping and constructing the very patterns being studied, along with the observing theorist herself.

Adorno argues that identity thinking also results in an undialectical separation between *actuality* and *potentiality*. In *Negative Dialectics*, he refers to the example of freedom to explain what he means: "Emphatically conceived, the judgment that a man is free refers to the concept of freedom." But as the individual encounters barriers to its actions, "the concept of freedom lags behind itself as soon as we apply it empirically." Such a confrontation forces the concept to contradict itself, as the particular individual seeks to be free, but must also diminish what the concept of freedom implies practically "for utility's sake" (1995:149–151). Adorno's social theory wrestles with this dilemma. The contradiction between the concept of freedom and the particular experience of social unfreedom cannot simply be resolved in thought. Instead, the "potential for freedom calls for criticizing what an inevitable formalization has made of the potential." The tension that arises because of the concept's unrealized *potentiality* results in a criticism of its *actuality*. For Adorno, "Dialectics is a protest lodged by our thinking against the archaisms of its conceptuality" (1995:152–154). It is the recognition of the mediated nature of all knowledge, and of the contradictions contained within human thought and society.

This perspective forms the basis of Adorno's concept of "social totality," which was discussed briefly above. Without a dialectical concept of society, he argues, one cannot distinguish between a society's actuality and its potentiality. The *status quo* will be taken to be society's only possible form. But in the contemporary world's current configuration, with ongoing disparities in distribution of wealth, access to education and health care, Adorno argues that one can only call modern society irrational:

> [T]he irrationality of institutions, and the irrational moments in our society, are to be understood only as functions of the continuing irrationality. While the means used by society are rational, this rationality of the means is really . . . only a means-ends rationality, that is, one which obtains between the set ends and the means used to achieve them, without having any relation to the real end or purpose of society, which is the preservation of the species as a whole in a way conferring fulfilment and happiness. That is the reason not only why irrationalities survive, but why they reproduce themselves further. (2000a:133)

This is to say that, even if the methodology of Stark and Innaccone resulted in some helpful initial empirical data (which Adorno's perspective might well challenge), without a broader concept of society – one more attentive to particularity and open to the critical sense of a different *potentiality* – their social theory risks ignoring internal social contradictions, exceptions, and diversity, while simply serving to support the established state of affairs:

> The process which supports life, which sociology has as its essential subject matter, is indeed the economic process, but the economic laws already stylize this process in accordance with a conceptual system of strictly rational actions, which asserts itself all the more insistently as an explanatory schema, the less it is actualized in the real world. Sociology is economics only as political economy, and that requires a theory of society. (Horkheimer and Adorno 1973:28)

Examining rational choice theory on religion through the lens of Horkheimer and Adorno's criticism of positivism demonstrates that the explication of human relations narrated in *A Beautiful Mind* amounts to what Hegel calls the "beautiful soul," who, "in order to preserve the purity of its heart, . . . flees from contact with the actual world" (1977:400). The "beautiful soul" is a consciousness that has withdrawn into itself, certain of its own validity, and unwilling to let the objectivity of the outside world threaten its self-certainty. The fictional male characters can walk out of the bar, confident in their new insights, without actually pausing to talk to the women in order to verify whether their assumptions about them are accurate.

In a manner of speaking, the notion of the "beautiful soul" serves to summarize the methodological criticisms raised in this essay against rational choice theory. By treating rationality and human desires as simple universal axioms, Stark and Iannaccone neglect diversities of culture and preference, and reduce reason to instrumental calculation. Ignoring the differences in and between distinct religious communities and traditions, the rational choice model proves to be based upon ideological presuppositions about human nature and social action. External concrete differences between different religious traditions and social locations receive little to no attention in its statistical analyses. Furthermore, the society in which the object of their study is found, particularly the dominant political economy of the United States, is subjectively unquestioned. Existing social forms are naturalized, ignoring the objectivity of what Adorno calls the broader social totality. For him, "the characteristic difference between a sociology oriented towards the objective structure and one guided merely by method" is that the former is not only concerned "with the actions of its test subjects," which is the sole focus of positivist theory. What this approach neglects, he continues, is that "these reactions, being something mediated, derivative and secondary, do not have anything like the certainty ascribed to them" (2000a:85). This neglect of the social structure behind the actions of individuals – the culture, ideology, class system, and modes of production that serve to influence the behavioral patterns constituting the social whole – results in an approach to the world that resembles Hegel's description of the beautiful soul:

> Its particularity consists in the fact that the two moments constituting its consciousness, the self and the in-itself, are held to be unequal in value within it, a disparity in which they are so determined that the certainty of itself is the essential being in face of the in-itself. (1977:401)

Adorno and Horkheimer on Religion

The different theoretical basis of the critical theory of Horkheimer and Adorno results in a very different approach to the study of religion from that of rational choice theory. Whereas Stark and his colleagues define religion exclusively as being "concerned with the supernatural" (Stark and Finke 2000:89), these two Frankfurt School theorists understand religion as being related to the concern for objective truth. This is not to say that they are uncritical of the frequent tendency of members of religious traditions to cling to supernatural and otherworldly ideas and aspirations. Along with Marx, Horkheimer and Adorno direct harsh criticisms against religion's ideological function. But unlike Stark and Iannaccone, they also aggressively oppose any appreciation for "compensation," or, in their language, "consolation." Horkheimer insists that such ideas are illusions, "the suffering of past generations receives no compensation" (1995b:26).

On this point, then, their critique of religion surpasses that of the rational choice theorists. Their scrutiny of religion's connection to compensation and suffering takes their analysis further than that of Stark and Iannaconne. As Horkheimer phrases it, "religion as consolation means more than might occur" to a religious leader or theorist. For, "it is not the truth of religion that dawns on the person in need, it is the need that constitutes its truth, not only individual, but social need as well" (1978:177). This perspective on religion has deep roots in the Marxian tradition. Marx's acknowledgment that religious suffering is both an expression of real suffering and a protest against it points in this direction. In "The Peasant War in Germany," Friedrich Engels interprets the religiosity of Thomas Münzer as a form of proto-communism, and his text "On the History of Early Christianity" analyzes how this "movement of oppressed people" shares similarities with the modern working class movement (Marx and Engels 1975:275–300).

Horkheimer approaches religious traditions in a similar spirit. Religion is for him a particular form of social expression that reveals in a unique way the inherent tensions and contradictions among individuals and communities in their social context. He states that, "religion is the record of the wishes, desires, and accusations of countless generations" (1995b:129). The argument here is that the task of the study of religion is to seek to explain why people require and depend on "compensators." A critical theory of religion intends to resist the temptation to conclude that the existence of these virtual-rewards is itself an "explanation" for religious behavior. From the perspective of

Adorno and Horkheimer, theorists like Stark and Iannaccone reduce religion to a theory of compensators, without probing into the conditions that make compensators necessary. This is exactly the approach to social analysis that Adorno accuses of "amputating" attention to historicity and the social totality.

Horkheimer and Adorno's approach to the issue of "consolation" is noteworthy for the fact that, although it certainly emphasizes the cognitive aspect of religious *belief*, it in no way limits itself to a cerebral understanding of "religion" to the same extent that rational choice narrowly restricts it to belief in immortality. These two members of the Frankfurt School recognize that the identity and experience of religious adherents involves far more than cognitive beliefs, but also emotional, social and psychological aspects of relation. For, although the metaphysical beliefs of the various religious traditions are considered to be illusions, Horkheimer argues that these same traditions are intimately linked to human aspirations, which, as they push beyond given social conditions, connect them to a longing for a better world, and for a connection to objective truth.

As we observed in Adorno's concept of social totality, his work is concerned to probe the contradictions and social forces that exist behind the "equilibrium" of the existing state of things. His understanding of the task of economics and sociology is that they involve "probing the wounds which this order has and which . . . it inflicts on us" (2000a:144). He suggests that these tensions testify to unresolved contradictions in the social order; "suffering is objectivity that weighs upon the subject," and so "the need to lend a voice to suffering is the condition of all truth" (1995:17–18). As with Horkheimer, Adorno conceives of religious discourse as a key expression of these wounds and suffering. He understands what he calls "metaphysical experience" to be closely related to religion. This claim is based on the view that conceptual thought, along with human experience, "has the curious characteristic that, although itself entrapped, locked inside the glasshouse of our constitution and language, it is nevertheless able constantly to think beyond itself and its limits, to think itself through the walls of its glasshouse" (2000:68).

This is to say that, in religious discourse, one can observe experiences and expressions that challenge the dominance of the current societal *actuality*, as religion both testifies to, and gives expression to, a concern for alternative *possibilities*. This is not by any means to suggest that religion is the only or the best social location to observe this phenomena, but, for Horkheimer and Adorno, the analysis of religion offers a richer resource for uncovering evidence of a deeper social experience than does a mere account of currently existing attitudes. It offers an opportunity to examine experiences that might "reflect the negation of the finite which finiteness requires" (Adorno 1995:392). Just as the concept of freedom challenges current experiences of unfreedom, religious expressions can be understood to challenge the foreclosure of the present on itself.

Horkheimer argues, therefore, that religion has provided Western culture with an invaluable inheritance:

> [Human]kind loses religion as it moves through history, but the loss leaves its mark behind. Part of the drives and desires which religious belief preserved and kept alive are detached from the inhibiting religious form and become productive forces in social practice. . . . In a really free mind the concept of infinity is preserved in an awareness of the finality of human life and of the inalterable aloneness of [human beings], and it keeps society from indulging in a thoughtless optimism, an inflation of its own knowledge into a new religion. (1995b:130–31)

The legacy Horkheimer points to in this statement is religion's relation to the concept of objective truth. He acknowledges that throughout history religious thought has also been intertwined with myth and illusion, so that, gradually, reason "aspires to replace traditional religion" (1974:13). But although Horkheimer appreciates this shift, he also laments it, for, as we have seen above, he observes that rationality often gets reduced to instrumentality and calculation. And so he writes, "the divorce of reason from religion marked a further step in the weakening of its objective aspect" (p. 14). With the rise and subsequent dominance of technical rationality, particularly in the form of modern science, human thought and social experience increasingly get locked into the confines of the *status quo*'s actuality. As the quotation at the outset of this paper laments, what the Enlightenment "killed was not the church but metaphysics and the objective content of reason itself" (p. 18). Suffering continues, and so individuals and communities continue to express it, sometimes in the form of religious discourse and practice. But what becomes increasingly difficult to articulate, in the view of Adorno and Horkheimer, is the hope for a better world, and an understanding of society that probes beneath the presuppositions of the current age.

This is the starting point for the study of religion offered by Adorno and Horkheimer; one that represents a marked contrast to the model presented by rational choice theory. For Adorno, "certainly a *ratio* that does not wantonly absolutize itself as a rigid means of domination requires self-reflection, some of which is expressed in the need for religion today" (1998a:138). But by this, he does not advocate a return to a religious or theological worldview. He observes that such a conclusion is often "cheaply marketed in order to provide one more so-called stimulus . . . by which the members of a calculating society are calculatingly made to forget the calculation under which they suffer" (1992:294). Rather, Adorno argues that part of the motivation behind religious practices, expressions, and longings, is to be understood as a longing for a better world, and for an objective truth. Because of this, the study of religion offers critical theory a rich site in which to analyze social contradictions and tensions. Thus, although far from advocating a 'return to religion', the Frankfurt School theorists call for a return to the criticism of religion, and for greater critical attention to the social conditions in which religious traditions function. For, in Horkheimer's estimation, a philosophy that seeks to be anything more than "scientism" is itself entangled with the same dilemmas as theology: "Knowledge is ultimately governed by purposes. Theology wants to be free of earthly ends. It is both lower and higher than any form of knowledge" (1995b:235). The problem with a rigid positivism is that, forgetting its own historicity, it clings to its narrow grasp of its object, which effectively reduces the object to an irrational myth based on subjective presuppositions, and results in a theory no more reliable than the metaphysical beliefs it seeks to escape.

To be sure, neither Adorno nor Horkheimer were able to develop thorough studies of particular religious communities in their lifetime. Adorno completed a few very sketchy examples, none of which encompasses the more detailed empirical work that he advocates in his methodological writings.[9] The failure to put forward a developed research programme was partially the result of their deepening despair over what they saw as the domination of social science and rationality by instrumental reason. Horkheimer in particular grew increasingly pessimistic in his later years about the possibility of resisting the snare of technical rationality's "iron cage." In a late aphorism, he writes, "to the extent that philosophy wants to be more than directions that can be confirmed, i.e. science, it disregards speaker and listener and

[9] For examples of Adorno's sociological writing on religion, see: Adorno 1994 and 2000b.

posits itself as absolute. Language in the emphatic sense, language which wants to be truth, is chattering silence" (1978:178).

This tone in his later writing is unfortunate, for it distracts from the strong emphasis throughout both his own writing and that of Adorno on the analysis of concrete particular manifestations of social experience. As their work increasingly focused on responding to the Holocaust and the challenges of post-war reconstruction, along with the emerging domination of technology and consumer advertising, Horkheimer and Adorno gradually set their interest in empirical social research and the study of religion to one side. Given the promise of their particular approach to an interdisciplinary social theory, along with the limitations of rational choice theory demonstrated in this essay, a return to the perspective they outline towards the study of religion will bear considerable fruit.

In the face of rational choice theory's rise to prominence in the study of religion in the 1990s, the time is ripe for such a return to analysing religion from an interdisciplinary perspective informed by the critical social theory of Horkheimer and Adorno. As this essay has illustrated, the latent neo-conservative economic assumptions of Stark and Iannaccone, along with their guiding premises about human individual and social action, are what shape their treatments of religion. Rational choice theory reduces religion to a theory of compensators that fails to account for why human beings require consolation in the first place. What is required, by contrast, is attention to the complex particularity of distinct communities that shape and are shaped by contemporary social and economic forces. A critical theory of religion challenges the slippage that leads from *A Beautiful Mind* to the "beautiful soul." As Adorno urged,

> What is called for is not only the assimilation of the mathematized market economy into sociology; economics, in its turn, is called upon to do precisely what it fails to do: to translate the economic laws back into congealed human relationships. (2000a:143)

Kenneth G. MacKendrick

Intersubjectivity and Religious Language: Toward a Critique of Regressive Trends in Thanatology[1]

We are often informed that we are living and dying in postmodern times. This claim is premised on the idea that there are characteristic attitudes toward life and death that can be distinguished and qualitatively divided into historical epochs, however synchronic or diachronic these epochs are conceived. Along these lines thanatologist Tony Walter (1994) has developed a topology that includes traditional, modern, and postmodern variants in our attitudes and practices accompanying dying and death. Walter argues that studying attitudes and practices pertaining to dying, death, and the disposal of the body are useful in articulating the plausibility of such distinctions and assist in policy decisions for caregivers and caregiving facilities. By way of a critical rejoinder to Walter's analysis I argue that more attention should also be given to the way in which such theoretical divisions and practices may negatively influence the attitudes and experiences of the people they are designed to inform. To this end my essay has two aims. First, to provide a sketch of traditional, modern, and postmodern strains of religious thought and practice,

[1] Kenneth MacKendrick: mackendr@ms.umanitoba.ca. I wish to thank Christopher Brittain for reviewing an early draft of this manuscript and Warren Goldstein for additional valuable comments throughout the editing process.

with an emphasis on death and dying and, second, to outline a critique of recent trends in thanatology that encourage or contribute to the mystification or spiritualization of death – discourses which perpetuate or create "death ideologies."

In *The Revival of Death* Tony Walter maintains that European and North American notions about death and dying have undergone significant transitions in recent years, moving along the path of secularization, punctuated by the disenchantment of death, the privatization of faith, and the decline of a belief in hell (Walter 1997:175–182). Walter encapsulates the qualitative transition in attitudes toward authority during the dying process, from religious to medical authorities and from medical authorities to the authority of the self, with the title of a Frank Sinatra song, "I did it my way." Although Walter favors recent developments in thanatology, he also observes that the gradual transition of death related behavior from acquiescence to an external authority (such as a priest) to the personal authority of the self arrives with a profound ambiguity. While the authority of the self may coincide with some conceptions of self-reflective autonomy he notes it may also be coincidental with a solipsistic and expressive individualism (Walter 1994:198) or what could be called the sovereignty of the individual. Walter's conclusions, which take the form of recommendations for future study and therapeutic practice, indicate that the institution of expressive individualism can be avoided through more interactive approaches to care. The kind of approach that Walter is hopeful about is exemplified but not exhausted by what he calls the postmodern response to death. For Walter, the postmodern model of care is, for the most part, a genuine advance in understanding dying and death; yet, he observes that while it is relatively "good on discourse" and the importance of narratively working through processes of dying, death, and bereavement, it is also "bad on ritual" and the final disposal of the body. He argues that although there is a growing awareness of the cathartic and therapeutic importance of ritual activity as a means of coping with dying and bereavement this has all too often been forgotten in the contemporary age of rapid rationalization and bureaucratic management. Rather than focus on the disposal of the body, my essay will further examine Walter's concerns about the individual and its relation to authority within postmodernism.

Traditional Death

Walter's analysis of the postmodern attitude toward death is situated as part of one of three schemas illustrating pervasive cultural responses to death in the west. He notes that these three schemas are ideal types emerging out of careful studies of death related practices and do not have fixed or absolute correspondences with historical experience. These ideal types capture the consistency of a cultural logic that can be theoretically differentiated in terms of its qualitative and institutional treatment of death and dying: traditional, modern, and neo-modern, with neo-modern responses to death divided into two strands, late modern and postmodern. Much of this schema shares common elements with Philippe Ariès analysis of western attitudes toward death, which read changing attitudes toward death and dying as a gradual coming into awareness of the self-conscious individual (Ariès 1981).

Walter maintains that the traditional response to death is rooted in and mediated by the norms of religious communities. The archetypal bodily context of death is a death that is rapid and frequent, typified by death brought about by plague or during birth or early childhood. The social context for dying and death is communal, theorized by Ariès as "tamed death," with each person seen not so much as an individual but as a participant in a dense web of social relations in which the community experiences death as a communal rather than individual loss. Death and dying are mediated by religious authorities and proscribed rituals of mourning. In traditional practices the body is the responsibility of religious officials and often immediately buried in a communal grave in the courtyard of a church, later being placed in a charnel house (ideally, *ad sanctos*). A death not mediated by these factors was viewed as "cursed." Death is wild, but tamed through religious ritual. The eschatological emphasis for most European Christian communities is not on the salvation of the individual soul, rather, is perceived in terms of communal salvation, the anticipation of the entire community being raised up together in the Final Judgment. It is not until much later, particularly after the Black Plague, that salvation is transformed into highly individualistic terms, with judgment occurring at the moment of death. Despite this turn toward the individual self, traditional death retains many of its characteristics well into the modern period. Traditional death can be charted in Europe from about the fourth century through until the late eighteenth or nineteenth century with qualitative changes around the thirteenth century.

One of the strongest indicators of the nature and coherence of "traditional death" is the relatively stable view of a prototypical "good death." The "good death" is the ideal death that is prescriptively regulated through social and religious norms. The rituals and practices surrounding *artes moriendi*, the art of dying well, exemplify the kind of authoritative norms governing the "good death" in Europe throughout this time period. A "bad death" is one that falls outside of these norms. To use another illustrative example regarding the significance of communal practice, some of the death rituals practiced in late imperial China, as James Watson notes, are such that they do not require that participants actually acknowledge the persistence of the spirit after life. What matters is that the rites are performed according to accepted procedure regardless of 'belief' (Watson 1988:9–10). Such rituals are traditional in the sense of falling under the auspices of cosmological and undifferentiated authority or religious tradition. A death accompanied by the proper rituals is "good." For the most part, accidental deaths, suicides, or murders are viewed as "cursed" or abnormal because they fall outside the norms prescribed by the cultural good death ideal. The accursed death is a death not tamed by ritual.

Modern Death

In stark contrast to the communal nature of "traditional death," modern death is hidden, and dying takes place within established medical institutions. The social context is marked by the separation of public and private spheres and is mediated by medical professionals and legal experts. As opposed to rituals of mourning and concern for the proper passage of the soul into the afterlife (e.g., purgatory or prolonged sleep prior to the resurrection), grief and emotional privacy become guiding norms. The soul is viewed, more or less, as the private property of the individual and not the responsibility of state or medical officials who often remain relatively silent about religious issues. Funeral experts often view the participation of religious experts as inconvenient or annoying. A Canadian funeral director writing with the pseudonym Coriolis notes, "Any effort of a clergyman [sic] to influence a family regarding anything from expenditure to service time are regarded as interference" (Coriolis 1967:49). In the modern age, religious participation is also muted by a dramatic decline in the belief in hell, a concept becoming virtually intolerable after WWI. Walter indicates, "No field chaplain could even so much as hint that the brave lad he was burying might be going to the wrong place"

(Walter 1994:15). In the modern context there is very little overall opposition to processes and procedures of rationalization and the medicalization of the body. Those who are dying, in general, seek technological assistance, expert medical care, and the involvement of professionals. As much as religious authorities (priests, laypeople) participate, the secularized body is essentially the property of the medical community along with state bureaucrats whose advice is taken as authoritative. Modern death is primarily secular and highly instrumental, largely indifferent to religious sensibilities. The modern attitude is one guided by the subject-object paradigm. In this context, which exaggerates anxieties about death by means of control, the dying person is viewed as an object of medical expertise and death is the result of a technological failure. Modern death is typified by Walter as cancer or coronary disease. Although burial of the body (often after embalming) is common, cremation becomes increasingly popular. Religious rites and authorities may be present but they are adjunct to the efficient and proper care and disposal of the body and are largely present for purposes of assisting the living with bereavement.

In the shift from traditional practices to modern practices, death ceases to be viewed as cursed but more often as tragic, and one could add the death of a child to the list of "bad" or particularly grief-ridden deaths. In the modern era there is a sustained silence regarding certain kinds of inappropriate deaths, including the death of infants and suicides. The model "good death" is one that is emotionally tolerable to the survivors and takes place within the confines of privacy and muted grief.

Neo-Modern Death

Walter then argues that the neo-modern experience of death and dying marks a decisive shift in western cultural attitudes. He indicates that there are two trends within this movement: one toward the increasing sophistication of methods of control and manipulation (late modern) and another toward individualization and expressive discourse (postmodern). Both are situated in the context of a growing awareness of the importance of communication, value pluralism, and the uniqueness of the experience of dying for the individual persons involved ('I've never done this before'). The neo-modern responses to death emerge out of experiential deficiencies in the modern attitude toward death, which became more prominent during the 60s. Since modern settings of instrumental and expert intervention are often constituted by an overall lack of emotional depth and communicative connection, what surfaces in these impersonal rational processes is the recognition of the importance of physical, emotional, and spiritual well-being, a factor in "grief management" that cannot be manipulated through the modernist subject-object paradigm. While in the late modern stream respect and the willingness to listen are decoys for manipulation, in the postmodern stream they are integral activities to ensure the autonomy of the self. Although there are two streams within neo-modernism sharing a similar context, Walter clearly favors the postmodern over the late modern. The late modern approach, he argues, intensifies the modern attitude through advanced and reflexive forms of mastery, especially psychology and grief management. What singularly distinguishes the late modern attitude from the modern and the postmodern is its "therapeutic conviction that we can master what we can touch or talk about" (Farrell quoted in Walter 1994:40). The postmodern attitude is driven not by a sense of mastery, but through the unfolding of selves in dialogue. In contrast to traditional and modern views, neo-modern death is neither rapid nor hidden but prolonged, and is best understood in the context of the mixture of traditionally divided public and private spheres (Walter indicates that cancer and AIDS are representative of this new paradigm). In particular, the private feelings and experiences of the dying person are now normatively viewed as part of the legitimate concerns of the public professional (Walter 1994:41). The new emphasis is on feelings and the expression of feelings and is governed by the normative expectation of choice and the autonomy of the dying individual. The prototypical religious attitude is pluralistic, prone to ritual mixing (with the cooperation and encouragement of medical experts) and religious syncretism. Narrative voice becomes the medium through which the dying person communicates their wishes which are to be respected and listened to. Within neo-modernism, the "bad death" is one in which the autonomy of the dying person is violated. The norm, contrary to traditional normative expectations, is that one is required to come up with their own "traditions" – a "personal mythology to live by" (Walter 1994:28).

As I will outline in my analysis of postmodern responses to death, it is my position that the encouragement to develop a "personal mythology to live by" during the process of dying may have the opposite effect of the intended means of care and consolation because mytho-poetic language, rooted in religious practice, is not necessarily communicative in nature. Mytho-poetic language is expressive, and while potentially recognizable may also be incomprehensible. Thus, religious language may be more of a hindrance to providing care to the dying and the bereaved. This is not to say that religious sensibilities should be ignored. Rather, that the use and encouragement of religious language within public institutions cannot reasonably expect to be recognized either by caregivers or by friends and family, and that caregivers may inadvertently encourage such obfuscation when encouraging the so-called spiritual dimension.

Critical Theory and Thanatology: Introduction

As a discourse interested in the emancipation of human beings from oppression, critical theory in the tradition of the Frankfurt School registers a political protest in the name of autonomy and human happiness alongside a social theoretical analysis of existing affairs. In the realm of thanatology, such a critique entails the analysis of death ideologies – regressive patterns in the way in which dying and death are viewed and experienced through processes of socialization and individuation. I think that a strong indicator of our cultural and philosophical attitudes toward death can be found in the narratives invoked when death is near. The modest aim of my essay is to provide a cursory critique of the kind of narratives taken up around death that Walter identifies as "postmodern," looking especially at recent trends in thanatology that privilege what might best be called expressive individualism – the authority, and the rationalization of this authority, conferred to an individual by caregivers during a process of prolonged dying. In what follows, I argue that the unchecked encouragement of the expression of feelings coupled with the treatment of individual decision making as "sacred" emerges out of a cultural attitude of ambivalence and anxiety, a strategic avoidance of death as real. Evidence of this cultural logic can be found in the trend toward the inclusion of "spirituality" as a preferential discourse for dealing with dying, death, and bereavement within the space of a secular environment. It is my contention that such encouragement may inadvertently have a disabling effect for those immediately involved in the process of dying and, at the same time, contribute to a social mystification or a spiritualized understanding of death in a wider social sense.

In order to support this claim I again draw on the studies of Walter, who provides an excellent analysis of contemporary responses to death and also conceptualizes the nature of authority in the dying and caregiving process.

According to Walter, one of the dangers of postmodern authority is that it eclipses the traditional separation of public and private domains by means of an unbridled support of expressive forms of discourse. After providing a summary of Walter's views on the possible authoritarian danger of expressive individualism I draw on Jürgen Habermas's critical social theory, focusing on his analysis of religion and rationality as a means of explaining the potentially authoritarian and mystifying dynamics of religious language. While religion has proven to be a powerful and pervasive discourse for dealing with dying and bereavement, it is important that the therapeutic ideals of consolation and working through not be confused with theoretical analysis. It is my assumption that how we talk about death, whether in terms of "grief management" or "death education," has a profound effect on how death is perceived and understood within society as a whole. Although it is readily evident that religious language may help dying individuals and survivors cope with the experience and trauma of death and loss, it is argued here that the privileging of religious or spiritual discourses in a highly individualized way has serious and perhaps unexpected effects. Our attitudes toward dying and death are culturally and politically significant since they often encapsulate our predominant attitudes toward subjectivity. An ill-conceived understanding of dying and death resulting in the spiritualization of death and thus a denial or an avoidance of its reality cannot but have serious and potentially harmful implications for everyday life. It is the task of critical theory to provide a critique of regressive forms of theoretical analysis and social practice. In this, I argue that a contemporary thanatology must confront what Habermas calls postmetaphysical thinking if it is not to lapse into the realm of ideology.

By means of an introduction, thanatology can be defined as the interdisciplinary study of death-related behavior including actions, attitudes, and emotions concerning issues of death, dying, and bereavement. Studies in thanatology have emerged since the 1940s and 1950s out of a relative silence on the topic – a silence that was often, and sometimes still, encouraged (Dean 1995). Although inevitably at the forefront of literature, art, and religious imagery, death, dying, and bereavement have not traditionally been the focus of sustained analysis. It was not until the path-breaking work and popularity of thinkers including Herman Feifel, Elisabeth Kübler-Ross, and Cicely Saunders that thanatology has become a serious topic of public discussion and inquiry. Today death education and death studies have become commonplace throughout the public sphere.

To be sure, the way in which death and dying are viewed, either philosophically or culturally, tells us something about the society that we live in. Geoffrey Gorer, for instance, has drawn attention to what he calls the "pornography of death" – the curios of a morbid fascination with decay, horror, and violence theorized as symptoms of cultural repression (Gorer 1995). According to Gorer, death is a taboo subject much like sex in Victorian times. He argues that when death is denied or normatively prohibited from public conversation, it nevertheless seeps into our everyday discourses in a more dramatic and seductive form, sometimes as humor and sometimes as horror, but always disassociated from reality and lived experience. An excellent example of this can be found in Bram Stoker's *Dracula*, when Mina Harker requests (and her request is granted) that she be read the Burial Service prior to her death (Stoker 2003). Not only is death portrayed as unreal in this gothic horror novel, it sheds light on the confusion between sex, death, and identity. Likewise, when Herbert Marcuse wrote about the "ideology of death" he argued that the ultimate compliance with death, sometimes haphazardly theorized as an attitude of acceptance in thanatology, may serve as a justification for a willingness or perhaps even an urge to die, further noting that when death and sacrifice are extolled as cultural values then 'working to death' becomes the norm: "earning a living rather than living becomes an end in itself" (Marcuse 1959). Similarly, Ernest Becker theorized that the repression of the fear of death leads to sacrificial heroism, a willingness to throw oneself into action uncritically and unthinkingly (Becker 1973). Thus, a society in which death is experienced as unreal may be more prone to sustain and create a culture of death in the form of militarism or colonialism. Philippe Ariès has also charted in some detail the way in which modern death has been rendered invisible and forbidden, perpetually creating an anxiety about death and dying and an avoidance of its reality (Ariès 1981). In light of the ideological significance of death, how dying and death are understood is of vital importance for the kind of society that we wish to live in, especially if the social taboos regarding death are prevalent and potentially harmful in the sense of either encouraging resignation towards suffering and dying, or glorifying death as heroic or sacrificial. Taken together, it is possible to see that how death is viewed ties into our predominant attitudes toward war, the economy, labor, and public policy.

Although western culture is often thought to be in denial about death, death being a social fact persistently rendered socially invisible because of its traumatic reality, Walter comments on the narrowness of this thesis, arguing that it is better to acknowledge that western society paradoxically denies death and affirms it simultaneously (Walter 1991). Given the long-standing theses regarding the multiple ways in which death is denied within cultural modernity, Walter's observation regarding the "revival of death" in the public sphere is all the more remarkable (Walter 1994). In what follows I argue that Walter's analysis, affirming the "authority of the self" in post-modernism, requires a more nuanced understanding of the dynamics of religious language to fully avoid the danger of authoritarian expressive individualism that he is concerned about. While he does note some of the problems that religious or spiritual language creates for health care workers I think it necessary to further clarify the relation between religious language and the supposed authority of the self.

Thanatology and Postmodernism

Part of my interest in Walter's thesis here has to do with the collapse of the distinction between public discourse and private faith (or belief) that is upheld in modernism and blurred in neo-modernism, and the re-emergence of "spirituality" or religion as a legitimate area of concern (and sometimes participation) for the secular professional. I am not seeking to criticize the division of labor within caregiving facilities – facilities that have professional religious authorities on staff to deal with the spiritual or religious concerns of their patients. My concern, rather, is with the intermingling of secular care with "spiritual care" which produces, in my view, a concept of the self that is individualistic and authoritarian rather than intersubjective and relational.

It is clear that the traditional approach to death and dying is inadequate, since we do not live in an age where people "bend at the knee" to religious authorities. Following Walter it is also evident that there are serious deficiencies in the modern view of death and dying. The impersonal nature of its approach, its intensely private norms and the exclusion of interactive forms of care has increased the traumatic impact that death has on the survivors. Although there may be a widespread nostalgia for the sacred canopy that traditional religious authorities provide, the required social institutions and cultural norms supporting this worldview have been weakened and in some instances are non-existent. That being said, it is with great irony that the post-modern approach to death involves the rejuvenation of religion, even if religious practices are conceived more in terms of their progressive function as mechanisms of support and comfort rather than as authoritative normative structures. The return of religion, within the sphere of what has come to be known as the postmodern condition, is not the return of traditional religious worldviews although it often appears this way. In postmodernism, religion returns not as an encompassing worldview, wherein the differentiations that modern thought provides are neglected altogether, but as one of several narratives that can be invoked for the functional purpose of comfort and the further expression of uniqueness and individuality. Postmodern religion punctuates and dedifferentiates some experiences but not all. It is a contradictory blend of modernism (rational differentiation, utilitarianism) and traditional forms of thought (the spellbinding power of the sacred, "magical-thinking"). One of the reasons that religion "returns" in such a pluralistic and contradictory way has to do with the unsettling disenchantment of the world brought about by secularization and the relative unpredictability of death combined with anxieties and fears the many people have, especially about personal failure and the desire not to be a source of concern or effort for others ('when I die I don't want to be a burden to my family'). The meaninglessness produced by a disenchanted universe, one where religious sensibilities are thrown on to an ever increasing tide of dwindling opportunities as technical mastery reduces the need for supernatural solutions to problems (the cell phone replaced the need to contact living friends and family through the use of a crystal ball) is often experienced as particularly intolerable during the dying process. The persistence of the idea of a "good death" is surely indicative of the discomfiture experienced by 'wild' death.

The neo-modern emphasis on the "good death" or "dying well" is highly paradoxical. First, because the logic of neo-modernism, with its emphasis on the autonomy of the individual, eliminates the traditional social dynamics of the "good death," a death taking place under the auspices and approval of religious authorities within a community. With the disenchantment of worldviews and the devaluing of tradition, something that can only be established with the recognition of value pluralism and an egalitarian outlook, the concept of the "good death" no longer has meaning. If it is acknowledged that there is no final supernatural arbiter of life and death or cosmological superstructure, then the concept of "good" no longer applies to death at all, apart from being a worn out social convention. If this is the case, then the concept fits better with Walter's conception of late modernism (the sophistication of methods of control) than to postmodernism. Second, the shift from religious authorities to medical authorities, and finally to the authority of the self, does not intrinsically change or challenge the nature of authority. It is here that I think a more careful understanding of authority is necessary. In neo-modernism there appears to be a paradoxical return of religion, but one that is potentially hollow and artificial. The encouragement and involvement of secular professionals in the development of a "personal myth to live by" during the process of dying is a paradoxical practice of sacralization amidst an already disenchanted and desacralized institutional setting, a revitalization of religion divested of its communal and authoritative trappings and transformed by a highly individualized outlook. It is the transformation of religion in the form of spirituality in relation to authority that I wish to discuss further.

As mentioned, within neo-modernism Walter distinguishes between late modern reflexive manipulation, the increasing secular desire to control the dying person, and postmodern double coding, the self-reflective and simultaneous and contradictory use of religious language and mixed ritual practice (e.g., Yogic meditation, Christian prayers, Buddhist chanting, New Age healing crystals, aromatherapy) and medical technology (e.g., chemotherapy). The incorporation of a wide variety of approaches to caregiving is viewed as part of a holistic response to the reality of value pluralism. What Walter does not address in detail within his theory regarding the revival of death (where death becomes a sustained topic of public conversation) is the curious move toward the re-enchantment of death that takes place within the postmodern strand of neo-modernism. In particular, the postmodern incorporation of a market mentality toward death and the spiritualization of dying, the dynamics of which I argue may lead to the dangers of expressive individualism – the authority of the self and the interior feelings of the self at the expense of others. Instead of religious authorities deciding what is and what is not a "good death," which is highly problematic in any regard, it is the individual who decides this. While this might seem to be part of respecting the autonomy of the individual, I think there is an important difference, especially in instances where the spirituality of the dying person is taken to be a sign of inward truth (private belief) over and above an external state of affairs (public knowledge). The authority invested in the dying narrative, about acceptable care, the diagnosis of symptoms, the management of pain, and the relation between medical and non-medical expertise is problematic because it may ultimately discourage open communication and threaten to become a one-sided form of expression, sheer assertion, forestalling the possibility of recognition and open context awareness (for an analysis of sado-masochism in one-sided relations, see Jessica Benjamin 1988). For example: although sensitive to this problem, Colin Murray Parkes, Pittu Laungani, and Bill Young argue, in an introductory essay to a volume dedicated to exploring religion and bereavement, that respect for the sacred is vital for developing healthy relations (Parkes *et al.* 1997:10–23). Similar claims can be found through the anthology *Death and Spirituality* edited by Kenneth J. Doka and John D. Morgan (1993). A reoccurring figure in much of the vast literature on spirituality and coping with death is Carl Jung, who, in his later years, encouraged his patients to actively explore and embrace their neuroses, particularly through religious imagery and language (Jung 1989). It is needless to point out that the encouragement of neurotic behavior will not be particularly helpful for the establishment of open context awareness. The painful tension between the possibility of relatively undistorted communication and distortions in language due to the presence of neuroses was the focus of much of Habermas's earlier work (1971). The emphasis on developing spiritual narratives during the process of dying neglects the fact that not all forms of respect for the sacred include open and reflective communication, nor does such respect itself guarantee non-alienating forms of interaction. In other words, the practice of respecting the sacred may not coincide with the normative ideals of reciprocity and mutual understanding in health care, and may in fact actively work against them. Following up on this, I think the dangers of the postmodern response to death can be explained by turning to the dynamics of religious language.

As a means of clarifying Walter's thesis regarding the revival of death in postmodernism, I think it is best situated alongside Habermas's notion of postmetaphysical thinking. By examining the semantic potentials of religious language as theorized by Habermas, it becomes evident that critical theory is in a position to offer a critical rejoinder to therapeutic recommendations suggesting that religion or spirituality is an invaluable resource for dealing with death and dying.

Communicative Action and Religious Language

Habermas argues that religious language is situated on the margins of philosophical translation, resistant to the tendencies of cultural modernity toward the reasoning discourses of the linguistification of the sacred. For Habermas, the linguistification of the sacred, the translation of spell-binding norms into discourses that respect autonomy and the constitution of the world through language, marks a transition from mythic to modern forms of thought, what he calls the move toward postmetaphysical thinking (Habermas 1987:77–111). This transition emerges out of the encounter with pluralism and the decentering of religious authority and tradition in favor of communicatively generated norms (norms that are chosen rather than dictated). According to Habermas, in modernity religion no longer holds cognitive or authoritative sway within rationalized communities. However, insofar as the translation of religious language into secular discourses has not occurred, religious language will retain an affective power for those belonging to a religious community and yield a kernel of incomprehensibility to those who do not share in the praxis driven collective representations.

Although Habermas is a relentless defender of cultural, philosophical, and political modernity, he notes that the defiant "syndrome of validity" that adheres to undifferentiated mythical and religious worldviews manifest in the form of religious language and can be understood as the bearer of a semantic content that is inspiring and, perhaps, indispensable (Habermas 1992:17, 51). In other words, religion continues to inspire and provide normative guidance despite its general displacement by rational discourses. Habermas maintains that since religious forms of identity lay claim to a transcendence that forestalls the "entropy of meaning" that is "necessarily banalized in political communication," religious identity-formation can serve as a kind of nourishment for the rejuvenation of the lifeworld threatened with disintegration and dissolution by rationalizing discourses (Habermas 1996:490). Considered in this light, religious language can be seen to mediate between impersonal processes of rationalization, however welcomed by participants, and social fragmentation via the emptying out of traditional values on the way toward a postconventional identity.

In terms of the schema outlined by Walter, this revivification of religion – not as an authoritative and proscribed tradition, but as the encouragement to develop a personal religious narrative – is constitutive of postmodernism. While Habermas notes that religion is a preservative against the collapse of meaning that rides in tandem with rationalization, he does not, unlike the postmodern approach, collapse the division between public discourse and private forms of expression along the way. I suggest that Habermas's conception of religious language has an advantage over a framework which accepts the collapse as constitutive of respecting the authority of the self. The preservation of this distinction, which I readily acknowledge needs to be reconsidered in many respects, is necessary if mutual understanding between those working in established health care institutions (hospitals, hospices, etc.) and the dying individual is to be possible.

While Habermas's comment that religious language is indispensable suggests that there is a grammatical uniqueness to religious language that stands apart from poetic expressions, this uniqueness should not be understood without ambivalence. What makes religious language "religious" requires careful elaboration. For Habermas, the unique character of religious language is not original in the sense of manifesting itself independently of human activity (Habermas 2002:74). Religious experience, from which religious language is typically thought to extend, is not accepted by Habermas as such, since such expressions are always caught up in structures of power and authority derived from the semantics of particular religious communities. A postmetaphysical approach, Habermas argues, must regard religious or mythic language operative within the framework of modernity in terms of its function rather than in terms of its normative validity, since it is the very validity structure of religious thinking that is subject to authoritative norms and an undifferentiated worldview (Habermas 2002:67–91). The distinction Habermas makes between intersubjective validity (the legitimacy of norms, for example) and subjective experience, as private and resistant to translation, is helpful. I have depicted this difference in terms of public knowledge and private faith or belief.

Owing to private character and cultic experiential basis of religious language, Habermas argues that it must be acknowledged that religious or theological forms of reflection have exhausted their rational potential because they are not open to critical scrutiny nor are they comprehensible within a public forum. This would not be the case if religious language was not resistant to translation into other discourses, an instance which would of course put an end to the grammatical uniqueness of religious language, its singular claims about transcendence and its spell-binding authority. Thus, religion, when considered from within the framework of postmetaphysical thinking, is theorized as rhetorical and functional, a semantic form of expression bereft of a communicative potential (open context awareness) and therefore a private or subjective concern. In short, religious discourse cannot reasonably be expected to lay claim to normative validity within a pluralistic and secular environment. Nor can it be reasonably expected that such discourses could be understood by "non-believers" within such an environment. According to Habermas, any future potential of religious expression to serve as a normative discourse hinges on its capacity to be translated into other discursive spheres, such as law, politics, sociology or, I would add, thanatology, a translation likely considered undesirable by religious adherents since it would render the perceived independence of religion as superfluous. Failing this, Habermas maintains that religion cannot but find its significance in modernity diminished, thrown irresistibly into the tide of secularization, however inspiring and rejuvenating it may in fact be. The persistence of religious language and mythic narratives within public institutions can only lead to breakdowns in communication, perhaps at times when such breakdowns are highly undesirable.

Although Habermas's claim regarding the uniqueness of religious language may be problematic, since it seems to privilege, or at least single out, religious semantics over other forms of expression, it is consistent with the premises of a moral theory of discourse affirming the autonomy of individuals to determine for themselves the parameters of the good life (and good death) based upon the modernist distinction between public morality and private ethical life without political prejudice or prejudgment (Habermas 1990a:98–109). Habermas accepts the right of individuals to draw upon religious language, but rejects its semantic capacity to be meaningful under the conditions of postmetaphysical thinking, as normatively binding for others. Any infraction of the spellbinding power of the sacred within the public sphere can be anticipated to have regressive tendencies. Nonetheless, as an ethical guide having to do with issues of the good life, in contradistinction to the impartial moral point of view that regulates the public sphere, religion may remain intact and, at least to some degree, is celebrated within the plurality of democratic societies. To be sure, private ethical life theorized by Habermas encompasses a wide range of social relations not the least of which is a public sphere wherein questions of semantic and rhetoric are debated.

Toward a Critique of Postmodern Thanatology

With the decline of religious authorities and growing resistance to the sovereignty of medical professions, there is evidence that the primacy of the individual within the postmodern response to death is accompanied by the emergence or re-emergence of new kinds of religious narratives based on the social expectation that the individual ought to articulate their own personal mythology, their own personal notion of the "good death." This narrative emphasizes the uniqueness of the individual but also is often taken to regulate their own private authority to determine, to whatever degree possible, their own death. It is the nature of this private authority that needs to be further explained and examined. It is argued here that the emergence of religious discourses must be uncoupled from the authoritative basis of an ill-conceived understanding of autonomy.

Under the rubric of the authority of the self, Walter (1994) notes that postmodernism encourages autonomy. The nature of autonomy and its relation to authority and religious language is what needs to be clarified. What I am interested in here is the way in which disenchantment is perceived of as being so threatening that the only remaining hope is to develop and encourage a renewal of mytho-poetic forms of expression. This renewal is mediated in a contradictory way within the postmodern paradigm. The result, for the postmodern response to death, is a kind of synthetic privileging of the sacred interiority of the individual. The postmodern revival of the sacred in terms of the individual should be distinguished from traditional religious forms, which situate the sacred as normative for the community. The rise of the rhetoric of re-enchantment can best be seen as the emergence of new forms of expression that entwine private feelings and perceptions and professional caregiving. The entwinement of private experience and public epistemology cannot be expected to find an easy balance when dying individuals are often encouraged to take on for themselves the creation of a personal mythology or a spiritual narrative, one which establishes the individual as a sacred sovereign. As I have argued, this can be highly disruptive and may lead to communicative breakdowns. The therapeutic aim of encouraging the articulation of individual sovereignty toward death, in the name of autonomy, may have the unintended consequence of making communication between those who are dying, family and friends, and those who are caregivers, more difficult.

It is worth pointing out that Habermas's conception of modernity is distinct from that of Walter. Walter understands modernism to operate along strategic lines, wherein late modernism continues this trend in a reflexive way. Habermas's conception is thoroughly intersubjective. The terminological issues should not prevent us from seeing that Habermas' conception of modernism is akin to Walter's theorization of postmodernism but does so without the danger of expressive individualism since it is based on recognition and reciprocity. The Habermasian view of modernity is therefore not coincidental with the view that modernity culminates in instrumental forms of rationality. Rational analysis, for Habermas, is not impersonal, since it relies on ongoing hermeneutic dialogue between experts and non-experts. It is also not conceived in terms of manipulation, since at the heart of a communicative theory is the idealization of an anticipated consensus on issues of public health and welfare. And, finally, it does not require the rejuvenation of religion in the form of spirituality because of the experiential basis of religious language as grounded in cultic praxis. It is symptomatic of postmodernism to perpetuate the subject-object model of human relations insofar as religious language is encouraged as part of individual expression rather than a more dialogical approach, since individuals are encouraged to relate to themselves and others through the realm of fantasy (subject-object) rather than sustained communicative action (consensus, dialogue). This being the case, Walter's distinctions between modernity, late modernity, and postmodernity all begin to blur, since they share a non-dialogical element, however "good on discourse" postmodernism may appear to be.

Given Habermas's comments about the difficulties in translating religious language, the conditions for recognition are foreclosed upon, rather than encouraged by, religious language. As psychoanalyst Jessica Benjamin notes, assertion expresses both authorship (moral accountability) and agency (autonomy) while recognition expresses the capacity to set limits to whatever is asserted – a way of establishing a boundary between self and other. When the delicate tension of mutual recognition breaks down, and Benjamin argues that this is both inevitable and common, assertion can become a destructive form of aggression (Benjamin 1988:28). The manifestation of aggression occurs when boundaries between individuals are rendered insubstantial (Benjamin 1988: 39). This is precisely why expressive individualism is a problem. When the individuals are encouraged to develop their own personal myths to live (and die) by, the utterly subjective nature of such expressions cannot be anything other than assertions until translated by others. Naturally, the laborious work of translation, when possible, takes time and energy. It is possible, even though religious language is resistant to translation, but given the context of dying, even when prolonged, time and translation skills are not necessarily something that health care professions have. In contrast to the postmodern vision of autonomy, the vision of autonomy shared by Habermas and Benjamin, is not solipsistic, in the sense that it recognizes the mutuality and necessary intersubjectivity required for subjectivity to develop and flourish.

The trend toward the sovereignty of the individual and the socializing tendency of various cultural communities toward a postmodern notion of the "good death" leaves the individual, in many instances, facing death, and perhaps controlling death, on their own terms, without the guidance of traditional religious or professional authorities. This is one of the weaknesses that Walter identifies with the postmodern revival of death. With the individual cast as a kind of sovereign, coupled with the encouragement of the use of religious language, the language of dying threatens to become singularized through its spiritualization – perhaps to the point of self-alienation. The individualist emphasis on the internalization of the sacred is something that Charles Taylor has theorized in detail. His analysis in *Sources of the Self* carefully outlines the way in which the intensification of a sense of inwardness forces one to adopt a stance of disengagement from one's own feelings, rendering inward reflection impossible (Taylor 1989:390).

In this sense, the postmodern move toward the 'forced' articulation of a death narrative or a personal mythology, the self-invention and guiding authority of a "good death," may have the inadvertent effect of isolating individuals from those around them or bringing about exaggerated forms of aggression. While I certainly agree that autonomy must be encouraged, it is necessary to grasp what this means with adequate sociological and philosophical concepts. Habermas's contention that religious language is not original is helpful here since it establishes a sociological basis for the conceptual ban on the sovereignty of the individual and takes up a skeptical position with regard to the sacred. Habermas argues that individuality is always socialized, the individual is itself a self-descriptive concept derived from processes of social recognition, affirmation, and contradiction. Under the premises of postmetaphysical thinking, religious language cannot be viewed as original, in the sense of an authentic manifestation of some form of ultimate reality, a sacredness that ought to be respected. While the philosophical and scientific discourses have disenchanted the social world, postmodern trends have renewed the power of the sacred in singular form, a form I argue is paradoxically encouraged by the reality of pluralism conceptualized in abstraction. What makes this renewal of religion postmodern is its optional and arbitrary nature coupled with expressive individualism. This transition might be understood along the lines of a shift from sacred ritual praxis within the context of a community to individual spiritual narrative. With the individual seen as the arbiter of his or her own death or way of dying, one potential consequence is isolation, the burdening of the individual with the articulation of a narrative that is neither self-motivated nor comprehensible by others.

One instance of this problematic encouragement can be seen as stemming from the use of stage models by health care professionals based on an evolutionary conception of rational subjectivity seeking to identify universal responses to death and bereavement (such as the stage model of Kübler-Ross). These generalized frameworks for dying (such frameworks are subject to different criteria in terms of cognition) are precisely the kind of approaches that must be avoided, or at least analyzed carefully. Such responses tend to sidestep the individual humanity and history of the dying or the bereaved by emphasizing a hierarchical model of stage development which, however descriptive, assumes the primacy of the end result: acceptance or reconciliation, the "good death." This end result is contextualized not in a life actually lived, but perceived through religious language and personal mythology (this is one of the crucial differences between Freud and Jung). In terms of stage models, the focus on the end result tends to create blindness toward the differentiated ways in which people die or grieve and, in fact, cumbersomely legislates appropriate attitudes and behaviors. Instead of a legislative approach to dying, the attribution of sacredness to the dying person, the hermeneutic and discursive models of recognition and intersubjectivity outlined by Habermas and Benjamin might prove more appropriate – models which encourages differentiation and see difference as part of a conflict of assertion and recognition. Within an intersubjective model the authority of "dying well" or the norm requiring a "good death" is diminished. The very notion of dying "correctly" becomes irrelevant. Balance between individuals relies on the creation of ways of communicating that avoid positing the self (or other) as an absolute authority. The ideal of autonomy cannot be understood in terms of sovereignty; rather, is derived from paradoxical relations of assertion and recognition – autonomy depends on recognition and contradiction for its communicative power, the capacity of the autonomous subject to cooperate with others. What is required, then, is not the instillation of a sacred interiority of the subject as a means of articulating a new version of the "good death," which emerges out of anxiety, the trauma of death and loss, but a communicative relationship that avoids the absence of intersubjectivity –

which very well may render such models irrelevant – an implication that would certainly weaken the excessive experience of trauma associated with 'unnatural' or 'bad' deaths and the social implications and stigmas that go along with them.

To summarize, if dying and bereavement come to be viewed as private within modernity, then the postmodern revival of death is borne in part out of resistance to the bureaucratization of dying and grief, a response where the distinction between public and private becomes blurred. What this resistance should signal is not the failure of modern thought as such, but the failure of one-sided forms of modern thought, those forms relying on a subject-object paradigm rather than more intersubjective orientations. The postmodern revival of death is a paradoxical way of taking back what rational discourses (in the narrow sense) have abstractly colonized or disenchanted by means of positing the sovereignty or sacredness of the individual. The problem is that when the individual is viewed as sacred, there is a tendency to suppress our mutual dependency and our linguistic and cognitive connections with one another. The supposed illegitimate separation of public and private interests is not the problem; rather, the problem resides in the attribution of authority in an undifferentiated way. There is no good reason why either medical authorities or the individual must be viewed as sovereign. A critical theoretical approach demonstrates the negative potentials of this approach. In Watler's theorization of modernity and postmodernity his concepts suffer from deficiencies and problems that, in practical terms, bring about the possibility of alienation and only heighten anxieties. As I have argued here, the use of religious language is one recent example of this. Perhaps thanatology needs to recognize that in modernity no death should be considered "good."

While the postmodern revival of death expresses an interest in death as an object of reflective and discursive control, this interest can be viewed as an inversion of the traditional response to death. In the traditional attitude death is ultimately the responsibility of the community, with the religious view that the community as a whole will be judged by supernatural powers in a life to come. In postmodernism, this responsibility is inverted in the sense of transferring responsibility for death from the community to the individual. The survivors are, in effect, acquitted of responsibility toward the dying because it is viewed as the responsibility of the solitary individual. Instead of being communicative partners, the self is viewed in opposition to others.

I would argue that postmodernism, in this instance, is not so much an expression of a post-secular or truly postmodern situation, but actually an inadvertent recuperation of an older form of authority within an alienated and alienating context. The historical connection between postmodernism and Protestant Christianity is something that Johannes Wolfart has discussed persuasively; namely, that the postmodernist remedy for the Enlightenment is little more than a revaluation of familiar premodern theological judgments (Wolfart 2000:395). Examined in this light, Walter's conception of postmodern attitudes toward death could harbor an unexpected return of magical behavior and premodern authority.

In contrast to traditional and postmodern attitudes toward death, modern death, theorized by Walter as the highly rationalizing discourse of the medical profession in the name of care, can be viewed as coming into conflict with its own mandate of care which ideally respects both the universal humanity and the individual integrity of the subject. The more disembodied that communicative forms of rationality become, the more distanced that expert cultures will be from lifeworld processes. This impersonal setting, what could be viewed of as the reification of the lifeworld, creates the context for a postmodern response, the social tendency toward re-enchantment. However, as Habermas shows, modernism need not be conceived only as rational manipulation. The abstract and bureaucratic mechanisms of modern institutions should not be viewed as indicative of the failure of modern thought as such, rather, as prejudicial and unwarranted institutions of authority. Thus, I think it is reasonable to say that it is not the secular emphasis of modernism that has failed, since it is through a public vocabulary that political and social institutions can be changed most efficiently, but the failure on the part of moderns to critically evaluate their own attitudes toward death and authority. In other words, in Habermas's critical social theory modernity is inadequately understood when theorized as a colonizing power of technical manipulation, since the ideals of modernity are inherent to communicative action, thus contradicting this tendency. According to Habermas, instrumental forms of reason are parasitic, dependent upon a more original, communicative use of reason.

Although medical institutions function with a high degree of authority, in postmodernism this authority has been gradually replaced or at least tempered by an almost mystical sovereignty of the individual and the supposed right of the individual to trump or ignore scientific expertise with mythological narrative. As Walter notes, this narrative approach has certain advantages but also arrives with certain disadvantages – "It is not so much that I have decided to do it my way: I am being required to" (Walter 1994:37). Dying persons become obligated to determine for themselves their own death. It should come as no surprise that this postmodern ethic mirrors the predominant ethic of consumerism. It is around these issues, the sovereignty of the individual and the re-enchantment of dying, that religious language has assumed new relevance. Given the post-traditional framework that emerges out of the contradictory expectations contained in a pluralistic world, there is a rush to fill the void of acceptable activities and attitudes. In other words, in order to deal with the ambiguity of death and dying, religion appears as one of several viable resources for dealing with death. Postmetaphysical thinking, in the tradition of Habermas, does not do away with religion but neither does it grant religious language a privileged place, thus avoiding the collapse of the distinction between public discourse and private experience and yet preserves respect for the autonomous individual. As Habermas argued in his debate with Hans-Georg Gadamer, impartial expertise need not be conflated with abstract authority (1973a). I might add the observation that religious language is scarcely a viable remedy to this entanglement. To this end, a critical theory of religion may assist in assessing the potentially disempowering or disabling practice of treating religious narrative as a discourse that sustains the authority of the self.

Part III: Religion

Warren S. Goldstein

Ancient Judaism and Early Christianity: A Critical Dialectical/Conflict Approach to Biblical History

If one wants to find historical documentation of religious conflict, there is certainly an overwhelming abundance of it in the Bible: the Hebrew slave revolt against the Egyptians, the wars against the Canaanites and Philistines, the tribal confederacy, the united monarchy, the division of the monarchy, the Babylonian exile, the occupation by the Persians and then the Greeks, the Maccabeean revolt, the Roman occupation, the emergence of Christianity, the Jewish War against the Romans, all of which culminated in the destruction of the second Temple and the second Diaspora. The conflicts were internal as well as external. The internal conflicts, whether between slave and master, patrician and plebian or prophet and priest, were dialectical; they took place within the society and were caused and exacerbated by external conflicts with other peoples. These conflicts were a source of tension, which made Ancient Judaism and Early Christianity, that emerged from it, into dynamic religions, which ideologically readjusted to ever changing political, social, and economic conditions.

This article will limit itself to an analysis of Ancient Judaism and Early Christianity primarily though the work of Max Weber, Karl Kautsky and Ernst Bloch.

Together they provide us with what is a dialectical/conflict approach to biblical history. This essay will use the following methodology. First, it will examine class conflict within ancient Jewish society, which drove the dynamic of that society forward. Second, its hypothesis is that the conflict was dialectical. There were conflicts between the elites, between classes, and with other kingdoms which were a source of social change. Finally, it shall use a critical perspective; it shall not selectively embrace nor reject these religious traditions but rather use critique as a form of self correction – pointing out the negative aspects while retaining the positive elements (Bloch 1995:1362).

Slave Revolt

The earliest history of the ancient Hebrews is shrouded in mystery and based on speculation. The Jews fell into debt because of a famine; this led to their slavery in Egypt (Antiq 2.7.7). What is likely is that at least some of the ancient Hebrews were enslaved in Egypt (Friedman 1987:82).

Moses is the messianic model; he led a slave revolt against the Egyptians. The royal family adopted Moses as an infant (Antiq 2.9.5–7). The leader of the slave rebellion grew up among the elites (Michels 1962). Moses' killing and burying of the slave master marked the beginning of the revolt (Exod 2:11–12). This class-based conflict expressed itself ideologically through religion. The transition from polytheism to monotheism represents a rationalization of religion. "The slave revolt in morality" begins with the Jews (Nietzsche 1967:34). Slave morality with the Jews took the form of the belief in freedom. The belief in freedom emerged in response to the condition of slavery.

Moses never made it to the Promised Land. The first prophet died in exile. The transition from Moses to Aaron was from prophet to priest.

The Tribal Confederacy and the United Monarchy

When God promised the land of milk and honey to Moses, there was one problem: it had to be occupied. The Hebrews went from being a class in slavery to a people attempting to gain territorial sovereignty. The Israelites led a series of battles against the Canaanite and the Philistines. The tactics used against the Canaanites were equivalent to ethnic cleansing. When Joshua took Makkedah and Libnah, "he left none remaining;" he smote "every person in it" (Joshua 10:28–30). The legitimation for mass murder was the claim that God was on their side. At least in one instance, as part of the battle ritual, the tribes brought the ark (which contained the tables of the Ten Commandments) into battle (1 Samuel 4). The Israelites, at least for a short period of time while they were politically independent, went from being an oppressed group to an oppressor.

Jacob had twelve sons each of whom was the original patriarch for the twelve tribes of Israel. Together they formed a tribal confederacy.

> The Hebrew tribes came as nomadic cattle-breeders, in constant conflict with the inhabitants of Palestine, the Canaanites, from whom they conquered one city after another, subjecting them more and more to their rule. (Kautsky 1919:190; 1925:192)

The occupation of Palestine by the Hebrews represents the end of nomadic wandering of the Semitic tribes and the emergence of a state (Kautsky 1925:190; Engels 1972). The ability of the twelve tribes to form a united monarchy was due to the temporary weaknesses of surrounding monarchies, in particular the Egyptians and Mesopotamians. Weber calls this period the *Zwischenzeit* (intermediate time) (Schluchter 1981:29).

In the development of the power structure of the united monarchy, both prophets and priests preexisted the first Jewish monarch. As a result, they retained a position of autonomy. The consequence of this was a separation of powers between king, prophet, and priest (Friedman 1987:37). Neither king, prophet nor priest was able to gain a monopoly over the power structure. Prophets had the ability to engage in a critique of both king and priest. The tensions between them were dynamic.

Samuel, one of the earliest prophets, anointed Saul the first King of Israel (Antiq 5.10.4). Saul united the tribes under a single monarchy. With him, there was a transition from a tribal society to a monarchy. Some of Saul's actions were considered immoral: "Saul also sent to Nob, the city of the priests, and slew all that were there, without sparing either women or children, or any other age, and burnt it" (Antiq 6.12.6). As a result, Saul fell out of favor with God, the prophet Samuel, and some of his people.

God left Saul and went to David. David's modest class origin gave him high moral standing. Originally, he was a poor man – a shepherd who was the son of Jesse, a Bethlehamite (1 Samuel 16; Antiq 6.8.1). David married into the royal family becoming Saul's son-in-law. Because of David's rise to power, Saul wanted to kill him. Saul and David each had their own army (1 Samuel 26). "There was a long war between the house of Saul and the house of David" (2 Samuel 3:1). The prophet Samuel sanctioned David's triumph (Friedman 1987:38).

David was ruthless toward his enemies. When he engaged in battles, he killed thousands. In his raids upon the Geshurites, Girzites and Amalekites, he took plunder and "left neither man nor woman alive" (1 Samuel 28:9). He took gold and silver from the nations he subdued (2 Samuel 8:11).

Although David was a messianic figure ruling by divine right, he had his moral imperfections. He fell in love with Bathsheeba, the wife of Uriah the Hittite, and she became pregnant by him; David had her husband killed (2 Samuel 11). David had wives and concubines (2 Samuel 5:13). Nevertheless, David is regarded as the Messianic ideal because his kingdom was the height of the United Monarchy.

Solomon, one of David's sons, continued to centralize the power of the state (Weber 1952:45; Bendix 1977:206–207, 213; Fahey 1982:68). "Solomon had seven hundred wives, princesses, and three hundred concubines" (1 Kings 11:3). Solomon's marriages were for political purposes. By marrying the daughters of other kings, he strengthened his alliances (Friedman 1987:42). Solomon's "wives turned away his heart" (1 Kings 11:3). "He grew mad in his love of women, and laid no restraint on himself in his lusts" (Antiq 8.7.5). Since Solomon even outdid David in wives and concubines, he was not as true to God (1 Kings 11:4). Both David and Solomon's sexual immorality were seen as turning away from God.

Under Solomon's rule, the first temple in Jerusalem was built. Despite the experience of slavery in Egypt, Solomon used forced labor to get stone from Lebanon to construct the temple (1 Kings 5:13). With the construction of the Temple, the Jerusalem priests established a cult monopoly. This led to a conflict with priests in the North (Weber 1952:161, 182–183). The urban monarchy supported the Jerusalem priests while the rural tribes supported the priests in the North.

The centralization of power in Jerusalem was also a result of the process of urbanization. A Patrician class emerged in Jerusalem and along with it a Plebeian class. After reducing the peasants to debt slavery, the patricians drove them off their land. The peasants went to the city of Jerusalem and in the process became a plebeian class. One of the factors that drove them into debt was mandatory military service. Some peasants continued to work on their land as debt slaves while others worked in large-scale agricultural enterprises (Weber 1952:27, 30–31, 65, 68, 111; Kautsky 1925:218).

The Divided Monarchy

The centralization of power in Jerusalem under the Monarchy, the Patricians, and Priests class, led to a revolt of the Northern tribes. After the death of Solomon, the Monarchy was divided into two kingdoms, each ruled by one of Solomon's sons. Jeroboam ruled the Northern Kingdom of Israel; its capital was Schechem and later Samaria. Rehoboam ruled the Southern kingdom of Judah; its capital was Jerusalem (1 Kings 11, 12:1, 16; Antiq 8.8.4; Bendix 1977:213, 233). The South retained its conception of God without image while the North established the Baal cult as a protest against the monopoly of the Jerusalem priesthood (Weber 1951:161; Bendix 1977:233). Ezekiel (23) equated the two kingdoms with two harlots whose lovers abuse and kill them and the idol worship practice by the Baal cult, with adultery. The sinful behavior of these two harlots led to their own wretched punishment.

In contrast with the more rationalistic conception of God in the South, the Baal cult was an ecstatic, orgiastic, and thus less purposively rationalized form of religion. They sacrificed humans and animals to God, burned incense on the altar, had male cult prostitutes in the temple, and worshipped idols, the sun, moon, constellations, etc. (2 Kings 23).

During the crises of the divided monarchy, a new type of prophet emerged: the prophet of doom (Weber 1921:238; Bendix 1977:237). Elijah, the first prophet of this type, killed his competitors: the prophets of Baal (1 Kings 18:40; Antiq 8.13.6). Weber (1952:97, 109, 178) saw this new type of prophecy as a response to the division of the Monarchy, which caused the weakness of the two kingdoms. During the divided Monarchy, the prophets oriented their criticisms primarily toward certain kings, particularly those in the Northern Monarchy of Israel, who, as a result of participating in the Baal cult, were seen as doing "what was evil in the sight of the Lord" (2 Kings 21:2).

Whereas the ecstatic Baal cult came from the North, the rational influence of the Levite priests and ethical prophets came from the South.

> This division (*Zwiespalt*) thus ran covertly throughout Israelite history since the beginning of the invasion. It became acute with the increasingly rational character of the mentalities of the two powers opposed to the orgy: the Levites and the prophets of disaster. (Weber 1921:207; 1952:193)

Weber sees ancient Israel as marked by a conflict between the Baal cult in the North and the prophets and priests in the South (Weber 1952:282).

Prophets together with priests contributed to the process of religious rationalization: "Prophets and priests are the twin bearers of the systematization and rationalization of religious ethics" (Weber 1963:45). The prophets worked with the rationalization of the Torah of the Levite priests (Weber 1952:332).

> Prophets systematized religion with a view to unifying the relationship of man to the world, by reference to an ultimate and integrated value position. On the other hand, priests systematized the content of prophecy or of the sacred traditions by supplying them with a casuistical, rationalistic framework of analysis, and by adapting them to the customs of life and thought of their own stratum and of the laity whom they controlled. (Weber 1963:69)

Prophets are guided by value rationality (ultimate ends), whose substance the priests rationalized in a casuist manner (Weber 1978:24–25; Kalberg 1980:1155). The priest substantively rationalizes the value rationality of the prophet. The value rationality of the prophets and the substantive rationality of the priests are of different types but together created a dynamic, which drove forward the process of religious rationalization. The tension and conflict between the prophets and priests was structural and ideological (Schluchter 1981:46; Eisenstadt 1981:148).

The prophet is charismatic while the priest represents a return to traditional domination (Schluchter 1981:46; Raphaël 1981:238). The prophet delivers the word; the priest interprets it. The prophet challenges the established order; the priest defends it. Both see themselves as defenders of tradition. Charismatic domination "becomes either traditionalized or rationalized, or a combination of both" (Weber 1978:246). "In this process the two basically antagonistic forces of charisma and tradition regularly merge with one another" (Weber 1978:1122; 1985:662). Charisma and tradition are antagonistic forces, which merge with each other resulting in a synthesis, which is contradictory and therefore dialectical.

The teachings of the prophets emerged within the context of a class conflict between the plebeians who were declassed peasants and the patricians who were aligned with the monarchy and the priest class. The prophets took the side of the poor against the rich and powerful (Weber 1952:206, 277; Schluchter 1989:191; Shmueli 1968:236).

Kautsky and Bloch provide two different quotations from Amos, both of which provide evidence of the economic exploitation and gross inequality that was prevalent during the reign of Jeroboam II (786–746 BC). Kautsky chooses this quotation from Amos:

> Hear this, you who trample upon the needy, and bring the poor of the land to an end, saying, "When will the new moon be over, that we may sell grain? And the Sabbath, that we may offer wheat for sale, that we may make the ephah small and the shekel great, and deal deceitfully with false balances, that we may buy the poor for silver and the needy for a pair of sandals, and sell the refuse of the wheat?" (Amos 8:4–8; Kautsky 1919:221; 1925:221)

When peasants brought their grain to market, they were not able to survive on the paltry sum which they received for it. As a result, the poor were driven into debt having to sell themselves while the rich took advantages of this situation. Bloch's choice of quotations from Amos provides further evidence of class antagonism:

> I will send a fire in Judah, that shall consume the palaces in Jerusalem . . . For that reason, that the righteous in order to be sold money and the poor in order to be sold a pair of shoes. They kick the head of the poor in the mud and hinder the ways of the miserable. (Amos 2:5–7; Bloch 1968:140)

Amos expresses his anger at the rich for taking financial advantage of the poor, who did not have enough to survive on. The teachings of the prophets were a response not only to political weakness of the divided monarchy but also to gross economic inequality between classes under a Jewish monarchy.

The Babylonian Exile

The prophets attributed the fall of the northern Kingdom to the Assyrians not to military weakness, but to turning away from God by practicing the Baal cult (2 Kings 13, 17). The fall of the southern Kingdom to the Chaldeans marked the beginning of the Babylonian exile (2 Kings 25). One of the tactics used by the Assyrians in their conquest of Samaria, which was later used by the Babylonians in their conquest of Judea, was to capture the elites, taking them into exile, thereby depriving the remaining poor of any political coherence (Kautsky 1925:221). Nebuchadnezzar, king of Babylon, "carried away all Jerusalem, and all the princes, and all the mighty men of valour, ten thousand captives, and all the craftsmen and the smiths; none remained, except the poorest people of the land" (2 Kings 24:14). While this event may seem unique, it was a common practice in antiquity for conquerors to take slaves during military conquest. What may be more unique is that Nebuchadnezzar attempted to bring an end to the Davidic line by executing Zedekiah's (the last king of Judah) sons in front of him and then blinding him (Friedman 1987:98).

The emergence of the belief in the Messiah corresponds to the loss of autonomy of the Jewish state (Taubes 1966:193). Messianism, with its central belief in redemption (*Erlösung*), arose in a historical context. The Messiah was the embodiment of the figure of David who would return the Jews out of exile and restore the autonomy of the Jewish kingdom (Weber 1978:1185).

The idea of the Messiah finds its original expression as the son of man: "And behold, with the clouds of heaven there came one like a son of man, and he came to the Ancient of Days and was presented before him. And to him was given dominion and glory and kingdom, that all peoples, nations and languages should serve him" (Dan. 7:13). The belief in the Messiah was used to galvanize opposition to foreign occupation after the return out of exile (Kautsky 1925:294–295).

Return out of Exile

Daniel engaged in dream interpretation; he interpreted a dream of Nebuchadnezzar, concerning his kingdom of Babylon. Its fate was to be conquered (Daniel 2; Antiq 10.10.3–4). After the defeat of the Babylonians by the Persians, Cyrus, King of Persia, allowed the Jews to return out of exile and rebuild the temple in Jerusalem (Ezra 1). Judah became "a vassal state of the Persian Empire" (Bendix 1977:237). The Monarchy was not restored but in its place a theocracy of the Jerusalem priesthood was established (Schluchter 1981:50; Fahey 1982:81–82). Despite the foreign occupation, the Jerusalem priests had a monopoly on power (Kautsky 1925:230, 236). The Levites collected tithes for the temple (Nehemiah 11:37–38). In an attempt to restore ethnic purity, all foreign wives and children were "put away" (Ezra 10:3). The return from the Babylonian exile brought an end not only to an autonomous Jewish monarchy but also to the prophecy that accompanied it (Schluchter 1989:197; Frend 1985:472; Eisenstadt 1981:158). The kings and prophets vanished; only the priests remained.

As befalls all empires, they go from being the conquerors to the vanquished. This is what happened to the Persians as well as the Greeks. Alexander the

Great's empire was broken up into several kingdoms one of which became ruled by King Antiochus. The weakness of the foreign occupation enabled the possibility for a successful rebellion against it. The Maccabeean revolt was against Hellenistic domination. In order to establish autonomy, the Maccabees employed the same tactics as any other conqueror in antiquity. Judas Maccabee's means included killing all males, plundering, taking spoils, and burning and razing cities (1 Maccabees 5,6). The Maccabees imposed Judaism on those people they conquered and forced them to pay taxes to support the temple in Jerusalem (Kautsky 1925:259). The Hasmonians (the Maccabees) were not and did not claim to be of the Davidic line. Judas Maccabee sent envoys to Rome successfully persuading them to enter into an alliance against the Greeks (1 Maccabees 9:21; Antiq 12.10.6). However, the alliance was only temporary. For a short period of time (about 100 years, 165–63 BC), the Maccabees were able to establish semi autonomy. After the Romans conquered the Greeks, Judea fell under their occupation.

Roman Occupation and the Emergence of Christianity

Christianity emerged in the context of a theocracy of the Jewish priests under Roman occupation. In the *Foundations of Christianity*, Karl Kautsky looks at the political and economic context in which Christianity emerged. Rodney Stark (1997:29) in *The Rise of Christianity* presents Kautsky's position in one sentence only to later dismiss it. He does not seriously engage it. Kautsky explains the economic base of the Roman Empire. With the increasing efficiency of agriculture, surpluses emerged which allowed increasing trade and the development of an artisan class. This created the opportunity for the accumulation of landed property and with it increasing inequality. This surplus made it possible for some to engage in intellectual labor (Kautsky 1925:48–49). Like most other empires in antiquity, the Roman Empire had a slave economy. Aside from the household, larger scale agricultural production as well as mining used slaves (Kautsky 1925:50–52). The larger the concern, the worse the condition of the slaves (Kautsky 1925:54). Slaves were obtained through warfare (Kautsky 1925:56). Ancient Judea was a colony of the Roman Empire, which exploited their colonies in two ways: usury and plundering (Kautsky 1925:86).

The idea of the Messiah, which is based on Moses and was prophesied as the Son of Man, became embodied in Jesus. The "Son of Man" was Jesus' name for himself, which he used as the title of the Messiah (Bloch 1972:146, 161). Jesus lived during a period of political unrest, prophecy, and expectations. The Jewish people waited for a king from the House of David who was capable of driving out the Roman occupiers (Bloch 1995:1256).

If the Gospels are an accurate historical account, Jesus referred to himself alternately as the Son of God and the Son of Man without any consistent pattern. The Judaic concept of the Son of Man is different from the Greek concept of the Son of God; although both concepts are theological, the Son of Man is more secularized and rationalized (Bloch 1968:161). The tension between the Son of God and the Son of Man is based on a contradiction between man's faith in God and man's faith in himself. The idea of the Son of Man is humanistic; it implies that humanity is the source of salvation (Bloch 1968:159; West 1991:205). Trust in God is given up and placed instead in the Son of Man (Bloch 1995:1238). In a simultaneous act of self-deification and secularization, Jesus "called God his own Father, making himself equal with God" (John 5:18). Jesus put himself on reciprocal and equal level to God: "no one knows the Son except the Father, and no one knows the Father except the Son" (Matthew 11:27). In a dialectical act of secularization, "that which men call God" becomes man (Bloch 1972:270). The Son of Man represents a move away from the belief in God and a dialectical secularization of faith into man.

The messianic figure was of a king riding on an ass (Zechariah 9:9). "Behold, your king is coming to you, humble, and mounted on an ass" (Matthew 21:5; see also John 12:15). He rode upon an ass because he was the prince of the poor (Weber 1952:18, 55–56, 368–369). The prophecy was of the messiah entering the gates of Jerusalem (Weber 1952:231, 322).

Even though the Davidic kings had disappeared for centuries, Jesus claimed to be "the son of David, the son of Abraham" (Matthew 1:1; Mark 10:47; 12:35; Luke 3:23–38). Claiming to be of the Davidic line, Jesus' aspiration was to ascend to the throne of the Jewish monarchy and lead Judea to break free of Roman occupation. Because of his failure, this is why the Romans sarcastically inscribed "this is the King of the Jews" on his crucifix (Luke 23:38; Kautsky 1925:405).

Whereas the Romans had a belief in Master morality, the Jews in opposition had slave morality.

> All that has been done on earth against "the noble," "the powerful," "the masters," "the rulers," fades into nothing compared with what the Jews have done against them; the Jews, that priestly people, who in opposing

> their enemies and conquerors were ultimately satisfied with nothing less than a radical revaluation of their enemies' values, that is to say, an act of the most spiritual revenge. (Nietzsche 1967:33–34)

Christianity is an extension of Jewish slave morality. Whereas slave morality with the Jews originally focused on the belief in freedom, with the emergence of Christianity, slave morality extended this to the belief in equality before God. While the belief in freedom was a response to slavery, the belief in equality was a response to inequality. The development of the Occident is an extended struggle – a dialectic between master morality and slave morality (Nietzsche 1968:52–54).

The development of Talmudic Judaism and early Christianity follows the dialectic of religious rationalization. A split occurred within Ancient Judaism. One of the paths toward which ancient Judaism developed was Talmudic Judaism; the other was early Christianity. Talmudic Judaism was a further rationalization of ancient Judaism while early Christianity was a charismatic movement driven by value rationality, which became routinized. The dialectic of prophet and priest in ancient Judaism continued in the conflict between Talmudic Judaism and early Christianity but it transcended it (Schluchter 1985:16; 1989:210). The history of ancient Judaism is a history of the development of rationalism. Rationalistic principles were taken over first by the prophets, then by the Pharisees and finally by the authors of the Talmud, who completed the rationalization of Judaism (Schiper 1959:252).

In contrast with ancient Judaism, the messianic beliefs of early Christianity took more of an otherworldly direction (Kautsky 1925:409). Neither Jesus nor his kingship was "of this world" (John 8:23; 17:14; 18:36). Nevertheless, Bloch (1972:131) argues that Jesus did not perceive the kingdom of God as being in the other world but in this world: "the kingdom of God is in the midst of you" (Luke 17:21). It is not clear that when Jesus spoke of the Kingdom of God, he meant in this world, which is more of a Jewish conception, or the other world, which has come to be more of a Christian conception.

Jesus did not come "to abolish the law and the prophets" "but to fulfill them" (Matthew 5:17). Jesus was called rabbi (teacher) (John 1:38; 3:2; 4:31). Jesus said "I have always taught in synagogues and in the temple, where all Jews come together" (John 18:20). His last supper was a Passover Seder with his twelve disciples (Mark 14:12–22; Luke 22:15). The son of man was crucified on Passach (Matthew 26:2). The central figures to whom Christians bow down and pray are four Jews: Jesus, Peter, Paul, and Mary (Nietzsche 1967:53).

When Jesus found moneylenders and trade being conducted in the temple, this was because the temple in Jerusalem collected a tax (domestically, as well as from Jews living in Diaspora). A large amount of money flowed through it (Kautsky 1925:271). Because of this temple tax, the Jerusalem priesthood's wealth grew tremendously (Kaustky 1925:276). This is why Jesus was upset about the moneylenders in the temple:

> And Jesus entered the temple of God and drove out all who sold and bought in the temple, and he overturned the tables of the moneychangers and the seats of those who sold pigeons. He said to them, "It is written, 'My house shall be called a house of prayer'; but you make it a den of robbers. (Matthew 21:12–13; see also Mark 12:15 and Luke 19:46; John 2:14–15)

Jesus, like Amos, thought that the moneylenders took unfair advantage of the poor and that the temple should not be a "house of trade" (John 2:16). Jesus thought that, under the conditions it was conducted, engaging in trade and money lending was a form of robbery.

Jesus led an uprising against the Jewish priest class who exercised a theocracy (albeit a puppet one) through the temple in Jerusalem (Nietzsche 1968:149). One of Jesus' major conflicts was with the Pharisees. The Pharisees, who have their origins in the Maccabeean revolt, were the heirs of the priesthood in the time of Jesus (Weber 1952:385; Abraham, 1992:253). Under the Romans, there was a proliferation of Jewish sects. Three of them mentioned by Josephus are the Pharisees, Saducees and Essenes (Antiq. 13.5.9). The Pharisees were intellectuals of upper-class origin, influenced by Hellenism, who inherited the rationalism of the prophets (Weber 1978:824; Kautsky 1925:297; Duncan and Derrett 1985:354; Schiper 1959:257).

Jesus stood in opposition to the Pharisees; he accused them and the scribes of being "the sons of those who murdered the prophets" (Matthew 23:31). He called them lovers of money (Luke 16:14). The Pharisees and scribes, in turn, accused Jesus of breaking the tradition. They said that he desecrated the Sabbath by feeding the hungry and healing the sick on the day of rest. Jesus, in response, called them hypocrites (Matthew 15:1–7; 23:13). Because of this conflict, "the Pharisees took counsel against him, how to destroy him" (Matthew 12:14; see also 3:6). They (along with the chief priests) sent officers to arrest him (John 7:31). Jesus' conflict with the Pharisees was of the prophet with the priests.

While Jesus attacked the Pharisees and Sadducees, he did not criticize the Essenes (Matthew 16:1–12; 22:23–46; Luke 6:31; 11:42–44). It is the love-communism of the Essenes that is related to early Christianity (Weber 1952:410).

While the Pharisees were complicit with the Roman occupation, the Zealots emerged against it. The Zealots stood in opposition to the Pharisees and received their support from the plebeians of Jerusalem. They had an alliance with the rebellious rural population in Galilee (Kautsky 1925: 298, 404–405). Mark (15:7) mentions rebels held in prison who had committed murder in the insurrection. One of Jesus' disciples was Simon the Zealot (Luke 6:15; Acts 1:13). This establishes a connection between Jesus and the Zealots who led multiple insurrections against the Roman occupation (Kautsky 1925: 298–299).

The teachings of Jesus played off the class structure; they appealed to the poor and attacked the rich and powerful. Like David, Jesus came from a modest background. Representing an agrarian past, David was the son of a shepherd whereas Jesus, in contrast, was a carpenter's son. Both came from Bethlehem (Matthew 13:55; 1 Samuel 16; Antiq 6.8.1). Jesus went to Jerusalem and challenged the chief priests, the elders, and the scribes (Matthew 16:21). Jesus consciously appealed to the poor: "Come to me, all who labor and are heavy laden, and I will give you rest" (Matthew 11:28). Jesus condemned the rich for their exploitation of the poor: "It is easier for a camel to go through the eye of a needle than for a rich man to enter the kingdom of God" (Matthew 19:24; Mark 10:25; Luke 18:25). While the kingdom of God belongs to the poor, it would be difficult for the rich to enter it (Luke 6:20). It is not clear whether the Kingdom of God is in heaven or something here on earth. Jesus advocated giving up material possessions and engaging in charity in order to be rewarded in heaven: "Sell what you possess and give to the poor, and you will have treasure in heaven" (Matthew 19:21; see also Mark 10:21 and Luke 18:22). The poor who suffer and die will go to heaven while the rich would go to hell (Luke 16:19–23). Although containing a moral condemnation of the rich and seeing the poor as more moral, his tone is simultaneously reconciliatory but sarcastic: "Forgive us our debts, as we also have forgiven our debtors" (Matthew 6:12). Jesus rejected the class structure and wanted to turn the world upside down: "the first will be last, and the last first" (Matthew 19:30; see also Mark 10:31 and Matthew 20:16).

Jesus spoke in parables which cannot be interpreted literally (Matthew 13:10, 13). He told one of his parables to the chief priests, elders, and scribes. It was of the vineyard owner, whose tenants beat and killed those he sent to collect taxes. Tax collectors were seen as being equally reprehensible as sinners (Luke 6:30). They were not sure what this meant but thought "he had told the parable against them." They attempted to arrest him, wanting to put him to death, but were afraid of the masses. So, they left "and went away" (Mark 12:12; Luke 22:2).

While Jesus' opposition to the Jewish theocracy (the Pharisees and the priests) is explicit, his opposition to Caesar and the Romans is watered down. Regarding the coin of tribute he said, "Render to Caesar the things that are Caesar's, and to God the things that are God's" (Mark 12:17; Luke 20:25). This can be interpreted either as acquiescence or as indifference to material things. Pilate is said to have only ordered Jesus to be crucified in order to satisfy the crowd (Mark 15:15). This appeasing attitude toward Rome is far removed from Jesus' originally rebellious attitude (Kautsky 1925:393). Jesus was not only an opponent of the ruling class in Judaism but also that of the Romans (Kautsky 1919:421–422).

Jesus' message about war and peace appears equally as contradictory. On the one hand, Jesus is associated with pacifism. He preached "love your enemies" (Matthew 5:44; Luke 6:27). His Sermon on the Mount warned of the consequences of violence: "All who take the sword will perish by the sword" (Matthew 26:52). But, he also said the exact opposite: "Do not think that I have come to bring peace on earth; I have not come to bring peace, but a sword" (Matthew 10:34). In his anger, he overturned the tables of the money-lenders in the temple. These contradictory statements are hard to reconcile.

Jesus' prophecies were apocalyptic: "nation will rise against nation, and kingdom against kingdom, and there will be famines, and earthquakes." This is "the beginning of the birth-pangs" (Matthew 24:7; see also Luke 21:10–11). Jerusalem will be surrounded by armies and the temple will be destroyed (Mark 13:2; Luke 22:20). We do not know whether this was written before or after the destruction of the second temple. One way to make a prophecy is to speak of an event which has already happened.

The early Christian community had a communistic character (Kautsky 1925:319, 331). Jesus lived together communally with his disciples (Kautsky 1925:334). The early Christians and the Essenes engaged in a communism of consumption (Kautsky 1925:410). Early Christian communism and the messianism, which brought it about, stood in opposition to the rule imposed by the Roman Empire (Kautsky 1925:380–381).

Both Jesus and Paul had questionable psychological states. People said of Jesus "'He is besides himself'" (Mark 3:21). Paul explained the reasons behind his psychological disturbance: "I am talking like a madman – with far greater labors, far more imprisonments, with countless beatings, and often near death"

(2 Corinthians 11:23). Paul tried to justify his madness: "If we are besides ourselves, it is for God" (2 Corinthians 5:13). Nietzsche (1968:165) commented that Paul expected others to believe his hallucinations which he himself did not believe. The value rationality of Jesus and Paul was driven to the point of irrationality.

The succession from Jesus to Paul represents the routinization of the charisma of Jesus (Schluchter 1989:232). There are differences between the teachings of Jesus and those of Paul. Jesus and Paul laid the foundations for two different movements. The Jesus movement was centered in Palestine. The movement of Paul, on the other hand, was located "in the eastern Mediterranean." It received its support from Jews in Diaspora who were an urban population composed of artisans and merchants (Schluchter 1989:214). While Jesus' message was oriented only toward the Jews, Paul extended it to the gentiles (Acts 11:2–3; Galatians 5:6; Ephesians 3:1, 5).

Rodney Stark (1997:49, 57) argues against Kautsky that early Christianity was not a proletarian movement but a religion which appealed to the Jewish middle class living in Diaspora. Yet, Kautsky and Stark deal with two different periods. Kautsky focuses on Christianity in its inception around the time of Jesus, whereas Stark's argument is only valid for Jews in Diaspora after the destruction of the second temple. Kautsky argues that early Christianity was a religion of the proletariat as long as one does not understand them as wage laborers (Kautsky 1919:viii; 1925:9). What Kautsky calls a proletariat, Weber calls plebeians. Weber follows Marx more closely in this respect; he prefers to use the term plebeian in the context of antiquity.

Paul's teachings, like those of Jesus, contain a hostility toward material wealth and an affinity with the poor. Although Jesus Christ was spiritually rich, "for your sake he became poor, so that by his poverty you might become rich" (2 Corinthians 8:9). Throughout the New Testament, there is an aversion towards an obsession with money and material wealth: "The Love of Money is the root of all evil" (1 Timothy 6:10). This rejection of money and material wealth is a detachment from this world. "Do not love the world or the things in the world" (1 John 2:15). Like with Jesus, there is an attack on the rich: it is "the rich who oppress you" and "drag you into court" (James 2:6). James (5:4–5) too condemns the rich:

> Behold the wages of the laborers who mowed your fields, which you kept back by fraud, cry out; and the cries of the harvesters have reached the ears of the Lord of hosts. You have lived on the earth in luxury and in pleasure; you have fattened your hearts in a day of slaughtered.

God has chosen the poor in this world "to be rich in faith" and heirs to the Kingdom of God (James 2:5). James' promises take on an increasingly otherworldly dimension.

While being concerned with the poor and having hostility against the rich, Paul's rejection of inequality had its limitations; he advocated a subordinate position for women, subjects and slaves. Paul's position toward women stands in contrast to Jesus who is lenient upon a woman who was an adulterer (John 8:7; 8:41). Like the Jewish tradition to which he belongs, Paul is "savagely antifeminist" (DeBeauvoir 1989:97). The husband is the head of the household and wives are to be subordinate to them (1 Corinthians 11:3). Wives should be submissive and subject to their husbands (Titus 2:5; 1 Peter 3:1; Ephesians 5:23): "Let a women learn in silence with all submissiveness. I permit no woman to teach or to have authority over men; she is to keep silent" (1 Timothy 2:11–12). Like women being subordinate to their husbands, slaves were to be subordinate to their masters (Titus 2:9; Colossians 3:22): "Let all who are under the yoke of slavery regard their masters as worthy of all honor" (1 Timothy 6:1). Because of this, Kautsky (1919:439; 413–414) argues that Early Christianity was more appealing to the plebeians (urban proletariat) than it was to the slaves. Along these same lines, subjects should "be submissive to rulers and authorities (Titus 3:1): "Obey your leaders and submit to them" (Hebrews 13:17). This is a complete inversion of the original rebellious spirit found in the prophets Moses and Jesus.

When examined closely, the teachings of both Jesus and Paul are contradictory. Jesus preached to be the Son of God and the Son of Man. He was a militant yet pacifist, rebellious yet acquiescent. He was more concerned with the Pharisees and the rich than with the Romans. Paul's egalitarianism only went so far. While condemning the rich and appealing to the poor, Paul supported a subordinate position for women, slaves and subjects. This leads to the suspicion of adulteration and watering down of the original text for those who later used it as the basis for their own power.

In 70 AD, Judea fought a war led by General Josephus Flavius against the Roman occupation. The Zealots were the most fervent in their resistance to the occupation. The war ended in 73 AD with the destruction of the Temple (and the beginning of the second exile). With this defeat, the revolutionary hope disappeared (Kautsky 1919:437; 1925:412). Nietzsche (1967:52) asks, "Rome against Judea, Judea against Rome." Who really won? Although Judea had been defeated, Christianity, which originated as a religion of opposition, grew within the Roman Empire only to undermine it. But in the process, most of Christianity itself became routinized and rationalized to the point where the historical context of its messianic roots have become unrecognizable and the original rebellious message has become inverted. Whereas the prophets Moses and Jesus stood in opposition to power, they have come to be used as legitimations of power.

Conclusion

In order to understand ancient Judaism and early Christianity, one needs to place their emergence within historical context. One can only understand the history of the ancient Jews when one looks at their relation to political power. If the ancient Jews were, for a time, a people in slavery, then the exodus was the consequence of a slave revolt. Yet the Promised Land, the land of milk and honey, could only be secured through military conquest. The height of the messianic ideal is that of David because he was king of a united Monarchy – the height of power. The prophets did not have any problem with a Monarchy, as long as it did what was right in the eyes of the Lord, and was their own. The division of the monarchy and the subsequent conquest of the two kingdoms by the Assyrians and Babylonians represent a fall from power. After the return out of the Babylonian exile, the Jerusalem priests established a puppet theocracy under the Persians. The Greeks and the Romans tolerated it. For a far greater period than it was independent and autonomous, Judea was an occupied colony. However, it was subject to repeated revolts – most notably the Maccabeean and the Zealot. The belief in the Messiah was a desire for a return to an autonomous kingdom.

The central beliefs of both Judaism and Christianity arose in response to concrete historical circumstances. The belief in freedom was a response to the condition of slavery. The belief in the Messiah expressed the collective desire of a political independence. The belief in equality before God was a response to the condition of inequality on earth.

It is an irony that, for people who were opposed to slavery, who had a belief in freedom, in equality before God and a hostility toward those in wealth and power, the only way they could obtain their autonomy was militarily, through violence. Joshua, David, and Judas Maccabee killed innocent civilians en mass and engaged in plunder. Solomon used forced labor to build the temple. The paradox is that only when the military leaders of the Jews used these tactics of conquest, plundering, and murder, did the Jews have political autonomy. Even so, the small kingdom of Judea could not sustain itself against the empires against whom they fought. They only thing that could was a belief system whose original meaning and historical context has been lost.

Jesus' teachings in relation to political power appear to be contradictory. He had a clear antagonism with the Jerusalem priests, appealed to the poor and condemned the rich, but appeared to be less willing to take on the Roman Empire. If he challenged the power structure, he was also killed by it. And, since he was unsuccessful in his bid for power, he never had to deal with the moral contradictions of using it. Paul's teachings were toned down and more other worldly in contrast with Jesus. His belief in equality was equality before God, not necessarily equality on earth. And while he was concerned with the equality of plebeians, he left women and slaves by the wayside.

Ancient Judaism and early Christianity were dynamic religions arising out of conditions of political and economic inequality. There were internal conflicts between the elites and between classes. Conflicts between the elites were those of the prophets against the kings and the priests. The charismatic prophets were carriers of value rationality while the priest's rationality was instrumental. The original class conflict was between master and slave in Egypt but, with the establishment of a Jewish kingdom, it developed into that of Patrician and Plebeian. Conflicts with other peoples exacerbated these class conflicts. The Jewish kingdoms were subject to continual occupation by foreign powers: the Assyrians, the Babylonians, the Persians, the Greeks, and the Romans. These internal and external conflicts were expressed ideologically through religion. Ancient Judaism and early Christianity, which were monotheistic, had a messianic belief in freedom and equality and stood in opposition to the polytheistic master morality of the occupying empires. Conflict, antagonisms, tensions, oppositions and contradictions marked the social relations of the adherents of ancient Judaism and early Christianity, which contributed to a development that was dialectical.

George Lundskow

The Concept of Choice in the Rise of Christianity: A Critique of Rational-Choice Theory

Many classical (modernist) sociologists, including Karl Marx, Emile Durkheim, Max and Marianne Weber, Jane Addams and Charlotte Perkins Gilman, hold that rational calculation – instrumental rationality – derives from the larger trend towards rationalization in modern society. Thus, the instrumental rationality of calculation, or rational decision making, rises to prominence and appears 'natural' specifically within the context of modern society. It is particular to the modern historical period. Predictably, a theoretical perspective, known as rational-choice theory, has arisen to account for the increasing influence of modern rationalization. Yet this theory, to the extent it has become a school of thought, has transformed itself into a new Grand Theory, a theory that claims exclusive explanatory power over all times and places, not only the modern context.

In this chapter, I develop a critique of rational choice theory; specifically, I challenge Rodney Stark's (1997) attempts to explain the rise of Christianity as a process of rational-choice – a book that deserves focused attention in that it is the first credible attempt to apply rational-choice theory beyond the modern world. Stark focuses on the crisis years of 300–476 CE, but discusses as necessary other periods as well. I will examine roughly the same timeframe.

To his credit, the book makes several important contributions, including a focus on socially transformative events like plague, drought, and sanitation in addition to the usual crises of political-economic disorder, civil war, and barbarian invasion. Stark also seriously considers the role of women as distinct from men, and this suggests important avenues of future investigation. Stark addresses many important and mostly neglected aspects of the ancient Greco-Roman world.

However, Stark uses history extremely selectively, citing only what supports his conclusions. The relevant history would consume far more than this one chapter, and Stark's book likewise lacks sufficient depth. Although somewhat attentive to history, Stark also embraces speculation, using an invented data set to represent ancient demographics in place of a thorough evaluation of the historical record. While imaginative, it remains purely speculative. Quantitative data is simply not available from antiquity. Thus, I will concentrate on the substantive historical aspects and his overall argument. This chapter does not allow the space to refute each individual component.

My critique counters Stark factually, that Stark lacks the necessary knowledge of the ancient world – and theoretically – that Stark's reasoning amounts only to assumptions. Stark essentially argues that the ancients recognized Christianity as an intrinsically superior religious product that, although it required greater personal commitment and sacrifice than its pagan competitors, compensated for the greater difficulty and risk with greater rewards – earthly charity and eternal life through divine salvation. Furthermore, he argues that the strong sense of self-sacrifice deeply impressed the pagans.

In opposition, I argue that the success of Christianity compared to paganism depended not on intrinsic quality of beliefs or membership criteria, but on extrinsic politics, an argument that Elaine Pagels makes about the triumph of Christian Orthodoxy over Christian Gnosticism in the same timeframe under discussion here (Pagels [1979] 2004). In place of rational-choice theory, I offer a class and culture based theory which argues that (Orthodox) Christianity succeeded because it became a direct expression of the power interests of the ruling class, and furthermore succeeded because it assimilated, rather than replaced or destroyed, pagan cultural traditions. Christianity arose gradually, and paganism died gradually, with extensive intermingling along the way. Eventually, as Christianity became the politically dominant religion well within Stark's 300–476 CE timeframe, his "years of crisis," it enforced a religious monopoly, a fact which renders the concept of rational-choice irrelevant.

I also counter Stark's assumptions, that religion is a matter of choice. My argument follows Daniel Bell in the *Cultural Contradictions of Capitalism* ([1976] 1996) that

> the force of religion does not derive from any utilitarian quality (of self-interest or individual need); religion is not a social contract . . . The power of religion derives from the fact that . . . it was the means of gathering together, in one overpowering vessel, the sense of the sacred – that which is set apart as the collective conscience of the people. (Bell [1976] 1996:154)

Religion serves to legitimate the social relations that constitute people's lives, and thus "to say then that 'God is dead' is, in effect, to say that the social bonds have snapped and that society is dead" (Bell [1976] 1996:155). Contrary to Stark, religion is never separate from the social relations that it represents. To the extent it exerts social control or inspires rebellion, religion exists as part of the social relations between people as Robert Merton ([1949] 1967:44) argued; it is not a fashion or commodity that a person can choose to accept or discard at any moment, any more than a person can simply accept or discard the social facts that constitute society.

Section I: Rational Choice Theory in Overview

Stark's work represents the latest and boldest installment of rational-choice theory. The following overview is not a summary or literature review, but a critique of rational-choice theory.

Over the last several decades, rational choice theory has battled with a variety of other theories to explain much of human behavior. Initially, scholars applied the concept of rational choice primarily to political issues, and then primarily to social movements with political objectives. Mancur Olson's ([1964] 1971) work on social movements is a foundational and well-known example. Even before Olson, however, some argued that all modern institutions, organizations, and even beliefs and values, not just social movements, are based on rational choice, including deeply held moral values. Among these values, Buchanan and Tullock (1962) argue that even, or especially, democracy is based on what they call the "calculus of consent." Democracy consists of nothing more or less than rational calculation of cost versus benefit, both at the operational level of institutions, and within the individual who votes for candidates, agendas, etc.

Using this cost-benefit model, subsequent work expanded the range of application for rational choice theory, synthesizing the political cost-benefit concept with the cost-benefit analysis of participation in movements that Olson pioneered. This produced a more comprehensive rational-choice theory, which Hirschman (1977, 1972) used to explain that, among other things, the rise of capitalism was, in essence, preordained, as it represents the ultimate expression of rational choice. Downs (1997) for example argues that capitalism and democracy are in essence, the same thing. However, capitalist society never seems to function in the rationally perfect, meritocratic manner its many proponents predict. Clearly, simple cost-benefit explanations focused solely on political-economy could not explain all aspects of human life.

Thus, rational-choice theorists directed attention to matters other than politics and economics – towards culture – yet still with the same economic rational-choice model in mind. Francis Fukuyama, one of the foremost theorists in this area, argues that trust, more than any other factor, constitutes the basis of modern social order. Following Talcott Parsons ([1951] 1991) Fukuyama (1996) and Barbara Misztal (1996) define trust as the expectation that people in general share a common set of values which serve as the basis for routine interaction. Although this involves a degree of risk, since the assumption of commonly shared values may be wrong, it is the only way a complex and diverse society can function. We must be willing to assume the risk (which investments, whether moral or material, always entail), in order to reap the benefits. Thus, trust in the face of risk constitutes the foundational element of rational choice-making.

Quite in vogue today, rational choice theorists view the value of trust, and its associated risk, as the foundation of modern capitalism and democracy. They oppose such things as governmental regulation and affirmative action, which inherently violate the principle of trust. Since all formal systems are inherently imperfect, they contend that bureaucratization limits the dynamic potential of social beings (Cook, et al. 2003; Ostrom and Walker 2003; Seligman 2000) because ever greater bureaucratization means simultaneously ever greater imperfection. Presently, rational-choice theorists believe that not only does cost-benefit of trust and risk motivate nearly all human decision-making in society today, but Fukuyama (1996) goes so far as to argue that rational choice as a cost (risk) versus benefit calculation constitutes the natural essence of the human species. Trust guarantees nothing, but rather expands our possibilities and inherently leads to progress because it transgresses the limits of codified procedure or tradition.

Contemporary rational-choice theory thus claims dominion over all human thought and action. Politics, economics, democracy, and all manner of interaction takes place on a rational basis, in accordance with rational-choice foundation of all social laws, which arise from the natural rational-choice essence of the human species.

This applies no less to religion than anything else.

Rational Choice Theory – Properly Qualified

Rational choice theory did not begin in the social sciences, but rather, in mathematics. Early attempts include a series of papers by John Forbes Nash in his *Essays on Game Theory* ([1953] 1997). Although game theory introduced the notion of rational-choice, game theory as such remained far more modest, at least among mathematicians, whereas rational-choice theory as such moved onto its own tangent, which became more ambitious and eventually, at least among its proponents in the social-sciences, all-encompassing.

In game theory, early developers such as Nash ([1953] 1997) and Luce and Raiffa (1958) premise "the game" as a series of *moves*. Each move constitutes one possible course of action, that, when chosen, precludes the other possible courses of action. Since in most situations many moves are possible, the person makes a choice, and this selection of a particular move over and against the others depends on the available information – sometimes this information is complete, sometimes not, but the person decides the move based on whatever information they have. A sequence of choices (moves) constitutes a *play*, which in social terms would be such things as lifestyles, political or economic agendas, educational and career choices, romantic partners, and so on. Each step of the way, the person pursues a course of rational utility, such that each move-selection, each step of the way as the game proceeds, may thus be called a rational choice.

However, game theory from mathematics emphasizes one decisive point that contemporary rational-choice theorists in the social sciences utterly ignore. For game theorists, rationality, or rational-choice, depends on various mitigating factors, most importantly, one's value system, through which one evaluates the available information. In game theory, there is no such thing as abstract and universal rationality:

> Certain cautions must be maintained in interpreting this concept [rational utility]. One alternative possesses a larger utility than another because it is more preferred, not the other way around. (Luce and Raiffa 1958:38)

The issue then, is not only rationality itself, but also, what sort of values shape a person's priorities, and thus for that person (or group) which choice constitutes the *preferred* choice, and in accordance with those values, therefore, the preferred outcome. The larger utility, the more preferred choice, depends on the values that shape the decision-making framework. Expediency and cost-benefit are only two of many possible value systems. This means that there can be, and typically is, more than one type of choice and action which depend on one's frame of reference. Cost-benefit calculation is one value reference, but as Alexander Pushkin famously wrote, "Better the illusions that exalt us than a thousand mundane truths." Feeling also counts.

In sociology, Max Weber (1978:24–25) sorted out different types long ago. Weber's concept of instrumental rationality most closely resembles "rational utility" from mathematics and rational-choice theory. Weber defines instrumental rationality as actions "determined by expectations as to the behavior of objects in the environment and of other human beings. These expectations are used as conditions or means for the attainment of the actor's own rationally pursued and calculated ends" (Weber 1978:24). That is, the person holds the quickest, most efficient and expeditious path towards an objective goal as the top priority, the most expedient means of accomplishment. The goal itself is not key here, but rather, the means by which the person strives towards it. It is the rationality of calculated procedure.

In other works, namely the *Protestant Ethic and the Spirit of Capitalism*, Weber argues that instrumental rationality, an attitude of rational calculation, rose to hegemonic prominence only with the rise of increasing calculated rationality generally, and capitalism specifically (Weber [1920] 2001). For Weber, instrumental rationality is the defining logic of modernity specifically, and definitely not some universal truth of humanity, in either a social or natural state. Rational choice theorists today thus strive to prove their theory in premodern contexts, as Stark attempts with the rise of Christianity, to counter critics that rational choice (that is, utilitarian instrumental rationality) is not just a modern phenomenon, but a universal fact of social life.

As Weber argues, the rise to prominence of one type does not automatically mean the demise of the others. Throughout his career, in various speeches (See "Science as a Vocation" and "Politics as a Vocation" in Gerth and Mills 1958) and in a closing section of the *Protestant Ethic*, Weber wonders what will become of humanity if nothing else remains except narrow expert specialization and cold calculation. Consistent with his professional perspective,

Weber argues that "it would be very unusual to find concrete cases of action, especially of social action, which were oriented only in one or another of these ways" (Weber 1978:26) referring to various types of action. Subjective emotions differ fundamentally from rational calculation, such that "formulation of subjective meaning in the case of erotic attraction or of personal loyalty or any other affectual type, than for example, in the case of a business contract" (Weber 1978:28) constitute very different types of motivation and action.

The business contract is limited in scope and is itself the direct product of modern instrumental rationality. In contrast, things like erotic attraction, loyalty, and spiritual devotion are far more complex, and of a different orientation to the world. Being different, the sensibility of faith may, and often is, in conflict with the means-end, cost-benefit calculation of instrumental rationality. Thus, rational-choice theory, as constituted today, cannot explain religion (or anything else) that is not of the instrumentally rational type. Rational-choice theory also cannot explain *irrational* decision-making, but that is also beyond the scope of this chapter.

Section II: The Failure of Rational Choice Theory Regarding Religion

Therefore I contend that rational-choice theory as used in sociology and as applied to religion begins from two major mistakes, which proponents take as assumptions: 1) that instrumental rationality is a universal truth, consistent among all times and places, and that 2) choice derived from a cost benefit assessment of risk versus trust enables all social behavior, which therefore consists only of cost-benefit decisions. Thus, rational-choice theory replaces different forms of decision-making with one form only. Rational-choice theory, as Stark applies it to Christianity, depends on similar assumptions: that 1) Christianity in the crisis years of 300–476 CE was clearly and essentially different from pagan traditions, and 2) a variety of choices were available for selection in an open religious market. My critique thus approaches rational-choice explanations on theoretical grounds and historical grounds. In short, it is neither a logical possibility nor historically accurate. Let us examine Stark's key conclusions.

In the search for universal evidence outside of modern society in order to demonstrate the trans-historical accuracy of rational-choice theory, Stark argues that, since spiritual rewards associated with religion are inherently risky, rational choice is the only and inherent reaction:

> Let us now consider how humans behave when confronted with risk and choice. The initial proposition is fundamental to the whole of social science. Individuals choose their actions rationally, including those actions which concern compensators.
>
> Rational choice involves weighing the anticipated costs and benefits of actions and then seeking to act so as to maximize net benefits. (Stark 1997:169)

In this case, Stark is discussing how people responded to the many calamities that plagued Roman civilization in the final 200 or so years before its 'fall' in 476 CE. Stark seeks to explain the Christianization of the Roman world during this period. For Stark, there is no need to justify rational-choice, because in his view, consistent with the history of the concept, it is the only factor of human behavior. Thus, the answer to any question is rational-choice; one need only show how the facts fit the predetermined explanation.

Stark argues that Christianity became the dominant religion of the empire because it offered the highest benefit, yet also with relatively high cost in the form of personal sacrifice. In the view of rational-choice theory, this was not a problem because collective action such as religion always must contend with the so-called free-rider problem, which Michael Hechter claims arises when people rationally realize that, "without participating, they can still reap the benefits of other people's activity in obtaining them. If every member of the group can share in the benefits, then the rational thing to do is to free-ride rather than to help attain the corporate interest" (Hechter 1987:27). Thus, the high cost of Christianity minimized the free-rider problem, such that early Christianity attracted only truly dedicated members, who in turn functioned more efficiently for the collective interests and who therefore raised the level of benefits for the members. This enabled Christianity to triumph over paganism, which could not muster the same degree of collective dedication or effective action to confront ongoing crisis because it suffered from rampant free-riders.

The Fallacy of Cost-Benefit Explanations in Stark's Rise of Christianity

An elegantly simple theory, to be sure. It assumes a cost-benefit foundation, which then only needs to control free-rider contamination. Stark assumes strong membership criteria of self-sacrifice that greatly inhibited free-riders. Second, he assumes high-costs coincided with high-benefits, and in times of crisis, Christianity offered extensive care of the poor and various other imperiled people. Third, he assumes a clear distinction between Christianity and paganism generally. Although religious elites argued such distinctions, no clear distinction existed in practice. As we will see, many pagan sects exacted high personal sacrifices, and Christian charity for the poor is mostly a modern practice.

Furthermore, did paganism die, as rational choice theory predicts any inferior product supposedly would in a competitive market? Stark states clearly that paganism "toppled over dead" (Stark 1997:94) once and for all in the crisis years 300–476. This is definitely not true. In fact, it prospered outside the major cities of Rome, Antioch, and Constantinople for several hundred years. Indeed, as I will show, paganism did not decisively disappear, but in fact continued quite influentially through the middle-ages and the Renaissance, perhaps even into modern times.

But let us also be fair. Stark argues that Christianity offered the "most rational" choice during the crisis centuries of 300–476 CE specifically, presumably not the only rational choice (he doesn't say what the others might be). As wars, invasions, plagues, droughts, famines, and infanticide depleted the population of the Roman Empire, especially of women, the Empire became increasingly unable to tend to the very same and ongoing social problems (Stark 1997:158–160). Chaos in general and plague in particular affected everyone, Stark argues, but it was the Christians, compared to the pagans, who offered both spiritual and physical solace to the suffering and dying.

According to Stark, the personal cost was high, in that all Christians must both tend to the ill and suffering, in order to receive help themselves, both in this world, and to receive salvation in the next. First, the Christians "deeply impressed" the pagans (Stark 1997:165) with their martyrs, who sacrificed themselves for the cause of Christianity and their belief in the loving God. Christianity supposedly offered rewards in the form of relief from suffering, and a very valuable compensator (something that is not the reward itself, but indicative of a favored condition) – immortality. Those unwilling to do so are thus denied the benefits – rewards and/or compensators. The particular combination of costs and benefits we may group together as a Christian way of life (Stark 1997:168–170). The Christian way of life meant service to the general community of Christians, and in times of crisis, service to everyone in need which typically involves great self-sacrifice in exchange for the compensator of salvation.

However, no uniquely Christian character emerged for at least the first six hundred years, except that both Pagan and early Christian writers agreed that the only uniquely Christian characteristic was sexual asceticism (Pagels 1989:58). All other characteristics, such as charity, were, at best, practiced inconsistently, and many early Christians argued that asceticism was fine for beginners and simpletons, but the greatest rival to early Christian Orthodoxy, the Gnostics, rejected asceticism in favor of higher spiritual accomplishment (Pagels 1989:60). Indeed, it appears that two different and competing Christian traditions developed as early as the mid Second Century – one known as Orthodoxy and one as Gnosticism. Both relied on scripture. Orthodoxy, the version of the emerging hierarchy of bishops, priests, and deacons, followed the scriptural tradition that traced back to the Twelve Apostles, the tradition that we know today as the New Testament. The Gnostics, in contrast, relied on accounts outside the Twelve, especially texts attributed to Mary Magdalene, Thomas, James (brother of Jesus) and Paul (also in the New Testament but not an apostle). Orthodox leaders, such as Tertullian (155–230 CE), Priest of Carthage, and Irenaeus (130–202), Bishop of Lugdunum in Gaul, aggressively attacked and persecuted the Gnostics, whom they condemned as heretics. Only those who traced their doctrine and authority to the Twelve were legitimate. Orthodoxy successfully suppressed the Gnostics, such that they disappear from the historical record, except as depicted in Orthodox attacks, until the discovery of the Nag Hammadi in 1945, a collection of Gnostic Gospels and other writings (Pagels [1979] 2004). In the crisis period of which Stark speaks, each side rivaled the other in terms of membership, with Orthodoxy dominant in the West and Gnosticism in the East. Orthodoxy eventually triumphed by applying its formal hierarchal power against the egalitarian Gnostics, who eschewed all authority. Despite Constantine's attempt to unite Christian theology in a way acceptable to all sides at the Council of Nicea in 325, widespread sectarian disagreement and often violent hostility intensified as more of the empire accepted diverse versions of Christianity (see Pagels 1989:98–126).

As a result, the notion of Christian charity, for example, as a defining feature does not appear until late in the Renaissance period or even into the Eighteenth Century (Waite 2003). Care of the poor and downtrodden, although present inconsistently in earlier times, is a uniquely modern Christian mission.

Furthermore, the supposed Christian ethic of self-sacrifice as part of the ascetic lifestyle did not impress the ancients, but rather, drew mostly amusement, as Lucian describes, writing around 170 CE:

> The poor Christian wretches have convinced themselves, first and foremost, that that they are going to be immortal and live for all time, in consequence of which they despise death and even willingly give themselves into custody, most of them. Furthermore, their first lawgiver [Jesus] persuaded them that they are all brothers of one another . . . by worshipping that crucified sophist himself and living under his laws. (Lucian of Samosata [c. 170 CE] 2001:15)

And so it appears that ancient pagans viewed Christians much as Stark believes. Yet Lucian does not admire their brotherhood and selflessness; on the contrary:

> Therefore they despise all things indiscriminately and consider all things common property, receiving their doctrines of faith without any evidence. So if any charlatan and trickster, able to profit by occasions, comes among them, he quickly acquires sudden wealth by imposing upon these simple folk. (Lucian of Samosata [c. 170 CE] 2001:15)

Rational-choice theory argues that the bane of all collective action is the free-riders, those who participate minimally but seek to accrue maximum benefit. Lucian observes that free-riders easily impose themselves on the Christians and even "acquire sudden wealth" whereas Stark, without references, argues that in the case of Christianity, "sacrifice and stigma mitigate the free-rider problems faced by religious groups" (Stark 1997:177) because they raise the costs of association. That is, a person must accept the stigma of being identified as a member, and also sacrifice of themselves. This raises the value of membership. Yet in addition to Lucian's testimony, and contrary to popular belief, the Romans persecuted Christians very irregularly, having killed only hundreds of people over roughly three hundred years of time, not thousands of people (Frend 1965:413). Moreover, patricians like Constantine the Great experienced neither stigma nor sacrifice upon his conversion shortly after October 28, 312 CE (battle of the Milvian bridge). If anything, his move towards Christianity only solidified his political power. It would seem that unscrupulous free-riders could readily exploit early Christians.

Even beyond the free-rider problem, Stark argues that the pagan world was crowded with far too many religious commodities, that the market was saturated with a dizzying array of choices as the result of "excessive pluralism" (Stark 1997:197). Christianity thus appeared as a superior product, because its monotheistic belief system clearly distinguished itself in comparison to pagan plurality. This only increased the value of Christian rewards, because it made them rare by comparison. A simple case of supply and demand. The religious marketplace would select Christianity because demand for this superior product would be high, and the market would likewise render paganism extinct as demand disappeared.

Factually, this did not happen. We know that Christianity triumphed, but we must avoid "the quite crude error of supposing the now familiar outline to have been already clear in the Fourth Century" (MacMullen 1981:136). If Christianity offered some special reward that would motivate great personal risk, it was not charity for the poor and succor for the sick and lonely. Stark's assertion that membership in early Christian groups was high in terms of personal sacrifice is likely not accurate. Barraclough, for example, shows that sincerity in Christian devotion for centuries often amounted to "the untaught, wandering prophet, naked and dirty, who appears often to have been regarded as a prophet simply because he was an unbalanced lunatic" (Barraclough 1976:24). Indeed, it was the ease of membership, rather than the trials and tribulations, that appealed to ruling elites who could convert easily, yet make a strong political statement in the process. Comparatively, the personal cost to join any number of pagan cults was often much higher. For any particular cult, initiation might require castration, self-flagellation, poisoning, lacerations, serving others in humility, or any number of combinations that often endured for days or even weeks (Turcan 1996). After initiation, ancient cults required regular demonstration of devotion, which typically involved repeated trials as well as monetary contributions. Again, Christianity was in practice simply one of many sects that exacted some form of commitment, and offered certain rewards in return, no greater or substantially different from the others.

We will return to a more likely motivation later (politics), but for now, we must reject Stark's further assumption that the Great Conversion of 313 CE (the year Constantine legalized Christianity) meant a decisive death for paganism.

The Fallacy that Paganism Simply Died

In reality, it is difficult to overestimate the enduring influence of pre-Christian (i.e. pagan) beliefs and practices. Despite "laws against sacrifices, seizures of idols by the state, and so back through the crowded chronicles of violence to suppress paganism . . . The pagans survived, unterrified" (MacMullen 1981:134). Many communities beyond the major cities in the late empire – Rome, Antioch, and Constantinople – refused to convert to Christianity, even when threatened with death and even when death was delivered. For example, as late as the Byzantine emperor Justinian (527–565 CE), successful warlord and devout Christian, conquered the southern half of the Italian peninsula, he discovered that the people still retained many pagan beliefs, including polytheism, and still celebrated many pagan holidays. He executed or starved out thousands to force conversion to Christianity, to little avail. Similarly, he and his successors never converted the communities of the African Mediterranean coast; they retained many pagan beliefs and practices well into the 1300s, long after even the Muslim conquest of the area, although the Muslim method of rule was far more civilized, and did not require conversion to Islam.

Ramsay MacMullen documents numerous pagan towns and communities well into the 800s CE, especially in Spain, rural Italy, and nearly all of North Africa (MacMullen 1997:74–77). Despite the best efforts of Roman and Byzantine emperors and their bishops, priests, and lay people to eradicate pagan cults, they endured. In fact, the ongoing pressure and frequent violence to crush paganism only increased its fervor. On numerous occasions, the local populace organized and resisted pressure and even military campaigns to defend their pagan cults. Where rational choice theory predicts its easy disappearance, paganism continued.

Furthermore, recent evidence now shows conclusively that paganism actually survived, if diminished, throughout the middle-ages, in nearly all parts of Europe if not elsewhere (Hutton 1999, 1991). The most popular rites and festivals were incorporated into Christianity, but also existed alongside of, and as far as church leaders were concerned, in opposition to Christianity. For example, the kalends, celebration common to nearly all of pagan Europe and the middle-east (MacMullen 1997:39) continued into the 700s if not later. Indeed, Boniface reports in 742 that "the annual parading, singing, shouting, and loaded banquet tables in the open squares in Rome around St. Peter's Cathedral on the traditional date follows the pagan custom" (cited in MacMullen 1997:37). The kalends are preserved today in festivals such as Mardi Gras in New Orleans and Carnevale in Rio de Janeiro. Although paganism lost its organizational structure, it assimilated into Christian culture as folk medicine, herbology, wise women and cunning men skilled in the arcane and often very practical arts of midwifery and animal husbandry.

Many places celebrated the solstices, equinoxes, and other times of the seasons perhaps to modern times. Even in the vehemently Christian Byzantine

Empire, celebrations such as the Maiouma (month-long nude bathing) in spring to celebrate the return of warm weather continued until at least the early 600s. Clearly, pagan culture lived well beyond the demise of pagan Rome, and shaped the cultural development of Christianity from its beginnings as an ascetic cult into the ostentatious pageantry and embrace of life by the time of the Renaissance. Indeed, the Renaissance – the Rebirth – was a rebirth of the ancient pagan arts and sciences, architecture, sculpture, and philosophy. For our purposes, this demonstrates that the relationship between paganism and Christianity was not an either/or proposition. Various and often competing priorities would eventually lead to a Christian Europe, yes, but along numerous and changing paths. Clearly, more than just rational calculation of gain and loss was in play.

Rural areas beyond Mediterranean Europe accepted Christianity only nominally, and blended it with many traditional pagan and folk beliefs and practices, including animal husbandry and farming (Kieckhefer 1989), herbology and medieval medicine (Barstow 1994), and trade guilds (Hutton 1999). Whether threatened with forced conversion or allowed to live peacefully, people held fast to deeply held paganism, both as a belief and as a tradition. If paganism was instrumentally irrational because it meant censure from office in both the east and west, confiscation of land and title, or death, it certainly proved its worth for much of the population in terms of emotional commitment. Using Bell's framework introduced earlier, the bonds of pagan society had not snapped, and hence its religious expression continued.

The Problem of Distinguishing Christianity

Long assumed that decisive dates could mark the end of one age and the beginning of another, Jonathan Smith instead identifies the inherent problems with such attempts, most of which rely on literature, written by Christian apologists. Most relevant here, the notion that pagan Rome ended with Constantine or with the final collapse of the imperial government in the West in 476 CE, and furthermore, that Christianity introduced a radically new system of beliefs and ethics that relied on the assumption that linguistical evidence, namely, scripture and related ancient documents, manifest actual radical change in society (Smith 1990). Smith demonstrates that such conclusions based on linguistical data are simply false, and arose from the pre-conceived belief that Christian scripture reflected a new and utterly unique religion (Smith 1990:37–53).

Beliefs likewise prove nothing. Indeed, notions of heaven, for example, the ultimate reward in Christianity, derived from various pagan sources, and continued to evolve in the Christian era, and thus no distinctly Christian notion of the after life exists separately from other religious cultures or the ongoing effect of time and place (McDannell and Lang 2001). As Riley indicates, historians have long since rejected the "Israel-alone" model (Riley 2001:5) in favor of syncretic explanations that Christianity formed from a synthesis of Judaism in combination with Greco-Roman and Syrian paganism and Persian Zoroastrianism. Both the pagan origins and effects of time and place on Christian thought, art, and literature are well-documented, as for example in a general perspective in the classic texts by Edward Gibbon ([1776] 1993) and in detail by Seznec ([1953] 1995) concerning the Renaissance period, which beyond artistic rebirth contributed to a new sense of humanism that Christianity has accepted only intermittently.

Even the most cherished aspects of Christian belief, such as the creation story, were adapted from paganism in both symbolism and morality (Pagels 1989) and the conflict between light and dark, good and evil, God and Satan derives from various pagan and non-Western sources (Messadie 1996) and especially from Zoroastrianism (Boyce [1979] 2001; Nigosian 1993; Riley 2001) which itself had assimilated and thus altered over time many other traditions, especially Manichaeanism (Stoyanov 2000). Even the Cain versus Abel story derives from the ancient Roman myth about how Romulus, who founded Rome, slew his brother Remus to become sole ruler of the Latins. Moreover, Romulus and Remus were twins, whose parents were the God Mars and the mortal Rhea Silvia, a Vestal Virgin (Titus Livius, 'Livy' c. 12 CE, cited in Lewis and Reinhold 1966:52–53). The Christian version parallels the Divine paternity and virgin maternity, with the difference that Romulus becomes a hero compared to Cain the apostate.

Thus, the development of and transition to Christianity was not a seamless linear series of instrumentally rational choices. Indeed, the affective- and value-rational choice to remain true to tradition and identity often prevailed over the instrumentally rational choice of submitting to the demands of the church and its champions. Under Christian oppression, the instrumental costs of paganism where high and its benefits low,[1] yet it persisted. Even after 312

[1] The benefits were low in the sense it delivered nothing beyond what people already had. In contrast, conversion to Christianity offered elevation in social status,

CE when Constantine created a Christian monopoly based on the Orthodox view, and later emperors actively suppressed a free religious market, paganism endured.

Crucially, Christianity blended with both Roman politics and culture, with great variations from one locale to another, which often led to bitter conflict among Christians. Indeed, the split between east and west after the fall of Rome in 476 CE followed every possible fissure: political, economic, cultural, linguistical, and of course, religious (Angold 2001:38–48). Christians of various types (including Catholic, Orthodox, Gnostic, monophysite, triphysite, and others) struggled both alongside and against each other (Pagels [1979] 2004), but also alongside and against Muslims and Pagans. Despite elite efforts on all sides for theological purity, and observable trends between east and west, the various religions of the era influenced each other syncretically. In all the major expressions of social life, such as art and culture (Soucek 1997; Tabbaa 1986; Thomas 1997; Thomson 1978; Vryonis 1997, 1985), economics and politics (Angold 2001; Nicol [1972] 1993; Norwich 1995; Runciman 1990), and religion (Cunningham 2002) east, west, Christianity, Paganism, and Islam each shaped the others. This blending is not a modern recreation of the past, but in fact a process recognized in medieval times as well, as for example in *The Alexiad* by Anna Comnena ([1120] 1969).

Thus it seems impossible to argue that Christianity somehow represented a unique and totally new system of belief, morality, or practice. Although some Roman cults were definitely elite institutions (especially the Emperor cults), many also appealed to and attracted the masses as Turcan (1996) shows regarding the cults of Mithra and Isis, for example, which embraced charity and the concept of everlasting life for its members (Meyer [1987] 1999). These cults offered a sense of meaning and belonging to the many displaced people in the major cities of the late Roman Empire (Turcan 1996:26). In this context, Christianity was one of many cults offering succor in this world and redemption in the next, provided that followers appeased the relevant god(s).

I contend, therefore, that the rational-choice factor of cost-benefit in times of loneliness or crisis is refuted. This aspect was not unique, or even primary, to Christianity. Indeed, Christianity would not develop a distinctive charac-

---

Imperial appointments, money, land, and power as rewards. None of this, however, made significant inroads in many areas for several hundred years, and even now, regional and local syncretic variations typify Christianity.

ter for several hundred years, and thus did not constitute a special commodity in a crowded marketplace of innumerable and undifferentiated pagan offerings during the crisis years of 300–476. Lastly, paganism did not clearly die but continued to influence Western civilization long after Christianity rose to dominance. The socio-historical facts do not support rational-choice theory as applied to the ancient world and the rise of Christianity. Yet, the discussion is not complete. Let us also build a theoretical counter-argument.

Section III: Multi-Dimensional Social Action

The Role of Class

Rather than assume that instrumental choice is a universal truth, I offer first a class distinction. Rational choice explains mostly the behavior of the ruling class, who have the power of choice at their disposal. For the subordinate classes, most of life is not a choice, but a fact of birth. As Angus noted long ago, the main benefit of Christianity after Constantine's acclamation was consistent with ancient pre-Christian practice; in the ancient world, "the attitude of that age toward authority was altogether different from that of the present day. The tendency of the age was to seek authority and rest in it" (Angus [1928] 1975:298). Through its attachment to the ruling classes in the Empire, Christianity gained newfound authority and thus attracted members on that basis. Far from a popular movement that rationally broke with the past, Christianity arose to dominance in the traditional Roman manner – association with power.

Thus, the assumption that Christian charity maximized the cost-benefit equation to favor active participation in early Christianity pretends that class inequality did not exist. Wealthy and powerful Romans had a much higher survivability in times of crisis (Chadwick [1967] 1993; MacMullen 1997) because they isolated themselves in vast estates far from the squalid and diseased urban areas. Indeed, early Christianity consisted mostly of patricians, not freemen or slaves (Martin 1990). As Martin shows, the metaphorical use of "slavery" in early Christianity applied to spiritual, not worldly relations, and thus imposed no particular constraints or obligations on the elite converts.

It is difficult to imagine, as Stark readily assumes, that Christians from the patrician class would directly give of themselves to alleviate the suffering of a member of the lower classes simply because their new religion dictated so.

Clearly, this did not happen in Christian Byzantium (Norwich 1989), the direct descendent of Christian Rome – they called themselves Romanaioi (the Romans) – and which maintained for over 1100 years (May 11, 330–May 29, 1453 CE) the same economic class and social status structure as ancient Rome. Although the Byzantine Empire maintained certain social institutions for the poor, such as an orphanage in Constantinople, a communal system of grain distribution, and a pension for soldier's widows (Norwich 1995), the concept of *personal* sacrifice for the poor, or as Stark argues, the notion of *personally* ministering to the needy, was unknown.

As the first Christian emperor (reigned 312–337 CE), Constantine the Great neither practiced nor encouraged anything even remotely approaching Christian charity and self-sacrifice. He and his successors, going all the way through the Byzantine period (476–1453 CE), wielded Christianity in typically Roman fashion – as a calculated instrument of control. Christianity survived and prospered because the ruling class upheld it, not because it ministered to the poor, plagued, and downtrodden masses. Rome and Byzantium survived for a collective 2100 or so years because the class structure survived, and the ruling class used its wealth and power to raise new armies or buy the loyalty of neighboring rulers, and at the same time used its military power to crush popular movements that threatened class privilege. In fact, the entire Byzantine period, the first and longest lived Christian empire, endured numerous internal battles, all of which pitted one elite group against another; there were no popular uprisings (Nicol [1972] 1993; Norwich 1995) in the name of religion. Elites invoked Christianity in the service of empire, and not to mitigate deprivation and oppression.

Stark is correct, that the elevation of Christianity as the new official religion of the Empire meant the political and economic demise of pagan temples and the priestly class (Stark 1997:199), especially after its ascendance in the Byzantine Empire. Yet Christianity did not prosper as a grass-roots movement as Stark depicts it, but moved significantly beyond the ruling class only after Constantine the Great (306–337 CE) decriminalized Christianity with the Edict of Milan in 313, and embraced it officially at the Council of Nicea in 325, although he did not do so personally until his deathbed (he was a Mithraist). Like Constantine, subsequent emperors realized the political utility of Christianity, as it now served as a loyalty test not to the one God, but to the emperor (Chadwick [1967] 1993). Constantine's successors, namely Constantine II, Constantius II, Constans, Valentinian, Valens, and Gratian all used Christianity like a bludgeon against political opponents, but not against opponents of Christianity specifically; they left pagan temples intact and priests alive. Not until Theodosius I in 392 does the emperor appear to hold Christianity as a goal in-itself (Norwich 1995), and not again until Justinian in the 500s. Although some subsequent emperors were personally pious, politics usually subsumed their piety.

If the emperors viewed Christianity in an instrumentally-rational fashion, they did so as characteristically Roman patricians and as emperors – the champion of the ruling patrician class. Far from showing Christian charity, late Roman and subsequent Byzantine emperors crushed peasant rebellions as ruthlessly as their pagan Roman predecessors crushed slave rebellions and barbarian uprisings. Even for the adherents from the lower classes, Christianity maintained the familiar social structure of Greco-Roman society in metaphorical terms (Martin 1990) even as it broke from other cultural traditions, namely, paganism. Still, Byzantium maintained the Hellenistic aspects of ancient society (Runciman 1987) and after the fall of Constantinople in 1453, intellectual refugees carried Hellenism back to the West and reintegrated it with Christianity to inspire the Renaissance (Runciman 1990).

Therefore, political gain and class dominance explains only the Imperial appeal of Christianity as an instrumentally rational tool of hegemony. The fact that numerous openly pagan beliefs and practices continued for centuries into the Christian era indicates that paganism offered something of value also. That is, it offered a different kind of rationality, or actually two kinds – traditional and affectual – neither of which exists in contemporary rational-choice theory.

The Role of Culture

Traditional celebrations in particular, especially when practiced in the face of persecution, indicate a deeper and more profound orientation to life than instrumental rationality. To sing, dance, laugh, feast, bathe nude, and, in general, to enjoy being alive, indicates a happiness and gratification in being human and alive in the world. In contrast to the dour and ascetic early Christian theologians (Pagels 1989), the pagan communities cherished life in this world, and through their celebrations, expressed contentment with life and the worldview that legitimated the social order, which sociologically is the celebration of idealized community (Berger [1967] 1990; Durkheim ([1912] 1995). If the temples were the domain of the priests, the larger pagan culture they represented was certainly the domain of popular participation in mass festivals (Ryan 1999). Although we do not know exactly what common people believed, they liked it enough to celebrate it several times a year.

Class and culture are always bound together, and no less so in ancient times. Even though the ruling class converted to Christianity, this conversion did not much change Roman/Byzantine Imperial culture. Similarly, official conversion to Christianity, nor in combination with extensive and persistent Christian efforts to convert the masses did not readily alter long-held traditional beliefs and celebrations. They still maintained the old festivals and rituals.

Beyond celebrations, evidence now suggests that natural philosophy, or what we now know as science, was associated with pagan mysteries from the fifth century to the Renaissance (MacMullen 1997) and thus continued in the middle-ages as magic or other arcane art. In the witch persecutions of 1450–1650 (Trevor-Roper 1969), the people typically persecuted were primarily unmarried or widowed women in cottage businesses, such as beer, bread, butter making, spinning, weaving, healing and midwifery (Barstow 1994) – all traditional roles for women. The healing/midwifery practitioners in particular were known as "wise-women," who some now believe possessed ancient knowledge associated with what medieval society understood as natural magic, itself a product of non-Christian, pagan mystery-cult traditions (Kieckhefer 1989). Also persecuted were "cunning men" whose skills pertained to animal husbandry and crop production – traditional roles for peasant men. Despite that fact that witch hunters translated the ancient practices into Christian imagery of Satan and Evil, the practices of pre-Christian knowledge and the associated class and gender roles remained from ancient times.

Thus, paganism as a cultural tradition, whether viewed positively or negatively, involved many cultural practices beyond a set of beliefs. Advanced, natural and philosophical knowledge was, even several hundred years later, viewed as pagan (and often interpreted as anti-Christian). Conceptual and practical knowledge, art, and joy of living were embodied as pagan, not as Christian traditions (Comnena [1120] 1969; Hutton 1999). Whatever belief a person may subscribe to during a crisis, these are only momentary associations, compared to their ongoing beliefs during routine times which reflect their history and social location – the traditions of their class and culture – the foundations of any society.

Class and Culture Convergence

To understand the rise of Christianity, we must understand two concepts that are much more complex than instrumental choice: 1) spirituality and 2) social conflict. Beginning with spirituality, Peter Berger ([1967] 1990) observes that spirituality, and the religious institutions that arise from it, are always an attempt to create meaning, an attempt to arrange the realities of life into a coherent unity with purpose and meaning. Chief among these realities is death. Regardless of how we live, we all die, and through spirituality, people seek to create meaning, and thereby emotional comfort, in order to live and, of course, to face death with some degree of reassurance. As long as death remains, as Shakespeare ([c. 1601] 1963) said, "the undiscovered country from whose bourn no traveler returns . . ." and which "puzzles the will" (Hamlet, III, I:79–80) so people will need spirituality in one form or another to make sense of the ultimate reality of life, which is death. Without a sense of meaning, the fact of death would render life absurd.

Thus, spirituality is a set of beliefs that connect the individual to a community, and in turn to a sense of being or purpose that transcends the individual and the mundane. In this way, people reassure themselves, through collective belief, that life is more than a series of events that ends in death, but part of something eternal, something important, something that assures the individual a place in this world, and in some larger scheme of being.

Spirituality is thus crucial for the long-term survival of any community, because it not only justifies the particular values and lifestyle of a community, but reinforces purpose and meaning, and thus connects the present with the past and future. Spiritual beliefs are thus the collective totality of social beliefs, which, precisely because they are collective and derived from social, not individual existence, appear to the individual as eternal and transcendent truths, as something outside of and beyond the individual, and which must, in a progressive form, empower the individual as an active member of the very same community. Thus humans create a feeling of the supernatural, of spiritual connections beyond what can be directly observed.

In the classic *Sacred Canopy* ([1967] 1990), Peter Berger identifies the central aspect of spirituality, deistic or not, as its ability to construct and maintain a nomos – a belief system that explains the meaning of life. This nomos arises specifically from actual social relations as well as visions of society as it ought to be. Without a nomos, a society falls into alienation and a-nomie (without values that explain the meaning of life),[2] which produces diverse and extensive social problems. For example, Native-Americans continued to live after Europeans destroyed their civilizations, but now, they lived as strangers in a homeland that was now a strange land, stripped of political power as well as cultural and personal identity.

Yet a firmly accepted nomos builds societies and can hold a social group together despite intolerance and persecution. Numerous historical examples exist: Christians under ancient Rome; the Jews in the Diaspora after 70 CE until the twentieth century; African-Americans during the civil rights struggle, the same aforementioned Native-Americans who rediscovered their cultural heritage – all of which united with a specifically religious nomos. Transcendent beliefs function affirmingly only to the extent they embody material conditions and promote realization of the self in conjunction with social interests. Thus, social conflict becomes relevant.

In Weber's well-known and often misunderstood *Protestant Ethic and the Spirit of Capitalism,* Weber argues that ascetic Protestantism became *both an expression of and justification for* material conditions, both socially and personally. Ideals and morality – religious or otherwise, arise from and in turn govern social life.

Similarly in Marxist perspective, in both socially specific and general terms, religion maintains social order through morals, customs, rituals, and belief about how the world ought to be (Marx [1843] 1978a:53) which, in oppressive forms, also justifies the world as it currently is. It connects the individual to established social order, and furthermore, justifies the established order as sacred and therefore inviolate. To rebel against the divine is to rebel against the established social order; the sacred virtues of the ruling class are the sacred virtues of heaven.

Thus, oppressive religion reflects an inverted social order, in which those who own property or hold title stand over those who work and actually build society. Since conscious realization of this inversion tends to challenge the

[2] Durkheim uses anomie in this sense, and not in the general sense of normlessness. The anomic person is normless, but specifically lacks a sense of meaning and purpose, but may have other norms and values. As Durkheim argues, anomie is found most intensely in successful business executives, who have a powerful normative standard – making money and having fun – but who lack a sense of meaning. In essence, Durkheim argues that money can buy property and thrills, but not happiness (See Durkheim [1897] 1979:247–250 and 253–257).

related hierarchy, religion places the Truth of existence beyond the grasp of real people, and into the hands of a supreme and unreachable being, into the hands of God, whose earthly representation is religion as an authoritative institution. Since religion, like any other institution, is inherently a socially constructed entity, the "struggle against religion is, therefore, indirectly a struggle against that world whose spiritual aroma is religion" (Marx [1843] 1978a:54). Thus, the struggle is against religion that supports – or fails to challenge – the established order of and suffering in this world. To the extent religious devotion is a form of compensatory satisfaction, Marx maintains that "religious suffering is at the same time an expression of real suffering and a protest against real suffering" (Marx [1843] 1978a54). It is thus not simply a drug or a diversion, but a type of insurance against popular discontent, and at the same time, an expression of the very same discontent and suffering. However much religion may pacify the masses, it also embodies their discontent. Class hierarchy cannot justify itself; it requires some other transcendent legitimization, whether God, Nature, The Nation, etc.

Despite the potential of religion to thwart political, economic, legal, and social change in general, Marx nevertheless relates religion as ideology directly to real dissatisfaction, to real suffering that arises from the inequality of life:

> Religion is the sigh of the oppressed creature, the sentiment of a heartless world, and the soul of soulless conditions . . . The abolition of the illusory happiness of men, is a demand for their real happiness. The call to abandon their illusions is a call to abandon the conditions which require illusions. (Marx [1843] 1978a:54)

The crucial point then follows that the task of Marxism is, "once the other-world of truth has vanished, to establish the truth of this world" and furthermore, to "unmask human self-alienation in its secular form now that it has been unmasked in its sacred form" (Marx [1843] 1978a:54). Marx addresses the criticism of religion toward those religious institutions that mask the suffering of this world, that maintain the oppression of this world, for the sake of a supposed truth from the "other-world" when in reality, the ruling class projects its legitimacy through religion in order to maintain its material advantage.

Rather than a general broadside and universal condemnation, Marx's attack on religion seems particularly focused; Marx criticizes the role of religion within particular social contexts, with particular social ramifications. He does not condemn all religion simply for being religious. For Marx, religion becomes oppressive to the extent it presents a universal and eternal truth over which an omnipotent and implacable Divinity presides. In this context, humans can only submit to such formidable power, and in turn, people can only submit to the authority of the real world. In this way, idealism dominates social life, such that real lives of real people become irrelevant.

In contrast to rational-choice theory, which acknowledges only one basis of thought and action, the Marxist tradition acknowledges the interaction of many social factors, especially class and culture. Following Marx and Weber, Bourdieu pursues through his concepts of symbolic power (1980) and cultural capital (1993, 1991, 1985) as a means to transcend the idealism-materialism dichotomy. For Bourdieu, culture – the realm of symbolic expression – strongly interacts with economics – the realm of class hierarchy – to shape society (1993, 1991, [1980] 1990). To the extent economics and culture are inseparable, theory and practice must likewise account for both sources of power, and in life, people require both economic means and cultural legitimization to live.

Similarly, Walter Benjamin noted that socialism "would never have entered the world if its proponents had sought only to excite the enthusiasm of the working class for a better order of things . . . Marx understood how to interest the workers in a social order which would both benefit them and appear to them as just" (Benjamin [c. 1927] 1999:395). Although socialism is a modern concept, the point applies to the ancient and medieval world under discussion, in that commitment to something new requires a sense of justice, that people will not commit to major changes in life just because it is abstractly rational. Although Christianity presented opportunities for the ruling class, the many practices and routines that included paganism remained just and meaningful for the masses, based on their logic of affect and tradition.

In other words, the rise of Christianity is relatively straightforward once one understands the forces of class and culture. As the legitimating belief system of the ruling class, Christianity served to enforce both elite submission to higher elites, and to enforce submission of the lower classes to the elite classes. Christianity only spread through the lower classes to the extent it assimilated or only gradually permeated established traditions and thus reflected and reinforced the reality of commoner life. Christianity required several hundred years to rise to popular social dominance beyond its initial political dominance.

Final Thoughts

In conclusion, rational-choice theory argues a simplistic version of instrumental-rationality. History, on the other hand, presents numerous complex events and processes that exhibit value-, affect-, and traditional rationality as well. Differentiating the types of rationality at work are a step up in sophistication, and especially in the case of the non-instrumental types, those not driven by immediate personal gain, require much greater attention and subtlety of analysis. Rational choice theory explains nothing about the origin of values, who benefits and who suffers, what the role of values in social order might be, and the relationship of values to their social realities, such as the distribution of wealth status, and power.

In the end, rational-choice theory is simply an expression of modern market-oriented rationality – the logic of late capitalism. It perhaps explains some things about religion today, and if it does, then the social bonds have snapped and society is dead. But Stark seriously stretches credulity to suggest that market relations in the United States explain religion in antiquity. Christianity did supersede paganism, but not perfectly, nor did it transform ancient culture or class relations. The patrician class often chose Christianity, but most other people had it forced on them. For those who refused to surrender their pagan traditions, Christianity obtained a compromise – change your beliefs and acknowledge the Christian God (and most importantly, his earthly ruler) as supreme, and you may continue with your pagan celebrations. In order to support their pre-determined rational-choice conclusions, Stark and others focus on moments of crisis, and in so doing overlook the social foundations of Roman pagan and early Christian society that define social relations over extended periods of time. At best, rational-choice theory explains choices people might make in a moment of crisis, when they seek the most expedient solution to an immediate problem.

But religion pertains to far more than crisis situations and the expediency of the moment. It addresses such things as the meaning of life, of things that can only be felt, of emotions, identity, and purpose, issues not immediately or easily answered unless one puts aside instrumental rationality in favor of other approaches. Like all things social, religion depends on what has come before, and develops syncretically and dialectically with the past; the rise and fall of institutions like religion do not hinge on instrumental decisions made in a moment, once and for all. Religious thought and practice develops over time, and changes with the times. One need only read *The Gorgias* or *The*

Apology by Socrates or the Vedic *Upanishads* to see Christian thinking – several hundred years before Christ. The task for scholars then is to identify the complex interaction of important variables of time and place, the social factors that define an age: the institutions of power and the forces of change. In comparison, rational-choice theory attempts to make the facts fit the narrow bounds of a simplistic theory which, in this case, amounts to little more than the ideology of modern capitalism.

Bonnie Wright and Anne Warfield Rawls

Speaking in Tongues: A Dialectic of Faith and Practice

We report on a six year ethnographic/ethnomethodological study of the local order details of religious services at two Assemblies of God (Pentecostal) Churches in Detroit, a major metropolitan area in the American Mid-West.[1] The research was designed to explore the relationship between local *Interaction Orders* of practices in details (Rawls 1987; Goffman 1983; Garfinkel 2002) and institutional orders of belief, narrative and account (Mills 1940; Durkheim 1912). The difference between an ethnomethodological and a more traditional ethnographic study is that ethnography aims for descriptions that illuminate the meanings, beliefs and values of actors and actions involved in the situations they study. Ethnomethodology, by contrast, focuses on those details that constitute the ways in which participants make their actions recognizable to one another as actions to which meaning, belief and value can be assigned in conventional ways. While beliefs are generally considered to be both the motivating and the organizing force behind religious behavior, we argue that local orders of religious practice are constitutive of beliefs – as they are of any meaning – and thus ultimately that practices are what give religion coherence and sustain shared belief.

[1] While extensive field observations were made in the two Assemblies of God Churches, the Full Bible Baptist Church was given considerably less attention and used primarily as a point of comparison with regard to practices associated with the speaking of tongues.

In this chapter we focus in particular on speaking in tongues, praise and prophecy as local orders of practice. Following Garfinkel's ([1948]2005) argument that action only has meaning if it achieves a recognizable order, we look for the ways in which the religious rituals we observed were made orderly and recognizable by participants (pastors and worshipers) for one another, as an ongoing matter, and not as a process of interpretation in a context of belief. In so doing, we treat actions that were incongruous – or problematic – to participants, as clues to the order properties of ordinary taken-for-granted action. Actions sanctioned as inappropriate demonstrate that beliefs and motives are not enough. It is necessary for participants to produce a recognizable form of practice.

In an attempt to access the constitutive details of recognizable and appropriate practice in the churches we studied, our analysis focuses on four cases of tongues, praise and prophecy (expressions of the Holy Spirit) which were treated as inappropriate by the congregations and their pastors. Through an analysis of these failed practices we attempt to elucidate the orders of detail that constitute recognizable and appropriate practices in each situation. When practices do not achieve a recognizable form, beliefs and motives are questioned and the participant sanctioned. In showing what does not count, such sanctions allow the researcher to observe and record the details of what does.

Recognizability is a key aspect of appropriateness. Practices must be recognizable in their details – as what is expected – before other parishioners can *recognize* them as appropriate expressions of belief in particular religious contexts. Participants only trust one another, and accept one another's actions as authentic, to the extent that they are able to produce practices that are recognizable as the expected and acceptable ones for "just this" local congregational situation. Trust – even in this religious and faith relevant context – is not based on beliefs, but on the ability to demonstrate competence in, and commitment to, the local orders of practice in which the others are also engaged.

In taking up the relationship between beliefs and practice we elaborate on an old difference between Weber and Durkheim over the relative importance of beliefs and practices. While Weber emphasized interpretive contexts of belief, Durkheim argued that practices come first, both as a logical and a historical matter, and that not understanding this had led, among other things, to ethnocentricism and the idea that western religions were superior because of their beliefs (Durkheim 1912; Rawls 2005). When beliefs are treated as the essence of religion, non-western religions that focus on practices and do not have a central deity, do not appear to be religions at all. Weber classified these forms of practice as "magic." From Durkheim's perspective this was a serious mistake. Because the essence of religion lies in its practices, Durkheim argued that the distinction between religion and magic must be based on an analysis of practices and not beliefs. According to Durkheim the popular view that religions are superior is wrong. The mistake results from not recognizing the priority of practice over belief. Durkheim had argued earlier, in *The Division of Labor in Society* (1895) that it was only through the development of social relations in which practices had once again been set free to run ahead of beliefs that modern western society showed the promise of progressing toward justice and democracy.

When the distinction between beliefs and practices becomes a focus it is apparent that practice and belief stand in a tension with one another that is essentially dialectical. This was Durkheim's position in *The Elementary Forms of The Religious Life* (Durkheim 1912; Rawls 2005). He argued that while accounts and beliefs can be achieved and sustained only through practice – once they have been achieved, beliefs (and their adherents) tend to treat practices as unimportant. Practices are no longer allowed to "run ahead" of beliefs, but become constrained by them. This is true not only in religion, but, as Garfinkel points out, is a characteristic of theoretical thinking in general (Garfinkel [1948]2006). For various reasons ideas have a strong tendency to obscure their own origins. Marx ([1845]1956) Durkheim (1912) and Garfinkel ([1948]2005) each took scholars to task for uncritically allowing this tendency to influence their thinking. They point out that social relationships in material details are the actual causes of social phenomena, and the cause of ideas – not the reverse.

Treating beliefs and narrative accounts as the causes of social orders, reifies ideas that result from social relations of practices and treats ideas as the cause of those social relations that create them. This inversion creates a false picture of practices that not only sustains the idea that religious beliefs are independent of the collective practice of religion, but also that social processes in general are in some profound way independent of the details of the local order practices that produce them. Most social science is based on this premise: the importance of generalizeability being just one indication. By contrast, both Marx and Durkheim advocated an approach to the study of social relations that focused on underlying relations concretely. Garfinkel argued that allowing *any* conceptual reification to *direct* the study of social order would result in that order remaining obscured by an overlay of abstraction.

Practices and Intelligibility: Inadequacy of Rules and Beliefs

Although it continues to be acceptable to explain social order and meaning as a matter of following rules, or being driven by institutionalized beliefs and values, the problems with this approach, first raised by Wittgenstein and C. Wright Mills in the 1930s, have not been resolved. In fact, it has become increasingly clear that the rule/belief driven view of social order and meaning is inadequate (Rawls 2002; 2003).[2] Rules cannot be followed and, therefore, a model of social order based on the idea of following rules, or conforming to beliefs, results in a problematic degree of abstraction, interpretation and contingency. The post modern abyss is one result of continuing to approach the problem of order and meaning in this way. Order is represented as comprised of actors' motives to use rules or conform to beliefs, or of institutions imposing conceptual frames, rather than viewing the problem of achieving recognizable orders of action (including rules and beliefs) in any particular situation as a serious problem in its own right, that carries its own order properties and, hence, motivation.

In spite of the seriousness of the debate over rules, most sociologists continue to proceed on the basis of the view that beliefs and conceptual typifications, or rules, drive both action and meaning. Studies of social phenomena then attempt to measure the effect of beliefs and values (variable

---

[2] A note on this complicated issue of rules seems in order at the outset. Beliefs, rules, concepts and institutions, or an institutionally driven view of social order, are being equated in this analysis. What is meant is that such approaches assume that an abstract conceptual formulae of some kind more or less guides action in some way. Either people try to follow it as a rule or principle, or are guided by, or to, it as a goal. In either case there is some conceptual type or category that the person is assumed to be trying to achieve. We argue that this approach neglects the demonstrated inadequacy of conceptual types/rules to work in this way. It overlooks as well the importance of the hearable and witnessable interactional details that are constitutive of whether or not something is recognized as a particular sort of something in any actual case. In speaking of "hearable and witnessable details" we are building on Garfinkel's (1967, 2002) argument that it is the details of local orders that constitute both social order and intelligibility (Rawls 2003). The argument is that the work of constituting recognizable local orders cannot be done via rules or conceptual typifications, but rather requires careful attention to empirical detail on the part of participants and therefore also on the part of researchers. For the original discussion of this problem readers should refer to Wittgenstein *Philosophical Investigations*, Saul Kripkie *On Rules*, C. Wright Mills "Situated Action and Vocabularies of Motive" 1940, and *The Journal of Classical Sociology* (forthcoming) for a special issue on the problem of constitutive rules in moral philosophy focusing on John Rawls' (1953) paper "Two Concepts of Rules," and the impact of that debate on contemporary social theory and the development of Ethnomethodology.

analysis) on action. This has the negative consequence of treating individual motivation and institutional belief and value as the two underlying poles of social order – when both are in actuality the reified results of social relations of practice. Beliefs are the result – not the cause – of social action. Once created, they can be used to justify action according to practice, but they cannot be used to order that action in the first place, prospectively.

Any reading of the resulting micro/macro divide will show that "micro" sociology, conceived in a context in which rules and institutionalized contexts of value and belief are given priority, appears to focus on issues involving individual belief and motivation in small scale interaction, while neglecting the so-called larger issues of "structure" associated with inequality and oppression. Macro sociology, in turn, treats essential social processes, such as religion, family, or the law, as formal institutions driven by a structure of rules or beliefs, rather than as sites in which practices must be enacted in detailed and recognizable ways in order for what we think of as institutions to have a continued existence.[3]

The idea that these are the only viable alternatives is unfortunate, because sociology, liberated from this dichotomy and focused on practice – instead of on concepts and beliefs – has the potential to address essential issues of inequality and structure, as features of the local order practices that are constitutive of situations. Focusing on either individual motivation or so-called macro structures glosses the details of practices – taking statistical accounts as a measure of action – and working from individual (survey/interview) accounts. Even when the problem of integrating individual beliefs and motives with institutional structures is taken seriously, as in Anthony Giddens' *Structuration Theory* (1981), institutional beliefs and values remain the central constraint and the problem of individual motivation is treated as essential.[4]

This tendency to focus on beliefs and motives, ignoring the powerful demonstrations of their inadequacy, has masked the importance of practice to essential

---

[3] The word "enacted" is an important one. Practices themselves are all too often equated with concepts, beliefs, or formal rituals. We use the word enacted to keep in front of the reader constantly the idea that practices only exist as and when they are done. They must be seen or heard, touched, smelt, tasted or felt. They must be recognizable in their material details. Concepts would be invisible in heads. Practices, to be witnessable, must be enacted.

[4] See Garfinkel Seeing Sociologically and discussion in Editor's Introduction of this problem. See also a special issue of Law and Society on methods for an extended discussion of this issue.

social forms, such as religion, obscuring the relationship between these social forms and the societies in which they are found, and obscuring also the relationship between social solidarity, inequality, and local orders of practice, in modern contexts in which beliefs and values are not shared.

Our empirical data are designed to illustrate the problems and confusions that arise when social phenomena which are ordered through practices in details are treated as if they were ordered by belief and value. We aim to show that even though speaking in tongues, praising, and prophesying are essential to the beliefs of both Assemblies of God Churches studied, and that their practice is justified in terms of those beliefs, beliefs are insufficient for actually producing those religious experiences. It is only when *as practices* they are enacted recognizably in local congregational settings that participants are enabled to have (and are accepted by others as having) the emotional and belief experiences associated with them.

There are ways of enacting the practices of expressing the Holy Spirit that are treated as inappropriate within a particular church's service and negatively sanctioned as a consequence. These same inappropriate ways would be considered appropriate in another church setting. The differences between appropriate and inappropriate instances of tongues, prophecy and praise are a matter of practices in detail and not of beliefs – which do not vary between these churches.

The varying local details of practices are consequential for the resulting belief experience, however, as people whose enactment of practice is judged to be inappropriate do not have the same experience as those whose practices are accepted and ratified by the group. Appropriate practices receive an interpretation from pastors and/or congregation through which the speaker's presentation (and hence their beliefs and moral status) are affirmed. By contrast, we have seen inappropriate practices drowned out by music, ignored and not given any interpretation, publicly chastised, and brought to a halt by ushers. In these cases participants did not have a positive experience (even though their practices would have been accepted elsewhere) and in being sanctioned their beliefs and their own moral status in the community, were called into question. Pastors would refer to the "need to get right with God," for instance, as an explanation for the inappropriateness of their performance.

Although the beliefs are the same at the two churches we studied, and both officially represent the same faith, their accepted form of practice differs. What is accepted as appropriate in one church is not accepted in the other. Thus, one could master the same beliefs, have the appropriate motives, and even have the corresponding belief experiences at both churches, by taking part in the general service,[5] but one would not be able to publicly (i.e., individually) perform essential parts of the service in an expected and recognizable way unless the practices were the same. Narratives are treated by some researchers as if they were practices in their own right. But, narratives and accounts can only be invoked after a problem develops – and thus are of no use in ordering practices prospectively. And, in the cases in our study, even having the appropriate account for one's actions would not help if the placement of the tongues and their tone do not fit expectations. Being disorderly is a sign that one is not truly spirit filled – and no "account" will alter this judgment. Thus, acceptance as a member and confirmation of both faith and moral status depend on a recognizable display of practice and not on a display of belief or narrative. A believer would have to participate for some time in order to master the differences between practices in detail in different congregations.

The ethnographic observations analyzed in this paper, are offered as a clarification of the distinction between belief and practice, which we argue is essential to sociology in general, but particularly germane to studies of religion, as religion would appear to offer the paramount case of a social form based on belief. The argument is intended to be analogous to that of Durkheim's *Suicide* (1897), which took an act that had been treated as essentially psychological and argued that it was, in fact, inherently social. In this case, religion is, of all social institutions, the one that, among western thinkers, is generally assumed to be the most purely based on belief and on the individual faith experience.

We hope to provide a demonstration that belief, without mastery of the details of practice, is not sufficient to enable persons to perform acceptably, in a public and individual way, in a religious service, any more than it is sufficient in a game of chess or football. The beliefs about religion in western life, like our beliefs about social order, run counter to actual practice – producing profound contradictions. The practices are constitutive of the beliefs.

---

[5] This important distinction between worshiping from the pew as a member of the larger "corporate" group (the term used by the church) and getting up as an individual to make a "public" expression of tongues, praising, or prophecy, will be elaborated in the body of this paper. Because public expressions of the spirit are taken as evidence of higher stages of conversion they are essential to the religious experience.

But, the study of social order and intelligibility are generally approached as though the beliefs were constitutive of practices. One may understand that the objective in football is to get into the end zone, but there are ways "in detail" of attempting to achieve this objective that umpires, players, and fans, will rule inappropriate.[6] Without constitutive practices in details there is no game and hence no objective. The same is true in a religious service.

The two Assemblies of God Churches that were the primary focus of the research constitute an interesting case study in this regard. In all three churches the pastors, during interviews, carefully tied practices to biblical justifications and interpretations, which would tend to support the more conventional view that beliefs are more important than practices. Yet, the forms of appropriate and recognizable practice accepted during services varied from church to church, even though the justifications, in terms of beliefs, official religion, and references to biblical texts, were the same. The interpretations of belief are in essential ways detached from, and secondary to, the practices. As C. Wright Mills argued, they function as justifications after the fact, but not as recipes for performing.

What we found is analogous to the situation within formal institutions, as described by C. Wright Mills (1940), wherein the rules, in this case biblical passages and corresponding beliefs, do not supply sufficient information to tell participants how to perform required religious practices. Since the validity of practices is not determined by a correspondence with belief, but rather depends on local orders of practice, that are quite different from one another in substance, and responsive to different local contingencies, the fact that they are all justified according to the same biblical passages and beliefs demonstrates that those beliefs do not organize the practices.

The texts and beliefs, which are demonstrably inadequate as directions for how to enact the practices, are inadequate because they are a second order phenomenon. They arise only after, and as a situated explanation for, prac-

[6] This is the essential flaw with a game theoretic analysis of practice. It leaves the essential problem of recognizeability unexamined. Unless practices are recognizable in their details they convey no intelligible (shared) meaning. Rules themselves are no help in constructing recognizeability. They are only available as a context of accountability that is oriented toward the possibility of being held accountable for the play, and are invoked only after the fact, but then as if they were in fact ordering principles in the first place. This is a magical sleight of hand – imparting the appearance of a rule following logic where there is in fact none.

tices. They do not order – nor is their purpose to order – the doing of practices. This explains their inadequacy, and in so doing speaks to the so-called postmodern dilemma. Texts, institutions and formal rules *are* inherently ambiguous as principles of order. But, this is *not in itself a problem*. Texts don't need to be adequate as instructions for action, or the interpretation of action, because they are not the driving force behind either the enactment, or the understanding, of practices. They are important as retrospective accounts. The problem arises when beliefs and rules are treated as the organizing principles of social action. Social order then becomes a mystery involving infinite levels of narrative interpretation of belief and value.

It follows that while beliefs are by necessity always ambiguous, the practices, which in detailed ways lead to the creation of those beliefs, are not. According to Durkheim (1912) the purpose, or function, of beliefs is to confirm the legitimacy of practices, so as to encourage people to participate in them, not to represent the truth about the origin and functions of such practices. Nor is it the work of beliefs to instruct people in how to perform practices.

Ironically, although Durkheim argued that practices should be the focus of an empirical sociology of social facts (Durkheim 1895; 1912; Rawls 2005) the discipline he helped to found has made the study of beliefs and values, and related variable analysis, its central focus, and done so in his name. Durkheim argued that, already in his own day, treating beliefs as primary had created the appearance of error and confusion, just as treating rules as primary had created a parallel ambiguity in the understanding of meaning and social structure. But, the ambiguity, or inadequacy, in each case, is not, and never was, a problem for social actors. It is practices that must be held to high standards of coherence and reproducibility, not beliefs. Beliefs merely provide a narrative account, or reason, for the enactment of practices that, as C. Wright Mills (1940) said, can be invoked retrospectively to maintain the appearance of formal *institutional* coherence.

The detailed analysis of religious services presented in this paper is designed to show that the specific practices of speaking in tongues, the interpretation of tongues, prophecy, and the discernment of spirits, involve a complex organization and presentation of practices that are treated by practitioners as evidence of a belief experience. It is important to note that conceptualizing expressions of the Spirit as socially structured does not negate the religious belief that these gifts are divine in origin. Although Pentecostals describe their public worship as a means of spiritually connecting individuals to God, they believe that the Holy Spirit works through people in a social context, in an orderly way, and that the details of that context facilitate this communication.[7] Therefore, the practitioners who were studied took the view that the concrete details of situated ritual practices are a spiritually directed orderly social means to a spiritual end. They sometimes talked explicitly about this aspect of the religious service. This makes Pentecostals different from many other Protestant religious groups in recognizing the importance of social practices to the individual faith experience.

In challenging the traditions and control of the Catholic Church the Protestant Reformation tended to reject both Catholic ritual and hierarchy, stripping religion down to individual faith and elevating the importance of a direct connection between deity and person. Religious reformers at the time represented a new middle class that challenged the existing status quo and its traditions, and advocated a form of worship that allowed more scope to the individual and to social change. For this reason most Protestant religions tend to stress beliefs and the individual interpretation of beliefs and downplay institutionalized ritual (even the Pentecostal and/or Revivalist focus on ritual is thought of as Spirit directed, not institutionally directed). In the same way that the tendency toward individualism set Protestants in conflict with the traditional status quo in Medieval Catholic Europe at the time, it now sets religions based on individualism in conflict with traditional religions worldwide in an age of globalization.

It is a consequence of this history that practices are more important than modern western thinking generally acknowledges. Ironically, in the modern era – when we no longer have common beliefs and have come to rely almost completely on shared practices – we place an increasingly heavy premium on shared beliefs. Most traditional and fundamentalist religions advocate a return to a "way" of worshiping, that is, to an earlier form of practice. But, our observations of the actual enactment of practices in a modern church show that practices in details remain essential. In the churches we studied, there is a time and place, and a way, in which religious practices are expected

[7] In fact one minister from the Full Bible Baptist Church studied in this paper, who worked with us as a researcher at the beginning of the project, examined his own ministry and argued that as a minister it was his job to socially construct a situation in which participants could become receptive to gifts of the spirit. The argument that recognizable practice necessarily came before belief was consistent with his deeply held faith.

to be done. When these expectations are not met, the religious expressions are not accepted as legitimate. Our analysis shows not only that two churches with the same basic beliefs exhibited variations in expected local orders of practice, but that these variations corresponded to the race and social class aspirations of the membership.[8]

In other words, there are practices that the parishioners treat as corresponding with class and race in consequential ways. One of the two Assemblies of God Churches, after moving from an urban to a suburban area, exhibited such changes, even though the pastor and much of the membership did not change. It was made clear that their new social class aspirations, and new location in a white suburb, required abandoning old practices and adopting a new set of practices geared toward the upward mobility of parishioners. This suggests that aspects of religious practices, can be geared toward both supporting and adapting to capitalist enterprise, while beliefs remain the same.

While Marx, Durkheim and Garfinkel are generally viewed as holding opposing views on religion, they all considered knowledge and social order to be the result of material relations; practice, or praxis. For each, the mistake of reifying beliefs and abstractions and then substituting them for underlying social relationships, threatened the understanding of modern social, religious and economic relations. Therefore, taking seriously the idea that religion consists primarily of practices, and that beliefs are only a consequence of those practices, has the potential to bring the positions of Marx and Durkheim together with Garfinkel's emphasis on practices in unexpected ways.

Pentecostal Worship as an Orderly Social Phenomenon

The high emotional content of Pentecostal worship services often makes them appear to outsiders to be spontaneous and unorganized. They are in fact highly orderly social events in specifiably detailed ways. Researchers have commented on the contrast between the apparent disorder and the actual orderliness of the services. John Wilson and Harvey Clow (1981:249) noted that, "Pentecostals do not simply abandon themselves in their worship services. Instead there is

[8] See Bonnie Wright, "Producing Legitimate Expressions of the Spirit in the Context of Racial Integration," *Journal for the Theory of Social Behavior* Volume 34(4) December 2005, for an extended discussion of this phenomenon. Among other changes, practices such as speaking in tongues were removed from Sunday services (done only on Wednesdays) and parishioners were expected to adapt to this change.

a controlled disorder." This "controlled disorder" does not take a traditional ritual form, however. Rather, it manifests itself in the enacted details of religious practice that, while specifiable, are also variable. Jeff Tilton (1978:582) points out that, "There is no printed program, no set order, but the people know what to expect." Similarly, Ezra Griffith, John Young and Dorothy Smith (1984:465) note that the ". . . services followed a definite pattern." According to Timothy Nelson (1996), Pentecostal worship services exhibit a pattern of ritual activities, feeling rules, and behavioral norms.

Pastors and practitioners of the religion treat the *order of practice* itself as the primary evidence of spiritual presence. Until an apparently spontaneous, but nevertheless expected and recognizable order to the service is evident, it is believed that spiritual presence cannot be and has not been achieved. Michael Harrison (1974:395) explained that Pentecostals characterize their services as involving a tension between spontaneity and order:

> The Pentecostals point to the remarkable spontaneity and unity of the meeting as evidence of the Spirit's guidance. The subtle influences of the leader and other older members on the character of the meeting and the reoccurrence of patterns of expression from week to week only become apparent after one attends several meetings.

Harrison argued that a surface appearance of social disorder masks the underlying importance of the social order of the service, because the apparently spontaneous achievement of order is interpreted as evidence that the Holy Spirit is directing the service. Thus, in an effective service the local order of practices remains what Garfinkel (1967) referred to as "taken for granted."[9]

The practices vary from church to church and have local congregational histories. Yet, in each case, achieving *just this* local order of practice is the criteria for believing that the Holy Spirit is directing the service.

Like other faiths, the Assemblies of God organization has official religious beliefs, or tenets. These tenets are referred to as "Fundamental Truths" (General Council of the Assemblies of God 2001). At the very top of the list, is the belief that the Bible is the inspired word of God, meaning that it is infallible, and that it is the ultimate authority on all matters of faith and conduct. Thus,

---

[9] Local Interaction Orders are always taken for granted as practices in details. But, in institutional contexts they usually develop elaborate systems of institutional justification and narrative.

members may view the entirety of the Bible as a book of rules that prescribe beliefs, attitudes and behaviors for all situations. Yet, there is as much variation in worship behavior between the two Assemblies of God Churches as there is similarity.

We argue that the relationship between the Assemblies of God doctrines and practices is one of retrospective justification of situated action, as described by C. Wright Mills (1940[1990]:207–218) and not a prospective ordering of practices by beliefs. While members of the Assemblies of God Church attend to the overarching doctrines as a context of accountable motivation for their worshipful behavior, those doctrines are not specific enough to specify the details of every practice expected in each next case.[10] Nor could they be. Members must develop a shared vocabulary of motive regarding how each tenet is to be fulfilled, and be able to use that vocabulary retrospectively to justify their actions. But, they must also be able to reproduce practices in recognizable details before they can associate those practices with their shared vocabularies.

It is through their participation in these material practices, which vary from church to church, that individuals internalize and learn to reproduce the orderliness of Spiritual gifts. As Mead (1938 [1964]:448–449) argued, when acting within the context of a social group, the worshiper internalizes the reactions of others to their own actions. Each group member's knowledge of the local order and their production of future action is then formulated in a reflection on this process. Garfinkel ([1948]2006) refers to this process as "reflexivity." Goffman (1956:13) argued that participants in social groups must commit themselves to a "working consensus," a condition that Garfinkel (1967) referred to as "Trust," interacting in ways that are expected by and acceptable to others. Through this commitment to the details of local practices, participants create an intelligible order of practice. But unless they are able to do this in witnessable material details, others will not be able to recognize what they are doing (Garfinkel 1967, 2002).

---

[10] Context of accountability is an idea developed elsewhere by Rawls and Meehan. It builds on both Mill's argument that institutional order is managed largely by acting in accordance with institutional vocabularies of motive, or accounts and on Garfinkel's idea (as elaborated primarily in "Good Reasons for Bad Clinic Records," (1967) that local practices are responsive for the need to account to institutional superiors for one's actions. It means basically that people operating in institutional contexts are sensitive to what they will be rewarded and sanctioned for doing and attend to this rather than following rules as they engage in practices in details.

Analysis of the worship services focused on distinguishing essential elements of the social process of the religious service in recognizable detail. The relationship between the elements of the process, and the order in which they occur was also a focus of analysis. Gifts of the Spirit, such as speaking in tongues, are important components of the worship process. While, as matters of faith, these gifts are often believed to be purely spiritual, in practice their coherence must be created in-situ. There are expectations associated with their enactment such that participants who have successfully spoken in tongues in another church may be unable to do so in a form that is recognized as appropriate within a particular congregation, and thus have their contribution ignored, or sanctioned by the pastor and the congregation, because it took an unrecognizable and, hence, for this congregation, "inappropriate" form.

We refer to these details as Interaction Orders of the religious service and argue that they are what makes particular religious experiences possible – not formal orders of belief or account. This paper delineates the details of the appropriate and inappropriate production of these Spiritual gifts in their social context, and relates their social construction to the religious beliefs formally given as accounts for them.

The Field Sites and Methodology

Both of the churches studied are Assemblies of God congregations. They are large complex organizations that may be categorized as mega-churches (Eisland 1998; Olson 1988; and Vaughn 1993). Each has well over a thousand participants in Sunday services, a large-specialized pastoral staff, a system of cell groups (smaller social units), and their own K-12 grade schools. One of the churches associates itself with the city of Detroit through a mission of urban outreach and racial reconciliation, so we refer to this as the Urban Church. Although initially a white suburban congregation, it currently has over fifty-percent African American membership. Conversely, the other church has identified itself with the northwestern suburbs of Detroit through a mission of evangelizing to those who have never been exposed to this particular form of Christian worship; we will refer to this as the Suburban Church.

Ethnographic, audiotape, interview, and census data were collected from 1996 to 2002 with permission of the church pastors. Field notes were taken during Sunday services at both churches and audiotapes were recorded (the churches also produced videotapes for sale). Six of the audio tapes were transcribed in sound-by-sound detail. Seven pastors were formally interviewed about their church's services, history, and mission. These interviews were also recorded and transcribed.

Practices and beliefs were analyzed and compared. Services were analyzed as a series of sequentially organized interactions between pastors and the congregation in which the pastor and congregation took recognizable turns. Patterns of similarity and difference in the expressions of accepted and rejected spiritual gifts were sought in order to uncover the in-situ characteristics of enacting recognizable practices. The general beliefs associated with these practices were explored through pastoral interviews, statements during worship, and the Assemblies of God national website (www.ag.org). While we found that the beliefs underlying these messages were essentially the same in both churches, the practices that members of the congregation enacted in conjunction with these beliefs differed significantly in their details.

Beliefs: Speaking in Tongues, the Interpretation of Tongues, Prophecy, and the Discernment of Spirits

While we argue that beliefs do not organize religious practice, they do provide a context of accountability for those practices, and the practices can be held accountable to the beliefs. Therefore, before examining the practices, it is important to know what the beliefs are and what authority they claim. After examining the beliefs we will go on to examine the practices and their violations in details.

Pentecostals, as well as Charismatic Christians, are distinguished from other Protestants by their stance on speaking in tongues. They believe that speaking in tongues is a form of spiritual baptism that is both available to true believers and necessary for a complete relationship with God. The first time a person speaks in tongues is referred to as their "baptism in the Spirit." This is their second initiation in the Holy Spirit. The first initiation experience is called being "saved" or "born again." When a person is born again they are urged through spiritual interaction to dedicate their lives to God. The belief is that the Holy Spirit plants the seed of the "new person" within the individual. Later, a worshiper hopes to become filled with the Spirit. Speaking in tongues is considered to be initial evidence of this overflowing of the Holy Spirit.

The second step in the believer's relationship with the Holy Spirit, Spiritual baptism, can either be simultaneous with Spiritual rebirth, or can happen fifty years after the initiate is born again. Furthermore, some Pentecostals who are born again never achieve ritual baptism in the Spirit. Yet, Pentecostals believe that everyone who makes themselves available to God and wishes to be baptized by the Spirit will receive Spiritual Baptism. So, a failure to produce these practices correctly can be a personal failure of faith.

Spiritual baptism is described as being filled with the conscious energy of God. "Filled" is the key term. People who are baptized in the Spirit are described as "spiritually energized." Believers expect to be refilled by the Spirit throughout their lives. It is described as an ongoing process in leading a "Spirit filled life."

Scriptural Supports for Beliefs

Scripture is used to support the belief in the presence of the Holy Spirit in worship through the practices of speaking in tongues, prophecy, the interpretation of tongues, and the discernment of these spiritual messages. The Bible describes two forms of tongues. The practice of Speaking in tongues is introduced in the book of Acts, which tells of the founding of Christianity after the death of Jesus. In Acts 1:3–5 Jesus speaks to his Apostles after his death and promises them that he will baptize them in the Spirit:

> 3. After his suffering [death], he [Jesus] appeared to these men [the apostles] and gave them many proofs that he was alive. He appeared to them over a period of forty days and spoke to them of the Kingdom of God. 4. On one occasion, while he was eating with them, he gave this commandment: "Do not leave Jerusalem, but wait for the gift that my Father has promised, which you have heard me speak about". 5. For John Baptized you with water, but in a few days you will be baptized with the Holy Spirit.

The Apostles are asked to remain in Jerusalem and wait for the Holy Spirit to baptize them. At this point in the text it is not clear what baptism in the Spirit means.

According to the Book of Acts, the Apostles receive this Spiritual baptism on the day of Pentecost. The event is described in Acts 2:1–4:

> 1. When the day of Pentecost came, they were all together in one place.
> 2. Suddenly a sound like the blowing of a violent wind came from the

> heaven and filled the whole house where they were sitting. 3. They saw what seemed to be tongues of fire that separated and came to rest on each of them. 4. All of them were filled with the Holy Spirit and began to speak in other tongues as the Spirit enabled them.

The Apostles were given this Gift of tongues when they were Spirit filled. They were filled with the Holy Spirit while they were worshiping together. The result was an experience described as "speaking in other tongues." According to Acts 2:5–13, those who were present at the Pentecost were given the ability to speak in human languages that were previously unknown to them, and to understand what was spoken without interpretation. This first form of tongues is referred to as "zenolalia" in the academic literature (Watson Mills 1986:2).

Later, in stories about Christian congregations that were founded after the death of Jesus, a second type of tongues is described. According to 1 Corinthians 14:1–25, this form of tongues cannot be understood without interpretation. In the first nine verses messages in tongues are contrasted with prophecies:

> 1. Follow the way of love and eagerly desire spiritual gifts, especially the gift of prophecy. 2. For any one who speaks in a tongue does not speak to men but to God. Indeed, no one understands him; he utters mysteries with his spirit. 3. But anyone who prophesies speaks to men for their strengthening, encouragement and comfort. 4. He who speaks in a tongue edifies himself, but he who prophesies edifies the church. 5. I would like every one of you to speak in tongues, but I would rather have you prophesy. He who prophesies is greater than one who speaks in tongues, unless he interprets, so that the church may be edified. 6. Now brothers, if I come to you and speak in tongues, what good will I be to you, unless I bring you some revelation or knowledge or prophecy or word of instruction? 7. Even in the case of lifeless things that make sounds, such as a flute or a harp, how will anyone know what tune is being played unless there is distinction in the notes? 8. Again, if the trumpet does not sound a clear call, who will get ready for battle? 9. So it is with you. Unless you speak intelligible words with your tongue, how will anyone know what you are saying? You will be speaking into the air.

While prophecies are spoken in a congregation's native language, messages delivered in tongues are not and need interpretation to be understood. This interpretation, like the Gift of tongues, is also a Gift of the Spirit. It is a form of prophecy. At this point in the Scriptures, a higher value is placed on interpretation than on the tongues themselves, because the message of the Spirit can only be understood through the interpretation.

The importance of interpretation is further discussed in 1 Corinthians 14:27–28:

> 27. If anyone speaks in a tongue, two – or at the most three – should speak, one at a time, and someone must interpret. 28. If there is no interpreter, the speaker should keep quiet in the church and speak to himself and God.

The academic literature refers to this form of tongues as "glossolalia" (Mills 1986:2). This is the form of tongues that is enacted in modern Pentecostal churches.

In churches, pastors discern the nature of spiritual messages. To discern means that they decide whether spiritual messages should be accepted as legitimate expressions of the Holy Spirit or treated as illegitimate expressions. Illegitimate expressions are described as stemming from an individual's fleshly desires, the impact of an unclean spiritual influence oppressing an individual, or from the possession of an individual by an unclean spirit. If they are legitimate they require interpretation. If they are illegitimate they do not.

There are three primary issues that come into play when discerning the spirit of public expressions displayed during worship services. First, a gift of tongues *must* be accompanied by an interpretation. The purpose of Spiritual gifts is to transmit Spiritual *guidance*, so the congregation needs to understand the message (1 Corinthians 14:1–25). Any public expressions that do not get interpretations are not considered appropriate. Second, any gift expressed must be *an expression of love*. It must offer support and comfort to the congregation. And, Third, all gifts must be expressed in an *orderly and uplifting* manner. Thus, *messages with a sad or disorderly tone will not be legitimated*.

The pastors give the second criterion, the expression of "love," a Biblical basis in 1 Corinthians. 1 Corinthians 13:1–13 speaks of the importance of faith, hope and love in relationship to spiritual gifts. Love is considered primary. Speaking in tongues and prophecy are mentioned specifically in 1 Corinthians 13:1–2.

> 1. If I speak in the tongues of men and angels, but I have not love, I am only a resounding gong or a clanging cymbal. 2. If I have the gift of prophecy and can fathom all mysteries and all knowledge, and if I have a faith that can move mountains, but I have not love, I am nothing.

Therefore, messages that are interpreted as unloving cannot be perceived as coming from God. Spiritual gifts are to uplift the congregation. This is discussed in 1 Corinthians 14:3–4 as follows:

> 2. But everyone who prophesies speaks to men for their strengthening, encouragement and comfort. 4. He who speaks in a tongue edifies himself, but he who prophesies edifies the church.

As a matter of practice this means that the sound and tempo of tongues are important, Messages that cause uneasiness, embarrassment, or discouragement in the congregation are, as a consequence, judged as not emanating from God. Thus, messages that publicly tear down the church's leadership do not edify the church and, therefore, are treated as not coming from God.

Finally, gifts of the spirit are *supposed to be expressed in an orderly manner.* The example of social order given in the Bible concerns the number of the people who may speak in tongues at any one time. Only two or three people should deliver public tongues, interpretation, or prophecy, during a single service (1 Corinthians 14:27). The relevant section of Corinthians concludes with the following statement: "But everything should be done in a fitting and orderly way" (1 Corinthians 14:40).

During interviews, pastors explained that this section of 1 Corinthians means that services should not be chaotic, but orderly. The pastors believe that each individual who is given Spiritual gifts is given some control over their expression. They do not believe there would be a situation in which the Holy Spirit would give a person a message that had to be delivered immediately. If necessary, they believe the messenger would be given the ability to wait until the appropriate time. 1 Corinthians 14:32–33 is used to support this argument. It indicates that: "the spirits of the prophets are subject to the control of the prophets. For God is not a God of disorder but of peace." Thus, there is Biblical support for perceivable social order in the enacted details of sacred spiritual practices.

Practices: The Social Order of Legitimate Spiritual Expressions

What the beliefs provide is a context of accountability in which order, harmony and positive messages are paramount. What the beliefs do not specify is what this might look like in any actual case. Yet it is just this local order that the beliefs treat as evidence of Spiritual presence. It is within local congregations that expectations regarding local orders of practice develop. What is to be considered orderly? When is the appropriate time and place? Which are appropriate messages? These are all matters decided by the conventions of local orders of practice.

In singling out local practices in details and discussing their legitimacy or illegitimacy we have followed the practice of the congregation in question in each case. In cases where pastors and congregation members displayed their acceptance of the expression of spiritual gifts as legitimate, these spiritual expressions were treated *by us* as having been appropriately produced for that social situation.[11] Conversely, when pastors and congregation members displayed their rejection of the expression of spiritual gifts, we treated those spiritual expressions as inappropriate for that specific social situation. We did not attempt to take a so-called "objective" stance. The legitimacy or illegitimacy of practices is a local matter determined by entirely local criteria. The participants are the experts in this regard and their judgment is the relevant objective judgment. As researchers, therefore, we attempted to understand how parishioners were making their judgments on the basis of how practices were performed and describe this process and its implications.

We describe the characteristics of appropriate expressions of the Holy Spirit first and then go on to describe the cases of inappropriate expressions of the Spirit that we found. We found that appropriate expressions of the Spirit occurred at a specific "point in the ritual process," in a certain "physical space," and used a "particular tone and content." Those spiritual expressions that were not demonstrably accepted as legitimate did not fit this pattern.

The Process of Spiritual Discernment

During the period of this study, public expressions of the spirit were discerned through different social mechanisms at each church (discernment is a process of accepting or rejecting messages; this is performed by pastors). Pastors at the Suburban Church discerned the messages in open view of the congregation, while this process was carried out in private, before the ser-

[11] We are using the term legitimate to refer to a visible public acceptance of a practice. This is distinct from Max Weber's use of the term in which he connects ideological justifications of leadership to ideal forms of authority structures. Legitimate is not a state of ideas – but of practices. Our research and analysis remain in the concrete situation of observed social practices. If the expression of a practice does not occasion problems, sanctions, or repair, then we consider it to be legitimate.

vice began, at the Urban Church. Once accepted, pastors at both churches reiterated and/or interpreted spiritual messages, holding them up as a display, and marking them as legitimate.

Public expressions of the Spirit that were accepted by the congregation and pastors at the Suburban Church emanated from the seat where the speaker was worshiping in the congregation "spontaneously." By spontaneously, we mean that congregation members did not have to receive formal permission to speak in this church and did not have to move up to a microphone at the front before doing so. At the Urban Church these same expressions if vocalized from the parishioners' seats would be judged illegitimate because prior permission had not been granted and they had not moved up to the microphone.

Pastors in the Suburban Church publicly judged the legitimacy of these expressions, as they occurred from the seats – by offering interpretations for them, calling attention to them – or when they were discerned to be illegitimate – by turning attention away from them. If the expression was spoken in tongues, an interpretation had to follow for it to be accepted as legitimate. If the pastor discerned that it was legitimate and an interpretation from the congregation did not follow immediately, then the pastor would ask for an interpretation, or produce one themselves. Either the original speaker or another person interpreted publicly spoken tongues.

At this Suburban Church the message in tongues and its interpretation were not evaluated for a "proper fit" with one another. During an interview, a pastor reported that the message in tongues could be five minutes long, and the interpretation could be as short as "God sends his blessings to us." While this was intended as an exaggeration, his point was that translations are not word for word, but renderings of the underlying meaning.

Pastors expressed acceptance of a spontaneous spiritual expression in two ways. First, when spoken tongues were immediately followed by an interpretation that was accepted, or when a prophecy was accepted, the pastor would restate the message for the congregation. For example, on one occasion a woman gave the following interpretation of tongues:

> You came here worried about your child. Your marriage troubles you. A traveling friend is on your mind. Give your cares to me. I will care for your ailing leg, missing loved one and your broken heart. Lay your burdens on me.

A pastor repeated the message from the pulpit: "For those of you who did not hear the message, it was that God knows your burdens and wants you to lay them at his feet, and give yourself over to praising Him." Thus, the pastor legitimated the tongues and their interpretation as a message from the Holy Spirit.

Secondly, at the Suburban Church, where tongues were spontaneous and discernment was public and not discerned in advance, pastors could indicate acceptance of a spoken message in tongues as legitimate by encouraging an interpretation when one did not immediately follow. On one such occasion, a pastor said, "I believe that there is an interpretation out there. These are gifts from God and they should be shared." The congregation continued to praise until an interpretation was offered. The pastor then reiterated the interpretation. Through this process the tongues spoken and their interpretation were accepted as legitimate.

Spiritual messages were more privately discerned – in advance – at the Urban Church. When a person wished to deliver a spiritual message to the congregation, they had to present their message to a pastor privately for discernment. This made the process of discernment very different at this church as the performance was not available for evaluation by the pastors. The pastor discerns the spirit of the message, and the character of the person making the request, and grants or denies permission. When discernment was done prior to the service in this way the pastor would be ready with the interpretation before the spiritual expressions were produced before the congregation. Since this process of discernment was private, we learned about it through interviews with pastors.

Once permission to deliver a message from the Holy Spirit was granted in the Urban Church, the message had to be spoken through a microphone at the front of the church at a point in time determined by a pastor. Just as at the Suburban Church, messages were positioned at praising peaks during worship. Not only must each speaker have prior permission to speak in this church, but messages in tongues had to be understood by and publicly interpreted by their own speaker before others gave them an interpretation. Any music that was playing was stopped, and people ceased their praising activities to hear the voice of the Holy Spirit spoken through one of His worshipers. After the message was delivered, a pastor would restate the message for the congregation. While members of the congregation may deliver tongues and prophecy loudly from their seats in this church during collective worship, the volume of praise and song is so high that their message would probably go unheard without a microphone and the secession of music.

Whether the initial discernment is public or private – when the spiritual expressions are spoken there still needs to be a public display of discernment and acceptance by the pastors and other aspects of the practice, tone, mood, content (of interpretation) timing etc., must be performed in acceptable ways.

The Appropriate "Point in the Ritual Process"

At both the Suburban and the Urban Churches appropriate expressions of the spirit were delivered during pauses in the worship service that were designated for praise and at altar calls – times during worship when it is appropriate for members of the congregation to express themselves at the alter. However "spirit filled" they are, worshipers must wait for those points to speak in tongues.

Worship services leading up to these points were composed of call-response interactions between religious leaders and the congregation. Leaders called out to the congregation, and the congregation replied by repeating either the song lines, or specific statements made by pastors. Pastors alternated periods of song and praise, building the intensity of worship sequentially until it peaked in an expression of the Spirit (i.e., someone praising, prophesying or speaking in tongues). At the peak of worship participation, volume and harmonization are at their highest point. Here leaders created pauses for praise in the call-response cycle of song and marked them as praise relevant with statements such as "Oh Holy God. Let us give our voices up in praise to Him."

Both "corporate" (in the group) and "public" (individual) expressions of the Spirit were produced during such pauses in the call-response cycle. Some people shouted out praises, raised their hands up, cried, prayed in their native language, or prayed in tongues. Pastors defined this as corporate praise because no one voice was attended to as separate from the corporate body of the congregation. Corporate praise is ironically seen as private because, while it is collective, it edifies only the worshipper, rather than edifying the congregation or its leadership.

After a period of corporate praise, pastors would re-initiate the call-response cycle. As the call-response song and praise cycle is repeated throughout worship, the congregational level of participation and harmonization in song and the level of corporate praise became heightened, with public expressions of the spirit beginning to punctuate peaks in the worship cycle. Public expressions of the Spirit are spoken by people individually, but are not private because they are heard above the corporate voice of the congregation. In the Suburban Church these were spoken from the worshipers' seats like corporate praise – while at the Urban church, worshipers were asked to make public expressions of the spirit from microphones at the front of the church.

The public form of speaking in tongues, the interpretation of tongues, and prophecy were the public expressions of the Spirit enacted during worship. These spiritual expressions were seen as public because they are expected to edify the congregations and their leadership. Pentecostals describe them as messages from God that are delivered by His Holy Spirit through members of the congregation. Spoken tongues sound like a foreign language made of familiar syllables that are connected into word-like components and organized into punctuated streams. They have a poetic character. Since tongues do not represent any known language, Pentecostals explain that they must be interpreted divinely either by the person who initially spoke in tongues or by another person who is present. These interpretations were also accepted as prophecies. Additionally, spiritual messages that were initially spoken in the congregation's native language were defined as prophecies as well.

All revivalistic services observed in our research resulted in expressions of the Spirit that were legitimated. Pastors legitimated public expressions of the Spirit by reiterating their meaning from the pulpit. If no appropriate public expressions of the Spirit were given, a pastor would address the congregation after the service peaked and remark on the "wonderful feeling of the Lord" that was evoked during worship. This "feeling of the Lord" was accepted as a corporate expression of the presence of the Holy Spirit. Thus, pastors worked to make an expression of the Spirit visible during every revivalistic service.

The Appropriate "Physical Space"

While the appropriate timing for expressions of the Spirit was found to be the same for both congregations, the spatial organization of accepted expressions of the spirit during worship services varied. At the Suburban Church, all appropriate corporate and public expressions of the Spirit were enacted from a person's place of worship, meaning from their pew, or from their position in the band or choir. Yet, at the Urban Church only corporate expressions were given from a person's place of worship. All public expressions of the Spirit in that church were appropriately expressed only from the front of the church through a microphone.

The Appropriate "Tone and Content"

Those expressions of the Spirit that were accepted as legitimate have a situation specific tone and content. Interpretations of prophecies may be evaluated on the basis of both tone and content, while tongues may only be evaluated on the basis of tone, because they have no textual meaning. Spiritual expressions that were accepted had a joyful, entreating, or praiseful tone. Further, their cadence was both melodic and poetic. Acceptable interpretations and prophecies had prophetic, encouraging or instructing content. Words of encouragement were more common than predictions. The only predictions that were heard were that the church will be blessed, revivals will sweep the nations, and sinners must ask God for forgiveness and change their ways or they will be brought out into public shame. Ironically, this last prophecy was given when Jim Baker was the guest speaker at the Urban Church. An instructive prophecy was heard on only one occasion, when the Suburban Church pastors were instructed to give communion. During an interview, a pastor said that messages should not be discouraging to the congregation, or publicly tear down its leadership. Since God's messages are expected to build or strengthen the church, discouraging messages are believed to originate with a source other than God. We found that only encouraging and supportive messages were discerned as legitimate during services.[12]

Inappropriate Expressions of the Spirit

We have described the character of legitimate expressions of the spirit and how they are legitimated by pastors and members of the congregation in some detail because it is only in contrast to these practices that expressions that are treated as illegitimate can be found and examined. What we looked for were the incongruous cases that were not treated as legitimate. In what

[12] This policy obviously allows pastors to censor criticism of church policy and leadership and indeed pastors explained in interviews that the policy had been adopted largely for this purpose. It seemed to eliminate most of the instances of tongues they considered inappropriate – and in so doing increased the orderliness of the service. Given that order is a sign of spiritual presence this is important.

ways did they not fit the congregations expectations? It is these illegitimate expressions in details and their treatment that provide a deeper understanding of the constitutive character of local orders of practice.

We identified inappropriate expressions of the spirit by the presence of negative sanctions and the absence of positive confirmation and interpretation. The timing, location, tone, and content of the messages that were negatively sanctioned differed from those that were accepted as appropriate.

While we were told about inappropriate spiritual expressions which had occurred at both churches, we were able to witness these only at the Suburban Church because the process of prescreening had eliminated them at the Urban church. Thus, we were able to learn about previously rejected spiritual expressions at the Urban Church only in generalities, through interviews with pastors.

Two pastors at the Urban Church explained that the prescreening process had been adopted because this congregation had a history of publicly spoken spiritual gifts that had to be rejected because the messages contained statements against the church's leadership and consequently did not uplift the congregation. The pastors held that people who were not living truly Christian lives had been delivering these messages. True messages would have been uplifting (i.e., any criticism is illegitimate). The pastors responded to this situation by discerning the spirit of messages prior to their delivery, using the content and tone of the message and the spiritual character of its messenger as the primary factors in their decisions. When asked if a person would be able to speak authentically in tongues after waiting to do so they replied that God was a God of order and that he would not force a worshiper to give his messages at a time that contradicted His Holy Spirit directed leadership (i.e., the pastors).

Because of this screening procedure, every public spiritual message that was heard at the Urban Church was accepted and was delivered at the appropriate time, in the appropriate space, and using the appropriate tone and content as we have described it.

According to pastors who were interviewed, illegitimate spiritual expressions of the spirit always had a personal and private origin, either stemming from "the flesh," meaning an individual's desires, or from demonic forces oppressing (i.e., surrounding and influencing) or possessing (i.e., inhabiting and acting through) an individual. It was the pastor's job to discern which expressions originated in the individual and which were true expressions of the Holy Spirit filling the individual. The distinction between demonic and fleshy sources of illegitimate expressions was never made publicly visible by pastors at either church. Instead, these spiritual expressions were uniformly negatively sanctioned through pastoral action that worked to make the acts invisible or to contradict the messages delivered. Counseling of individuals who produced these inappropriate expressions was private.

While attending services at the Suburban Church, four expressions of the spirit were discerned as illegitimate and negatively sanctioned. The four occasions of illegitimate expressions included: (1) An inappropriate expression of praise, (2) An inappropriate occasion of speaking in tongues, (3) An inappropriate prophecy, and (4) An inappropriate occurrence of shouting accompanied by dancing in the spirit. These four inappropriate expressions will be described and analyzed in terms of their timing, spatial location, and the public response that each received. We focus our discussion on those aspects of these expressions that were relevant to why they were not considered legitimate expressions of the Spirit within the local congregational order of practice.

An Occasion of Inappropriate Praise

On one occasion, a woman was observed being removed from the sanctuary by a pastor and an usher after she had been praising in a spirited manner. The woman had walked around the periphery of the sanctuary, while crying, waving her hands in front of her waist and shouting, "Thank you Lord. Thank you Jesus." After circling the sanctuary alone, a female usher followed her. A male pastor later joined them. They each put an arm around the woman, whispered in her ear, and gently walked her out. The congregation did not appear to notice this event, and continued to worship.

The woman's praise did not fit the characteristics of legitimated public expressions of the Spirit in this church. Although the tone of her praise was uplifting, the ritual timing and spatial location were off. Other worshipers cry, wave their arms, and shout out praises from their pew during the points in the service between songs that are designated for praise. By contrast, this woman's praise was enacted during the song portion of the worship service, rather than in the pauses designated for praise. Furthermore, moving around the periphery of the sanctuary, which is acceptable and even preferred in some churches, is not expected here and drew the attention of the leadership, leading to her removal from the sanctuary.

People were not expected to move around the periphery of the sanctuary either at this church or in the Urban Church. In these congregations such behavior is considered disorderly. Yet, this is not the case at all Pentecostal churches. For example, when visiting a Full Bible Baptist church, we observed that actual running around the periphery of the sanctuary was considered an orderly and accepted expression of the Holy Spirit, called "running in the Spirit." But, being unexpected in this church it is disorderly and being disorderly it cannot be an authentic expression of the Spirit – the main evidence of whose presence is considered to be the order of the service.

An Occasion of Inappropriate Tongues

On another occasion, a man who was praising in tongues inappropriately was joined by two pastors who put their arms around him and motioned to the music pastor on stage to increase the volume of the music. The man's expression of tongues was initially loud enough to be heard over the congregation's singing. This is too loud for expressions of the spirit that are not produced in pauses designed for such expressions. Furthermore, his voice was deep and anguished. Once the volume of the music was raised on the instruction of the pastor, however, he could not be heard.

The man's spoken tongues did not match either the timing or the tone of the tongues that were accepted as legitimate in this church. Publicly spoken tongues that were legitimated by the pastors were spoken over the voice of others during pauses in singing designated for praise, in a melodic, imploring, or joyful tone. By contrast, this man's tongues were spoken loudly during song, rather than in a pause. Appropriate tongues are supposed to have an uplifting and loving tone. This man's voice had an anguished tone. Once his spiritual expression was discerned as inappropriate, the pastors worked quickly to minimize its appearance without drawing attention to the man by increasing the volume of the music. There was no interruption, either positive or negative, and the congregation continued to worship without pause.

An Inappropriate Prophecy, Accompanied by Dancing and Shouting in the Spirit

When a woman delivered a prophecy that criticized the level of the congregation's praise, another woman joined her by both shouting and dancing in the spirit. The congregation decreased their praise and appeared to be confused. In response, the head pastor contradicted the prophetic message and criticized the act of shouting and dancing at that time. Appropriate prophecies emanating from the speaker's place of worship that were heard over the voice of worshipers during praise, relayed uplifting messages to the congregation in an imploring or joyful tone. In this case, the speaker's message and tone broke with these expectations. She cried out: "Why aren't you praising me? There is no high praise here. I will not send my Spirit if there is no high praise. Why do you not praise me?" Both her message and tone were critical.

Criticism is not considered to be orderly because it is not uplifting. The congregation became quiet. Another woman moved away from her pew into the aisle and shouted out praises loudly and danced in place. While the second woman's public spiritual expression was delivered at an apparently appropriate ritual moment (in a pause after a prophecy), she was physically out of place (in the aisle), the message had an inappropriate tone for a public expression of the spirit (dancing and shouting), and the prophecy she was amplifying was inappropriate. Appropriate public and corporate spiritual expressions in this church were expected to be delivered from one's pew. Shouting and dancing were not accepted as appropriate public expressions of the spirit.

The congregation and the pastors responded negatively to the prophecy (criticism), the shouting, and the dancing. Rather than increasing their praise in response to a message from God, the congregation's praise declined, indicating that they reacted quickly to the inappropriateness of the expression. There seemed to be a sense of confusion. The congregation was not uplifted by the message. The head pastor responded to the situation by saying, (paraphrased): "A time for shouting and dancing is coming. We will be able to give high praise when the divisions in the congregation are healed and when more people get right with God." The pastor's words explained that high praise was important. But indicated that he did not accept the legitimacy of the prophecy. From interviews we understand that such comments refer directly to those who have produced inappropriate tongues.

In this case, by delivering inappropriate expressions of the spirit, the two women demonstrate that they are "not right with God." They are the problem – not a lack of high praise by the congregation. The pastor was able to bridge the gulf between the message and the congregation's behavior by saying that the congregation would be able to give high praise when they filled their deeper spiritual needs: "getting right with God" and "healing the divisions in the church." "Getting right with God" involves asking for forgiveness of sins, reading one's bible, and following biblical principles. "Healing divisions in the church" involves acceptance of differences, forgiving others of any wrongs that they may have committed, and involving people outside of one's intimate social circle in activities.

Summary

In contemporary social science it has become commonplace to think of problems of social order in terms of theorized concepts and to think of beliefs and values as driving social action. Social solidarity is viewed as a matter of consensus about beliefs and values and not a matter of enacting the same practices cooperatively in a context of mutual commitment and trust. Looked at in this way social orders become elusive. Individual behavior is supposed to be unpredictable, and in order to get a sense of some underlying patterns of order, researchers attempt to model objectives, beliefs, or projects that actors may be orienting toward that would explain their behavior.

If, however, one begins with the premise that social orders are produced through practices enacted in common and that solidarity does not require a consensus of belief – then the object of study becomes very different. What actors think, believe or want is no longer the issue. Abstractions and generalizations lose their importance. Social actors are engaged in producing orders for one another. These orders are external and can be studied as orders without reference to abstractions. The empirical recognizeability of practices is the objective of actors. Their motivation is to communicate with one another. Like moves in a game, social actions are only intelligible against a background of finely ordered and witnessably recognizable local practices.

If, in the traditional way of social science, social action is assumed to be loosely oriented toward beliefs and values, then the actual details of particular situations are uninformative. What researchers would look for are the generalizeable underlying orientations toward value and their variable relationships. Beginning with a focus on beliefs, researchers then focus on definitions, clarifying concepts and setting out the relationship between theory and method involved in their work. They ask actors what they believe and why they act the way they do.

With respect to religious scholarship in particular, the focus is not only on getting a clear conceptualization of the material – but the subject itself is considered to be primarily conceptual. What, after all, is religion, if it does not consist of some basic beliefs and concepts?

Our research challenges this general emphasis on concepts, taking a detailed study of religious practice as a demonstration of the independence of practices in their details from beliefs: and the independence of religious solidarities themselves from beliefs. Although we conducted some interviews with pastors, in general we do not expect that participants are aware of the details of the practices that they engage in. These details are what Garfinkel (1967) has called "taken for granted." Nor do they need to understand the accountable relationship between beliefs and practices. This is a matter for pastors.

Although we are constrained to use language, we resist the tendency toward conceptual reduction, and attempt instead to see what about the practices that we observe is treated as orderly (and disorderly) in-situ by participants. The aim is not to describe things in endless detail so that variations in meaning and tone might be conveyed. Rather, we focus on what about the production of practices made them recognizable to participants in that setting as practices of a particular sort. The analysis then focuses on the significance of the details we found in the production of those orders. We assume that if we asked practitioners about what they were doing they would give us belief based answers that do not explain the details of the local orders that they actually produce.

Our analysis of the local order of services in the two Pentecostal churches studied revealed enacted spiritual expressions that were treated as inappropriate by participants in the situation. If a person claims that the Holy Spirit is speaking through them – how are others to judge the validity of this claim? We found that validity in this regard was largely a matter of how the practices were produced. The details of what was expected were tied to particular local contexts of practice and could not be explained in terms of beliefs alone. We observed that legitimated expressions of the spirit at these two churches were delivered in particular ritual moments and spatial locations, and had a specifiable tone and content. When these aspects of the local order of practices were missing they were not treated as legitimate. Illegitimate expressions were not only treated as violations of the local order, but as evidence of moral flaws in the person producing them – a finding consistent with Garfinkel's argument that Trust is implicated in the production of orderly and expected practice and with Goffman's treatment of spoiled identities. Public expressions of the Spirit were subjected to more scrutiny in this regard than corporate expressions in both churches.

There were some significant differences in the way practices were expected to be performed in the two churches. Congregational variation in the production of legitimate expressions of the spirit is evidence of the importance of ritual practice and its distinction from spiritual belief. All Pentecostal churches, of various denominations, share the belief that God will manifest Himself through worshipers by giving them spiritual gifts. Yet, there is variation between churches in the type of spiritual gifts displayed, their manner or method of legitimate expression, and the process whereby they are discerned as legitimate. Consensus of belief bore little relationship to the actual details of those practices through which the solidarity of the congregational religious experience was produced. We found that even different churches, of the same denomination, in the same metropolitan area, vary in the acceptable details of the production of legitimate spiritual gifts. This means that participants must learn how to appropriately produce their spiritual gifts through participation in congregational worship, not through faith, and that each time a member shifts to another congregation they must learn new ritual practices on site.

Pentecostal congregations are interacting social groups with interactional expectations deeply embedded in the details of ritual practice. Newcomers who do not know the local order of practice and consequently can not meet these interactional expectations may be negatively sanctioned until they are able to meet the new group's situated expectations with regard to practice. Knowledge of, and commitment to, a set of beliefs will not help the parishioner in this regard. On the other hand, it is not necessary to master the beliefs in order to have a meaningful spiritual experience through enacting practices appropriately.

Moreover, the interactional expectations in their details have an association with the sacred and are designed to edify the congregation and its leadership. Whether intended or not, *a failure to meet situated interactional expectations is a challenge to the status quo of sacred authority* and will be treated as evidence of the parishioner's moral shortcomings. Thus, members who are dissatisfied with leadership, as well as newcomers who are not socialized into the congregation, could find their spiritual expressions discerned as illegitimate.

There is an interesting paradox in this. Ironically, belief and faith are emphasized as the key to the individual "born again experience" that facilitates "baptism of the Spirit," through the initial experience of speaking in tongues. Yet, the experience of speaking in tongues, as well as the interpretation of tongues, and prophecy, are practices that must be produced in publicly recognizable ways in order to be discerned (another organized and detailed practice) and accepted as legitimate.

Our position is consistent with Garfinkel's argument that the detailed and recognizable features of embodied action are essential to intelligibility and elaborates his idea that in order to be witnessably recognizable, action must also be instructable, that is, it must be learned as recognizably reproducible details of practices *in-situ*. It also underscores the relevance of local orders of practice to Marx's treatment of religion as ideology, demonstrating the reliance of systems of belief (ideology) on underlying systems of witnessably enacted practice (praxis). Praxis ultimately must come first. As Durkheim argued (1912), it is practices that first produce the beliefs. We examine the details of praxis/practice, not only in relations of labor, but also in the labor of constructing beliefs.

Social practices were the focus at each step of the research process. Instead of analyzing social practices as expressions of belief we treated expressed belief as practices to be analyzed. Motivation, faith in this case, is a feature of situated interactions and their expectations in details. Failing to enact the practice correctly leads to a different attribution of motive than a correct enactment. Thus, the primary motivation must be to enact the practice correctly. Thus, we do not treat motivation as a value or belief belonging to individuals, organizations or institutions. When, in more conventional research, the focus is removed from situated action and situated social actors, and conceived of as values and beliefs and variables related to them, social structure becomes an abstract concept devoid of lived details. Structures appear deterministic, lacking room for agency. Attempts to account for agency then seem to require the interpretation of abstract structures and abstractions of individual motives. Attempts to account for structure seem to require the aggregation of individual motives.

All abstractions – beliefs, narratives, rules – invoke this dialectic. It is not peculiar to studies of religion. It is a problem for the analysis of all social orders that their theorized appearances come to be treated as the *real* thing, obscuring actual social processes and relations from view. Both Durkheim and Marx recognized this problem and argued that the truth of social practices of various sorts lies in the actual concrete relationships between persons that they enact – or make possible – not in their end products.

The general practice of taking the end product – beliefs and narrative accounts – and treating them as the motivational and organizing principles of religion and other social orders, constitutes a dialectic of belief and practice: a contradiction that substitutes belief for practice and obscures both the purpose and the order of social relations – because it treats the result as the cause. This reification creates the appearance of both structural determinism and the need for an infinite regress of interpretation: a picture of things that is the reverse of the actual concrete relationships in which they stand.

Marx argued that in focusing on *things* as *ideas*, as finished products – one ends up with the idea that history developed backwards. In the preface to *The Holy Family*, Marx ([1845]1956:15, emphasis in original) outlined his objections to allowing "*self-consciousness*" to substitute for the "*real individual man.*" The argument is complicated by the fact that Marx is criticizing Hegel, taking on a particular form of German Idealism, and criticizing what he calls "Critical Criticism," a form of Christian Germanic argument. But, his fundamental point is one that Durkheim, C. Wright Mills and Garfinkel will later take up: that focusing on the end product of social relations creates the appearance that the end product (beliefs or developments like industrialism) was the purpose and effective stimulant of social action – when in actuality it came after and was caused by something else. The something else consists of social relations that are in Marx's terms both "real" and "material."

According to Marx ([1845]1956:21, emphasis in original) "In material history there were *no industrial towns* before there were *factories*; but in Critical history, in which the son begets his father, as already in Hegel, *Manchester, Bolton*, and *Preston* were flourishing industrial towns before factories were even thought of." Marx is taking exception to both a particular way of treating religion and a particular way of looking at history. His point in both cases is that the result is treated as the cause, and that this contradiction is the consequence of looking at things in terms of resulting ideas (reification) – rather than looking at the "materialness" of social relations in their details. In trying to rise above the particular – the critical focus on ideas loses sight of the real altogether – and as if there were no real social relations the result is allowed to substitute for its cause.

In current terminology it is generally said that social relations – material relations – are in their concreteness messy and contingent. As social scientists we are supposed to be preoccupied with how to get a pattern out of these details that is generalizeable across cases by performing some sort of conceptual reduction. In spite of a long and important debate over the efficacy of rules, institutions and motives – and their relationship to social order – there has been a general failure to take seriously the argument that social practices would not work in the first place unless there were a recognizable pattern in their enacted details that participants could work with. Conceptual reductions lose these patterns – they do not recover them.

What Marx, Durkheim, Mills and Garfinkel all have in common is a recognition that any workable pattern of social practices must lie in the details in ways that are accessible to participants. They recognize that the conceptual reductions we are so fond of as "scientists" are not *objective* representations of these relations, but rather, are separate social entities belonging to society – as end-products. As Mills pointed out, these conceptual reductions provide for participants convenient excuses and justifications for action – but turning to them for a scientific explanation of the ongoing order of social relations is backwards.

This substitution of abstractions for concrete social relations creates a false consciousness about beliefs and abstractions and about religious belief in particular – that obscures what is important about religious practice. People focus on beliefs – and fight one another over them – trying to use them as transcendent moral values – when in fact it is the underlying practices that generated those beliefs in the first place. There is a strong tendency also to overlook the fact that the underlying practices make transcendent moral requirements of their own: "Trust" and a "Working Consensus" with regard to practice (Rawls 1987, Garfinkel 1967, Goffman 1959) – treating such interactional arrangements instead as "merely" secular and amoral – and treating research focused on them as trivial.

But, treating the narrative accounts that result from practices as more moral and more important than the local moral imperatives and order issues of the practices on which they depend, and which created them, strips both modern society and the social science of modernity of their moral center. As beliefs, religions separate people – but as practices, in-situ, through the ways in which practices depend on mutual reciprocity and trust, like all practices, they bind people together: creating solidarities of practice that do not depend on consensus of belief and value. In a pre-modern world conflicting solidarities based on belief were not a problem. They served to strengthen the boundaries between societies and to produce and maintain the solidarity of small groups. But, as societies become more diverse – and people of differing values and beliefs are brought into increasing daily contact with one another – social and moral orders that transcend belief, belonging instead to situated actions, become essential. A sociology that focuses on local orders of morality is a critically needed enterprise in a modern global context.

It was Durkheim's argument, in *The Elementary Forms of The Religious Life*, that most of the serious misperceptions about religion have come from treating it as a system of ideas, when it is in fact a system of practices. He argued that, as practices, religions have many things in common that in terms of their beliefs appear to be completely different. He set out in *The Elementary Forms* (Durkheim 1912, Rawls 2005) to show how – if religion was treated as a system of practices – instead of as a system of ideas – it could be shown that all religions have a common purpose in their practices, and that even so-called primitive religions that appeared to western scholars to have magical aspects – and consequently were not considered to be really religions – turn out to be religions in just the same ways as modern religions when approached in terms of practices. This reduces ethnocentricism and discovers a common moral center in human social practices.

To treat the result of material activity as real – while treating the activity itself as inconsequential – is to let ideology replace the concrete social relations that comprise social and economic life. This is a dialectical contradiction resulting from and consistent with the tendency of modern society to replace all concrete social relations with reified conceptual "things" that are treated as independent when they are not. Durkheim argued (1895) that this view of social order belongs to the past and locks us into an emphasis on belief and value that threatens our ability to maintain solidarity in a modern context (Rawls 2003). Social solidarity is a matter of practice not consensus of belief and value. Trust is required by the necessity to cooperatively enact practices – it is not a belief state. Marx also argued that instead of focusing on ideas, we must focus on social relationships themselves – concretely as material relations and in details – in order to avoid the absurd reifications of the economists, philosophers and religious thinkers of his day.

With regard to religion and the study of religion, however, this dialectical contradiction is even more deeply ironic than with other social facts, as religion has come, rather uniquely, to be treated as primarily about beliefs – and not about the practices that constitute it. In subjecting religion to an examination of practices in their witnessable details, we hope to illuminate the dialectical contradiction involved in all relationships between ideology and practice. It is through a focus on practice that Marx and Durkheim hoped that Sociology could resolve these issues. Contemporary sociologies of practice inspired by Garfinkel and Goffman carry on this tradition.

Lauren Langman

From the Caliphate to the *Shaheedim*: Toward a Critical Theory of Islam

Allah is Great-and the Caliphate Preferable to Modernity

A specter is haunting the Islamic world, the specter of fundamentalism. In the face of the Great Powers of the world, and even greater powers of transnational capital, the relative economic stagnation, political weakness and intellectual stagnation of contemporary Muslim societies becomes more and more evident to those both within and without.[1] Buffeted by larger economic forces, powerless in face of Western hegemony, throughout the Islamic world, fundamentalism, as political Islam, has become the typical response and a growing force. Following the failure of modernist, often secular political movements to establish strong democratic States with robust economies, various Islamisms from Salafism to the Khomeini theocracy promise that moral renewal can and will lead to political empowerment. From the Islamic Brotherhood to Hamas to Jamaat Islamiya and a resurgent Taliban, political Islam has garnered a great deal of popular support. In the Western world, the promise of nationalism was to control the political in order to realize the cultural (cf. Gellner 1983).

[1] As will be evident, there are vast differences within Islamic societies; Algeria is not Yemen is not Indonesia is not Pakistan. Turkey has embraced modernity; Yemen remains feudal. The various Islamisms are not part of a unified movement. This paper is a more abstract, "ideal typical" analysis of Islam.

In much the same way, Islamisms, while rejecting nationalism as a modernist ideology, would seek autonomous control of the State to realize the community of virtue. In their own words, their goal is to dispatch the "infidels" from within or without, take over the Muslim world, restore the Caliphate, and reclaim a greatness lost. These Islamisms stand dedicated to ending the domination of outsiders and/or obeisance to local autocrats who are either directly serving the West and/or tolerating, if not supporting, Western companies, banks etc. The American invasion of Iraq has inspired widespread hatred and loathing and in turn, much of the resistance to the occupation has been expressed by fundamentalist groups. (There is secular opposition as well but that is not the present concern.)

Calls for the condemnation of evil Others, merciless retribution to the "guilty", and restoration of a former greatness resonate within our memories to nightmares of earlier moments that return and return. Our ears hearken back to the 1920s and 30's when, amidst the shouting masses and charismatic fanatics, large numbers of people embraced Fascist political doctrines that, like contemporary Islamisms, preached anti-modern irrationality, disdained human freedom, and vowed retribution to evil Others who "stabbed the people" in the back. Shrill voices promised a Reich that would last 1,000 years. Fascism would not only prove to be contrary to the rational self interest of Germany, but indeed, its valorized irrationality led to unprecedented death, destruction and devastation. How could this anti-modernist irrationality be understood? How can this understanding shed light on the "clerical Fascisms" within certain Islamisms?

The seminal work of the Frankfurt School of Critical Theory charted the rise of the modern world and its contradictions. In the 1920's the dominant response to the contradictions of modernity was Fascism that was widely embraced. The foundational analysis of modernity, qua the "immanent critique" of rationality, remains the *Dialectic of Enlightenment* (Horkheimer and Adorno 1991). They argued that market society and its legitimating Enlightenment ideology that valorized Reason led to the demise of absolutism. The emancipatory promise of the Enlightenment, freedom as the consequence of Reason was soon belied as "Instrumental Reason", *qua* the ideological authority of purposive reason, itself became a new basis for domination. Their imminent critique of ideological domination was supplemented by the incorporation of Freudian psychodynamics (Fromm 1941). In their view, the modern family fostered an authoritarian character that was prone to powerlessness and meaningless. Such a character was disposed to embrace authoritarian ideologies that allowed an "escape from freedom", yet assured subjugation to authority. Their understanding of early twentieth-century. Fascism now provides us with beginnings of a heuristic framework to reveal key elements of contemporary Islamist movements and their extremist ideologies. The Frankfurt School's analyses of alienation, domination, authoritarianism, character, and Reason yet provide a powerful theoretical understanding of political extremism cloaked in religious garb.

As shall be argued, however different classical Fascism and its contemporary clerical forms, however irrational their logics of and goals of moral renewal through subjugation to "higher powers", these anti-modernisms share underlying similarities and common themes. In their attempt to understand the rise of Fascism, these scholars first pointed out how political economic crises intersected with social character, how authoritarian dispositions facilitated the obedience to authority and how that authority, in command of the means of then modern information technologies, extolled anti modernisms, found scapegoats for blame and extolled violence to enemies. In each case, leaders resurrected a mythological Golden Age and promised its restoration. While much has been written on the rise of Nazi Germany and the more recent ascent of the rise of the Christian right, Critical theory has had less to say about the rise of Islamism, political Islam, as "clerical fascism" (Berlet, 2005). As will be argued, while on the one hand, the embrace of Islamism provides individuals with a variety of emotional gratifications, at the same time, xenophobic hostility to foreign "infidels" and collective barriers limit modernity and purposive rationality that might ameliorate the stagnation, poverty and backwardness that engender Islamisms.

In the following chapter, I will argue that 1), Islam grew and its Caliphate prospered, in part due to its *Shariah*-based commercial law, backed up by its armies. But 2), such laws created "limits to growth" and the "backward" barbarians to the North, embracing evidentiary-based law, capitalism and an ascetic "inner determination" in sacralized vocationalism, began to overtake the Caliphate and eventually colonized much of the Muslim world. 3) Between traditional barriers to modern rationality, and various expressions of colonialism and neo-imperialism, despite various (subverted) attempts at modernization, most Islamic societies have remained autocratic, economically stagnant, patriarchal and intellectually backward. 4) As a result of *ressentement* to the West and enduring domination, Islamisms have flourished and, at times, shaded into terrorism. 5) To explain the various moments of decline, *ressentement* and terrorism, I will attempt to show how the syntheses of Marx and Weber by the Frankfurt School of Critical Theory, further informed by Freud, provide crucial insights.

From Islam to Islamism

Sociology represented the attempt of post Enlightenment society to become conscious of itself as a society and valorize its dominant values of Reason and Progress. Its theories of sequential, progressive development assumed that religion would decline in the face of science and Reason. Marx and Weber suggested that while religion had played a major role in human history, its power was on the wane. These early versions of secularization theory were ultimately confirmed, in Western Europe. While rationality has been essential for the rise and legitimation of Western modernity, the irrationality of its rationality dehumanizes the person, fragments the social and disenchants the world while its hubris of progress leaves people bereft of transcendental meanings. Religions, however, provide a number of emotional gratifications through integration into an identity-granting community of meaning with powerful rituals, while providing believers with explanations of adversity, means of assuaging hardships, and often promises of a better life to come.

As events have shown, proclaiming the demise of religion was a bit premature, especially given the wide spread rise of fundamentalism that would seem to belie the predictions of decline. Fundamentalist religion can be understood as a critique of rationality, a rejection of its efficient, albeit sterile, worldview, as well as an alternative framework of belief and action. That said, fundamentalism fosters moral and cultural barriers to goal rationality that refluxes back upon the society and in turn sustains poverty, ignorance, illness degradation and breeds a corrosive atmosphere that, unchecked, legitimates terrorism, the violence of non state actors. Fundamentalisms can be seen in Christian, Jewish, Muslim or Hindu forms.[2] These fundamentalisms have condoned if not fostered violence and killing. But today, Islamic fundamentalism, Islamism, or political Islam has become the most important expression. Political Islam seeks control of States in order to impose its religiously extreme worldviews and agenda. It readily uses violence and destruc-

[2] This is not to ignore various secular fundmentalisms from Maoism on the left to the free market visions of the right.

tion, to establish its goals. Fundamentalist beliefs have been used to justify martyrdom operations e.g. *shaheeden* (suicide bombings)as a tactic.[3]

Part I Critical Theory as Enlightenment

A comprehensive sociological understanding of Islam from a Critical perspective should attempt to understand how and why it emerged as a world religion. How and why has Islam taken particular forms in different cultural and historical contexts? The present essay interrogates fundamentalism as a powerful social and political force. It will be argued that understanding the rise of Islamic fundamentalism must go beyond mainstreams of the sociology of religion for two reasons. Firstly, one must have an interdisciplinary perspective that starts with historically specific economic conditions and then further considers political, cultural and social-psychological factors. Furthermore, to understand most societies, especially Islamic societies, we must also consider geo-political factors from without, as well as local class-based structures of power and belief. I will argue that the Frankfurt School of Critical Theory provides a comprehensive multi-perspectival, multi-dimensional critique of domination in which intertwined economic, political, cultural (historical) and social psychological perspectives become illuminated (Kellner 1989). Moreover, considerations of the depth psychology of character and desire, first sketched by Nietzsche, provide a richness of explanation lacking in other perspectives. Secondly, the dominant position of "value neutrality" of mainstream sociology makes it not only difficult to critique domination, but thwarts envisioning possibilities of emancipation based on immanent critique of existing conditions.

It will be argued that early Islam's theocratic-based domination enabled the rise of a vast and powerful civilization from the Andalus to China. But at a later time, internal contradictions would not only stifle continued growth, but foster stagnation, demise and military weakness. Certain aspects of cultural traditions that privileged family, clan and tribe, as well as the nature of Islamic theology and law, acted as barriers to the influx of modernist thought

[3] It will be argued that Islamic theology is **not** the cause of martyrdom, but rather certain social conditions have fostered "martyrdom" as a military tactic, a "weapons of the weak" and an instrument of terror are employed against dominant powers. They are not promoted by religious doctrines, rather, religious doctrines have been created to legitimate and valorize what are basically political or military acts.

that, despite having made various inroads that might overcome these barriers, has remained limited in impact. As a result, most Muslim societies typically pose formidable barriers to political democratization and economic growth. One consequence of these factors has been fundamentalism. Ironically, fundamentalisms, while anti-modern, adroitly use modern technologies to gain voice and/or secure popular political power, which are modern notions.

Critical Theory

In the early years of the twentieth-century, market society (rational capitalism), was riven with multiple crises of legitimacy. In Germany, unemployment, inflation, and its military defeat in WWI engendered fear, shame, humiliation and rage. Its ideological support of Reason, freedom and democracy were belied by irrationality, domination and elite power. Fascism, as a mass movement and compensatory ideology that promised amelioration, flourished. Its emotional appeals to unreason, charismatic leadership and anti-modernist ideology sutured totalitarianism governance and modern technologies with intense emotions of loyalty to the State and hatred to "blameworthy" Others. The emergence of totalitarianism in the early twentieth-century, in Fascist and Communist forms was not easily understood within the then available theoretical frameworks. Critical Theorists rested on Marx's critique of capitalist political economy, but in reaction to various notions of economic reductionism, they stressed the role of Marx's cultural concerns with alienation, ideology and politics. More specifically, they found that Marx's (1963a) analysis of Bonapartism anticipated the rise of Fascism as an alienated petty bourgeois peasantry supported a "farcical" military hero/ruler. Louis Napoleon staged a *coup d'etat* and seized control of the French State, acting as a "representative" of the bourgeoisie who united monarchists and *lumpenproletariat* against workers and fears of communism.

For the Frankfurt School, while Marxism addressed the economic malaise of the working classes, it *failed* to address the role of culture and psychosocial yearnings of some segments of the workers, as well as other groups, especially the petit bourgeoisie. National Socialism, an authoritarian ideology, led by "powerful" yet "ordinary men", "erased" the notion of class, and promised economic prosperity and restoration of a once glorious nation that had been usurped and/or betrayed. Nazism promised to repair the "damaged" community and provide the "people" [*volk*] with recognition, pride, dignity and agency. Moreover, Nazism named a vile, blameworthy enemy culprit responsible for the social adversities. The eternal Jew deserved all blame and hated. His/her very existence polluted all that was good and pure. Given psychosocial dispositions to submit to authority inculcated by the bourgeois family, Nazism offered an "escape from freedom", a surrender to powerful leaders who articulated ideologies of submission to authority and retribution against enemies (Fromm 1941). The parallels with contemporary Islamisms are striking.

Critical Theorists attempted to locate Weber's understanding of Rationality as a value, and its expression in goal oriented action, within the critique of domination. More specifically, they saw Instrumental Reason, purposive rationality, as the legitimating ideology of capitalism that ensured an efficient, predictable, calculable capitalist economy and administrative organization. Moreover, while for Marx, alienation expressed the extent to which proletarian labor power was commodified, for Weber, the "disenchantment" of the modern world meant that everyone was dehumanized in a society of "technicians with heart" and "specialists without feelings". Further, Weber noted that in such societies, people might find meaning by following charismatic leaders-the kinds that emerge in times of crisis. Politics as a realm of passion and meaning was a way out of the "iron cage" of sterile rationality. Further, Critical Theory took Freud's psychoanalytic theory seriously, especially noting how authority became internalized as character. This, in turn, disposed a complex of domination and subordination that led to a glorification of leaders, rule, and uncritical obedience to their dictates.

In the following pages, I will suggest that the Frankfurt School analysis of the rise of Fascism crafted in the 1930s and 40s, offers important insights into the nature of contemporary theological absolutism. Marx's critique of political economy notes how capital has radically changed economic and social life; today, for many traditional societies, globalization has precipitated reactionary solutions. Weber's concern with religion, especially the "elective affinity" for charismatic leadership at moments of crisis, suggests that fundamentalism can be a palliative reaction to the adverse consequences of economic change. But further, as Habermas (1975) suggested, crises in the political or economic sphere can migrate to the realms of culture, identity and motivation-identity. The passionate embrace of fundamentalist identities, and the ferocity of hatred to the secular Other, requires us to not only consider the political economic factors, but examine the depth psychological moments of identity, emotion and desire. Moreover, identities and motivations emergent under conditions of crisis can reflux back and impact the political and economic. Finally, if the Instrumental Reason of the West, with its dehumanized, totalitarian logic of efficiency, enabled a fusion of advanced technology and atavistic barbarism, the rejection of that same modernity, cloaked in theological justifications, similarly sustains domination and can culminate in terrorism and mass murder. As I shall argue, understanding Islamic fundamentalism, a modern ideology cloaked as "religious tradition" reveals the enduring explanatory power of Critical Theory. As will be seen, the embrace of modern Western values in Muslim societies in the nineteenth-century, remained limited and encapsulated. More often than not, the modernizers failed to establish long lasting reforms. As a result, the failure to embrace Post-Enlightenment modernity, and the continuing resistance to rationality, can be seen in the persistence of authoritarian governments, economic stagnation and cultural ossification. Limited economic opportunities and political powerlessness has led some people to a fervent embrace of fundamentalist expressions of anti-modernity. Notwithstanding the radically different political contexts and realities of the present age, and the vast differences between Western and Islamic cultures, the Frankfurt School analysis of Fascism hints at a complex and nuanced understanding of the path from seventh century Mecca to NYC on 9/11/02.

Rationality and the Rise of the West

What factors led to the "rise of the West"? What impact did its Christian values play, and what was the role of its major institutions in fostering its ascent? How and why did a bourgeois class emerge? What was the role of its distinct values rooted in Christianity in fostering the conditions leading to the Renaissance, Reformation and Enlightenment and in turn, rational, capitalist societies that saw Science and Reason as enabling progress?[4] Rational commerce, bureaucratic administration, and a distinctly novel form of "inner determination" enabled the rapid ascent of market society, science and in turn, industrialization. In the contemporary world of globalized capital, as different countries or regions have shown differential rates of economic growth, the role of cultural values, especially religion fostering or impeding the diffusion of rationality, has again become an explanatory variable. While devel-

[4] The notion of "progress" assumes that societies are neither static nor perfect; they can be changed, for the better, by human effort. This notion lies at the heart of Comte, Marx and most of the sociological legacy.

oping nations such as Hindu India or Confucian/Communist China rush forward into technologically-based economic growth, the vast swath of Islamic countries remain mired in stagnation and poverty.[5]

Weber attempted to explain why, of perhaps thirty or more major civilizations, only Western Christendom fostered goal rational economic action, (*zweckrational*) and in turn rational modernity with its technologically based economic growth and eventually, world domination. His analysis showed that the unique legacy of Judeo-Christian monotheism included an activist notion of God that intervened in human history. Christianity, unlike Islam, valorized asceticism. This in turn fostered monastic orders that later inspired a Protestant "inner determination" (salvation anxiety), a "this worldly" vocationalism/sacralized as a "calling" with promises of salvation, and in turn, a "methodological orientation" to everyday life seen as a career rather than a collection of isolated moments. These values catalyzed the growth of the bourgeois classes that would embrace a "disenchantment of the world"; purposive rationality would become the dominant value in the economic, political and cultural spheres of modernity. For the Frankfurt School, informed by Lukács, capitalism fostered bourgeois categories of thought colonized by Formal Reason, purposive rationality that in turn legitimated new forms of domination. This rationality, as both a logic and form of goal oriented action, served as both a catalyst for the growth of capitalism and its own legitimation. But it also led to dehumanization and a carceral society. As such, this rationality invited various critiques ranging from romanticism to fascism, and in our current age, various fundamentalisms would re-enchant the world.

Islamic Exceptionalism

Many of the elements of purposive rationality were present in other societies. In the West, this could be seen with the introduction of the "concept" in Greek philosophy and the discipline of the Hoplites (Weber, 1978). Rome developed a number of advanced technologies from weaponry to civil engineering and architecture based on the arch and cement. But at the same time, most advanced civilizations had specific structural and/or ideological barriers to rational modernity. While, to be sure, aspects of Reason could be found in many early

[5] The embrace of Islamisms may thus be "rational choices" for the individual, but since these choices are to seek emotional gratifications, collectively, the "choices" may not be all that rational.

civilizations, especially in their sciences and technologies, its embodiment in secular law, as in Rome or India, was quite rare. Patrimonialism (the unity of family and State) was the typical form of administration; rationally organized, meritocratically staffed, bureaucratically regulated administration carrying out the policies of political parties, was little developed elsewhere.[6] It was only in Renaissance Europe where rational commerce dependent on rational law, rational administration and a rational culture came together to foster the Reformation, and in turn, the Enlightenment, industrialization and democratization.

For Weber, Hinduism and Confucianism, much like Islam, had various cultural barriers to rational modernization and change. Neither Hindu India nor Confucian China had a Reformation. Yet India and China have shorn themselves of the weight of tradition and are now at the leading edges of modern commerce and advanced technologies. But in Islamic societies, the limited diffusion and subsequent encapsulation of rationality has meant economic and scientific stagnation. More specifically, the traditionalist barriers to rationality in Hindu and Confucian religion tended to be limited to specific realms. In India, the ascriptive-based caste system limited social intercourse, imposed a heredity-based division of labor that thwarted individual talent and slowed the emergence of the factory system, lest higher classes face ritual pollution. Its pantheist Hinduism created a "magic garden". It did not allow a secular, demystified realm. In China, Confucianism, more a set of ritual practices than a complex theology, did not have religious-based barriers to science or rational commerce.[7] The emphasis on aesthetics and cultural learning required for qualification as literati, the privileged stratum of "gentlemen administrators", thwarted the embrace of rational, meritocratic governance or commerce. Further, the aristocracy maintained itself by limiting the emergence of other classes such as merchants that might challenge its power and legitimacy.

From what has been said, a fundamental difference between Islam and Protestantism, Hinduism and Confucianism, as well as Buddhism, has been

[6] For Weber (1978), the Turkish Janissaries, European born, yet trained in Turkey, came close to a more rational form of administration, and indeed "Turkish Exceptionalism", e.g., a multiparty Islamic Nation-state, with a modernizing economy, strong ties to Israel, and Westward orientation reflects both geographic location and the historical legacies of Turkey that markedly set it apart from the Arabic Middle East.

[7] Indeed in the sixteenth century, with the growth of oceanic trade and incipient industrialization, the Emperor abruptly halted these before they might engender political classes that might challenge his authority.

the unity of religion, community and everyday life. This seamless web of Islamic faith, law and commerce, had little room for rational law or philosophy that were safely sequestered in centers of learning. And in the Muslim world, fundamentalism has become a major determinant of social life. While Rodinson (1966) has argued contra Weber, Islamic commerce was rational, and Muslim merchants were as motivated, avaricious, and as willing to exploit workers as their Protestant counterparts. But he added, the capitalist trading sector of merchants never fostered a full scale capitalist social formation. Rodinson suggested that Weber's analysis of the Protestant disdain of magic and Islamic prohibitions upon usury that were typically circumvented, failed to explain why Protestantism fostered capitalism and Islam was not conducive to the expansion of its capitalist sector. (He argues that the European colonizers restricted potential competition.) As I will argue, the crucial indigenous factors were not magic or usury prohibitions, but Islamic commercial law and the Protestant "this worldly, asceticism". Together, these enabled the emergence of an autonomous, secular, commercial realm as well and the "inner determination" of individuals to pursue worldly success without creatural indulgences. Asceticism for Weber was a necessary and sufficient basis for early capitalism; but there must also be "the physical means of production by the entrepreneur, freedom of the market, rational technology, rational law, free labour and finally the commercialization of economic life" (cited in Turner 1974:12).

Shariah-based commercial law did not enable the growth of large scale trading enterprises as did European (Italian) law based on secular Roman commercial law. Thus asceticism, a crucial aspect of the "inner determinism" of the Protestant merchant that fostered investment in long-term, large-scale, private economic enterprises, was absent in most other societies, including Islam. Finally, the patrimonial forms of governancethwarted the path to rational capitalism. Thus, contra Rodinson, I will argue that there were inherent aspects of Islam that prevented capitalism from emerging. On the other hand, I would agree with Rodinson, that the classical *imperialism and colonization of the nineteenth and early twentieth centuries, also served to thwart efforts at modernization. Following WWII, between the Cold War and quests for oil, various progressive movements from Nasser's Pan-Arab socialism to Mossadeq's democratic socialism were systematically undermined by the United States and Britain. Finally, contemporary neo-colonialization by global capital, has sought resources and markets, but has been little concerned with supporting actual democratic and or modernizing movements.*

To understand the appeal of contemporary Islamism, we will note that not only did early Islam pose specific impediments to the expansion of rational markets and/or meritocratic administration, but these legacies have endured. The central feature of Islam was its seamless web of religious faith and moral regulation with law, commerce and administration. While *kadi* justice, based on the Quran, regulated commerce, so too were commerce and culture infused with religious codes. Insofar as sacred law, *shariah,* was global and all pervasive, rather than sectorial, there was little space for secular discourses and debates. Moreover, while Islam, like Christianity was a salvation religion, it did not valorize asceticism and self denial, nor did it engender "salvation anxiety". Thus, for both its warriors and merchants, Islam did not foster the conditions that led to self-denial, asceticism *qua* rational control of affect as an aspect of individual character. To be sure, while there is an obsessive concern with cleanliness, the "anal-compulsive" character, wrought by anxiety, was typically Western. In sum, Islam fostered structural barriers to the incursions of modernity *qua* rational commerce, rational administration and secular world views. Nor did Islam engender the kind of individual character structure well suited to that kind of rational control. Islamic rationality was cloistered in its schools and centers of learning. Thus despite the efforts of foreign colonizers or indigenous elites to introduce rationality into the Islamic world, despite the many modernizing and/or nationalist movements that did in fact take place in the nineteenth and twentieth centuries, the impetus for modernization has more often than not been thwarted. The limiting case, however, remains Turkey where the Western-oriented Kemalist revolution succeeded. Despite various modernization movements, there are still many limits to the diffusion of modernity. As a result, the relative weakness of Islamic countries, vis a vis other nations, is a daily reminder of underdevelopment. (The economic and military power of Israel makes this blatant.)

British imperialism in India and China, and the embrace of communism in the Chinese case, often led to some folks getting educations in the West and/or exposure to Western ideas (see below, p. 308). This in turn often encouraged the emergence of indigenous cadres dedicated to modernization-especially political self determination. Eventually, as part of independence/revolutionary struggles, there was broad public support for independence and modernization. Chinese and Indian elites created spaces for purposive rationality in the commercial sectors that in turn fostered transformations that created spaces for rational administration and secular culture. The revolutions of both Gandhi and Mao, anti-colonialism in one case, a civil war between communists and nationalists in the other, resulted in modern States with secular realms and expanded spaces for rational science and commerce-even when opposed to the traditionalism of either the Indian caste system with its notions of ritual purity or the Chinese clan system that depended on filial devotion. Thus Hindu and Confucian societies have nevertheless been able to accommodate themselves to modernity and indeed have become major actors in the world. In turn, they have rapidly growing economies. They accommodated themselves to modernity by providing significant spaces for rational, purposive action, as evident in secular procedures for business, political administration and scientific endeavors.[8] While Hindus may not eat beef, they may well write software and/or answer callers from the US. India has-a functioning democracy and a large middle class-the world's largest. Confucians may respect the spirits of elders, yet they have introduced economic rationality to produce much of the clothes and electronic *tschoschkes* for the West. Most recently, they have initiated leading edge research in computers, pharmaceuticals and electronics. But the Islamic societies of the Middle East, noting great variations between Lebanon and Sudan, Morocco and Yemen, have remained economically stagnant, politically torpid and intellectually moribund.[9] Save oil production or terrorism, they are irrelevant to the larger world economy.

The Dialectic of Un-enlightenment

The sociology of religion, as outlined by Weber and Durkheim, said little about Islam. Moreover, fundamentalism had not yet become a major social force. Weber's scattered writings on Islam as a "salvation religion" noted its "elective affinity" for warriors (Weber 1978). Muslim knights, unlike their medieval Christian counterparts, were less inclined to asceticism. Moreover, its legal system was based on religiously schooled professional jurists, *kadi* justice based on the Quran stood in contradistinction to the secular nature of evidentiary-based Western justice. Despite his insights, Weber did not offer

---

[8] We do not assume that modernity means democratic, and based on "popular sovereignty", rather, modern forms of political legitimacy do not rest on God's will, as interpreted by clerics and religious virtuosos. As will be argued, this separation of Church (Temple, Pagoda or Mosque) and State has been essential for modernity. So too are double entry bookkeeping and commercial transparency.

[9] To be sure, Turkey, while Muslim, is progressing toward modernity and someday, EU membership. Similarly, Lebanon and some of the smaller Gulf states, openly embracing rational commerce, are also showing growth. Moreover, they support free, and often critical media like Al Ahram and Al Jazeera.

a systematic analysis of Islam. It is necessary to note that while certain aspects of Islam were highly conducive to building extensive caravan-based trade and a vast theocratically based Empire, there were a number of structural and cultural barriers to a Reformation, and later, resistance to an Enlightenment-based secular modernity, if not morality.[10] More specifically, the ruling elites used *Shariah*-based laws to secure the hegemony of their rule and stability of their community (*Umma*), just as the merchants depended on fair, ethical trade.

More recent scholars inspired by Weber, from Turner (1974) to Schluchter (1999), have attempted to more fully develop his perspective. Notwithstanding, the value neutrality of this tradition has had certain important consequences in framing certain questions. More specifically, Weber, emphasizing the universality of domination, eschewed an emancipatory vision of society and/or a telos of freedom and democracy. Therefore, his critiques of the social order were quite subtle. Islam, as a salvation religion, like Christianity, believed in an after life and an activist God that intervened in human affairs. While Islam, as "warrior religion," in Weber's view may have encouraged "territorial expansion", or conquest, to save the souls of "infidels", Islam, did not foster either "salvation anxiety" or sacralize a "this worldly", vocational asceticism among its merchant classes. Husain (N.d.) argues that, while like Protestantism, Islam encouraged hard work:

> Weber shows that rational law, autonomous cities, an independent burgher class and political stability were totally absent in Islam. But, as it is, he does not seem to link the absence of capitalism in Islam to the nonexistence of the prerequisites identified by him. On the contrary, he lists at least two factors responsible for preventing Islam from evolving naturally. The monotheistic Islam of Makkah failed to develop into an ascetic this-worldly religion because its main carrier was a warrior group. The content of the religious message was transformed into a set of values compatible with the mundane needs of this warrior group. The spiritual element of Islam as a belief system with emphasis on salvation was transformed into the secular quest for mundane gains. The result was that Islam became a religion of accommodation rather than of transformation. Second, the original message of

[10] While this is not the place to develop the argument, given Italian humanism, following Kant we can find a basis for morality that is not dependent on a God or religious legitimation.

> monotheism was subjected to change under the impact of Sufism which catered for the emotional and orgiastic needs of the masses. In consequence, Islam was pulled in two opposite directions by these two groups. The warrior group pulled Islam in the direction of a militaristic ethic; and the Sufis in that of mystical flight. Both the directions of Islam, representing, as it were, a bifurcated Islamic ethic failed to produce, as Weber will have us believe, the prerequisites congruent with the rise of rational capitalism.

Moreover, despite the legacies of the Greco-Roman civilization, its advanced sciences, medicine and philosophy, rationality remained limited to virtuosos encapsulated within its centers of learning. Thus, Islamic theology was little transformed by either internal contradictions or challenges from without. Despite the sophistication of Muslim science, philosophy and medicine, there did not emerge a class that would either challenge religious orthodoxy or embrace rationality and in turn foster a Muslim Reformation. While beliefs and practices may well vary by time and region, like most legitimations of traditional authority, Islam has often stood as a barrier to the purposive rationality that is an essential moment of modernity. This was as evident in it patrimonialism that stunted the move to rational administration as much as the absence of asceticism as a moment of inner determination seen in "salvation anxiety" that in turn impelled work, not to seek wealth, but confirm salvation.

But let us at the same time note that the religiously-based ideological barriers are typically materially-based and often used and fostered by certain groups to sustain their own powers. The contemporary political classes (mostly autocratic dictatorships), as well as clerics and theologians, typically on State payrolls, generally do not want an open, critical press, genuine grassroots democracy and open debates that might redress grievances or challenge their power. Nor do they wish to open their economies to genuine competition that might undermine local businesses, read reduce corruption. Few of these countries can be said to have a truly representative government, grass root political organizations, or a free, uncensored press.[11] As a result, much of the

[11] Lebanon has a much more open press, for example, Dar Al Hayat, compared to the tightly controlled press of Iran that routinely closes dissenting newspapers. Further, the emergence of Al Jazeera, the television network, provides information more open than typical of Middle Eastern news sources. It is also worth noting that comparatively speaking the Middle East has fewer NGOs than other areas of the world. Prodemocracy NGOs are typically harrassed. On the other hand, the explosion of the Internet has become a means of creating open, democratic spaces where free communication is possible.

Middle East, save oil kingdoms, remains mired in economic stagnation and political ossification in which there is growing urban poverty and social malaise. Nor have any of these countries shown either much curiosity about the outside world or produced much in the way of intellectual innovation.[12] Otherwise said, Islam, which was once one of the great civilizations in history, has not only remained economically stagnant, politically repressed, and intellectually ossified, but these conditions have bred particularly virulent Islamisms extolling theocratic governance, fundamentalist versions of Shariah law and intense animosity to Western modernity. This has been seen in the Algerian civil war, the Iranian theocracy, organizations such as Muslim Brotherhood, Hezbollah, Hamas, and above all, the rise of Al Queda. Understanding the rise, fall and stagnation of Islam and its contemporary embrace of fervent Islamic fundamentalisms, requires a consideration of the interaction of history and biography, a "sociological imagination", sensitive to economic, political and depth psychological considerations of "human variety" (Mills 1959).

Given the failures of modernist ideologies, as a result of internal barriers specific to Islam, compounded by European interventionism and imperialism, fundamentalism, political Islam, has flourished in the last few decades. Fundamentalism has taken especially virulent forms in the Islamic societies of the Middle East and South Asia that have on occasion led to violent acts ranging from the Palestinian *intifada*, the tragedy of 9/11 and the bombings of the Madrid Railroad Station and London tube.[13] The resistance to American occupation in Iraq has also been seen as an expression of Islamism, political Islam.[14] But as I will also argue, while religious fundamentalism may be the expression of anger, alienation and frustration, it is not the cause.

---

[12] Arab intellectuals, commissioned by the United Nations found their societies crippled by a lack of political freedom, repression of women and isolated from the world of ideas that stifled creativity. For example, with a population of 280 million, 330 books were translated into Arabic, about 10% of the number translated into Greek, with 20 million readers. In the last twenty years, there have been 350 patents compared to 14,000 for S. Korea. See *Arab Human Development Report 2002*. The United Nations Development Program and the Arab Fund for Economic and Social Development. New York: United Nations Publications, 2002.

[13] As I shall argue, the relationship between fundamentalism and the embrace of violence is not as simple as mass media often suggest. Indeed, the Marty and Applebee (1991–95) fundamentalism project alone has five volumes. Further, many terrorists are left wing and secular, NOT religious.

[14] This is not to suggest that the resistance was inspired by Islam. There are a number of groups that oppose the occupation; some are quite secular like the Communists. Rather, Islamism is often used to legitimate the struggle against foreign domination.

Part II The Ascent and Decline of the Islamic Caliphate

Muhammad, Mecca and Beyond

In the sixth century, conflicts between Persia and Byzantium pushed caravan routes southerly into the Saudi Peninsula (Turner 1974). But the chronic rivalries and wars between the nomadic tribes made orderly, predictable trade precarious. It was in this context that the Prophet Muhammad, a trader, received the word of Allah from the archangel Gabriel that was written down as the Quran. Muhammad began to spread the holy words of Allah that would bring a monotheistic religion to the pagan tribes who would become unified through a monotheistic "world religion". Although Islam began as a form of quietist piety among urban merchants, it would change to a more activist expression as it gained followers.

> At the time of its origin in Mecca, the eschatological religion of Muhammad developed in pietistic urban conventicles that were likely to withdraw from the world: subsequently in Medina and in the evolution of early Islamic communities, the religion was transformed into a widespread Arabic, status oriented, warrior religion.[15]

Muhammad, as a prophet and skilled arbiter, found a ready audience among the growing classes of traders and merchants, whose status disposed an "elective affinity" for a salvation religion that would establish an "imagined community" of people united by faith that provided members with valorized, sacralized identities, and a God ordained ethical regulation of everyday conduct conducive to the expansion of commerce. The Middle East would become safe for the expansion of trade. But that expansion was also dependent on a warrior class that cast a decided stamp on its worldly ethic.

As Weber noted in the case of Protestantism, shared and upheld ethical standards between members of the religious "brotherhood", between members of a common "world" religion, enabled trust in strangers that was essential for the conduct of business in large, widespread markets. Islam, as a "world religion" of warriors and merchants, pacified the area and established universal moral codes for regulating everyday life and orderly commerce; this in turn facilitated mercantile-based economic growth. Thus, the economic conditions of the time disposed an "elective affinity" for a "world religion"

[15] Wolfgang Schluchter, "Hindrances to Modernity, Max Weber and Islam." Toby Huff and Wolfgang Schlucter, *Max Weber and Islam* (New Brunswick, N.J., 1999) 79.

to pacify the region and routinize caravan trade. This trust made possible a complex banking system that enabled a check drawn in Spain to be cashed in China.

Islam, as a salvation religion with an activist God, concerned with just whom might be found in heaven, fostered the "saving of souls" by converting infidels, which in turn sacralized military efforts and created vast territorial expansion and a wealthy Empire ruled by a Caliphate, followers and descendents of the Prophet. The Caliphate was the combination of temporal and spiritual rule begun by Muhammad, and subsequently carried out by his followers, Abu Bakr (his father-in-law), Umar, Uthman and Ali, collectively the *Rashidun* (the rightly guided). After the death of the Prophet, power moved from Mecca to Damascus, headed by the Omayyad Caliphate (Damascus, 661–750). The Caliphs, however, unlike the Prophet, did not have the power of prophecy. Selection was based on his being a devout follower.

The descendents or followers of Muhammad claimed authority as both secular and religious leaders of the community of faithful, the *umma*. With talented leadership, skilled and brave warriors, military conquest and expanded trade, within 100 years, Islam had spread from Gibraltar to the Indus. Its merchant classes grew in size, wealth and power. Following the triumph of the Abbasid Caliphate (Baghdad, 750–1248), and a number of military conquests, the Muslims recovered Greco-Roman philosophy and science, learned paper making from the Chinese and embraced numbering and math from India. There was a period of cultural efflorescence. With peace came prosperity, and with prosperity came centers of learning devoted to philosophy, arts, sciences and medicine. This would come to be seen as the Golden Age as cities like Cairo, Baghdad, Damascus and Cordoba also became affluent cities and great intellectual centers. Islam became one of the great civilizations. Islam indeed survived the sacking of Baghdad and continued to foster science and learning. But meanwhile, a long dormant Christendom was ascendant. As its merchant classes grew, Muslim and Jews were expelled from Spain in 1492. Soon the Europeans were able to circumnavigate the globe and bypass the caravan trade of the Muslims. The Arabic Middle East would go into decline as the Turkish Ottomans expanded their empire. But by the nineteenth century, that empire was in decline as industrial Europe flourished. With WWI came the *coup de grace* of the Ottomans, now so weakened that the Kemalists seized power and imposed a modernist course in Turkey.

Islamic Law

For Islam, the word of Allah as revealed in the Quran and the teachings in the *hadith*, were the basis of sacred law, *shariah*. There was no distinction of sacred and secular law, all law was sacred. For Islam, economic life was regulated by commercial codes derived from the Quran, more specifically the *Hanafi* commercial codes.[16] Islam, with its *shariah*, laws and ethical regulations that applied to all pacified and unified diverse peoples, enabled the expansion of vast trade networks throughout the region. While this would routinize commerce, it would also mitigate against the emergence of a secular space and the extent to which rational commercial law might emerge. The institutionalization of a sacred commercial law resting on theological justifications stood as a barrier to rational, predictable legal procedures and standards of evidence such as in Indian law or Roman commercial law.

As Weber (1978) noted, in the Western system, legislative bodies passed laws based on formal rationality, rules of evidence and prior cases. Western judges dispensed justice based on abstract laws and precedents. But Islamic law, as interpreted by trained *mufti*, legal scholars, and administered by *kadi* judges, was jurist in nature. The great jurists who established the legal traditions of Islam were more "legal prophets", establishing substantive-theological "stereotyped jurist law . . . that opposed secularization". Formal-juridical (rational) legal codes were wanting.[17] Its system of jurists appointed by the central authority, were frequently antagonistic to the central authority. This often gave the judge administrative authority that nevertheless made him loyal to the central authority and prevented local powers or landed classes from emerging.[18] In sum, Islamic law was conducive to the establishment of large scale patrimonial State organizations such as the military or government organizations, but it did not foster large scale autonomous institutions such as mercantile organizations or, perish the thought, civil society organizations or political groupings such as estates or parties.

The Muslim jurists, *mufti* scholars and *kadi* administrators, were religiously trained experts, thoroughly qualified through examinations. But they were

---

[16] See Kuran, 2001.

[17] Wolfgang Schlucter, "Hindrances to Modernity, Max Weber and Islam." In Huff, Toby, and Wolfgang, Schlucter, Eds., *Max Weber and Islam* (New Brunswick, N.J., 1999) 108.

[18] Haim Gerber, The Social Origins of the Modern Middle East (Boulder, CO., 1987).

not clerics, e.g., *immans, mullahs* or religious virtuosos. While they may have been appointed by the State, absent legislative bodies, jurism in Islam was not centrally legislated or litigated; it was based on particular interpretation and local conditions.[19] Quranic commercial law was based on the *Shariah* legal codes and regulations that were the product of the *Hanafi* School and were based in large part on what had been local commercial practices and traditions. *Kadis* offered the interpretations of these commercial codes and settled conflicts. It was highly important that, for Islamic societies, social [legal] rationality was closely tied to the foundations of specific religious categories, beliefs, and exercises in relation to everyday life, commerce, and governance. This is not to imply that such justice was random, haphazard or without extensive formal training. Agricultural commerce and caravan-based, merchant trade were highly regulated by religiously-based laws. This established predictable conditions that were highly conducive to economic growth. Indeed from the time of the Prophet and the holy Caliphs, trade was highly valued and its traders acted very much like Protestant capitalists (Rodinson, 1966). The unity of sacred and secular law enabled an ethically regulated trade that flourished. But while this commerce was routinized *it was not* rationalized in the Weberian sense. Nevertheless, within a couple of centuries, Islam quickly spread and its trade networks spanned from Iberia to China.

Eventually, however, the religiously-based legal codes would acquire a fixity that would act to prevent later generations from making fundamental revisions as material conditions changed.[20] While Islamic commercial laws would at first facilitate the rapid growth of Islamic commerce, these same laws became impediments to the expansion of the economy both from within and without. On the one hand there were limits to the size of commercial enterprises. This in turn meant that Muslim traders would be less able to compete with later Europeans. Firstly, Islamic merchant trading associations, whether or not familial, could not assume the legal form of a joint stock corporation with juridical rights *independent of the owners*. Moreover, Muslim merchants did not employ the kinds of economic rationality, e.g., double entry bookkeeping, or risk insurance as did the upstart Italian merchants who were

---

[19] It is important to note that Islam did not have a centralized clerical hierarchy.

[20] Timur Kuran, *The Islamic Commercial Crisis: Institutional Roots of the Delay in the Middle East's Economic Modernization*. (Los Angeles, California, 2001): USC Center for Law, Economics and Organization, Research paper, CO01–12, http://papers.srn.com/abstract _id+276377

able to forge large scale commercial enterprises that flourished over time. Thus, an Italian business enterprise could continue to grow and amass fortunes long after the death of a founder(s). Indeed many of the successful merchants of Italy were large family enterprises such as the Medicis, Borhgeses, Peruzzis, or the Bardis. Islamic legal codes kept business small, limited and ephemeral. No great merchant families emerged, let alone the vast trading companies typical of Europe.[21] The subsequent growth of Portuguese and Spanish trade, and later the Netherlands and England, all depended on these large-scale enterprises.[22] Secondly, Islamic inheritance laws meant that when one of the associates died, a partnership was terminated and inheritance was divided in egalitarian ways, as opposed to European laws that allowed limited inheritance, e.g., a single person could inherit a share of an enterprise that nevertheless survived the loss of an owner-partner. Finally, the prohibitions on "excessive" interest, *rabī* and the lack of rational accounting meant that business enterprises could not borrow money for investment purposes.[23] Quranic-based laws thus thwarted the growth of a secular, commercial, sphere. As a result, while vast Islamic trade networks would create great wealth, that wealth was not centralized by large, powerful economic actors. It would never have the large, rationally regulated, large scale, international economic enterprises that led to the affluence of the West.

The Decline of the Crescent

A number of internal and external factors led to the decline of the [Abbasid] Caliphate and the waning of Islam's Golden Age. Thus, for example, Islam survived and rebounded from the Mongol sackings of Baghdad and the destructions of the libraries of the foremost cultural center of Islam. Following the first Mongol invasion by Hulagu Khan in 1258, the Abbasid Caliphate was destroyed. The city rebounded, but was again attacked in 1401 by

[21] Timur Kuran, *The Islamic Commercial Crisis: Institutional Roots of the Delay in the Middle East's Economic Modernization*. (Los Angeles, California, 2001): USC Center for Law, Economics and Organization, Research paper, CO01–12, http://papers.srn.com/abstract _id+276377

[22] Thus for example, the Dutch East India Company, or the British East India Company became important motors for economic growth and imperialism. See http://en.wikipedia.org/wiki/Dutch_East_India_Company http://59.1911encyclopedia.org/E/EA/EAST_INDIA_COMPANY.htm

[23] Rodinson (1966) argues that the prohibition was not absolute, what was disdained was excessive interest.

Tamerlane. Meanwhile, political power was fragmented and dispersed to local groups such as the Fatimids, Ayyubids and Mamluks in North Africa, the Ottoman Turks, Persian Safavids or the Timurids of Mogul India. Although many of these local powers prospered, the vast Caliphate ruled by the Umayyads or Abbasids, would fade into history. The Ottoman Turks claimed the mantle of the Caliphs, ending the Arabic domination of Islam. By the fifteenth century, between political fragmentation and growing competition with a rapidly rising Europe, Islamic economic growth began to sputter and decline. Ibn Khaldun (1969) noted endless cycles of conflict between the rich urbanites and rural tribes that would thwart economic growth. Finally, by the sixteenth century, European merchants with their vast ocean-going fleets, undercut the caravan trade that had been the lifeblood of Islamic wealth.

Thus, we might note that in 1453, Mehmet II's Ottoman army conquered Constantinople. But by 1492, with the *Reconquista*,the Muslims were forced out of Spain. In any event, in 1492, the expulsion of the Muslims from Spain and the Spanish discovery of the New World, might mark the point in which an ascendant Christian Europe would overtake a waning Islamic Caliphate.[24] A century and a half later came the Turkish defeat at the gates of Vienna, by Sobieski in 1683, the defeat of the Ottoman army by Prince Eugene in 1697 and again in 1716. Further, the colonialization of Muslim countries that began in 1798 meant Muslim societies would be ruled by European powers. The colonization of Islamic societies by the great imperial power wrested local control of the lands from North Africa to the Indus and beyond. The destruction of the Turkish fleet at Navarino in 1827, foretold the end of the Ottoman Empire almost a century later.

In more recent times, further evidence of military, technological and economic weakness was seen in the establishment of the State of Israel in 1948 that led to a number of subsequent military defeats of massive Arab armies by the far smaller IDF (1948, '56, '67 and '73). The consequences of economic weakness and political fragmentation have endured till this very day and have kept most Muslim countries from prospering in the contemporary world.

[24] Of course the Ottoman Caliphate, a truncated remnant of a much larger empire endured for 700 years until 1918.

What Went Wrong

As most historians note, the growth of the Italian city-States depended on trade with the Levant. The cultural efflorescence of Renaissance depended on the preservation of Greco-Roman philosophy by Moslem scholars. But while the Italian Renaissance established the conditions that would lead to the Reformation in Christendom, why didn't these same ideas foster a Reformation within Islam that would create spaces for secular commercial law and practices, for a democratic civil society, and in turn, public spheres for the expression of diverse ideas? As Lewis (2002) put it, what went wrong? The answer must consider material, geographical factors and ideological factors. 1) While there were many rifts within Muslim societies, for example, between nomads and city dwellers, the merchants and warriors were integral parts of the same ruling strata. Further, the religious leaders were themselves often traders and/or members of trading families. Thus, the conditions were not present for the rise of an upstart merchant class that would become carriers of a secular social ethic that might challenge the dominant classes. Moreover, insofar as its knightly classes were more likely to be term limited tax farmers whose land tenures were at the pleasure of the State rather than landowners as in Europe, vassalage did not develop. Perhaps class conflict may be the moving force of history, but in the Muslim world, an upstart rival class did not emerge. 2) Unlike Christianity in Rome or Byzantium, Islam was a relatively decentralized religion. There did not exist an Islamic pope or dominant "Rome" that might become a central focus for theological administration, critique and dissent (Collins 1998). Rather, there were major theological centers in Damascus, Baghdad, Cairo, and Cordoba etc. 3) While there have long been variations in scholarly interpretations both in religion (*ijtihad*) and philosophy, the mainstreams of Islam political thought were rooted in Plato's *Republic*, that legitimated a theocrat-king model of rulership that in turn mitigated against political input from other stratum.

Given Islamic theology, asceticism did not play a role commensurate with its place in Christianity. Muslim merchants were not unlikely to become bearers of a "worldly ethic of practical action". Nor might "salvation anxiety" foster an obsessive compulsive, methodological orientation to everyday work as a religious calling, a moment of a career. Given the then prevalent ideology, the theologically derived, commercial-legal *Hanafi* codes that had once promoted expansion and regional trade, patrimonial power arrangements and its class structure, there was little space for the emergence of a new class of challengers to the existing system. After a certain point, perhaps with European military ascendance and circumnavigation that reduced the role of caravan based trade, further economic growth was thwarted. Islamic economies then began to wane and stagnate.[25]

Meanwhile, given the unique qualities and histories of Christian Europe such as 1) "constitutionalism" that began with the Magna Carta limiting the authority of the king, and 2) the "military revolution" in which technological advances/innovations in the kinds of gun powder weapons, the rifling of barrels, as well as combat tactics, together with the re-organization of the military, slowly but surely gave Europeans military superiority. As Christendom thrived and Islamic societies stagnated, there was a wide spread *ressentement* to the Western world extending to the point of issuing *fatwas* against Muslims traveling to Europe. As a result of this, as Islam was overshadowed by ascendant Christendom, the *ressentement* to the West has acted a cultural barrier to embracing Western knowledge and techniques that has acted as a brake upon modernization. The prosperity of Israel stands in sharp contrast with its poor neighbors. The recent conquests of Afghanistan in 2002 and Iraq in 2004 reveal the military impotence of Muslim countries.[26] The *ressentement* has grown.

Part III Colonialism and Reform

The Fate of Reform

As is typical of colonization, indigenous subjects frequently went to study in the mother country. Quite often, they not only learned science, engineering and medicine, but also learned about Western democracy, resistance and even socialism. Indeed the writings of Marx and/or socialist parties influenced a number of colonized people who attended Oxford, the Sorbonne or, in the twentieth century, Patrice Lumumba University. Despite the legacies and barriers posed by cultural traditions and structural impediments to modernity,

---

[25] Timur Kuran, *The Islamic Commercial Crisis: Institutional Roots of the Delay in the Middle East's Economic Modernization*. (Los Angeles, California, 2001): USC Center for Law, Economics and Organization, Research paper, CO01–12, http://papers.srn.com/abstract _id+276377

[26] The "conquest" of Iraq may be a bit problematic. Despite declarations of "mission accomplished", the Iraqis have not seemed to have accepted the "benign" occupation by the US military.

often upheld by religious laws and *fatwas*, there have been various progressive movements and attempts have been made to embrace Western science and introduce purposive rationality, *qua* modernity, progressive ideologies and rational, democratic governance. A number of efforts at modernization and democratization have been undertaken beginning in the nineteenth-century (Moaddel 2005).

In the nineteenth-century, it did not seem that there were insurmountable conflicts between Islam and the West; even some nineteenth-century fundamentalists such as Jamal Al Din in Iran and Muhammad Abduh did not see incompatibility between Islam and Western science, philosophy and law. Rather, they opposed colonialism and foreign domination. While there were many critiques of of the West, its imperialist ambitions and colonial practices, they did embrace Enlightenment notions of general political participation and willing assent by the governed. Even one party dictatorships with staged rallies claimed to represent the will of the people. At this point, there are a number of unique histories in Egypt, Persia or India, each with its own social, political and cultural narratives where certain Muslim leaders and intellectuals were seeking new syntheses of Enlightenment rationality with Islamic religion, laws and customs (Moaddel 2005). European influences grew and certain modernist-based opposition to traditional authority and hereditary rule emerged. Various versions of Europe's secular modernity and liberalism began to impact Islamic societies. Such efforts often achieved temporary success, but for the most part failed to foster lasting structural changes.[27] Turkey is often invoked as the exemplar of Islamic modernity. But the Kemalist revolution indeed shows that in the face of cultural barriers and the obstacles of tradition, it required a military takeover and a secular army to "sustain" modernity. Since 1960, three military coups have deposed elected governments, often banning political parties and imposing sharp limits on political and personal rights.

Various reformist and democratizing movements have come, and more important, gone in Islamic countries. The post-colonial independence movements were often led by military leaders such as Ataturk, Nasser or Kessem

[27] In Turkey, it was not until the twentieth century that the Sultan, ruler of a waning hegemon defeated in a war, was overthrown by a petty bourgeois military class who embraced modernization to restore military power. Similarly, in Egypt, Nasser overthrew the king, but his secular socialism was short lived. Yet autocratic rule has endured, even ratified in elections.

who imposed various modernist, nationalist, socialist, or even royalist regimes.[28] In some cases, anti-colonial independence movements from the democratic socialism of Mossadeq, to the Pan-Arab socialism of Nasser or Kessem, variants of secular nationalism, socialism or communism were undermined by Western (American) interventions and coups. Without underlying mass constituencies of either a rational bourgeoisie or internationalist proletariat classes seeking reform and democratization, the result was powerful central States with autocratic rule that was typically intolerant of an open public sphere, democratic participation or popular dissent (Moaddel 2005). In some cases, e.g., Turkey, Egypt, Syria, Libya, and even Iraq, following the military overthrow of a monarchy, there have been spaces for secularism and separation of Mosque and State. But, except for Turkey and its "enforced democratization" from above, despite various modernizing efforts, without traditions of "popular sovereignty" embraced by a powerful class, there has been very little in the way of genuine democratic governance with competing political parties, support for human rights and a free, critical press that can criticize the government and its leaders. Indeed thousands of political dissidents languished in prisons and/or faced torture in Egyptian prisons, while others have often been murdered en mass as in Syria and Iraq. And it should be noted, that quite often such governments, however unpopular among their own people, have often been sustained by US largesse to secure bases and/or allies in wars against "communism" and more recently, terrorism.[29]

Material and ideological barriers to change

As Moore (1966) argued, the nature of pre-modern authority/land owner-renter relationships shaped modern governance. Between its religiously-based commercial laws/practices and *kadi* justice, Islam did not foster a merchant class like the European bourgeoisie who made capitalism both dynamic *and* inequitable. There were no Islamic equivalents to either the European anti-clerical secular intelligentsia (the *philosophes*) who valorized Reason or the commercial bourgeoisie, driven by an "inner determination" rooted in "salvation anxiety", who became the bearers of a rational, secular modernity who

[28] Turkey of course was never colonized, rather with the fall of the Ottoman Caliphate, Ataturk took over.

[29] It is thus not surprising that many of the Islamic groups oppose the US for supporting governments like the Saudis, the Egyptians or the Israelis who are seen as serving the US and maintaining an illegal occupation of the West Bank.

would contest the hegemony of Church and demand separation of Church and State.[30] In practice, Islam legitimated a system of values and community such that clerics, landowners, merchants, warriors and even intellectuals each had a stake in the perpetuation of the system. Thus, a class-based challenge to the Caliphate demanding either a critique of religion, or a secular space within the community and/or demands for democratic rule and personal rights did not emerge.

There are fundamental ideological tensions, if not conflicts, between Islamic orthodoxy and secular modernities (Moaddel 2005). Islam has certain core beliefs and principles; Allah is the one God, Muhammad was his messenger, and there is a unity of faith, community (*ulamma*) and governance. As a result, throughout the Islamic world, especially in the Arab Middle East, "secular modernity" has not been widely embraced outside of a few academic and/or commercial realms.[31] More specifically, despite many local differences in interpretation, there are several aspects of Islam that have acted as barriers to the diffusion of modern, rational values that might confront and challenge aspects of Islamic laws, custom and tradition. These are 1) the status of rational, empirical sciences and their relation to Islam, 2) the relation between religion and politics, 3) the ideal form of government, 4) national identity, 5) the relations of Muslim nations to the outside world and 6), the status of women (Moaddel 2005:7).

Science: In Weber's time, Catholics were more likely to study art, philosophy and literature while Protestants were more likely to study math and science. Similarly, the Islamic pursuit of science is often secondary to other interests. Rationalism and science are often seen as opposed to God, faith and belief. Much like many American evangelicals, science is regarded as contrary to scripture. Today, Islamic educational systems provide a huge number of graduates in religion or Quranic studies rather than modern commerce, science and technologies that sustain economic growth.[32] Notwithstanding, we might note that while many world-class scientists and doctors may come

---

[30] It is of course interesting that at the time of this writing, a major issue in France is the toleration for the *hijab, yarmulke* or crucifix in the secular, public school system.

[31] As will be noted however below, a number of efforts toward modernization have been stifled from either within by traditional authorities or undermined from without by imperialist forces, the latest being the USA. Further, there are many examples where Islamic modernities are emergent such as Lebanon or Turkey.

[32] It should be noted, however, that there are not many opportunities for science and technology graduates in the Muslim countries. The few such jobs that exist, are likely to go to graduates of Western schools, namely the children of the rich.

from Muslim backgrounds; most, however, are likely to be found in Western societies.

Religion and Politics: Among the primary tenets of Islam, despite many regional variations, there has been the widespread endurance of *Shariah* based religious codes, and the unity of religion, commerce, governance and everyday life. For Islam, the idea that laws were made by men, rather than based on the revealed word of Allah, was heresy. Muhammad was both a trader and a Prophet; there was no conflict between commercial and religious activities. As was noted, given the traditional class systems, there did not emerge the kinds of relationships that led to a bifurcation of mosque and a trading class, whether the relationship was cooperative, as in the Italian city-states as the Church grew richer, or contentious, as when free peasants and petit bourgeoisie embraced Luther or Calvin. As such, we did not see the conditions that gave rise to "constitutionalism", recognition of legal rights that might sustain secular authority challenged by other bodies or estates. Islam did not create a separation of mosque and State and spaces where "people" might legitimately challenge State rule. Islamic fundamentalists accept this unity of faith and power, but challenge existing systems so that they might take power and restore a lost unity.

Government: The ideal form of Islamic government was the Caliphate, a form of traditional authority, in which theologically qualified elites were selected as rulers in which *Shariah* based Islamic rules prevailed. Muhammad as the founder, and the Rightful Holy Caliphs (Abu Bakr, Umar, Uthman and Ali), established principles of theocratic governance that were given legitimacy and coherence by embracing Plato's concept of a "natural" ruling elite. Other forms of government were precluded. The Caliphate, much like hereditary kingship, was not based on popular assent, representative government or democratic secular values typical of modern "rational" Nation-States. Traditional Islamic governance thus precluded secular nationalism that fostered citizen-based identities on the basis of "the rights of man". Nor was there a space for popular representation and assent of the governed. Man-made law was not seen as acceptable.[33] The bourgeois political imaginary embraced "popular sovereignty", republicanism and secular nationalism as principles of legitimate authority reflecting the "will of the people", constructed as cit-

[33] Indeed as Weber has shown, the preconditions for democratic governance were unique to European Christendom, save for a few brief moments among Greek and Roman elite landowners, democracy has not been a typical form of governance.

izens, members of an "imaginary community" the Nation-State. Secular Western style governments separate from the Church, with representatives and elected leaders rested on Western traditions ranging from "constitutionalism" to the self-governance of autonomous Protestant churches. Democracy, with popular elections of representative lawmakers is seen as contrary to traditional Islam.

Identity: While most Muslim societies today are quite diverse, despite encapsulated realms of cosmopolitan elites, for most people in Muslim societies, identities remain based on traditional, ascriptive factors, primarily religious and localist – family, clan, tribe or village that are typically more salient. There are few alternative sites for the negotiation and transformation of identities. Neither the spread of industrial labor, nor the growth of advanced services (medicine, sciences, technologies), nor even the various branches of Western corporations have spurred the rise of classes (status groups) bearing a rational social ethic and/or pressures for renegotiating identities. Further, more so than other developing countries, in Islamic societies, especially in the Middle East, the masses tend to have remained quite insular. As was earlier noted, more so than most societies, the Islamic world translates very little of the publications of other countries. There are, however, some spheres conducive to alternative identities. Naturally, the universities, especially liberal arts and social sciences linked to the larger disciplines that transcend national boundaries – sociology, for example – are conducive to the erosion of tradition. Similarly, various civil society organizations, NGOs, and local branches of INGOs that link the local to the global, erode traditionalism. While there are important segments of military and political classes committed to reform, and some academics and many of the growing educated classes that do embrace modernist democratic governance, they remain a minority and are often challenged by fundamentalists.[34]

Outside world: For many Muslims, there are a number of grievances toward the West in general and the US in particular. Islamic societies, like most others, have a certain degree of ethnocentrism, but in many such societies, there is a disdain toward non-believers, the Others, of infidel nations. Now while this may not be typical among elites it is interesting to note the extent to which the knowledge and cultures of other nations is of little interest (except

[34] This was clear in the Algerian civil war in which modernist nationalists battled fundamentalists – almost a million people died.

the interest in many of the young in Western popular culture, much to the chagrin of their elders). There have been progressive movements, but American and/or British intervention into domestic politics thwarted these movements or processes, often through coups, assassinations, and/or the installation of compliant intermediary authoritarians. The intervention and/meddling into local politics is typically resented. Further, there is resentment over the influx of decadent Western ideas from gender equality to democracy to human rights to pornography, though at the same time, there is a large market for Western film and videotapes, especially those considered erotic, if not pornographic. It should be noted that the Islamic societies are sources of raw materials (oil), markets for Western goods and popular tourist destinations. These are not closed societies like N. Korea or Burma. There have been large Diasporas of Turks in Germany, Pakistanis in England, Algerians in France and Indonesians in Holland. And a few of everyone comes to the US. As many second generation immigrants have access to the Internet and maintain ties with home, they often act as culture brokers spreading Western media like metallic rock, porn etc. This does erode some barriers.

Women: Finally, in no Muslim society do Muslim women have equal rights or status with men. To be sure, there is a great deal of difference between Saudi Arabia, where women cannot drive, and Pakistan or Indonesia, that have had a woman prime minister, while nevertheless most women languish. In Lebanon or Turkey there are fairly large numbers of educated women working in diverse fields. Prewar Iraq had a number of women as government ministers. While patriarchal traditionalism is indeed changing, it does serve as both a barrier to the influx of Westerners and an inducement for some of the more talented women to leave their native countries for the West. The attitudes and practices regarding women from legal right to FGM are often matters of contention and focal points of resistance to change. The position of women is, and will remain a barrier to the embrace of a genuine modernity that includes gender equality. As Inglehardt and Norris (2003) argue:

> However, when it comes to attitudes toward gender equality and sexual liberalization, the cultural gap between Islam and the West widens into a chasm. On the matter of equal rights and opportunities for women – measured by such questions as whether men make better political leaders than women or whether university education is more important for boys than for girls – Western and Muslim countries score 82 percent and 55 percent,

> respectively. Muslim societies are also distinctively less permissive toward homosexuality, abortion, and divorce. . . . These issues are part of a broader syndrome of tolerance, trust, political activism, and emphasis on individual autonomy that constitutes "self-expression values." The extent to which a society emphasizes these self-expression values has a surprisingly strong bearing on the emergence and survival of democratic institutions. Among all the countries included in the WVS, support for gender equality – a key indicator of tolerance and personal freedom – is closely linked with a society's level of democracy.[35]

A central moment of one's identity is gender, and as long as gender is both essentialized and difference valorized, there will be barriers to modernity.

Without either material contradictions articulated by a class, or an ideological basis to impel a critical stance toward religion born by a powerful class, or pressures toward the renegotiation of identities, save in Kemalist Turkey, there have been few forces to foster a differentiation of Mosque, State and everyday life.[36] While there has been a complex interplay of ideas and influences in different Islamic societies, most European ideas from socialism to nationalism, to popular democracy and, above all, secularism, neither produced new and lasting democratic changes nor were widely institutionalized.[37] Without the existence of a class or status group that might embrace such a stance and embrace a critique and/or renegotiate identities, there was neither a Reformation, nor strong indigenous pressures toward modernization and secularization. Nor were there the kinds of checks and balances in governance that might either constrain arbitrary power or share power with other groups or even the community.

There are 47 countries with a Muslim majority; perhaps 12 are electoral democracies, and none of the core Arabic-speaking has representative governments. Autocratic governance such as in Saudi Arabia or Kuwait, often with a very thin veneer of democracy, e.g., Egypt, Jordan or Pakistan, is more typical than genuine multi-party competition for parliamentary governance. Yes there are elections, yet the process is so controlled that the sitting autocrat

---

[35] http://www.globalpolicy.org/globaliz/cultural/2003/0304clash.htm

[36] This is not to assume that all Muslims are devoutly religious, but rather, there are few spaces where critical or secular discourses can be publicly articulated.

[37] While there were a number of modernist and reformist movements, Turkey is always the "exceptional" case due to the modernist military revolt of Kemal Ataturk and "enforced" modernization.

wins. And often their sons assume power after them. While for the West this is considered anti-democratic despotism, nepotism and rampant corruption, indeed it is a long-standing cultural pattern of rulership in many such societies. In this way, there has been little change from the Caliphs of yesterday to modern presidents who are elected for life, who use their political power to amass fortunes for themselves and their friends. Loyalty is sustained through gifts and personal obligations. While these patterns are often typical in traditional societies, in modern societies this is considered graft and corruption.

Thus, as can be seen, there are a number of aspects of Islam that have worked individually and in concert as barriers to the infusion of purposive rationality and structural reform. The barriers to rational commerce, democratic governance and the limited size and power of modernizing classes, as bearers of a rational social ethic, has meant the failures of efforts to modernize the economy or find space for reformist politics to foster democratization. In the end the only channel available for social mobilizations articulating local discontents and general grievances toward the West has been fundamentalism. In sum, the relative stagnation of Islamic societies has been a product of religiously based, cultural/historical legacies, dictatorial governments, or foreign policies (read: imperialist interventions) from without, that sustained repressive governments that, however corrupt, however inefficient, have been "friendly" to Western governments. In turn, there has been little economic benefit for the masses, nor secular channels to redress grievances.

Part IV Fundamentalism

Globalization and Social Change

As both Marx and Schumpeter noted, capitalism, spearheaded "creative destruction"; it fostered massive transformations and upheavals as the feudal class structure was torn asunder. Lords and serfs exited from the stage of world history as the bourgeoisie and proletarians entered. The demise of feudalism fostered various stresses and strains of economic displacement, unemployment, migration of populations, etc. In its current instantiation, global capitalism, like its earlier forms, has led to rapid economic changes, major social changes and massive dislocations (rural-urban migrations, Diasporas, job loss, class mobility, most often downward). Globalization has led to a constriction of opportunities for meaningful work. Traditional forms of agriculture, artisan labor and petty bourgeois trade are rendered obsolete. Further, in many countries, there are limited opportunities even for educated classes.

Globalization has encouraged the diffusion of modernity, as the cultural expression of capitalism, with its secular worldviews and values of Reason, progress, and in some cases freedom, democracy, and equality.[38] So too, do the global culture industries, intertwined with consumerism as the hegemonic ideology of our age, widely disseminate mass mediated forms of privatized hedonism from shopping to eroticism (Cf. Sklair 2002). This hedonistic self-indulgence and valorization of the erotic, spread through satellite television and the Internet, challenge traditional patriarchal authority and moral norms of sexual modesty and constraint. Patriarchy has been sustained by economic power on the one hand and ideologies of gender essentialism that restrict women on the other. The globalization of MTV culture thus erodes the authority of elders, at least male elders, and interrogates the subordinated role of women, now seeking, if not demanding, political, economic and even gender-based voice and agency. Such media are an acute affront to the values and identities of many traditional people, especially those already disadvantaged by the global economy for whom traditional male status (patriarchy) and religious piety served as a basis for status and self esteem. Between its economic changes that erode traditional authority and its hedonistic popular culture, modernity challenges essentialist notions of gender that sustain patriarchy and hierarchical gender relations.

Fundamentalism as a Response to Globalization

Globalization has fostered alienation and distress at economic, political, cultural and social psychological levels. Fundamentalism is an anti-modernist compensatory response to rapid social and cultural changes and the stresses and strains of a global age. Fundamentalist religion is a *reaction* to these rapid transformations, dislocations and adverse economic consequences, as well as a critique of the superficiality of a materialistic culture, and the problematic nature of individualistic, self-critical forms of de-centered, hedonistic selfhood (see Marty and Applebee 1991; Juergensmeyer 2001). The growth of

[38] Global capital often works through some of the more authoritarian governments in the world, and indeed, American capital has often been responsible for installing and sustaining these governments.

fundamentalism in the last several decades is a wail that reflects the real pain and suffering of the oppressed, downtrodden and marginalized in a global age. Fundamentalism is the opiate of displaced, alienated people. It emerges as an attempt to redress real and imaginary grievances when other channels are blocked. We have thus witnessed the rapid rise of fundamentalist religious orientations throughout the world as a defense against the adversities and failures of modernity to improve life in many traditional societies. It appeals to "invented traditions", returning to "roots", and paving a path to moral renewal, promising the restoration of an earlier and better imaginary Golden Age. Some popular understandings of fundamentalism claim it is an age old phenomenon tied to ancient conflicts. Rather, it is a modern phenomenon, a movement that must be understood as a reaction to current events, conditions and political struggles in the curent era.

When we conjoin economic adversity and political domination that does not allow voice, redress or amelioration, with 1) attenuated social ties and challenges to traditional male domination, and 2) cultural challenges to traditional morals, values and beliefs, we see fertile ground for fundamentalism as reactionary compensation that would "turn back the clock". While on the one hand, globalization has fostered progressive changes such as pressures for transparency, democracy, and has also mobilized progressive resistance movements such as global justice movements and/or workers and feminists challenging inequality and exploitation, on the other hand, far more often and for far more people, globalization has fostered various reactionary fundamentalisms that would sustain traditional sources of status, honor and dignity, while defending communities from "immoral" influences.

Religion, as Marx pointed out, while appearing as a set of ideas, is shaped by material conditions, class arrangements. Fundamentalism has been a wide spread movement found in many religions that calls for the primacy of religious laws and religiously-based ways life. Fundamentalism proclaims a religious absolutism that demands scripturally derived belief and practices must be the basis of civil law and the general way of life for all. For Martin and Appleby (1991), there are certain common "family resemblances" of fundamentalism regardless of its denomination:

1. Religious idealism is the basis for personal and communal identity;
2. Fundamentalists understand truth to be revealed and unified;
3. It is intentionally scandalous – outsiders cannot understand it;
4. Fundamentalists envision themselves as part of a cosmic struggle;

5. They seize on historical moments and reinterpret them in light of this cosmic struggle;
6. They demonize their opposition and are reactionary;
7. Fundamentalists are selective in what parts of their tradition and heritage they stress;
8. They are led by males;
9. They envy modernist cultural hegemony and try to overturn the distribution of power.

Further, they argue that there are five ideological characteristics.

1. Fundamentalists are concerned with the erosion of religion and its proper role in society.
2. Fundamentalism is selective of their tradition and what part of modernity they accept or choose to react against.
3. They embrace some form of Manichean (dualism.)
4. Fundamentalists stress absolutism and inerrancy in their sources of revelation; and
5. They opt for some form of Millennialism or Messianism.

There are certain characteristics of fundamental religion *common to all its variants*. Fundamentalism as a reaction to contemporary social, cultural and moral stresses and strains associated with modernity – though it is quite selective about which aspects of modernity to utilize or condemn. (It can use technologies such as computers, the Internet, tapes and cell phones, but it abhors democracy, secular law and/or hedonistic popular culture.) Fundamentalism as a reaction against the decline and marginalization of religion and what has traditionally been a moral life. It would reclaim what is believed to be traditional morality and virtues as the path to a golden future. Its leadership tends to be quite authoritarian, demanding obedience and subordination of members. It is scriptural and its "holy book" is absolutist, without error, and its morality requires its elect believers adhere to a strict code of ethical behavior founded on a Manichean moral dualism that maintains strict boundaries between the moral insider and infidel outsider. Writing for the twentieth-century Fund, Grant Wacker has put it quite succinctly. Fundamentalism can be seen as:

> . . . a global religious impulse, particularly evident in the twentieth century, that seeks to recover and publicly institutionalize aspects of the past that modern life has obscured. It typically sees the secular state as the primary

> enemy, for the latter is more interested in education, democratic reforms, and economic progress than in preserving the spiritual dimension of life. Generic fundamentalism takes its cues from a sacred text that stands above criticism. It sees time-honored social distinctions and cultural patterns as rooted in the very nature of things, in the order of creation itself. That means clear-cut and stratified roles for men and women, parents and children, clergy and laity. On the other hand, generic fundamentalism seeks to minimize the distinction between the state and the church. To hold that the state should operate according to one set of publicly shared principles, while individuals should operate according to multiple sets of privately shared principles, is morally pernicious and ends up harming everyone, believers and nonbelievers alike. Religious truths are no different from the truths of medical science or aeronautical engineering: if they hold for anyone they hold for everyone.[39]

Fundamentalisms claim that tragic consequences have befallen the world as religious based values, identities and interpersonal relationships have been undermined, especially by scientific world views and secular states. Fundamentalisms, as compensatory ideologies rejecting modernity, provide alternative "world views" that "explain" social, cultural, economic or economic malaise and adversity on the basis of deviations from moral virtue. Fundamentalists interpret current political events and/or natural phenomenon as expressions of God's will that can range from the rights of Brooklyn Jews to claim ownership of Palestine, to seeing 9/11 as evidence of God's displeasure of gays, abortions and wanton sexuality, especially that of women. Some fundamentalists saw Katrina as retribution for the sex, nudity and erotic licentiousness of New Orleans and an impending gay rights festival.[40]

Fundamentalisms typically regard an ethically based "good life" as based on a 1) literal reading of a holy scripture, 2) clear cut hierarchies of age and gender domination, and 3) strict moral codes of behavior and severe punishments for infractions, e.g., amputations for theft, stoning for adultery. Sexual codes are central to fundamentalists. Impurities, especially female sexuality, represent danger, dirt and disorder that must be controlled and violations harshly avenged (Douglas 1966). Every expression of fundamentalism

---

[39] http://www.nhc.rtp.nc.us:8080/tserve/twenty/tkeyinfo/fundam.htm

[40] It should be noted that the French Quarter where these celebrations take place was relatively unscathed, while Biloxi, a more subdued city, was devastated. Seems like God's aim is not too precise.

attempts to reinscribe and reinforce "essential" male/female differences and privilege male authority.[41] Fundamentalist religion provides clear-cut rules of moral conduct, fixed narratives of identity and clear-cut gender roles. This not only gives a sense of certainty and stability in face of rapid social change and cultural contestations, but a transcendentally based system of meaning. Adherents believe that if people pursued strict moral codes based on absolute adherence to scriptural doctrines and lives of purity, while rigid gender hierarchies are sustained, a glorious future will befall the community of virtue, notwithstanding existing conditions. For Christians, after the Rapture and the return of Christ, the Kingdom of God will be restored. For Jews, the Messiah will return and the Temple rebuilt. For Muslims, the Caliphate will be re-established.

Fundamentalisms take at least two forms, retreatist and transformative. Retreatists seek to isolate themselves from the larger, secular and indeed profane community. Thus various rural Christian sects or communities seek to withdraw from the larger world and remove themselves from its influences. Similarly, various ultra Orthodox Jews seek "autonomous" communities, but insofar as some are likely to work outside their communities and engage in the political process, their isolation is only partial. Transformative fundamentalists would seek to overthrow existing societies and/or governments and establish theocracies such as Iran, or for awhile, the Taliban rulers of Afghanistan. In countries with open electoral systems, fundamentalists typically seek political power to advance their moral positions. This has been clear in alliances of the Republican Party and the Christian Evangelicals as well as the BJP in India. Fundamentalism has become a major factor in American, Israeli, Indian and Islamic politics.

Understanding Islamic Fundamentalism

Throughout the Muslim world we have witnessed growing fundamentalist movements seeking political rule in accordance with strict adherence to Islam. Islamisms generally assume an anti-Western form rejecting Western modernity in terms of democratic rule, freedom, equality and progress. In recent years, the diffusion of Western popular culture and consumerism throughout the Muslim world has been experienced as a major affront to Islamic

---

[41] This is clear in the resistance to attempts to stop FGM, *shariah* justice for female infidelity and the use of rape as punishment.

orthodoxy. But it is not simply modern values that are disdained; there are a number of actual grievances ranging from the support of unjust rulers to the support of Israel. While there are common threads in most fundamentalisms, Islamisms have taken a particularly onerous and violent direction in various forms of violent struggle seen as *jihad*, ranging from armed militias to martyrdom (*shaheeden*) operations, from hijacking planes to bus bombings as a strategy. Why has this occurred?

A Critical Theoretical approach to fundamentalism, political Islam, *qua* religious ideology, must chart the political, economic and cultural determinants that give rise to an "elective affinity" with authoritarian precepts and its proclivities to foster, or perhaps only legitimate violence. As such, I would suggest that there are a number of underlying similarities between classical fascism and Islamism as a form of clerical fascism (Berlet 2005). Just as fascism grew out of economic dislocations, blocked economic opportunities and political humiliation over military defeats, so too have Islamisms emerged in societies with, limited economic futures, few job opportunities and legacies of political domination that often endure after independence. Large swaths of the Islamic Middle East remain mired in stagnation and, often, abject poverty. Not surprisingly, fundamentalism can often be found in classes and communities where certain populations, especially young and often unmarried men, are unemployed, underemployed and face social discrimination. Without a livelihood, they cannot marry. Such men often find solace in compensatory ideologies that provide dignity. This is often true for the better educated as well. Both Fascism and Islamism, as reactionary, compensatory ideologies, promise a glorious future both individually and collectively if people are obedient, subservient to charismatic leaders, and willing to sacrifice, and, if needed, use violence to achieve transformative/restorative goals. Both ideologies appealed primarily to the petty bourgeoisie, but found many followers in other classes.

Thus, to consider Islamism as a general response to the economic consequences of globalization and its cultural values, we need to look at its "elective affinity" for people at particular class locations especially vulnerable to social strains. Following Marx, Weber and Freud, religion provides compensations (opiates) and psychological gratifications For Marx, religion both sustained and assuaged the consequences of class domination. It was "the opiate of the people". But at the same time, it was an expression of "real", material suffering. For Weber, religion offered a theodicy (a theology of benevolence and evil) that explained the distributions of fortune and why they were typically unequal. For Weber, suffering came not simply from class domination, but the human condition, death, misery and sadness; religion served ameliorative functions for the person, while at the same time it was a central factor directing an "economic ethic". For Weber, religion provided explanations of reality, orientations to the world, and prescribed ethical codes of conduct. Thus Islamisms can now explain the economic adversity and humiliation that have befallen Muslim societies on the basis of foreign domination and the incursions of immorality from without. But this was made possible by their own failures of faith and loss of virtue. Islamisms give voice to the alienated, explanations for their conditions and solutions for overcoming adversities.

From Jihad to Terrorism

While fundamentalisms divide the world into the chosen and the damned, most fundamentalists are typically ethnocentric and denigrating toward the infidel Other. However, they do not typically embrace actual violence.[42] But today, the political Islam that is often seen as the basis of *jihad* qua religious war, terrorism is seen as primary tactic to influence another State. But terrorism is a label for those who employ violence in political struggles; it is a military tactic used in low intensity warfare by non State actors. Thus, when Menachim Begin was in *Irgun*, bombing the King David hotel was seen as part of a struggle for independence. Those Iraqis who seek the explusion of American troops are labeled terrorists.

For Islam, *jihad* connotes struggle, typically the individual's own struggle to be moral and virtuous. But the notion of lesser *jihad*, holy military war, violence toward others, has been revived to legitimate terrorism in the name of God.[43] Small numbers of Islamicist *Jihadis* have embraced terrorism, typically the "weapon of the weak" to articulate a variety of grievances of economic and political powerlessness ranging from Israel's occupation of the West Bank, Russia's domination of Afghanistan or Chechnya, America's invasion of Iraq

---

[42] Of course ethnocentrism and denigration of the other, whether on the basis of religious, racial, ethnic or class, can, and often does, become mobilized as actual violence from lynching to genocide.

[43] Many Muslim scholars have decried the use of Islamic theology by Islamicists, whom they say have corrupted the Quran by justifying suicide, and/or the murder of non-combatants, especially women and children.

and its general support for dictatorships, or Indian control of Kashmir. To be sure, the *jihadi* agenda is often nihilistic. Terrorist acts are heinous and despicable and more often than not, terrorism does not achieve its goals. Terrorism is used as a weapon against a militarily superior power to attain political goals, typically eliminating domination, and oppression. But for those with strong religious convictions, who have been angered, denigrated and rendered powerless, who are without voice or other means of political redress, it becomes quite easy to frame political conflict in the religious terms of virtue vs infidel, and find scriptural justifications for the use of violence.

To be sure, between the Bible and Quran, there are many justifications for smiting the enemy, just as there are entreaties for peace, justice, compassion, and even charity to the stranger. The belief that terrorists/insurgents are seeking heaven and the services of 72 virgins as the incentive for martyrdom operations, represents a form of Orientalism that ignores the political injustice that engenders terrorism – many terrorist are not religious, or have only recently become so. What must be noted, Huntington (1996) notwithstanding, is that the goal of the *jihadis* is not religious war but rather overcoming what is regarded as unjust forms of foreign or domestic domination that leaves expressive violence as the only way to deal with the structural violence that results from domination. As Fanon (1963) put it, violence turns the violence of the colonizer upon the colonized and back to the colonizer. Such violence is cathartic.

But further, in a number of cases, we have seen the role of *shaheeden*, martyrdom operations (suicide bombings as a strategy). This is not unique to Islam. Many Japanese, practicing Shinto, committed kamikaze (suicide) missions in WWII. The use of suicide bombers was initiated by the Tamil Tigers, a secular Marxist group that used suicide bombings long before the tactic was used by Muslim *jihadis*. Moreover, the *hadith* (sayings and actions of the Prophet) specifically prohibit suicide. Life or death is determined by Allah. Thus these operations are not seen as suicide missions but acts of martyrdom. Yet there are certain reasons why Islamisms are conducive to martyrdom.[44] Let us first note that the basis for jihad and in turn shahadeen operations is not due to Islam per se, but the consequences of Islam's earlier decline and subsequent barriers to modernity from both within and without. Facing dom-

[44] Of course not all martyrs have been Muslim.

ination by foreigners, especially the Great Satan, or local proxies allied to the Great Satan, from Saudi princes to Israeli PMs, they would seek voice and redress though legitimate channels, and failing that, through violence.[45] Seeking entrance to heaven in the next world, is not the goal.

A number of scholarly studies have shown that most *jihadis* are not motivated by religion. In his analysis, Papes (2005) analyzed thousands of cases of suicide-terrorism. In his interview with the American Conservative, he summarized his findings:

> The central fact is that overwhelmingly suicide-terrorist attacks are not driven by religion as much as they are by a clear strategic objective: to compel modern democracies to withdraw military forces from the territory that the terrorists view as their homeland. . . . Since suicide terrorism is mainly a response to foreign occupation and not Islamic fundamentalism, the use of heavy military force to transform Muslim societies over there, if you would, is only likely to increase the number of suicide terrorists coming at us.[46]

Similarly, for theWashington-based Center for Strategic and International Studies (CSIS):

> Most were motivated by "revulsion at the idea of an Arab land being occupied by a non-Arab country." [They are] often from middle class families of prominent conservative tribes. Many were well-educated and had jobs.[47]

For Islam, martyrdom has a strong historical precedent, much like Christianity that sees its founder and early followers as martyrs from either crucifixion or their fates in the Roman spectacles. While Shia and Sunni Muslims diverge on the question of Ali as the successor, both find his death in battle as martyrdom, a highly praised virtue.[48]

[45] The Israeli occupation of the West Bank has been declared a violation of UN law, just as the World court claimed the separation barrier illegal. Yet Israel has ignored all legal challenges to its occupation. In much the same way, the invasion of Iraq by GW Bush was not approved by the UN. This did not stop the invasion. In both cases, without armies to fight the US, *shaheeden* operation are the only available weapon.

[46] http://www.amconmag.com/2005_07_18/article.html

[47] http://abcnews.go.com/US/print?id=1136691

[48] So too does Christianity rest on the martyrdom of Jesus and the fate of his followers in the Roman arenas. Even Judaism, in its recent constructions of history have seen Masada as the symbol of its willingness to die before surrender.

The Fun of Fundamentalism

One of the key points of the Frankfurt School was to incorporate depth psychology into the critique of domination. Specifically, the emotional allure of fascism and the power of its propaganda depended on its resonance with individual character structure, namely certain authoritarian character types at particular class and or social locations, etc. While earlier theories of fundamentalism saw it as a typical reaction of the poorer and less educated to marginality, downward mobility etc, it is now clear that many people, often highly educated (in sciences and technology), can well experience alienation and stress. In turn, they may and might embrace fundamentalisms of various stripes.

Harman (2003) has identified four different class fragments prone to embrace fundamentalism, starting with 1) the classical petty bourgeoisie of small traders (*bazaaris*) and landowners, often clergy, who attempt to defend their economic resources and self esteem against the larger forces of globalization. 2) Some elements of the newly rich, anxious in their new status, find security in the embrace of Islam that disdains the secular socialism that might emerge. 3) The rural poor, flocking to the cities, face poverty and alienation. Lubeck and Britts (2001) note that these groups find solace and comfort in fundamentalist mosques. Finally, 4), many members of the "new middle class", often sons of professionals, failing to find places in the new economy commensurate with their levels of education, are not only likely to find compensatory gratifications in fundamentalism, they are, moreover, most likely to provide the activist cadres. For example, Muhammad Atta and the leaders of the 9/11 attack were highly educated. But they were unable to find work in Europe, let alone Accah, one of the poorest parts of Saudi Arabia. Similarly, leaders such as Osama Bin Laden, Ayman al Zawahiri or Abu Musab al-Zarqawi are generally from affluent, educated, privileged classes. In the Palestinian struggles and Iraqi resistance, it is often the educated yet still marginalized and powerless that opt for fundamentalism and then terrorism. Moreover, such acts are not so much impelled by psychopathology or desires for hatred and revenge, but rather a moral, ethical cause.[49]

One of the most central contributions of the Frankfurt School was its voluminous studies on authoritarianism; specifically, how did the bourgeois author-

[49] See Clark McCauley's analysis of the 9/11 perpetrators http://ideologiesofwar.com/papers/cm_understanding.htm

ity relations (of earlier generations) become internalized as an enduring part of character, and in turn, how does the socialization process and resulting authoritarian character structure (super-ego) secure and reproduce domination. Authoritarianism, *qua* characterological dimension, disposed the embrace of authoritarian ideologies, especially those with Manichean values and xenophobic "us/them" views of the world. Authoritarian personalities typically display a great deal of conformity and conventionalism, and willingly submit to authorities and authority figures. S/he projects aggression to outsiders or those with "different" lifestyles and/or values and justifies his/her hatred to the Other for that reason. Authoritarians tend to be anti-intraceptive, unimaginative and prone to stereotypes and clichés as opposed to more complex and ambiguous understandings. They much value power, especially those who are in power. They have a destructive, hostile, cynical attitude to the world, and an exaggerated concern with sexuality due to their own repression. Beneath the vast historical and cultural differences of Nazism, Christian Fundamentalism and Islamism, there are common social psychological underpinnings beginning with the tendencies for authoritarian submission. I would suggest there are four, overlapping themes, 1) alienated desires, "submission to higher authority" and redemptive violence, 2) *ressentement*, 3) the simplification of reality and 4) the articulation of hope.

1. *Alienation, Desire and Self*: In the 1844 manuscripts, there is an implicit philosophical anthropology of motivation that rested on essentialist assumptions that clearly anticipated much of Freud's theories of desires and dreams. Marx's critique of alienated labor argued that selling one's labor power as a commodity by producing commodities produces a system that stands outside the person and refluxes back upon him/her rendering him/her powerless. Similarly, workers became alienated from their very species being and their community. The worker lost all sense of dignity as his/her self was truncated by economic necessity and s/he was reduced to little more than a beast of burden. S/he was further humiliated living in a bourgeois society where money was the basis of pride and respect and the power to buy not only material wealth, but beauty, health and wisdom. As a result of living so close to the edge, life was rendered meaningless. Otherwise said, within the 1844 Manuscripts there is an implicit theory of fundamental human needs for 1) agency, being in control of one's life, 2) attachments and connections to people, 3) self-esteem and dignity, and 4) anxiety-reducing shared meanings.

These "desires" have been better theorized within psychoanalytic frameworks. Beginning with Wilhelm Reich's insights on the psychology of Fascism,

Eric Fromm initiated the incorporation of depth psychology into the Frankfurt School's critique of domination. To do so, he moved from Freud's biologically rooted drive-object theory, to a more social/interactional notion of historically-based desires for creative self-transcendence (agency), loving attachments to Others, for genuine self love (dignity) and a framework of meaning and devotion. For Fromm, frustrations of such desires often led to anxiety and in turn, he argued that submission to powerful authorities and/or a love of death and destruction could assuage fears and anxiety. In his terms, the "escape from freedom", and "necrophilia" were the essence of fascist leanings (Fromm 1941; 1973). In the present context, fundamentalism as political Islam, what can be called "clerical fascism" (Berlet 2005), can be theorized as the psychosocial reaction structural crises, as well as crises of identity-motivation. Fundamentalism speaks to frustrated longings. In the face of powerlessness, attenuated social ties, humiliation and challenges to traditional frameworks of meaning, people are prone to join subcultures with ideologies of redemptive violence against evil doers that yet provide a sense of voice (agency), community, dignity and meaning. Fundamentalisms provide membership in a valorized, dignity-granting community of meaning that has been constructed on the basis of "imagined" traditions and values in face of enemy non-believers.[50]

Further, it should be noted that in most societies, powerlessness and humiliation are experienced as incompatible with certain notions of assertive masculinity. When men are rendered powerless and humiliated, the combination of castration anxiety and narcissistic insult elicit shame and in turn, engender rage and intense desires for compensatory amelioration. For Scheff (1994), the failure to recognize this unconscious shame becomes the basis for irrational rage. Fundamentalisms typically valorize the dignity of the believer and privilege essentialist notions of masculinity. Thus, membership in certain kinds of identity-granting communities of meaning that embrace violence as both a means to an end and identity, from Nazis to skinheads to Islamism can provide alternative visions and valorize esteemed identities

[50] Fundamentalisms, like religion in general, provide solidarity and a positive valuation of the self, feelings of agency and, of course, frameworks of meaning. The difference between fundamentalism and "ordinary" religion, however, is the demand for compliance to superior powers and intense hatred to evil others. Much the same can be said about extreme nationalisms that can often turn xenophobic and aggressive.

compared to harsh realities and denigrated selfhood, through its promises of a better life to come.

How and why do people, especially male people, come to valorize death over life in the pursuit of compensatory masculinity? Fromm (1973) argued that the conditions of domination, powerlessness and isolation, led to impairments of self-love and the thwarting of self-constitution and realization. This in turn leads to the embrace of nihilism and "necrophilia" that he defines as the love of death and destruction whether of self or Others.[51] Let us remember the famous words of Usama bin Laden, "You love life, we love death." Men, otherwise thwarted in self-realization, with attenuated attachments and limited capacities to love others, find that the only basis of agency and meaning is through the expression of violence.[52] Perhaps we might note Theweleit's (1989) study of the *Freikorps*, the veterans of WWI, petty bourgeois men without jobs or job prospects who disdained women and erotic love. They sought war, death and destruction as their purpose in life. To die in combat as a hero was preferable to living in peace.

Thus, if fundamentalism is psychologically compensatory, it must be seen as not only gratifying frustrated desires and longings, but also providing a valorized identity in which dignity is based on a combination of piety and assertive masculinity. Whether Christian or Jew, Hindu or Muslim, the respected, indeed idealized, pious warrior has long been a exemplary role model. Moreover, in premodern times, the warrior needed to have a long period of training to develop the requisite physical strength and warrior skills of horsemanship, handling weapons etc. Often such training began in childhood While modern soldiers require a great deal of technological skills to handle the leading edge technologically sophisticated weapons of advanced modern armies, it takes much less skill and training to handle easily available AK 47s or RPGs.[53] Then, given some theological justifications of a small minority of clerics, *jihadi* operations become highly moral forms of masculine

---

[51] I am not suggesting a psychological basis for terrorism; indeed, most studies suggest a "banality" of terror, and most terrorists tend to be relatively normal people, free of evident psychopathologies.

[52] It is worth noting that most terrorists tend to be unattached males, typically blocked or thwarted by limited alternatives, prejudices and/or injustices.

[53] This is not to suggest that all such "soldiers" are unskilled, indeed the manufacture of bombs, rockets and even improvised explosives requires a good deal of skill. Moreover, many *jihadis* have been highly trained in military strategy and tactics.

prowess. For a number of fundamentalists, donning a military uniform, carrying a gun, and willingness to die in combat, provide a valuable compensatory identity that provide piety and aggressive masculinity when the more typical channels are blocked or limited.[54] Thus give the current conditions of degradation and despair, many young men, and some women, find community, dignity and agency by linking themselves with the legacies of the "heroic warriors" who created one of the great civilizations of the world. Terrorism, when seen as the action of a "heroic warrior", serves to empower the person and restores his/her honor.

Fundamentalism provides a number of compensations for frustrated longings and desires, not the least of which is valorizing a self-identity based on moral virtue rather than material accomplishments. One of the fundamental challenges to traditional expressions of selfhood has been the rate of technological and social change that has made a stable, cohesive sense of self problematic. The pluralization of self that is so highly celebrated by Western postmodernists, brings a great deal of anxiety, and even shame and self denigration for those without the resources to take advantage of the opportunities of modern societies. Moreover, an essential moment of later modernity has been gender equality and erotic hedonism in both its life styles and popular culture. Fundamentalisms provide a stable, cohesive self identity, bound by fixed rules and regulations, sustaining essentialist notions of gender hierarchy, and clear-cut meaning systems that decry hedonism and any sexuality outside of heterosexual male control.

2. *Ressentement*: For Nietzsche, the subjugation of the Christians by the Romans fostered *ressentement* on the part of the weak and powerless as a form of self hatred. The slaves suppressed desire for revenge against their masters and repressed their envy for the wealth, power and emotional/sexual freedom of the Romans. This inward hate and loathing by the powerless leads to the desire for revenge through the deaths and/or destruction of the powerful and their material and psychic advantages. But unable to express that anger, the slave embraced the values of kindness, mercy, charity and humility in face of the power of his/her master. But in so doing, s/he hated him/herself. His/her redirection of aggression to the self, embodied in the internalization of the slave morality, sustained his/her subjugation.

[54] It might be also noted that the deeply ingrained gun culture of the US is not simply a product of the NRA and gun makers, but endures as a symbol of empowered manhood.

Following Nietzsche's suggestive insights, Fanon (1963), moved the argument from Master-Slave to colonizer and colonized. He argued that the affluent and powerful colonizer not only dominated the colonized, but denigrated the indigenous culture and deemed inferior the identities of the colonized in order to legitimate their colonization. The "white man's burden" was to bring (Western/Christian) civilization to the uncivilized. Colonization of land, culture and mind, of course, leads to the rage and *ressentement* of the colonized, but his/her rage was often turned inward, upon his/her very self and expressed in self destructive behavior. The violence done to the culture of the colonized, to the "wretched of the earth" fostered self-hatred and destructive behavior such as crime, addiction or interpersonal violence. When Fanon (1963) wrote, his context was colonialization, especially the French control of Algeria and his homeland Martinique. Today, naked colonial power no longer endures as such, yet much of his analysis remains cogent (Scatamburlo and Langman, 2001). Rather, globalization as a form of neo-colonialization that controls investments, raw material prices, trade, investment etc. Moreover, the identities and cultures of the global elite are seen as superior to those of the underdeveloped. Violence to the oppressor is not only cathartic, but becomes viewed as the means to overcome political, economic or cultural domination.

This analysis suggests that the Islamic world has faced three major insults and humiliations that have in turn bred *ressentement* toward the West. 1) When Islam was one of the three most advanced cultures in the world, Christendom was in its Dark Ages, superstition ruled and its peoples ran around in forests in animal skins. But with the growth of trade, Europe was ascendant. The defeat of the Muslims in Spain was emblematic of the declining power of the Islamic world in the face of Christendom. Following its defeats at the outskirts of Vienna, Islam would continue to decline vis a vis Europe, especially after merchant fleets circumvented caravan-based trade, the lifeblood of the Muslim trading classes. 2) In the nineteenth century, European colonizers took over many Muslim states. The last major Islamic power, the Ottoman Caliphate, eventually succumbed, following a number of defeats by European armies. Following the various independence movements after WWII, even when nominally "independent", the leadership of many Muslim countries was still controlled by foreigners, especially the US that had secured power and influence throughout the Muslim world, as for example in Saudi Arabia, Egypt, and Persia. Often this power was secured through unscrupulous means from bribery to coups. 3) The creation of the State of Israel was seen as a daily reminder of Arabic political weakness that enabled the UN to establish the state of Israel. Further, despite vastly larger Arab armies, the more technologically advanced IDF was the victor in all its military conflicts. But what is more, Israel has become a leader in global business, its GDP/person is about the same as England; its wealth is greater than all its neighbors combined. It is a world leader in technology providing the world with the cell phone, MMX/Pentium chips, IM and voice mail, etc. Much the same can be said about its medicine and agriculture. 4) Finally, the impact of globalization has been such that the insularity of people from the larger world has waned and the import of foreign goods, often undercutting local artisan production, symbolizes the technological stagnation while much of the products of the Western culture industry portray vast wealth.

The attempts to secure dignified work and in turn, life styles through education has become especially difficult in many Islamic countries where there are few demands for the technologically skilled. While many young people do pursue higher education, for those trained in Arabic or Quranic studies, there are many more college graduates than there are jobs for them. The universities that were once the breeding grounds for socialist revolution are now spaces where Islamisms are becoming widely studied and embraced. Moreover, there are a number of Muslim students who go to European universities and even move to Europe. But Europe, facing high unemployment, regards such Muslims with anger and contempt. They are denied jobs, relegated to inferior housing, and treated with disdain. Without dignity, hope or honor, they turn to fundamentalist mosques for solace and repair. And some embrace causes and action that provide "heroic masculinities."

These various sources of *ressentement* and shame from internal legacies and the domination of foreign States, past and current, have been conducive to the embrace of violence as a compensatory tactic to secure voice, agency and dignity. A number of factors ranging from historical myth and actual legacies of ascent and demise have now resulted in a *ressentement* that valorizes violence as a compensation for frustration. Fundamentalist ideology joins with *ressentement* as a reaction to subjugation, as an attempt to restore a shamed and denigrated self and community. The warrior of past glories has been resurrected as the foot soldier of fundamentalism as seen in the extent to which even young boys in fundamentalist communities "naturally" embrace the warrior as the model of the faithful. In many Muslim countries small numbers of mostly young, unattached, males, projecting their anger outwards, seeking compensation for subjugation, embrace fundamentalism as a legitimation (not cause) for militancy and embrace terrorism. And of these *jihadis*, an even smaller number become suicide bombers, fully accepting the belief that fallen warriors, martyred in battle, *shaheeden*, get a special place in heaven. While often such *shaheeden* tend to be boys from poor and destitute classes, there are as many better educated young people, and even some women, willing to die for their cause. In sum, many who suffer from various forms of domination and social constraints, who glean little honorific status or dignity but instead experience shame and humiliation, find solace in hate, revenge and destruction of the Other, even at the cost of one's life.

3. *Simplification of reality*: Following what has been said, fundamentalisms simplify vastly complex realities that are fraught with ambiguities, into a few basic understandings, beginning with a Manichean good/bad view of the world and other people. Complex events are personalized as the actions of a specific people, typically involved in a conspiracy of some sort. And as so often happens, the evil doers for fascists or Islamic fundamentalists tend to be the Jews.[55] The fundamentalist world view reduces complex social realities to simple explanations ranging from conspiracies of infidels to the "moral decline" of the community. Punishment of the infidels, and/or the "renewal of faith," becomes the solution to all problems.

4. *Hope*: For Marx, religion expressed both real pain and genuine hope for something better. But the workers could only imagine a better life in the next world, thus preserving existing social conditions. Horkhiemer's critical theory of religion has said much the same. Finally, noting the communality of Freud's theories of dreams and daydreams as wish fulfillments, Bloch (1986) has argued that hope was an intrinsic human quality. People were motivated by dreams of a better life, they yearned for utopian moments without the stresses and strains of actually existing social life.[56] In the face of the oppressions, humiliations, *ressentement* and victimhood, imaginary histories become refashioned into a desirable future. At such moments, cultures resurrect archaic legacies of empowerment and dignity. These legacies often invoke tales of "heroic masculinity". For Nazis, there were the gods of Valhalla populated by Wagnerian depictions of *ubermenchen*, courageous supermen whose will to power (Nietzsche) was not fettered by the banalities of underlings. For

[55] This is not to anyway exonerate Israel's heinous policies toward the Palestinians, but rather the tendency to blame all the economic problems of close to a billion Muslims on Jewish plots and conspiracies.

[56] See http://www.uta.edu/english/dab/illuminations/kell1.html for an excellent summary/introduction to Block by Keller (N.d.).

Imperial Japan there were the Samurai of the Shoguns. Islamisms, as expressions of clerical fascism, promise to restore the early Caliphate, purify the community (*umma*) and restore the greatness of the heroic knight who dies a martyr. Such legacies of collective memory are reconstructed and reinterpreted by various leaders who convince others, not themselves or their own family members, to give their lives to the noble causes.

Conclusion

Marx, Weber and Freud-The Enduring Power of Theory

For Marx, alienation was a consequence of wage labor, commodified labor power, understood as fostering the system of commodity exchange that stood outside the person and refluxed back upon him/her, to act as an outside power that rendered the person powerless, thwarted his/her selfhood, dehumanized him/her (estranged from species being) and condemned him/her to live in a fragmented social world. His analysis has had a lasting impact for the critical understanding of society. But Marx also showed how ideologies might assuage alienation in ways that served to reproduce the system of class domination. His comments on religion noted how it expressed the real pain and suffering of economic privation and alienation. But religion also promised ameliorative hope, albeit for the proletariat, the "better life" was to be found in the afterlife. While penned over 160 years ago, Marx's insights remain seminal. On the one hand religion, as an expression of material interests, spoken as ideology, sustained domination. But religion also stood as a critique of domination and the articulation of hope as it promised to overcome alienation, domination and exploitation.

For Weber, concerned with subjective meanings of social action rather than objective functions of organized groups and/or classes, religion was a more complex phenomenon; it offered explanations for the distribution of fortunes. Further, it was not always the ruling class that shaped religion, certain critical strata, be they warriors, merchants or prebendaries were likely to have an "elective affinity" for a particular kind of religion, and strongly embrace it and, in turn, stamp the society in certain ways, especially insofar as religions fostered a certain "economic ethic". As Weber then showed, urban artisans in the Roman empire were the group most likely to embrace early Christianity, a salvation religion that promised a better life in the next world if they accepted their subordinated status to Rome in this life. Following Nietzsche, this valorization of the "slave mentality", replete with its repressive asceticism came out of the *ressentement* toward the Roman elites (Kellner N.d. a). Yet that mentality endured thousands of years till this very day.[57] But insofar as that Christianity emerged from Judaism, it held an implicit rationality in its rejection of magic that was obscured by the Catholic Church. Further, Christianity, as a "slave mentality" that found virtue in self denial, preached asceticism, quite atypical of Romans in that era.[58] Over a millennium later, these elements of salvation, rationality (rejection of magic) and asceticism would become central elements of Protestantism.

In contrast, for Weber, Islam was embraced by warriors who held an elective affinity for a salvation religion. As such, warrior classes stamped Islam in two important ways. Unlike Christians, Muslim warriors, were not disposed to asceticism. Nor in turn were the merchants. From the martyrdom of Ali, to the wars against crusaders, martyrdom would play a significant role in Islamic culture. Further, for Weber, the system of religiously based law interpreted by *mufti* scholars and administered by *kadi* judges meant that commerce was based on *vertrational* rather than *zweckrational* goals. Thus for example, Islam never fostered the vast commercial organizations typical of Europe.

We might also recall Freud's comments on religion beginning with the notion that religion served as an illusion that a benevolent Father would grant people the happiness that was denied, thwarted, ironically, by the demands for repression imposed by Civilization (Freud, 1961). Ironically, the demands were mandated by religion and ultimately became internalized as the superego. At certain times, certain charismatic leaders who embodied the group's values might act like a cultural superego such that submitting to his authority might gain the love of the leader as well as cement ties between believers. Thus Freud showed how authority not only became part of the psyche, but played a central role in social life, insuring social bonds were maintained and that necessary labor, as well as the specialized, creative labor was done.

[57] The dialectic of religion, the contradiction of domination and religion as hope, especially evident in Christianity, is a central premise for a critical theory of religion See for example Siebert (this volume).

[58] While the infamous sex orgy was largely a leisure activity for the rich, prostitution was not only legal, but there were many state-owned, public brothels.

The Frankfurt Synthesis

These legacies informed the development of Frankfurt School Critical Theory that melded the insights of Marx's critiques of alienation and exploitation with Weber's discussions of rationality, dehumanization, and religion, with Freudian depth psychology, especially his analysis of authority, submission and the superego.[59] Their approach to the critique of ideology (*ideologiekritic*-immanent critique of the contradictions within an ideology) provided theoretical tools that not only illuminated what was cloaked by ideology and/or defense mechanisms, but held an implicit emancipatory hope for the overcoming of alienation, dehumanization and repression and a better future (see Jacoby 2005). Identification with parents ensured that the legitimations of traditional, rational and charismatic authority were internalized and became enduring moments of character.

Thus one of the most useful legacies of Critical Theory was to see that materially determined values were not simple emanations from factories, but as embraced by certain actors, could act as material forces that stamp the society such that certain values can act in autonomous ways that yet served economic interests. In their words, Instrumental Reason, as the legitimating ideology of capitalism, stood as the dominant form of authority; the king was replaced by manuals of bureaucratic regulations and procedures. Nevertheless, that rationality produced advanced technologies of production/distribution, wealthy market societies and highly efficient forms of administration. Yet that efficiency demanded compliance and the erosion of critical thought. The legitimacy of capitalism was ultimately sustained by its purposive rationality *zweckrationality*, which held promises of wealth, freedom, community, self determination and creative self fulfillment. But in order for that market society to produce vast wealth, it has spread the logic of Instrumental Reason, as well as its economic and/or military power throughout the world. But ultimately that rationality subverted itself; it not only led to dehumanization of those living in sterile, empty "iron cages" but, in certain cases, led to the ultimate of irrationality, the Holocaust.

---

[59] To be sure there were many other influences from Nietzsche and Schopenhauer – indeed the entire history of philosophy, as well as their contemporaries. Lukacs, for example, introduced Marxists to Weber.

From Fascism to Fundamentalism

Critical Theory said very little about religion *per se*. Its primary focus was the rise of Fascism, and following WWII, mass society, mass culture and the demise of emancipatory reason in "one dimensional" society. But as I have argued, not only are there many underlying psycho-cultural similarities between Fascism and fundamentalism, but certain authors use the very term "clerical fascism".[60] The fundamental theoretical premise of this analysis has argued that fascisms and fundamentalisms in general are both responses to alienation and ways that would assuage that alienation. A long tradition of alienation theory and research has noted that there can be other material bases to alienation, not the least of which can be political domination, which itself often sustains economic domination, deprivation and immiseration. Fundamentalism has been a growing response to the adversities of the now globalized world. Its demands for submission to its absolutist and simplistic world views and compliance with its essentialist codes of gender hierarchy and rigid morality promise moral renewal and social regeneration. As was noted, submission to authority, rigid social hierarchies, moralism and simplification of reality, offer solace and comfort in world seemingly out of control.

Neither Weber nor the Frankfurt School said much about Islam in general, let alone Islamism and its extreme forms of martyrdom/terrorism.[61] Nevertheless, the Critical Theory tradition provides a framework for theorizing the rise and I would argue immanent demise of Islam and, in turn, the move to fundamentalism. As was noted, we need to begin with the critique of political economy and simply note that throughout the world fundamentalism began to flourish at the same time as globalization began to create a unified world market. But while globalization created enormous wealth, for the few, it did not bring benefits to the multitudes buffeted by the winds of social change as many established forms of commerce and employment waned while new products and methods of doing business came

[60] There are differences between classical fascism and fundamentalisms over the nature of governance, eg fascisms did not use religious texts as the basis of law. See Harman, 2003.

[61] Although his scattered references did indeed inspire a number of scholars such as Turner, and Schlucter etc, to focus on Weber, he did not offer a systematic account as he did with China or India.

forth as well as new political realities Not only did many people suffer economic losses, but the basis of their status and dignity were lost as well. Globalization and all that has gone with it has undermined traditional anchors of self, community and meaning. The ties of community were attenuated, traditional values assaulted, while a mass mediated youth culture of self indulgent hedonism spread throughout the world. In sum, with globalization came new forms of alienation.

Much like Fascism, religious fundamentalisms, as palliatives, are responses to real suffering. If one accepts one's subjugation to the larger cause of moral renewal based on absolutist, Manichean values rooted in a holy scripture, fundamentalisms provide alternative identity granting communities of meaning and recognition premised on a morally based critique of existing conditions and promises of moral restoration. In short, fundamentalism provides cohesive communities bound by religious beliefs and rituals, stable identities rooted in fixed notions of gender in which dignity and esteem are based on absolutist moral criteria. Fundamentalisms provide frameworks of meaning based on the inerrancy of scripture in a world ever more meaningless, rationalized and depersonalized, and seemingly in moral decline through the embrace of relativism. For fundamentalists, an absolutist scriptural morality counteracts the waning of community ties, the fluidity of identities and relativism of meaning.

Islamisms

As was argued, with the decline of the Caliphate, in face of an ascendant Christendom, just as early Christians felt *ressentement* to the more powerful Romans, so too did waning Islam feel *ressentement* toward the rising West. While this served to keep Islamic societies weak, with the colonization of the Muslim Middle East, and indeed Mogul India and SE Asia, it was in the self interest of European colonizers to keep the colonized weak, passive and submissive.[62] Much of this was done through the use of local authorities as intermediates, but some of these local elites, to be effective administrators, were educated in the mother countries. While this did work for awhile, nevertheless, as many of the colonized attended European schools they brought back ideas of the Enlightenment and modern governance. In the late nineteenth

[62] Many of the nineteenth-century fundamentalist movements, especially Wahabism, emerged as critiques of foreign influences as well as indigenous Sufism.

and early twentieth centuries, there were indeed a number of modernist revolutions, but with the exception of Kemalist Turkey, they did not endure in the form of democratic, representative governments.[63] Rather, given post war geo-political and economic agendas, Muslim States, themselves often created by European powers drawing lines in the sand, became subjected to various forms of neo colonialism. Notwithstanding independence movements and even a variety of indigenous modernizing movements, the societies remained economically stagnant, politically ossified and recalcitrant to change.

Much of the post war history of the world could be seen as alienated people attempting to take charge of their lives and fight, even die, if need be, for self-determination. And indeed while the global maps were redrawn, in many countries, autonomy and independence from colonial authorities did not bring freedom and self determination. This has been especially true in the Islamic world, and especially the Arab states. Islamic fundamentalism can be understood as an expression of alienation from political power, the fragmentation of communities, thwarted self determination and challenges to a traditional moral order. Just as Hitler promised a 1000 year Reich free of Jews, Islamisms promise restoring a Caliphate free from political domination by alien powers and without the corrupting influences of infidel Others.

While Islamic societies faced these global winds of change, they began at a different place. As was argued, between the legacies of decline and defeat, internal barriers to Western values, ideas and commercial practices, and often colonization, there was a lingering *ressentement* to the West. This was followed by neo-imperialist interventions that subverted progressive mobilizations. As a result, Muslim societies have been both economically stagnant and autocratically ruled, often at the behest of neo-imperial powers seeking either resources (oil), geo political influence or both. Thus Islamism, a fusion of politics and fundamentalism, not only stressed spiritual renewal, but promises a restoration of the community of virtue, the *umma,* as it was, or is imagined it was, at the time of the Caliphate.

While most fundamentalisms see themselves in conflict with the creatural world, and remain content to pray and perhaps exert political pressure where possible, as we have stated, in many Muslim countries, there are few channels for independent political action. Such conditions lead to certain people

[63] Turkish Exceptionalism has always been used to critique other Muslim countries for not having "modernized". This, for example, has shaped the views of Bernard Lewis. Turkey has been used to justify Orientalism.

of certain classes willing to take up arms against their "enemies" from within or without. Islamisms, however, have framed their grievances in religious terms and invoke holy war. *Jihad,* and its extreme form, *shaheeden* martyrdom, are responses to the economic despair catalyzed by globalization, oppression and/or the political powerlessness of oppressed people. Given the lack of decent jobs and/or political voice through independent "grass roots" political institutions and/or opposition parties or democratic NGOs, and in the face of economic and political adversities, facing assaults by Western culture from its dehumanizing rationality to its hedonistic self indulgence and blatant sexuality, mosques become places of solace and Islamism is the only likely response.

Political grievances that are often quite legitimate become articulated through religious discourses. Moreover, there are times when fundamentalists actually take over the State such as in Taliban Afghanistan, Khomeini's Iraq or Bush's United States. But governance based on religion and scripture cannot govern very well in a globalized world dependent on advanced technologies. Fundamentalisms, while responses to economic and/or political deprivations, cannot foster the rational policies that produce wealth within and promote co-operation with other States. Such forms of governance will either implode or lose legitimacy. To embrace fundamentalism, whatever its short term gratifications may be, is a very irrational choice. But this contradiction is only evident to those whose dialectical understanding of society was informed by the Frankfurt School.

Epilogue-After Jihad

Various scenarios suggest that the foreseeable future portend nothing but endless war and conflict between the West and Islamic *jihadi* for several generations. But the analysis presented suggests that while Islamisms are likely to continue in the short run, and the *jihadis* power will grow, *at* some point, between their growing numbers and sheer violence, they and their issues will force recognition and acknowledgement. I would suggest that just as the Chinese communists and British colonizers of India played key roles in fostering Indian and Chinese modernities, so too will Islamisms wane and foster Islamic modernities (See Langman and Morris 2002). Fundamentalisms can never address their basic contradictions; their anti-modernity exacerbates the very problems they would seek to ameliorate (Cf. Roy 1994). Critical

Theory suggests that if Islamisms actually attain political power and voice, that will lead to their demise. With power comes needs to produce wealth, secure legitimacy and to negotiate with other States. But if and when they get to run schools, health care systems and hospitals, postal systems, public works, etc, most often on limited budgets, violence tends to wane, in deed if not in rhetoric. To overcome the conditions they would ameliorate, they will need to incorporate the very purposive rationality which they so much abhor. That is the central insight of history. But Reason should become the basis of freedom and emancipation, not the source of domination. That is the central insight of Critical Theory.

David Gay, Warren S. Goldstein, and Anna Campbell Buck

Operationalizing The Critical Theory of Religion

The Critical Theory of Religion, as it has been articulated by Rudolf Siebert (2001) and Michael Ott (2001), has remained an exegesis on a theoretical level. While most of the work of the Frankfurt School was theoretical, they also engaged in survey research (see Adorno et al. 1950). A critical theory needs to reflect the changing conditions of society. The validity of a theory is dependent "on the derived propositions being consonant with the actual facts" (Horkheimer 1982[1937]:188). If a theory is valid, it should be capable of being empirically verified.

The first generation of the Frankfurt School engaged in a synthesis of the theories of Marx, Weber, and Freud. In an attempt to operationalize the critical theory of religion, we will go back to some of their insights on religion.

Unlike Max Weber and Emile Durkheim, Karl Marx is not perceived by most sociologists of religion to provide one of the foundations for the subdiscipline. While the number of those adhering to a Marxist sociology of religion has been limited, the potential contributions of Marx to the subdiscipline should not be ignored (O'Toole 1984:69). While Marx's most well known statement about religion is that it is the "opium of the people," this quotation is taken out of textual and historical context and misunderstood (Bloch 1972:62; Goldstein 2001:66; McKinnon 2005). One needs to understand opium within the context of the nineteenth century when it was legal. Opium was not only a narcotic but it was used for medicinal purposes (Marx himself used opium). It was a source of profit and a cause of conflict (the opium wars and the temperance movement) (McKinnon 2005). Marx expresses a two-way relationship between religiosity and suffering which is dialectical. Religious suffering is "an expression of real suffering" and a protest against it (Marx 1992[1844]:244). If this is true, then religion arises as a response to suffering and should help to alleviate the experience of it but not necessarily the conditions that cause it. But how do we measure suffering? Some suffering may have direct economic causes while other suffering may be due to illness or psychological factors that are not directly caused by socioeconomic factors.

One of the major contributions that Max Weber (who, along with Marx and Freud, is another theoretical foundation of critical theory) makes to this discussion is that the underprivileged have a greater need for salvation. "Since, every need of salvation is an expression of some distress, social or economic oppression is an effective source of salvation beliefs, though by no means the exclusive source" (Weber 1978:491). Social and economic oppression are one of the sources of the belief in salvation. The upper classes use religion to legitimize their own position and have less of a need for salvation. From this, we can derive the hypothesis that the lower the socio-economic status, the stronger beliefs one would have in salvation. This may translate into the lower the income, the greater the belief in the afterlife.

Freud thought that religion was a form of "compulsive neurosis" (Freud 1991:20). Childhood traumatic experiences, which have been forgotten and repressed, are the cause of this neurosis (Freud 1939:91). Freud suggests that similar to the psychological history of the individual, the origins of religion are the result of a primeval collective traumatic experience, which is no longer conscious. Religion is a form of collective neurosis, which is a result of the oedipal guilt, which the son feels in murdering the father (Freud 1939:101–102). While some of this is highly speculative and has a fictitious quality, what remains relevant is the hypothesis that religion is a response to trauma.

Aside from the classics, contemporary sociologists have discussed the relationship between economic and psychological stress, and religiosity. Stark and Bainbridge (1985) in their pendulum theory of secularization argue that due to the secularizing effects of wealth, sects, which become institutionalized into churches, move from a state of higher tension with this world to a state of lower tension. Higher tension churches are lower down on the Socio-Economic Scale than lower tension churches. Roof and McKinney (1987) in their analysis of mainline American denominations find that the members of stricter conservative denominations are less educated and have lower incomes while the members of less religious liberal denominations are more educated and have higher incomes. Baptist churches, which are higher tension, have incomes lower than the national average (Wuthnow 1988:84). We expect to have similar findings, that the lower the income, the more religious people will be, while the higher the income, the less religious.

In this article, we shall be examining some of these ideas about the association between trauma and religion. Trauma may have underlying economic causes but they are not necessarily the only ones. Some trauma may be purely psychological although it may have underlying social causes. We speculate that the more severe the trauma, the higher the religiosity as measured by variables such as belief in god, belief in the afterlife, belief in hell, etc. However, at the same time, since religion is a response to suffering and may help to alleviate it, we may find that those who are more religious report less trauma.

Religion, Rational Choice, and Well Being

Rodney Stark and Roger Finke reject the premises of the critical theory of religion made by Marx, Weber, and Freud. First, they argue against Marx's quotation that "religion is the opium of the people" (Stark and Finke 2000:30). However, they have a very flat reading of this text, which as we have discussed, is more nuanced and multidimensional. Second, they cite data that indicate the higher the income, the higher the level of church attendance (Stark and Finke 2000:30). When contrasting rich and poor, church attendance may not always be an indicator of religiosity. The poor may be deterred from church attendance due to the hidden costs of church attendance. But, they may have also given up hope.

Stark and Finke (2000:30) arguing against Freud that religion is a "psychopathology" and basing themselves on Chris Ellison, report that religiosity has positive effects on mental health: "Religious belief and practice greatly improve self-esteem, life satisfaction, the ability to withstand major social stressors, and even physical health" (Stark and Finke 2000:46). We do not dispute that religion may have a beneficial impact on mental health. What we would question is the conditions that give rise to the stressors with which religion helps people to cope. Much of the survey data may not accurately measure the stressors (trauma) that give rise to the need to turn to religion as coping mechanism.

A closer examination of the articles they cite by Ellison (1991:80) reveals that he does see religion as enhancing well being although in a more restricted sense. Basing himself on Berger's religious phenomenology, Ellison (1991:82) argues that religion provides "existential coherence" for people confronting "high levels of stress". Ellison seeks to understand the relationship between religiosity, stress and psychological well-being. In order to get at this relationship, he uses a group of "Trauma" variables from the General Social Survey (hereafter GSS) (e.g., divorce, unemployment, bereavement, and hospitalization/disability) (Ellison 1991:84). He finds that "religious faith buffers the negative effects of trauma on well-being" (Ellison 1991:89). This effect is greater upon individuals with less "sophisticated cognitive skills" (i.e. "lower levels of formal education"). According to Ellison, "Religious faith makes traumatic events easier to bear" (1991:90).

In a later article, Ellison (1994) takes this argument even further. He argues that the involvement in religion may have beneficial effects on mental health by decreasing the risk of several social stressors. These include "1) chronic acute health problems, (2) marital discord and dissolution, (3) occupational conflicts, (4) legal difficulties, and (5) parent-child conflicts" (Ellison 1994:91). He concludes that religious involvement particularly in some conservative denominations reduces the risk of social stressors (Ellison 1994:111).

We do not disagree with Ellison's findings but with the way that Stark and Finke interpret them. These findings do not disprove the theories of Marx, Weber, and Freud on religion, but rather validate them. If religion helps people deal with traumatic experiences, then couldn't one see religion as a response to trauma? If the wealthy and educated have higher attendance levels, they would report lower levels of stress although this may be due to factors other than religion (for example, income provides access to better health care, etc.). The poor and uneducated, who have higher levels of stress, particularly if they are not turning to religion (i.e., attendance), would have a more despondent outlook.

This paper attempts to augment the existing literature in the following ways: (1) we examine the effects of economic considerations on religiosity, (2) we explore the extent to which economic factors vary by urban versus more rural residence, (3) we assess the degree to which religiosity is a response to psychological trauma, and (4) we use a quantitative approach to analyze these relationships at three different intervals over a twenty-year period.

Data and Measures

Like many previous studies of differences in social attitudes addressing a wide range of social phenomena, our investigation uses data from the GSS. The GSS is an appropriate data set because it contains survey items tapping attitudes toward psychological trauma and economic concerns, as well as information on the various background characteristics of respondents. In order to examine the questions of interest, the 1978, 1988, and 1998 survey years are employed for the analysis. We select these years because the items of interest are asked in each of these years, and the survey years represent a twenty year time comparison. Separate analyses are run for each of the survey years.

Dependent Variables

Religiosity. Frequency of attendance at religious services is measured through an eight-point ordinal scale with higher scores indicating more frequent attendance. A score of zero means that the respondent did not attend religious services at all during the last year. A score of eight (8) represents respondents who attended religious services several times a week.

Independent Variables

Psychological variables. Separate items were selected to represent psychological trauma. For the 1978 and 1988 GSS, the question (similar to Ellison – see above) pertaining to the number of traumatic events (deaths, divorces, unemployment, or hospitalizations – disabilities) happening to the respondent last year is used to construct a dummy variable. The variable represents respondents who experienced one or more of the events either directly or indirectly.

The 1998 GSS does not contain the same item above but does include six items gauging negative affect in the last thirty days. The first item addresses the extent to which respondents feel that nothing could cheer them up. The GSS asks the following question: "In the past 30 days, about how often do you feel so sad that nothing could cheer you up?" The response categories for the item are (1) all of the time, (2) most of the time, (3) some of the time, (4) a little of the time, and (5) none of the time. The same response categories and wording of the question are used for "nervous," "restless or fidgety," "hopeless," "that everything was an effort," and "worthless." To construct an index, the coding for the six items is reversed, and the responses are summed (reliability coefficient = .85). This strategy yields an index that ranges from 6 to 30 with higher scores reflecting greater psychological distress.

Economic variable. Economic difficulties are measured using the income scales employed by the GSS for the survey years. The scales are then rescaled to percentages. Drawing from a variety of sources, the decision was made to use the 13 to 14 percentile as the cut point for those falling below the poverty line. In addition, an interaction term to represent the urban poor is also included in the models.

Control Variables. Recent studies demonstrate that attendance at religious services varies by a number of sociodemographic and background factors. Dummy variables representing southern residence (South = 1, U.S. Census designation), married respondents (married = 1), households with children under the age of eighteen living at home, gender (female = 1), and African American respondents are used as control variables, along with age (in years), educational attainment (in years) and community size (six-point ordinal measure, with more urban areas receiving higher scores).

Analytical Strategy and Results

Multiple regression is used to analyze attendance at religious services since the scale is not significantly skewed and meets the basic criteria for this type of analysis. Two models for each time period are used to examine the main effects of the independent variables, with and without controls, on attendance at religious services.

Results

Table 1 shows the means and standard deviations for all variables in each of the three time periods. For the dummy variables or dichotomous variables, the mean reflects the proportion of respondents on that item that are coded one. Tables two, three, and four display the bivariate correlations for all variables in the analysis.

Table 5 shows the models for the three time periods. Model I for the 1978 time period displays the coefficients for the main effects and the interaction term for urban poverty. The model is statistically significant but explains a very small proportion of the variance. Living in poverty has no significant effect on attendance but does show a positive coefficient. The model does show that the urban poor are less likely to attend. The coefficient of psychological trauma exhibits a statistically significant negative effect. Model II includes control variables and accounts for 8.9 percent of the variance. Once controls are entered into the equation, the effects for poverty and the urban poor are no longer evident. However, trauma and attendance demonstrate a negative relationship net of the effect of covariates. That is, respondents who experience greater psychological trauma attend religious services at lower rates. The analysis also shows that older and more educated respondents report more frequent attendance. Southern residents and African American respondents are more likely to attend religious services than their counterparts. Married respondents, respondents with children under the age of eighteen living at home, and females are also more likely to attend. The coefficient for the urban scale shows that respondents living in more urban areas attend services less than those in small communities.

Table 5 shows that Model I for 1988 is not statistically significant. Hence, there are no main effects in this model. Once controls are included in Model II, psychological trauma has a statistically significant effect on attendance. The economic factors show no significant effect. The effect of control variables varies from the 1978 model. Age and education remain significant predictors of attendance while an increase in community size leads to a decrease. Married and female respondents are also similar to the 1978 model. However, southern residents are no more likely than their nonsouthern counterparts to attend. Finally, having children at home is not a significant predictor.

The third set of models in Table five exhibits the main effects model and the model with controls for 1998. Model I is statistically significant but explains a small percentage of the overall variance. Like the 1978 model, the main effects for psychological trauma exhibit a negative relationship with attendance. The coefficients for the economic variables are not statistically significant. Model II includes covariates. This model shows that the relationship between trauma and attendance remains statistically significant net the effect of covariates in the model. In addition, the economic effect is evident as well. Respondents with incomes below the poverty line are less likely to attend. Conversely, the more urban poor are more likely to attend religious services.

Discussion and Conclusion

The analysis generates a few somewhat limited conclusions and raises a number of theoretical and empirical questions.

First, consistent with the extant literature, the effect of control variables such as education, marital status, urban residence and residence of the south are in the expected direction. With respect to psychological trauma and the economic conditions of respondents, the analysis indicates that some of the main effects are not consistent with our hypothesis. For example, our economic variable, poverty, is negatively correlated with attendance at religious services. This is the case for the main effects model in 1978 and the main effects and full models in 1998. This indicates that those in poverty are not necessarily turning to religious participation in an effort to ease their plight in life. Such a result requires an explanation as to why this is the case. One of our speculations is that people living below the poverty level may be less inclined to go to church due to the capital investment required for attending (tithing, proper attire, etc.). Additional research is needed to investigate potential explanations for this relationship.

William Julius Wilson (1987:20) describes the growth of the hyper ghetto and increasing social dislocations ("crime, drug addiction, out-of-wedlock births, female-headed families, and welfare dependency"), as a result of the transition from an industrial to a post industrial economy. If religiosity is a response to social trauma, then one would expect to see increasing religiosity in the inner-city ghetto as a response to the increasing social dislocations. Elijah Anderson argues, on the other hand, building on the framework provided by Wilson, that because of this shift, there has been a transition in role models from the old head to the new old head: "Traditionally the 'old head' was a man of stable means who believed in hard work, family life, and the church" (Anderson 1990:3). The new old head, who is the antithesis of this Protestant work ethic, is the drug dealer. Given this logic, with the replacement of the old head by the new old head, one would expect to see a decline in church attendance. This raises the question whether the urban underclass is turning to religion to ameliorate the stress caused by increased social dislocations.

Our analysis demonstrates that the relationship between the urban poor and public religious participation moves from a negative relationship in 1978 (i.e., life in urban poverty is associated with lower frequency of attendance) to a positive relationship in 1998. The analysis for 1998 lends support for Wilson's position. This pattern is evident for those in urban poverty but not for those below the poverty level in the general population.

Our analysis demonstrates a consistent, significant relationship between psychological trauma and attendance at religious services. The coefficients are negative in all models in each survey year. Those who have recently experienced trauma and feel that life is hopeless and nothing can cheer them up are not the people who are attending religious services. At the same time, those attending church are less likely to give up hope and more likely to report higher levels of subjective well-being. People who join others in religious activities are generally more likely to believe in life after death. Such beliefs are likely to promote provisions of meaning that afford people the opportunity to place their lives in a context that makes them feel comfortable. The question that we cannot answer in this analysis is which comes first. Does participation over the life course (or some part of it) buffer the effects of trauma when it occurs and hence provide a framework for coping with the problem? If this were the case, then we would expect continued attendance at the onset of various negative life events. However, higher attendance rates may not be the case if the order is reversed. That is, do people attend religious services as a reaction to psychological trauma? Our results suggest that those who experience negative psychological experiences do not necessarily turn to places of worship as coping mechanism or reaction to these negative life events. Instead, they appear less likely to attend.

Clearly, employing data such as the General Social Surveys has its strengths and limitations. The GSS is one of the few data sources that addresses a wide range of issues and taps a number of attitudinal and behavioral dimensions. The GSS includes a number of items concerning religiosity, subjective well-being, and other sociodemographic information. The GSS also spans an approximate twenty-year time period and affords opportunity to examine trends in attitudes across these years. This analysis addresses attendance at religious services as an indicator of the participatory dimension of religiosity. The same question is asked in all years included in the study. We are also able to tap the psychological trauma dimension across this time period as well. While a slightly different measure is employed in 1998 than in 1978 and 1988, the two measures are highly correlated, indicating that both measures are addressing similar concerns. Finally, the GSS includes consistent items across the years concerning sociodemographic characteristics.

There are of course limitations to using these types of data. Our dependent variable is limited to attendance at religious services as a proxy for public participation in church or synagogue. Other items that tap ideational or devotional dimensions were not available in all survey years. In addition, the combination of psychological trauma and religiosity items were not included in the same years or asked to the same respondents.

Another limitation is that we were restricted to a twenty-year time frame for the analysis. While significant changes in the social and economic fabric of our society occurred over this time period, a trend comparison with other time periods (e.g., the 1950s and 1960s) would provide more depth to the analysis. A related limitation is that surveys of this type cannot measure historic events and their impact on psychological trauma, economic conditions, and religiosity.

We hope to initiate a dialogue to bridge the gap between critical theory and positivistic social sciences. One of the problems involved in doing so is how to take a dialectical theory and test it. In dialectical relationships, there are "feedback loops" and these feedback loops need to be operationalized. Such analyses would require various nonrecursive models to estimate reciprocal effects. We invite others to test the hypothesis of a critical theory of religion with survey research and data analysis.

Table 1
Means and Standard Deviations for Religiosity, Psychological Trauma, Poverty, and Controls

	1978		1988		1998	
	Mean	Std.Dev.	Mean	Std.Dev.	Mean	Std.Dev.
Attendance at Religious Services	3.63	2.77	3.92	2.66	3.64	2.79
Psychological Trauma	.38	.49	.43	.50	11.28	4.46
Life in Poverty	.14	.35	.11	.31	.14	.35
Urban Poverty	.38	1.13	.30	.98	.48	1.32
Age	44.01	17.85	45.90	18.39	46.40	16.99
Urban Residence	2.84	1.54	3.00	1.44	3.07	1.53
Southern Residence	.33	.47	.34	.47	.37	.48
Married Respondents	.72	.45	.67	.47	.59	.49
Highest Year of Education Completed	11.93	3.18	12.58	2.96	13.28	2.92
Children Under Age of 18 Living at Home	.45	.49	.36	.48	.33	.47
African American Respondents	.10	.30	.12	.32	.14	.35
Female Respondents	.57	.49	.55	.50	.54	.50

Table 2
1978 Bivariate Correlations: Religiosity, Psychological Trauma, Poverty, and Controls

	Attend	Trauma	Poverty	UrbPoor	Age	Urban	South	Married	Educ	Kids	Black	Female
Attendance at Religious Services	1.00	–.065	–.019	–.048	.134	–.083	.088	.141	–.003	.066	.070	.136
Psychological Trauma		1.00	.138	.144	–.009	.026	.006	–.094	–.113	–.037	.061	.035
Life in Poverty			1.00	.839	.221	–.042	.033	–.170	–.312	–.144	.103	.138
Life in Urban Poverty				1.00	.135	.181	–.016	–.174	–.249	–.092	.149	.118
Age					1.00	–.072	.001	.248	–.306	–.404	–.087	.027
Urban Residence						1.00	–.066	–.175	.097	–.022	.254	.010
Southern Residence							1.00	.058	–.144	.027	.136	.034
Married Respondents								1.00	–.114	.158	–.128	–.018
Educational Attainment									1.00	.034	–.103	–.081
Children Living at Home										1.00	.058	.029
African American Respondents											1.00	–.011
Female Respondents Education Completed												1.00

Table 3

1988 Bivariate Correlations: Religiosity, Psychological Trauma, Poverty, and Controls

	Attend	Trauma	Poverty	UrbPoor	Age	Urban	South	Married	Educ	Kids	Black	Female
Attendance at Religious Services	1.00	–.070	–.046	–.057	.151	–.144	.064	.204	–.030	.054	.034	.167
Psychological Trauma		1.00	.085	.098	.097	–.001	–.007	.009	–.171	–.023	.037	.070
Life in Poverty			1.00	.866	.032	–.072	.100	–.179	–.219	–.024	.145	.063
Life in Urban Poverty				1.00	.029	.109	.031	–.173	–.188	–.007	.200	.074
Age					1.00	–.084	.076	.357	–.293	–.392	–.077	.089
Urban Residence						1.00	–.183	–.142	.102	–.047	.221	.034
Southern Residence							1.00	.076	–.150	–.052	–.033	–.062
Married Respondents								1.00	–.093	.109	–.167	.061
Educational Attainment									1.00	.057	–.088	–.050
Children Living at Home										1.00	.012	.035
African American Respondents											1.00	.011
Female Respondents Education Completed												1.00

Table 4
1998 Bivariate Correlations: Religiosity, Psychological Trauma, Poverty, and Controls

	Attend	Trauma	Poverty	UrbPoor	Age	Urban	South	Married	Educ	Kids	Black	Female
Attendance at Religious Services	1.00	–.114	–.036	–.0147	.128	–.061	.132	.227	.047	.080	.155	.120
Psychological Trauma		1.00	.163	.162	–.133	.039	–.011	–.148	–.163	.033	.025	.003
Life in Poverty			1.00	.879	.053	.063	–.011	–.168	–.243	–.049	.178	.099
Life in Urban Poverty				1.00	.046	.251	–.049	–.163	–.197	–.037	.219	.104
Age					1.00	–.053	.028	.384	–.176	–.354	–.078	.046
Urban Residence						1.00	–.090	–.163	.086	–.044	.221	.023
Southern Residence							1.00	.001	–.062	–.023	.129	–.016
Married Respondents								1.00	–.055	.114	–.089	.040
Educational Attainment									1.00	–.002	–.119	–.027
Children Living at Home										1.00	.156	.088
African American Respondents											1.00	.048
Female Respondents Education Completed												1.00

Table 5
Multiple Regression: The Effects of Psychological Trauma, Poverty, and Control Variables on Religiosity for the 1978, 1988, and 1998 Survey Years

	1978				1988				1998			
	Model I		Model II		Model I		Model II		Model I		Model II	
Psychological Trauma	–.335	(.147)*	–.260	(.143)@	–.348	(.179)@	–.421	(.171)*	–.070	(.018)*	–.039	(.017)*
Life in Poverty	.601	(.370)@	–.047	(.398)	.107	(.562)	–.314	(.569)	–.765	(.463)@	–.960	(.470)@
Life in Urban Poverty	–.253	(.116)*	–.090	(.122)	–.168	(.180)	.018	(.181)	.187	(.123)	.267	(.128)*
Age			.029	(.005)*			.019	(.006)*			.014	(.005)*
Urban Residence			–.143	(.051)*			–.261	(.064)*			–.156	(.054)*
Southern Residence			.378	(.149)*			.281	(.182)			.643	(.154)*
Married Respondents			.454	(.173)*			.998	(.205)*			1.028	(.173)*
Educational Attainment			.073	(.024)*			.091	(.031)*			.091	(.027)*
Children Living at Home			.587	(.158)*			.369	(.198)@			.315	(.177)@
African Americans			1.113	(.247)*			.994	(.273)*			1.397	(.224)*
Female Respondents			.784	(.140)*			.862	(.169)*			.568	(.148)*
Constant	4.020		.996		4.109		1.398		4.456		1.237	
R-Square	.008*		.089*		.007@		.131*		.015*		.130*	
N	1455		1455		903		903		1288		1288	

Cell entries are given as unstandardized regression coefficients with standard errors in parentheses.

@ = $p < .10$

* = $p < .05$ or beyond

About the Authors

CHRISTOPHER CRAIG BRITTAIN is Assistant Professor of Ethics and Theology at the Atlantic School of Theology in Halifax, Nova Scotia. His research includes the critical social theory of the Frankfurt School, political theology, and the nature of secularism. He has published articles on Max Horkheimer and on Slavoj Zizek, and his dissertation focuses on the thought of Theodor W. Adorno. He recently published "The 'Secular' as a Tragic Category: On Talal Asad, Religion and Representation," in *Method and Theory in the Study of Religion* 17.2 (2005). Currently, he serves on the executive of the Canadian Society for the Study of Religion, and is working on a book project with the working title: *The Weight of Objectivity: Adorno and the Refusal of the 'Return to Religion'*.

ANNA CAMPBELL BUCK is Assistant Professor of Sociology at the University of Central Florida. Her teaching and research interests include religion, health, and aging, as well as statistics and quantitative methods. Her recent work focuses primarily on the relationship between religiosity and mental and physical health outcomes, especially among older adults and Hispanics. Examples of current papers include, the effect of church attendance on functional health status among elderly, Mexican Americans, and the use of individual growth curve models to analyze age and changes in religiosity.

DAVID A. GAY is Associate Professor of Sociology at the University of Central Florida. He received his Ph.D. from Duke University. His published work has examined variations in attitudes among American mainline denominations, the relationship between region, religion, and life satisfaction, the effects of switching on denominational subcultures, and variations in religiosity across the depression era, baby boom, and generation X birth cohorts. His work has appeared in the *Journal for the Scientific Study of Religion, Review of Religious Research, Social Forces, and Social Science Quarterly.*

WARREN S. GOLDSTEIN is Assistant Professor of Sociology at the University of Central Florida in Orlando. He received his Ph.D. from the New School for Social Research in 1998. He has published several articles which come out of his doctoral dissertation, "Messianism and Marxism: Walter Benjamin and Ernst Bloch's Dialectical Theories of Secularization." His research interests are in the sociological theory of religion. He is currently working on developing a dialectical theory of secularization as part of a critical theory of religion.

LAUREN LANGMAN is a professor of sociology at Loyola University of Chicago. He has long worked in the tradition of the Frankfurt school of critical theory, especially on issues of alienation and relationships between culture, politics and the psychosocial. His most recent publications include a special issue of *American Behavioral Politics* devoted to the presidency in a television age, and, co-edited with Devorah Kalekin, *The Evolution of Alienation: Trauma, Promise, and the Millennium. He ha*s also published on the alternative globalization movements, and the many forms of identity that emerge in the current age from fundamentalists to the extremes of body modification. More recently, he has published several book chapters on Islam and fundamentalism.

He has been chair of the Marxist section of ASA, is currently president of the alienation research committee of the International Sociological Association and on the editorial boards of *Critical Sociology*.

GEORGE LUNDSKOW is Associate Professor of Sociology at Grand Valley State University in Michigan. His longstanding interest in religion and Marxist theory began academically at the Jesuit high school he attended. Since then, professor Lundskow's work has examined religion in the context of social change, both reactionary and progressive. C. Wright Mills' *The Sociological Imagination* informs his general approach to sociology, that sociology should contribute progressively to vital issues of the day. His current research examines the rise of charismatic Christianity and anti-science movements.

KENNETH G. MACKENDRICK is Assistant Professor in the Department of Religion, University of Manitoba. In addition to Critical Theory his research interests include death and mourning rituals, concepts of evil and impurity, and food and religious practices. He is currently working on a monograph entitled *Discourse, Desire, and Fantasy*, a philosophical and psychoanalytic study of Jürgen Habermas's critical social theory.

ANDREW MCKINNON has a Ph.D. in Sociology from the University of Toronto. He has published in *Method and Theory in the Study of Religion*, *The Journal for the Scientific Study of Religion*, and *The Companion to Modern French Thought*. His doctoral dissertation analyses the relationship of religion and emergent consumer-capitalism in the United States, with a focus on the 1925 bestseller by Bruce Barton, *The Man Nobody Knows*, a book which told the story of Jesus as a master advertiser and the founder of modern business. He is a member of the Toronto Book Review Collective for *Critical Sociology*.

MICHAEL R. OTT is an Assistant Professor of Sociology at Grand Valley State University, Allendale, Michigan. He received his Master of Divinity degree from Princeton Theological Seminary in 1975 and his Ph.D. in Sociology from Western Michigan University in 1998, where he studied with Dr. Rudolf J. Siebert. Dr. Ott is also an ordained minister of the United Church of Christ, having served the church as a full-time pastor for 25 years prior to his becoming a professor. As a minister, he developed in both theory and praxis the connection between the Frankfurt School's critical theory of society and religion and a critical, political theology of social critique and liberation toward a more reconciled future society. His book, *Max Horkheimer's Critical Theory of Religion: The Meaning of Religion in the Struggle for Human Emancipation* gives expression to this dialectical development. As a professor, he continues to research, teach and write on the liberational negative or inverse theology of the critical theory of society and religion as a critique of neo-liberal globalization. His writings have been published in the United States, France, and the Ukraine. His most recent work, *Reclaiming the Revolutionary Substance and Potential of Religion: The Critical Theory of Religion* was just published in the Michigan Sociological Review, Fall 2005. Dr. Ott is also a Coordinator of the international course "The Future of Religion" held annually at the Inter-University Centre in Dubrovnik, Croatia. He is presently completing a manuscript from this course entitled *The Future of Religion: Toward a Reconciled Society*.

ANNE WARFIELD RAWLS is an Associate Professor of Sociology at Bentley College. Her career has focused on working out the distinction between Interaction Orders and Institutional Orders and her research on religion, social work, blindness, race and intercultural interaction (much in collaboration with students) explores the details of interaction orders and their relationship to institutional contexts of accountability in these areas. Her work focuses on the importance of practices, as opposed to beliefs and theorized accounts, in both classical and contemporary sociological theory and research. Her particular focus has been on the work of Durkheim and Marx, among the classics, and Goffman and Garfinkel among contemporary sociologists. Her publications include *Epistemology and Practice: Durkheim's Elementary Forms,* (2005) Cambridge University Press, "Orders of Interaction and Intelligibility" in Javier Trevino 2002 *Goffman's Legacy,* Rowman and Littlefield. She also edited and introduced Harold Garfinkel's *Ethnomethodology's Program: Working Out Durkheim's Aphorism,* 2002 Rowman and Littlefield and *Seeing Sociologically,* Paradigm Publishers 2006. Published articles include "Interaction Orders of Race," 2000, *Sociological* Theory, "The Interaction Order Sui Generis" 1987, *Sociological Theory,* and "Durkheim's Epistemology: the Neglected Argument", 1996, *American Journal of Sociology.* Translations of her work on Garfinkel and Durkheim have appeared in Russian, French, Italian, and Czech.

WILLIAM CLARE ROBERTS is Assistant Professor of Philosophy at Washington and Jefferson College, in western Pennsylvania. His primary research interests include Marx and Nietzsche, Ancient Greek philosophy, and the relationship between philosophy and literature.

RUDOLF J. SIEBERT was born in Frankfurt am Main, Germany, in 1927. He studied history, philology, philosophy, sociology, psychology, social work and theology at the Universities of Frankfurt am Main, Mainz and Münster, and at the Catholic University of America, Washington D.C. He is Professor of Religion and Society, Director of the Center for Humanistic Future Studies at Western Michigan University, Kalamazoo, Michigan, and, since 1975, Director of the international course on the "Future of Religion: Jerusalem, Athens and Rome – Seedbed Societies of the Modern West" in the Inter University Center, Dubrovnik, Croatia, and he is director of the international course on "Religion and Civil Society: Toward a Global Ethos" in Yalta, Crimea, Ukraine. Siebert has taught and lectured at many universities in Western and Eastern Europe, the United States and Canada. His mayor works are: *From Critical Theory of Society to Theology of Communicative Praxis; Hegel's Philosophy of History: Theological, Humanistic and Scientific Elements; Horkheimer's Critical Sociology of Religion: The Relative and the Transcendent; Hegel's Concept of Marriage and Family: The Principle of Free Subjectivity; The Critical Theory of Religion: Frankfurt School; Recht Macht und Liebe: Georg W. Rudolphi's Prophetische Politische Theologie; From Critical Theory to Critical Political Theology: Personal Autonomy and Universal Solidarity; The Longing for the Entirely Other: The Rescue of the Hopeless; Hitler's Theodicy: Merciless Fate and Human Defiance.* Siebert and his late wife Margareth had 8 children.

BONNIE WRIGHT teaches at Ferris State University. She completed her graduate work at Wayne State University in 2003 with a doctoral dissertation that examined the role of practices in various dimensions of religious worship. Her perspective blends a deep commitment to problems of class, gender and racial inequality with a detailed study of practice that is ethnomethodological in orientation. In addition to presenting a detailed analysis of the importance of practice in constructing the essence of religious experience, working through the idea of praxis as an interaction order, her paper "Discerning the Spirit in the Context of Racial Integration and Conflict at Two Assemblies of God Churches," in *The Journal for Theory of Social Behavior,* explores ways in which issues of race and class manifest themselves in the details of religious practices.

References

Abraham, Gary. 1992. *Max Weber and the Jewish Question.* Urbana: University of Illinois Press.

Abrams, M. H. 1971 [1934]. *The Milk of Paradise: The Effect of Opium Visions on the Works of De Quincey, Crabbe, Francis, Thompson, and Coleridge.* New York: Octagon.

Adorno, Theodor W. 2003. *Vorlesungen über Negative Dialektik.* Frankfurt am Main: Suhrkamp Verlag.

Adorno, Theodor W. 2001. *Zur Lehre von der Geschichte und von der Freiheit (1964/1965).* Frankfurt am Main: Suhrkamp Verlag.

Adorno, Theodor W. 2000. *Metaphysics. Concept and Problems.* trans. Edmund Jephcott. Stanford, California: Stanford University Press.

Adorno, Theodor W. 2000a. *Introduction to Sociology.* trans. Edmund Jephcott. Stanford: Stanford University Press.

Adorno, Theodor W. 2000b. *The Psychological Technique of Luther Martin Thomas' Radio Addresses.* Stanford: Stanford University Press.

Adorno, Theodor W. 1998. *Metaphysik: Begriff und Probleme.* Frankfurt am Main: Suhrkamp Verlag.

Adorno, Theodor W. 1998a. *Critical Model.* trans. Henry W. Pickford. New York: Columbia University Press.

Adorno, Theodor W. 1997. *Zur Metakritik der Erkenntnistheorie: Drei Studien zu Hegel.* Frankfurt am Main: Suhrkamp Verlag.

Adorno, Theodor W. 1997a. *Negative Dialektik: Jargon der Eigentlichkeit.* Frankfurt am Main: Suhrkamp Verlag.

Adorno, Theodor W. 1997b. *Kulturkritik und Gesellschaft.* Frankfurt am Main: Suhrkamp Verlag.

Adorno, Theodor W. 1997c. *Kierkegaard.* Frankfurt am Main: Suhrkamp Verlag.

Adorno, Theodor W. 1997d. *Soziologische Schriften.* Frankfurt am Main: Suhrkamp Verlag.

Adorno, Theodor W. 1997e. *Ob nach Auschwitz noch sich leben lasse.* Frankfurt am Main: Suhrkamp Verlag.

Adorno, Theodor W. 1995. *Negative Dialectics.* trans. E. B. Ashton. New York: Continuum.

Adorno, Theodor W. 1994. *The Stars Down to Earth and Other Essays on the Irrational in Culture,* edited by Stephen Crook. London: Routledge.

Adorno, Theodor W. 1993. *Einleitung in die Soziologie, 1968.* Frankfurt am Main: Suhrkamp Verlag.

Adorno, Theodor W. 1992. *Notes to Literature.* vol. 2, trans. Shierry Weber Nicholson. NY: Columbia University Press.

Adorno, Theodor W. 1980. *Minima Moralia.* Frankfurt am Main: Suhrkamp Verlag.

Adorno, Theodor W. 1979. *Soziologische Schriften I.* Frankfurt am Main: Suhrkamp Verlag.

Adorno, Theodor W. 1976a. "Introduction." Pp. 1–67 in *The Positivist Dispute in German Sociology.* trans. Glyn Adey & David Frisby. London: Heinemann.

Adorno, Theodor W. 1976b. "Sociology and Empirical Research." Pp. 68–86 in *The Positivist Dispute in German Sociology*. trans. Glyn Adey & David Frisby. London: Heinemann.

Adorno, Theodor W. 1974. *Minima Moralia*. New York: Schocken Books.

Adorno, Theodor W. 1973. *Negative Dialectics*. New York: The Seabury Press.

Adorno, Theodor W. 1970. *Der Positivismusstreit in der deutschen Soziologie*. Neuwied und Berlin: Herrmann Luchterhand Verlag.

Adorno, Theodor W. 1970a. *Über Walter Benjamin*. Frankfurt am Main: Suhrkamp Verlag.

Adorno, Theodor W. 1966. *Negative Dialektik*. Frankfurt am Main: Suhrkamp Verlag.

Adorno, T. W. et al. 1950. *The Authoritarian Personality*. New York: Harper & Brothers.

Adorno, Theodor W. & Eugen Kogon. 1958. *Frankfurter Hefte. Zeitschrift für Kultur und Politik*.

Alighieri, Dante. 1996. *The Divine Comedy of Dante Alighieri*. trans. Robert M. Durling. New York & Oxford: Oxford University Press.

Althusser, Louis and Etienne Balibar. 1970. *Reading Capital*. trans. Ben Brewster. London & New York: Verso.

Anderson, Elijah. 1990. *Streetwise: Race, Class, and Change in an Urban Community*. Chicago: University of Chicago Press.

Angold, Michael. 2001. *Byzantium: The Bridge from Antiquity to the Middle Ages*. New York: St. Martin's Press.

Angus, Samuel. 1975 [1928]. *The Mystery-Religions*. New York: Dover Publications.

Anselm of Canterburry, Saint. 1962. *Basic Writings*. Las Salle, IL: Open Court Publishing Company.

Arato, Andrew and Eike Gebhardt (eds.). 1982. *The Essential Frankfurt School Reader*. New York: Continuum.

Ariès, Philippe. 1981. *The Hour of Our Death*. New York: Oxford University Press.

Arrow, Kenneth J. 1987. "Rationality of Self and Others in an Economic System." Pp. 201–16 in *Rational Choice: The Contrast between Economics and Psychology*, edited by Robin M. Hogarth & Melvin W. Reder. Chicago: University of Chicago Press.

Arthur, Christopher J. 2004. *The New Dialectic and Marx's Capital*. Leiden, NL & Boston: Brill.

Arthur, Christopher J. 1986. *Dialectics of Labor: Marx and His Relation to Hegel*. Oxford: Basil Blackwell.

Arthur, Christopher J. and James White. 2001. "Debate: Chris Arthur and James White on History, Logic, and Expanded Reproduction in *Capital*." *Studies in Marxism* 8: 127–135.

Asad, Talal. 1993. *Genealogies of Religion*. Baltimore: John Hopkins University Press.

Baldwin, N. 2001. *Henry Ford and the Jews: The Mass Production of Hate*. New York: Public Affairs.

Barraclough, Geoffrey. 1976. *The Crucible of Europe*. Berkeley: University of California Press.

Barstow, Anne Llewellyn. 1994. *Witchcraze: A New History of the European Witch Hunts*. San Francisco: Pandora/HarperCollins.

Becker, Ernest. 1973. *The Denial of Death*. New York: The Free Press.

Bell, Daniel. 1996 [1976]. *The Cultural Contradictions of Capitalism*, Twentieth Anniversary Edition. New York: Perseus/Basic Books.

Bendix, Reinhard. 1977. *Max Weber: An Intellectual Portrait*. Berkeley: University of California Press.

Benjamin, Jessica. 1988. *The Bonds of Love: Psychoanalysis, Feminism, and the Problem of Domination*. New York: Pantheon Books.

Benjamin, Walter. 1999 [c. 1927]. *The Arcades Project*. Cambridge, MA: Harvard University Press.

Benjamin, Walter. 1996. *Selected Writings: Volume 1 – 1913–1926*. Cambridge, MA: The Belknap Press of Harvard University Press.

Benjamin, Walter. 1985. *Das Passagen – Werk: Zweiter Band*. Frankfurt am Main: Suhrkamp Verlag.

Benjamin, Walter. 1983. *Das Passagen – Werk: Erster Band*. Frankfurt am Main: Suhrkamp Verlag.

Benjamin, Walter. 1978a. *Briefe 2*. Herausgegeben und mit Anmerkungen versehen von Gershom Scholem und Theodor W. Adorno. Frankfurt am Main: Suhrkamp Verlag.

Benjamin, Walter. 1978b. *Ursprung des deutschen Trauerspiels*. Frankfurt am Main: Suhrkamp Verlag.

Benjamin, Walter. 1977. *Illuminationen*. Frankfurt am Main: Suhrkamp Verlag.

Benjamin, Walter. 1968. *Illuminations*. New York: Schocken Books.

Berger, Peter. 1990 [1967]. *The Sacred Canopy: Elements of a Sociology of Religion*. New York: Anchor Books/Random House.

Berlet, Chip. 2005. "When Alienation Turns Right: Populist Conspiracism, the Apocalyptic Style, and Neo-Fascist Movements." In *The Evolution of Alienation: Trauma, Promise, and the Millennium*, edited by Lauren Langman and Devorah Kalekin. Lanham, MD: Rowman and Littlefield.

Berridge, Victoria and Griffith Edwards. 1980. *Opium and the People*. London: Allen Lane.

Bible: New International Version. 1978. New York: The American Bible Society.

Bloch, Ernst. 1995. *The Principle of Hope*, 3 Vols. trans. Neville Plaice, Stephen Plaice and Paul Knight. Cambridge: MIT Press.

Bloch, Ernst. 1986. *The Principle of Hope*, 3 Vols. Cambridge: MIT Press.

Bloch, Ernst. 1985. *Das Prinzip Hoffnung*. Frankfurt am Main: Suhrkamp Verlag.

Bloch, Ernst. 1972. *Atheism in Christianity: the religion of the Exodus and the Kingdom*. trans. J. T. Swann. New York: Herder and Herder.

Bloch, Ernst. 1971. *On Karl Marx*. New York: Herder and Herder.

Bloch, Ernst. 1970a. *Man on His Own: Essays in the Philosophy of Religion*. New York: Herder and Herder.

Bloch, Ernst. 1970b. *Man Philosophy of the Future*. New York: Herder and Herder.

Bloch, Ernst. 1968. *Atheismus im Christentum*. Frankfurt am Main: Suhrkamp Verlag.

Bloch, Ernst. 1964. *Thomas Münzer: Theologien de la revolution*. trans. Maurice de Gandillac. Paris: Éditions Julliard.

Bloch, Karola and Adelbert Reif (eds.). 1978. *Denken heisst Überschreiten: In Memoriam Ernst Bloch 1885–1977*. Köln/Frankfurt am Main: Europäische Verlagsanstalt.

Blumberg, Albert and Herbert Feigl. 1931. "Logical Positivism: a New Movement in European Philosophy." *Journal of Philosophy* 28: 281–96.

Bolz, N. and. W. van Reijen (eds.). 1996. *Walter Benjamin*. New Jersey: Humanities Press.

Bourdieu, Pierre. 1993. *The Field of Cultural Production*. New York: Columbia University Press.

Bourdieu, Pierre. 1991. *Language and Symbolic Power*. Cambridge, MA: Harvard University Press.

Bourdieu, Pierre. 1990 [1980]. *The Logic of Practice*. Stanford, CA: Stanford University Press.

Bourdieu, Pierre. 1985. "The Market of Symbolic Goods." *Poetics* 14 (April): 13–44.

Bourdieu, Pierre. 1980. "The Production of Belief: Contribution to an Economy of Symbolic Goods." *Media, Culture, and Society* 2: 261–293.

Boyce, Mary. 2001 [1979]. *Zoroastrians: Their Religious Beliefs and Practices*. London and New York: Routledge.

Brecht, Bertolt. 1961. *Seven Plays*. New York: Grove Press.

Brenner, Lenni. 2002. *51 Documents: Zionist Collaboration with the Nazis*. Fort Lee, NJ: Barricade Publishers.

Brenner, Lenni. 1983. *Zionism in the Age of Dictators*. Westport, CT: Lawrence Hill Publishers.

Brittain, Christopher Craig. 2005. "Social Theory and the Premise of all Criticism: Max Horkheimer on Religion." *Critical Sociology* 31(1–2): 153–168.

Bruce, Steve. 2000. "The Supply-Side Model of Religion: The Nordic and Baltic States." *Journal for the Scientific Study of Religion* 39(1): 32–46.

Bruce, Steve. 1999. *Choice and Religion: A Critique of Rational Choice Theory*. New York and Oxford: Oxford University Press.

Buchanan, James and Gordon Tullock. 1962. *The Calculus of Consent*. Ann Arbor: University of Michigan Press.

Butel, Paula. 1995. *L'Opium: Histoire d'une fascination*. Paris: Perrin.

Carver, Terrell. 1998. *The Postmodern Marx*. University Park, PA: Pennsylvania State University Press.

Chadwick, Henry. 1993 [1967]. *The Early Church*, Revised Edition. London: Penguin Classics.

Cleaver, Harry. 2000. *Reading Capital Politically*, 2nd ed. Leeds & Edinburgh: Anti/Theses & AK Press.

Coleman, James S. 1990. *Foundations of Social Theory*. Cambridge: Harvard University Press.

Collins, Randall. 1998. *The Sociology of Philosophies*. Cambridge: Harvard University Press.

Comnena, Anna. 1969 [1120]. *The Alexiad*. New York: Penguin Books.

Cook, Karen S. (ed.). 2003. *Trust in Society*. Washington, DC: Russell Sage Foundation.

Coriolis. 1967. *Death, Here is Thy Sting*. Toronto: McClelland and Stewart.

Cox, Michael. 2002. "The Search for Relevance: Historical Materialism after the Cold War." Pp. 59–74 in *Historical Materialism and Globalization*, edited by Mark Rupert and Hazel Smith. New York: Routledge.

Cunningham, Mary. 2002. *Faith in the Byzantine World*. Downer's Grove, IL: InterVarsity Press.

De Quincey, Thomas. 1956 [1821]. "Confessions of An English Opium Eater: Original version." In *Confessions of An English Opium Eater*, edited by Malcolm Elwin. London: McDonald.

Dean, Patrick Vernon. 1995. "Is Death Education a 'Nasty Little Secret'? A Call to Break the Alleged Silence." Pp. 322–326 in *The Path Ahead: Readings in Death and Dying*, edited by Lynne Ann Despelder and Albert Lee Strickland. Toronto: Mayfield Publishing.

DeBeauvoir, Simone. 1989. *The Second Sex*. New York: Vintage Books.

Demerath, N. J. 1995. "Rational Paradigms, A-Rational Religion, and the Debate over Secularization." *Journal for the Scientific Study of Religion*, 34(1): 105–112.

Descartes, Rene. 1958. *Descartes Philosophical Writings*. New York: The Modern Library, Random House, Inc.

Devigne, Robert. 1994. *Recasting Conservatism: Oakeshott, Strauss, and the Response to Postmodernism*. New Haven: Yale University Press.

Doka, Kenneth J. and John D. Morgan. 1993. *Death and Spirituality*. Amityville: Baywood Publishing Company.

Douglas, Mary. 1966. *Purity and Dange.* London: Routledge and Kegan Paul.

Downs, Anthony. 1997. *An Economic Theory of Democracy*. New York: Addison-Wesley Publishing.

Dubiel, Helmut. 1992. *Kritische Theorie der Gesellschaft*. Weinheim/München: Juventa Verlag.

Dubiel, Helmut, Ludwig v. Friedeburg & Wilhelm Schumm. Institute für Sozialforschung. 1994. *Rechtsextremismus und Fremdenfeindlichkeit. Studien zur aktuellen Entwicklung*. Frankfurt/New York: Campus Verlag.

Duncan, J. and M. Derrett. 1985. "Recht und Religion im Neuen Testament (bis zum Jahr 135). Pp. 317–362 in *Max Webers Sicht des antiken Christentum*, edited by Wolfgang Schluchter. Frankfurt am Main: Suhrkamp Verlag.

Durkheim, Emile. 1995 [1912]. *Elementary Forms of the Religious Life*. trans. Karen Fields. Glencoe, IL: The Free Press.

Durkheim, Emile. 1895. *The Division of Labor in Society*. Free Press: Chicago.

Eisenstadt, Shmuel N. 1981. "Max Webers antikes Judentum und der Charakter der jüdischen Zivilisation." Pp. 134–184 in *Max Webers Studie über das Antike Judentum*, edited by Wolfgang Schluchter. Frankfurt am Main: Suhrkamp Verlag.

Eisland, Nancy. 1998. "Contending with a Giant: The Impact of a Megachurch on Exurban Religious Institutions." Pp. 190–219 in *Contemporary American Religion: An Ethnographic Reader*, edited by Penny Edgell-Becker. Walnut Creek, CA: AltaMira Press.

Eliade, Mircea. 1961. *The Sacred and the Profane*. trans. Williard R. Trunk. New York: Harper.

Ellison, Christopher G. 1994. "Religion, the Life Stress Paradigm, and the Study of Depression." Pp. 78–121. In *Religion in Aging and Mental Health: Theoretical Foundations and Methodological Frontiers*, edited by Jeffrey S. Levin. Thousand Oaks, CA: Sage Publications.

Ellison, Christopher G. 1991. "Religious Involvement and Subjective Well-Being." *Journal of Health and Social Behavior* 32(1): 80–99.

Elster, Jon. 1985. *Making Sense of Marx*. Cambridge, UK & Paris: Cambridge University Press & Editiones de la Maison des Sciences de'l Homme.

Engels, Friedrich. 1972. *The Origin of the Family, Private Property and the State*. New York: International Publishers.

Engels, Friedrich. 1969. *Anti-Dühring*. London: Lawrence and Wishart.

Engels, Friedrich. 1954. *Socialism: Utopian and Scientific*. Moscow: Foreign Languages Publishing.

Fahey, Tony. 1982. "Max Weber's *Ancient Judaism*." *American Journal of Sociology* 88: 62–87.

Fanon, Frantz. 1963. *The Wretched of the Earth*. New York, Grove Press.

Feuerbach, Ludwig. 1972. *Principles of the Philosophy of the Future*. Indianapolis: Bobbs-Merrill.

Feuerbach, Ludwig. 1967. *Lectures on the Essence of Religion*. trans. Ralph Mannheim. New York: Harper and Row.

Feuerbach, Ludwig. 1957. *The Essence of Christianity*. New York: Harper & Row, Publishers.

Fisher, Jan. 2005. "Limbo, an Afterlife Tradition, May Be Doomed by the Vatican" in *The New York Times*. VOL CLV. No 53,442. Wednesday, December 28.

Fishermann, Thomas. 2004. "Der Präsident spielt Poker: Den Amerikanern droht noch mehr Ungleichheit und Unsicherheit." in *Die Zeit*, Nr. 47, 11. November 2004.

Flechtheim, Ossip, K. 1985. "Die Herausforderung der Zukunft und die Futurologie." in *Neue Gesellschaft/ Frankfurter Hefte* 2/32/Februar.

Flechtheim, Ossip, K. 1971. *Futurologie: Der Kampf um die Zukunft*. Köln. Verlag Wissenschaft und Politik.

Flechtheim, Ossip, K. 1966. "Widerstände gegen Abrüstung." in *Frankfurter Hefte* 21/7/Juli.

Flechtheim, Ossip, K. 1962. "Die radikale Alternative/1. August 1914 – 1. September 1939 – Wann zum letztenmal?" in *Frankfurter Hefte* 17/9/September.

Flechtheim, Ossip K., Lohmann, Hans-Martin. 2003. *Marx zur Einführung*. Hamburg: Junius Verlag.

Foucault, Michel. 1978. *The History of Sexuality: An Introduction*. New York: Random House.

Freccero, John. 1986. *Dante: The Poetics of Conversion*, edited by Rachel Jacoff. Cambridge, MA: Harvard University Press

Frend, William H. C. 1985. "Die Bedeutung von Max Webers Ansatz für die Untersuchung der frühen Christlichen Sektenbewegung." Pp. 466–485 in *Max Webers Sicht des antiken Christentum*, edited by Wolfgang Shluchter. Frankfurt am Main: Suhrkamp Verlag.

Frend, William H. C. 1965. *Martyrdom and Persecution in the Early Church*. London: Basil Blackwell.

Freud, Sigmund. 1992. *Das Ich und das Es: Metapsychologische Schriften*. Frankfurt am Main: Fischer Verlag.

Freud, Sigmund. 1991. *Totem und Tabu*. Frankfurt am Main: Fischer Taschenbuch Verlag.

Freud, Sigmund. 1964. *The Future of an Illusion*. Garden City, NY: Double Day and Company.

Freud, Sigmund. 1961. *Civilization and its Discontents*. New York: W. W. Norton & Company.

Freud, Sigmund. 1939. *Moses and Monotheism*. New York: Vintage Books.

Friedman, Richard Elliott. 1987. *Who Wrote the Bible?* San Francisco: HarperSanFrancisco.

Fromm, Erich. 2001. *Haben oder Sein*. München: Deutscher Taschenbuch Verlag.

Fromm, Erich. 1999. *Love, Sexuality and Matriarchy: About Gender*. New York: Fromm International Publishing Corporation.

Fromm, Erich. 1992. *The Dogma of Christ*. New York: Henry Holt and Company.

Fromm, Erich. 1990. *The Sane Society*. New York: Henry Holt and Company.

Fromm, Erich. 1981. *On Disobedience and other essays*. New York: The Seabury Press.

Fromm, Erich. 1980. *Greatness and Limitations of Freud's Thought*. New York: The New American Library.

Fromm, Erich. 1976. *To Have Or To Be?*. New York: Harper & Row.

Fromm, Erich. 1973. *The Anatomy of Human Destructiveness*. New York/Chicago/San Francisco: Holt, Rinehart and Winston.

Fromm, Erich. 1970a. *Zen Buddhism and Psychoanalysis*. New York: Harper and Row.

Fromm, Erich. 1970b. *Psychoanalysis and Religion*. New Haven: Yale University Press.

Fromm, Erich. 1969. *The Nature of Man*. London: MacMillan Company.

Fromm, Erich. 1968. *The Revolution of Hope Toward a Humanized Technology*. New York/Evanston/London: Harper and Row, Publishers.

Fromm, Erich. 1941. *Escape From Freedom*. New York: Holt, Rinehart.

Fukuyama, Francis. 1996. *Trust: Human Nature and the Reconstitution of Social Order.* Touchstone Books.

Fukuyama, Francis. 1992. *The End of History and The Last Man*. New York: The Free Press.

Furfey, Paul Hanley. 1966. *The Respectable Murderers: Social Evil and Christian Conscience.* New York: Herder and Herder.

Gadamer, Hans-Georg and Jürgen Habermas. 1979. *Das Erbe Hegels*. Frankfurt am Main: Suhrkamp Verlag.

Garfinkel, Harold. 2002. *Ethnomethodology's Program: Working Out Durkheim's Aphorism.* New York: Roman and Littlefield.

Garfinkel, Harold. 1967. *Studies in Ethnomethodology*. Englewood Cliffs, NJ: Prentice Hall.

Garfinkel, Harold. 1941. "Color Trouble." in *The Best Short Stories*, edited by Edward J. O'Brien. Boston: Houghton Mifflin.

General Council of the Assemblies of God. 2001. Assemblies of God USA Online. (www.ag.org).

Gerber, Haim. 1987. *The Social Origins of the Modern Middle East.* Boulder: Lynne Rienner Publishers.

Gellner, Ernst. 1983. *Nations and Nationalism*. Ithaca, NY: Cornell University Press.

Gerth, H. H. and C. Wright Mills (eds.). 1958. *From Max Weber: Essays in Sociology*. New York: Oxford University Press.

Gibbon, Edward. 1993 [1776]. *The History of the Decline and Fall of the Roman Empire*, 3 Vols. New York: Alfred A. Knopf/Everyman's Library.

Giddens, Anthony. 1984. *The Constitution of Society: Outline of the Theory of Structuration*. Cambridge UK: Polity Press.

Goffman, Erving. 1983. "The Interaction Order." *American Sociological Review* 48: 1–17.

Goffman, Erving. 1956. *The Presentation of Self in Everyday Life*. Chicago: The Free Press.

Goldhagen, Daniel J. 2002. *A Moral Reckoning: The Role of the Catholic Church in the Holocaust and its Unfulfilled Duty of Repair*. New York: Alfred Knopf.

Goldstein, Warren S. 2001. "Messianism and Marxism: Walter Benjamin and Ernst Bloch's Dialectical Theories of Secularization." *Critical Sociology* 27(2): 246–281.

Goldstein, Warren S. 2005. "The Dialectics of Religious Rationalization and Secularization: Max Weber and Ernst Bloch." *Critical Sociology* 31(1–2): 115–151.

Gorer, Geoffrey. 1995. "The Pornography of Death." Pp. 18–22 in *Death: Current Perspectives*, 4th ed., edited by J. B. Williamson and E. S. Schneidman. Toronto: Mayfield Publishing Company.

Gould, Carol C. 1978. *Marx's Social Ontology: Individuality and Community in Marx's Theory of Social Reality*. Cambridge, MA: MIT Press.

Goux, Jean Joseph. 1990. *Symbolic Economies: After Marx and Freud*. trans. J. C. Gage. Ithaca NY: Cornell University Press.

Greenbury, Donald P. and Ian Shapiro. 1994. *Pathologies of Rational Choice Theory: A Critique of Applications in Political Science*. New Haven: Yale University Press.

Greinacher, Norbert. 1986. *Der Schrei nach Gerechtigkeit: Elemente einer prophetischen politischen Theologie*. München: Piper Verlag.

Griffith, Ezra; John Griffith, and Dorothy Smith. 1984. "An Analysis of the Therapeutic Elements in a Black Church Service." *Hospital and Community Psychiatry* 35(5): 464–469.

Haag, Karl Heinz. 1983. *Der Fortschritt in der Philosophie*. Frankfurt am Main: Suhrkamp Verlag.

Haan, Michael D. 2005. "Numbers in Nirvana: How the 1872–1921 Indian censuses helped operationalise 'Hinduism.'" *Religion* 35(1): 13–30.

Habermas, Jürgen. 2002. *Religion and Rationality: Essays on Reason, God, and Modernity*. Cambridge, MA: MIT Press.

Habermas, Jürgen. 2001. *Glauben und Wissen: Friedenspreis des Deutschen Buchhandels 2001. Laudatio: Jan Philipp Reemtsma*. Frankfurt am Main: Suhrkamp Verlag.

Habermas, Jürgen. 1998. *Die postnationale Konstellation: Politische Essays*. Frankfurt am Main: Suhrkamp Verlag.

Habermas, Jürgen. 1996. *Between Facts and Norms: Contributions to a Discourse Theory of Law and Democracy*. trans. William Rehg. Cambridge, MA: MIT Press.

Habermas, Jürgen. 1993a. *Justification and Application: Remarks on Discourse Ethics*. Cambridge, MA: MIT Press.

Habermas, Jürgen. 1993b. "Remarks on the Development of Horkheimer's Work." Pp. 49–65 in *On Max Horkheimer: New Perspectives*, edited by Seyla Benhabib, Wolfgang Bonß, and John McCole. Cambridge, MA: MIT Press.

Habermas, Jürgen. 1992. *Postmetaphysical Thinking: Philosophical Essays*. trans. William Mark Hohengarten. Cambridge, MA: MIT Press.

Habermas, Jürgen. 1991. *Texte und Kontexte*. Frankfurt am Main: Suhrkamp Verlag.

Habermas, Jürgen. 1990. *Die nachholende Revolution*. Frankfurt am Main: Suhrkamp Verlag.

Habermas, Jürgen. 1990a. *Moral Consciousness and Communicative Action*. trans. Christian Lenhardt and Shierry Weber Nicholsen. Cambridge, MA: MIT Press.

Habermas, Jürgen. 1988. *Nachmetaphysisches Denken: Philosophische Aufsätze*. Frankfurt am Main: Suhrkamp Verlag.

Habermas, Jürgen. 1987. *Philosophisch-politische Profile*. Frankfurt am Main: Suhrkamp Verlag.

Habermas, Jürgen. 1986. *Autonomie und Solidarität*. London: Verso.

Habermas, Jürgen. 1984/1987. *Theory of Communicative Action*, 2 Vols. trans. Thomas McCarthy. Boston: Beacon Press.

Habermas, Jürgen. 1982. *Politik, Kunst, Religion*. Stuttgart: Philipp Reclam Verlag.

Habermas, Jürgen. 1981. *Theorie des kommunikativen Handelns: Band 2. Zur Kritik der funktionalistischen Vernunft*. Frankfurt am Main: Suhrkamp Verlag.

Habermas, Jürgen. 1976. *Zur Rekonstruktion des Historischen Materialismus*. Frankfurt am Main: Suhrkamp Verlag.

Habermas, Jürgen. 1975. *Legitimation Crisis*. Boston: Beacon Press.

Habermas, Jürgen. 1973. *Theory and Practice*. trans. John Viertel. Boston: Beacon Press.

Habermas, Jürgen. 1971. *Knowledge and Human Interests*. Boston: Beacon Press.

Haffner, Sebastian. 2001. *Anmerkungen zu Hitler*. Frankfurt am Main: Fischer Verlag.

Halliday, Fred. 2002. "The Pertinence of Imperialism." Pp. 75–89 in *Historical Materialism and Globalization*, edited by Mark Rupert and Hazel Smith. New York: Routledge.

Hanfling, Oswald. 1981. *Logical Positivism*. New York: Columbia University Press.

Harman, Chris. 2003. *Prophet and the Proletariat: Islamic Fundamentalism, Class and Revolution*. London: Socialist Workers Party.

Harries, Martin. 2000. *Scare Quotes from Shakespeare: Marx, Keynes, and the Language of Reenchantment*. Stanford: Stanford University Press.

Harrison, Michael. 1974. "Preparation for Life in the Spirit: the Process of Initial Commitment to a Religious Movement." *Urban Life and Culture* 2(4): 387–396.

Harvey, David. 2003. *The New Imperialism*. New York: Oxford University Press.

Hechter, Michael. 1987. *Principles of Group Solidarity*. Berkeley and Los Angles: University of California Press.

Hegel, Georg W. F. 1994. *Hegel's Phenomenology of Spirit*. trans. Howard P. Kainz. University Park, PA: Penn State Press.

Hegel, Georg W. F. 1986a. *Frühe Schriften*. Frankfurt am Main: Suhrkamp Verlag.

Hegel, Georg W. F. 1986b. *Jenaer Schriften 1801–1807*. Frankfurt am Main: Suhrkamp Verlag.

Hegel, Georg W. F. 1986c. *Phänomenologie des Geistes*. Frankfurt am Main: Suhrkamp Verlag.

Hegel, Georg W. F. 1986d. *Nürnberger und Heidelberger Schriften 1808–1817*. Frankfurt am Main: Suhrkamp Verlag.

Hegel, Georg W. F. 1986e. *Wissenschaft der Logik I*. Frankfurt am Main: Suhrkamp Verlag.

Hegel, Georg W. F. 1986f. *Wissenschaft der Logik II*. Frankfurt am Main: Suhrkamp Verlag.

Hegel, Georg W. F. 1986g. *Grundlinien der Philosophie des Rechts oder Naturrecht und Staatswissenschaft im Grundriss*. Frankfurt am Main: Suhrkamp Verlag.

Hegel, Georg W. F. 1986h. *Enzyklopädie der philosophischen Wissenschaften I*. Frankfurt am Main: Suhrkamp Verlag.

Hegel, Georg W. F. 1986i. *Enzyklopädie der philosophischen Wissenschaften II*. Frankfurt am Main: Suhrkamp Verlag.

Hegel, Georg W. F. 1986j. *Enzyklopädie der philosophischen Wissenschaften III*. Frankfurt am Main: Suhrkamp Verlag.

Hegel, Georg W. F. 1986k. *Vorlesungen über die Philosophie der Geschichte*. Frankfurt am Main: Suhrkamp Verlag.

Hegel, Georg W. F. 1986l. *Vorlesungen über die Aesthetik I*. Frankfurt am Main: Suhrkamp Verlag.

Hegel, Georg W. F. 1986m. *Vorlesungen über die Philosophie der Religion I*. Frankfurt am Main: Suhrkamp Verlag.

Hegel, Georg W. F. 1986n. *Vorlesungen über die Philosophie der Religion II*. Frankfurt am Main: Suhrkamp Verlag.

Hegel, Georg W. F. 1986o. *Vorlesungen über die Geschichte der Philosophie I*. Frankfurt am Main: Suhrkamp Verlag.

Hegel, Georg W. F. 1986p. *Vorlesungen über die Geschichte der Philosophie II*. Frankfurt am Main: Suhrkamp Verlag.

Hegel, Georg W. F. 1986q. *Vorlesungen über die Geschichte der Philosophie III*. Frankfurt am Main: Suhrkamp Verlag.

Hegel, Georg W. F. 1977. *Phenomenology of Spirit*. trans. A. V. Miller. Oxford: Oxford University Press.

Hegel, Georg W. F. 1967a. *The Phenomenology of Mind*. New York: Harper Torchbooks.

Hegel, Georg W. F. 1967b. *Hegel's Philosophy of Right*. New York: Oxford University Press.

Hegel, Georg W. F. 1956. *The Philosophy of History*. trans. J. Sibree. New York: Dover Publications.

Heinrich, Michael. 1996. "Engels' Edition of the Third Volume of *Capital* and Marx's Original Manuscript." *Science and Society* 60: 452–66.

Hertz, J. H. 1956. *The Pentateuch and Haftorahs*. London: Soncino Press.

Higham, Ch. 1983. *Trading with the Enemy: The Nazi-American Money Plot 1933–1949*. New York: Barnes and Noble.

Hirschman, Albert O. 1977. *The Passions and the Interests: Political Arguments for Capitalism before its Triumph*. Princeton, NJ: Princeton University Press.

Hirschman, Albert O. 1972. *Exit Voice and Loyalty: Exit Voice in Firms, Organizations, and States*. Cambridge, MA: Harvard University Press.

Hitler, Adolf. 1971. *Mein Kampf.* Boston: Houghton Mifflin Company.

Hitler, Adolf. 1943. *Mein Kampf.* Boston: Houghton Mifflin Company.

Hollis, Martin. 1994. *The Philosophy of Social Science: An Introduction*. Cambridge: Cambridge University Press.

Holy Bible. 1990. New Revised Standard Version. Grand Rapids, MI: Zondervan Corporation.

Horkheimer, Max. 1996. *Nachträge, Verzeichnisse und Register*. Frankfurt am Main: Fischer Verlag.

Horkheimer, Max. 1996a. *Briefwechsel 1941–1948*. Frankfurt am Main: Fischer Verlag.

Horkheimer, Max. 1995a. *Between Philosophy and Social Science*. trans. G. Frederick Hunter *et al.* Cambridge: MIT Press.

Horkheimer, Max. 1995b. *Critical Theory*. trans. Matthew J. O'Connell. New York: Continuum.

Horkheimer, Max. 1993. "The Present Situation of Social Philosophy and the Tasks of an Institute for Social Research." Pp. 1–14 in *Between Philosophy and Social Science Selected Early Writings*. trans. G. Frederick Hunter, Matthew S. Kramer, & John Torpey. Cambridge, MA: The MIT Press.

Horkheimer, Max. 1990. *Nachgelassene Schriften 1914–1931*. Frankfurt am Main: Suhrkamp Verlag.

Horkheimer, Max. 1989. "The Jews and Europe." Pp. 77–94 in *Critical Theory and Society: A Reader*, edited by Stephen Eric Bronner and Douglas MacKay Kellner. New York: Routledge.

Horkheimer, Max. 1988a. *Nachgelassene Schriften 1949–1972*. Frankfurt am Main: Suhrkamp Verlag.

Horkheimer, Max. 1988b. *Schriften 1931–1936*. Frankfurt am Main: Fischer Verlag.

Horkheimer, Max. 1988c. *Schriften 1936–1941*. Frankfurt am Main: Fischer Verlag.

Horkheimer, Max. 1988d. *Aus der Pubertät: Novellen und Tagebuchblätter 1914–1918*. Frankfurt am Main: Suhrkamp Verlag.

Horkheimer, Max. 1987. *Nachgelassene Schriften 1914–1931*. Frankfurt am Main: Fischer Verlag.

Horkheimer, Max. 1985. "Zur Zukunft der Kritischen Theorie: Gespräch mit Claus Grossner." Pp. 419–434 in *Max Horkheimer, Gesammelte Schriften Band 7: Vorträge und Aufzeichnungen, 1949–1973*. Frankfurt am Main: Fischer Taschenbuch Verlag.

Horkheimer, Max. 1985a. *Vorträge und Aufzeichnungen 1949–1973*. Frankfurt am Main: Fischer Verlag.

Horkheimer, Max. 1985b. *Nachgelassene Schriften 1931–1949*. Frankfurt am Main: Fischer Verlag.

Horkheimer, Max. 1982 [1937]. "Traditional and Critical Theory." Pp. 188–243 in *Critical Theory: Selected Essays*. New York: Continuum.

Horkheimer, Max. 1978. *Dawn & Decline: Notes 1926–1931 & 1950–1969*. trans. Michael Shaw. New York: The Seabury Press.

Horkheimer, Max. 1974. *Eclipse of Reason*. New York: The Seabury Press.

Horkheimer, Max. 1973. *Aspects of Sociology*. trans. John Viertel. London: Heinemann.

Horkheimer, Max. 1973a. "Forward." Pp. xi–xii in Martin Jay's *The Dialectical Imagination: A History of the Frankfurt School and the Institute of Social Research, 1923–1950*. Boston, MA: Little, Brown and Company.

Horkheimer, Max. 1972. "Traditional and Critical Theory." Pp. 188–243 in *Critical Theory: Selected Essays*. trans. Matthew J. O'Connell and Others. New York, NY: The Seabury Press.

Horkheimer, Max. 1970. *Die Sehnsucht nach dem ganz Anderen: Ein Interview mit Kommentar von Helmut Gumnior*. Hamburg: Furdie-Verlag H. Rennebach KG.

Horkheimer, Max. 1947. *Eclipse of Reason*. New York: The Seabury Press.

Horkheimer, Max and Theodor W. Adorno. 2002. *Dialectic of Enlightenment: Philosophical Fragments*. trans. Edmund Jephcott. Stanford University Press.

Horkheimer, Max. 1991. *The Dialectic of Enlightenment*. New York: Continuum.

Horkheimer, Max. 1969. *Dialektik der Aufklärung*. Frankfurt am Main: S. Fischer Verlag.

Horkheimer, Max. 1973. *Aspects of Sociology*. trans. John Viertel. London: Heinemann.

Horkheimer, Max. 1972. *Dialectic of Enlightenment*. New York: The Seabury Press.

Howard, Ron (director). 2001. *A Beautiful Mind*. Screenplay by Akiva Goldsman and Sylvia Nasar. USA: Universal Pictures.

Huff, Toby and Wolfgang Schluchter. 1999. *Max Weber and Islam*. New Brunswick, NJ.: Transaction Publishers.

Huntington, Samuel. 1996. *The Clash of Civilization and the Remaking of the World Order*. New York: Simon and Schuster.

Husain, Sayed, Anwar. N.d. "Max Weber's Sociology of Islam." http://www.bangladesh-sociology.org/Max%20Weber-Anwar%20Hosain.htm

Hutton, Ronald. 1999. *The Triumph of the Moon: A History of Modern Pagan Witchcraft*. New York: Oxford.

Hutton, Ronald. 1991. *The Pagan Religions of the Ancient British Isles*. New York: Ballantine.

Iannaccone, Laurence R. 1997. "Framework for the Scientific Study of Religion." Pp. 25–44 in *Rational Choice Theory and Religion: Summary and Assessment*, edited by Lawrence A. Young. New York and London: Routledge.

Iannaccone, Laurence R. 1995. "Voodoo Economics? Reviewing the Rational Choice Approach to Religion." *Journal for the Scientific Study of Religion* 34(1): 76–89.

Iannaccone, Laurence R. 1994. "Why Strict Churches are Strong." *American Journal of Sociology* 99(5): 1180–1211.

Iannaccone, Laurence R. 1990. "Religious Practices: A Human Capital Approach." *Journal for the Scientific Study of Religion* 29(3): 297–314.

Inglehardt, Ronald and Pippa Norris. 2003. "The True Clash of Civilizations." *Foreign Policy* 135: 62–71.

Jacoby, Russell. 2005. *Past Imperfect*. New York: Colombia University Press.

Jameson, Frederic. 1981. *The Political Unconscious: Narrative as a Socially Symbolic Act*. Ithaca NY: Cornell University Press.

Jay, Martin. 1981. *Dialektische Phantasie: Die Geschichte der Frankfurter Schule und des Instituts für Sozialforschung 1923–1950*. Frankfurt am Main: Fischer Verlag.

Jay, Martin. 1971. *The Dialectical Imagination: A History of the Frankfurt School and the Institute of Social Research, 1923–1950*. Boston: Little Brown and Company.

Jones. E. 1961. *Sigmund Freud*. Basic Books. New York.

Jung, Carl, G. 1990. *Archetypen*. München: Deutscher Buch Verlag.

Jung, Carl, G. 1989. *Memories, Dreams, Reflections*. trans. Richard and Clara Winston. New York: Vintage.

Jung, Carl, G. 1958. *Psyche & Symbol*. Garden City, NY: Double Day Anchor Books.

Jung, Carl, G. 1933. *Modern Man in Search of a Soul*. New York: Harcourt Brace Janovich.

Jurgensmeyer, Mark. 2001. *Terror in the Mind of God: The Global Rise of Religious Violence*. Berkeley: University of California Press.

Kain, Philip J. 1986. *Marx's Method, Epistemology, and Humanism: A Study in the Development of His Thought*. Dordrecht, NL: D. Reidel Publishing Co.

Kalberg, Stephen 1980. "Max Weber's Types of Rationality: Cornerstones for the Analysis of Rationalization Process." *American Journal of Sociology* 85(5): 1145–1179.

Kant, Immanuel. 1965. *Critique of Pure Reason*. New York: St. Martins Press.

Kant, Immanuel. 1929. *Critique of Pure Reason*. New York: St. Martin's Press.

Karakayali, Nedim. 2004. "Reading Bourdieu with Adorno: The Limits of Critical Theory and Reflexive Sociology." *Sociology* 38(2): 351–368.

Kautsky, Karl. 1925. *Foundations of Christianity*. New York and London: Monthly Review Press.

Kautsky, Karl. 1919. *Der Ursprung des Christentums*. Neunte Auflage. Stuttgart: Verlag von J.h. W. Dietz.

Kellner, Douglas. 1989. *Critical Theory, Marxism and Modernity*. Baltimore: Johns Hopkins Press.

Kellner, Douglas. N.d. a. *Modernity and Its Discontents: Nietzsche's Critique*. http://www.gseis.ucla.edu/faculty/kellner/papers/FNmod.htm

Kellner, Douglas. N.d. b. *Ernst Bloch, Utopia and Ideology Critique*. http://www.uta.edu/english/dab/illuminations/kell1.html

Kemple, Thomas M. 1995. *Reading Marx Writing: Melodrama, the Market and the 'Grundrisse'*. Stanford: Stanford University Press.

Kershaw, Ian. 2001. *The 'Hitler Myth': Image and Reality in the Third Reich*. Oxford: University Press.

Kertzer, David. I. 2001. *The Pope Against The Jews: The Vatican's Role in the Rise of Modern Anti-Semitism*. New York: Alfred Knopf.

Khaldun, Ibn. 1969. *The Muqaddimah*. Princeton: Princeton University Press.

Kieckhefer, Richard. 1989. *Magic in the Middle Ages*. Cambridge: Cambridge University Press.

Kielmansegg, Peter Graf. 2004. "Drei Regeln für den Frieden," in *Die Zeit*, Nr. 53. Politik, Essay, December 22. S.10.

Kohn, Hans. 1961. *American Nationalism: An Interpretative Essay*. New York: Collier Books.

Kogon, Eugen. 1979. "Der Neonazismus in Bedrängnis und Angriff," in *Frankfurter Hefte* 34/3/März.

Kogon, Eugen. 1967. "Revolution und Theologie – Das Neue in unserem Zeitalter/ Symposion," in *Frankfurter Hefte* 22/9. September.

Kogon, Eugen. 1965. *Der SS Staat. Das System der deutschen Konzentrationslager*. Frankfurt am Main: Europäische Verlagsanstalt.

Kracauer, Siegfried. 1995. *Mass Ornament: Weimar Essays*. Cambridge, MA: Harvard University Press.

Küng, Hans. 2004. *Der Islam: Geschichte, Gegenwart, Zukunft*. München/Zürich: Piper Verlag.

Küng, Hans. 1994. *Das Christentum. Wesen und Geschichte.*

Küng, Hans. 1991. *Das Judentum*. München/Zürich: Piper Verlag.

Küng, Hans. 1990. *Projekt Weltethos*. München/Zürich: Piper Verlag.

Küng, Hans. 1981. *Does God Exist: An Answer for Today*. New York: Vintage Publisher.

Küng, Hans. 1978. *Existiert Gott? Antwort auf die Gottesfrage der Neuzeit*. München/ Zürich: Piper Verlag.

Kuran, Timur. 2001. *The Islamic Commercial Crisis: Institutional Roots of the Delay in the Middle East's Economic Modernization*. Los Angeles: USC CLEO Research Paper No. C01–12.

LaCapra, Dominick. 1983. *Rethinking Intellectual History: Texts, Contexts, Language*. Ithaca & London: Cornell University Press.

Lambert, Yves. 1991. "La 'Tour de Babel' des definitions de la religion." *Social Compass* 38: 73–85.

Langman, Lauren and Douglas Morris. 2002. "Islamic Modernity: Barriers and Possibilities." *Logos Online*, Spring, 61–74.

Levesque, Paul, J. and Siptroth, Stephen M. 2005. "The Correlation Between Political and Ecclesial Ideologies of Catholic Priests: A Research Note." in *Sociology of Religion*. 66(4): 419–429.

Lewis, Bernard. 2002. *What went wrong?: Western impact and Middle Eastern Response*. New York: Oxford University Press.

Lewis, Bernard. 1993. *Islam and the West*. New York: Oxford University Press.

Lonitz, Henri. 1994. *Theodor Adorno and Walter Benjamin: Briefwechsel 1928–1940*. Frankfurt am Main: Suhrkamp Verlag.

Löwenthal, Leo. 1989. *Critical Theory and Frankfurt Theorists: Lectures-Correspondence-Conversations*. New Brunswick: Transaction Publishers.

Lubeck, Paul and Bryana Britts. 2001. "Muslim Civil Society in Urban Public Spaces: Globalization, Discursive Shifts, and Social Movements." Pp. 175–202 in *Urban Studies: Contemporary and Future Perspectives*, edited by J. Eade and C. Mele. Oxford: Blackwell Publishers.

Luce, R. Duncan and Howard Raiffa. 1958 [1957]. *Games and Decisions: Introduction and Critical Survey*. New York: Dover Publications.

Lucian of Samosata. 2001 [c. 170 AD]. "The Passing of Peregrinus." *Loeb Classical Library: Lucian, Vol. V*, edited by Jeffrey Henderson. Cambridge, MA: Harvard University Press.

Machtan, Lothar. 2001. *The Hidden Hitler*. New York: Basic Books.

MacMullen, Ramsay. 1997. *Christianity and Paganism in the Fourth to Eighth Centuries.* New Haven and London: Yale University Press.

MacMullen, Ramsay. 1981. *Paganism in the Roman Empire*. New Haven and London: Yale University Press.

Marcuse, Herbert. 1995. *Triebstruktur und Gesellschaft*. Frankfurt am Main: Suhrkamp Verlag.

Marcuse, Herbert. 1984. *Aufsätze und Vorlesungen 1948–1969: Versuch über die Befreiung*. Frankfurt am Main: Suhrkamp Verlag.

Marcuse, Herbert. 1980. *Psychoanalyse und Politik*. Frankfurt am Main: Europäische Verlagsanstalt.

Marcuse, Herbert. 1970. *Five Lectures: Psychoanalysis, Politics, and Utopia*. Boston: Beacon Press.

Marcuse, Herbert. 1966. *Reason and Revolution: Hegel and the Rise of Social Theory*. Boston: Beacon Press.

Marcuse, Herbert. 1964. *One-Dimensional Man*. Boston: Beacon Press.

Marcuse, Herbert. 1962. *Eros and Civilization: A Philosophical Inquiry into Freud*. New York: Vintage Books.

Marcuse, Herbert. 1961. *Soviet Marxism: A Critical Analysis*. New York: Vintage Books.

Marcuse, Herbert. 1960. *Reason and Revolution: Hegel and the Rise of Social Theory*. Boston: Beacon Press.

Marcuse, Herbert. 1959. "The Ideology of Death." Pp. 64–76 in *The Meaning of Death*, edited by H. Feifel. Toronto: McGraw Hill.

Marsden, Richard. 1999. *The Nature of Capital: Marx after Foucault*. London & New York: Routledge.

Martin, Dale B. 1990. *Slavery as Salvation: The Metaphor of Slavery in Pauline Christianity*. New Haven: Yale University Press.

Marty, Martin and R. Scott Applebee. 1991–95. *The Fundamentalism Project*, 5 vols. Chicago: University of Chicago Press.

Marx, Karl. 2002 [1844]. *Marx on Religion*, edited by John Raines. Philadelphia: Temple University Press.

Marx, Karl. 1996. *Later Political Writings*. trans. Terrell Carver. Cambridge, UK: Cambridge University Press.

Marx, Karl. 1992 [1844]. "A Contribution to the Critique of Hegel's Philosophy of Right: An Introduction" in *Early Writings*. trans. Rodney Livingstone and Gregor Benton. London: Penguin Books.

Marx, Karl. 1983 [1844]. "Contribution to Hegel's Philosophy of Right." trans. Annette Jolin and Joseph O'Malley, in *The Young Hegelians: An Anthology*, edited by Lawrence Stepelvitch. Cambridge: Cambridge University Press.

Marx, Karl. 1978 [1845]. "Theses on Feuerbach." *The Marx-Engels Reader*, 2nd ed. New York: W. W. Norton.

Marx, Karl. 1978a [1843]. "Contribution to the Critique of Hegel's Philosophy of Right." *The Marx-Engels Reader*, 2nd ed. New York: W. W. Norton.

Marx, Karl. 1977a [1844]. "Towards a Critique of Hegel's Philosophy of Right:

Introduction." trans. David McLellan, in *Karl Marx: Selected Writings,* edited by David McLellan. New York: Oxford University Press.

Marx, Karl. 1977b. "Theses on Feuerbach." trans. David McLellan, in *Karl Marx: Selected Writings,* edited by David McLellan. New York: Oxford University Press.

Marx, Karl. 1977c. "On the Jewish Question." trans. David McLellan, in *Karl Marx: Selected Writings,* edited by David McLellan. New York: Oxford University Press.

Marx, Karl. 1976 [1844]. "Zur Kritik der Hegelschen Rechtsphilosophie: Einleitung." in *Karl Marx Friedrich Engels Werke* (MEW). Dietz Verlag, Berlin. Band 1.

Marx, Karl. 1976a [1867]. *Capital: A Critique of Political Economy,* vol. 1. trans. Ben Fowkes. New York: Vintage Books.

Marx, Karl. 1975 [1844]. "Contribution to the Critique of Hegel's Philosophy of Law. Introduction." in *Marx and Engels.*

Marx, Karl. 1972. *The Eighteenth Brumaire of Louis Bonaparte.* New York: International Publishers.

Marx, Karl. 1970 [1859]. *A Contribution to the Critique of Political Economy.* New York: International Publishers.

Marx, Karl. 1967. *Capital: A Critique of Political Economy,* vol. 1. trans. Samuel Moore and Edward Aveling. New York: International Publishers.

Marx, Karl. 1964. *Early Writing.* New York/Toronto/London: McGraw-Hill Book Company.

Marx, Karl. 1963 [1844]. "Contribution to Hegel's Philosophy of Right. Introduction." in *Karl Marx: Early Writings.* trans. Tom Bottomore. New York: McGraw Hill.

Marx, Karl. 1963a. The Eighteenth Brumaire of Louis Bonaparte. New York: International Publishers Co.

Marx, Karl. 1961. *Das Kapital: Kritik der politischen Ökonomie.* Berlin: Dietz Verlag.

Marx, Karl. 1953. *Frühschriften.* Stuttgart: Alfred Kröner Verlag.

Marx, Karl. IISG. Archives. Amsterdam: Internationaal Instituut voor Sociale Geschiedenis.

Marx, Karl and Fredrick Engles. 1845 [1956]. *The Holy Family or Critique of Critical Critique.* Moscow: Foreign Language Publishing House.

Marx, Karl and Friedrich Engels. 1978. *The Marx-Engels Reader.* 2nd ed., edited by Robert C. Tucker. New York: W. W. Norton.

Marx, Karl and Friedrich Engels. 1975. *On Religion.* Moscow: Progress Publishers.

Marx, Karl and Friedrich Engels. 1975a. *Marx-Engels Collected Works.* New York: International Publishers.

Marx, Karl and Friedrich Engels. 1956. *Werke.* Berlin: Dietz-Verlag.

Matheson, Peter. 1981. *The Third Reich and the Christian Churches.* Edinburgh: T & T Clark, Scholder.

McCutcheon, Russell T. 1999. *The Insider/Outsider Debate in the Study of Religion: a Reader.* London & New York: Cassell.

McCutcheon, Russell T. 1997. *Manufacturing Religion.* New York: Oxford University Press.

McDannell, Colleen and Bernard Lang. 2001. *Heaven: A History.* New Haven and London: Yale University Press.

McKinnon, Andrew M. 2005. "Reading 'Opium of the People': Expression, Protest, and the Dialectics of Suffering." *Critical Sociology* 31(1–2): 13–36.

McKinnon, Andrew M. 2002. "Sociological Definitions, Language Games and the 'Essence' of Religion." *Method and Theory in the Study of Religion* 14: 61–83.

McLellan, David. 1973. *Karl Marx: His Life and Thought.* New York: Harper and Row.

McLellan, David. 1970. *Marx Before Marxism.* New York & Evanston, IL: Harper & Row.

McLoughlin, William. 1978. *Revivals, Awakenings, and Reform: An Essay on Religion and Social Change in America 1707–1977.* Chicago: University of Chicago Press.

Mead, George Herbert. 1938 [1964]. *The Philosophy of the Act.* Chicago and London: University of Chicago Press.

Mendieta, Eduardo. 2005. *The Frankfurt School on Religion.* New York: Routledge.

Merton, Robert K. 1967 [1949]. *Social Theory and Social Structure.* New York: The Free Press.

Messadié, Gerald. 1996. *A History of the Devil.* New York: Kodansha International.

Metz, Johann Baptist. 1995. *Landschaft aus Schreien: Zur Dramatik der Theodizeefrage.* Mainz: Matthias Grünewald Verlag.

Metz, Johann Baptist. 1980. *Faith in History & Society: Toward a Practical Fundamental Theology.* New York: The Seabury Press.

Meyer, Marvin W. 1999 [1987]. *The Ancient Mysteries: A Sourcebook of Sacred Texts.* Philadelphia: University of Pennsylvania Press.

Michels, Robert. 1962. *Political Parties: A Sociological Study of the Oligarchical Tendencies of Modern Democracy.* New York: The Free Press.

The New Oxford Annotated Bible with the Apocrypha. 1977. Revised Standard Version, edited by Herbert G. May and Bruce Metzger. New York: Oxford University Press.

Mills, C. Wright. 1959. *The Sociological Imagination.* New York: Oxford University Press.

Mills, C. Wright. 1940 [1990]. "Situated Actions and Vocabularies of Motive." *American Sociological Review.* Reprinted in *Life as Theater: A Dramaturgical Sourcebook,* 2nd ed., edited by Dennis Brissett and Charles Edgley. New York: Aldine de Gruyter.

Mills, Watson E. (eds.). 1986. *Speaking in Tongues: A Guide to Research on Glossolalia.* Grand Rapids, MI. William B. Erdman's Publishing Company.

Misztal, Barbara A. 1996. *Trust in Modern Societies: The Search for the Bases of Social Order.* Polity Press.

Moaddel, Mansoor. 2005. *Islamic Modernism, Nationalism, and Fundamentalism.* Chicago: University of Chicago Press.

Moore, Barrington. 1966. *The Origins of Dictatorship and Democracy.* Boston: Beacon Press.

Moseley, Fred (ed.) 1993. *Marx's Method in Capital: A Reexamination.* Atlantic Highlands, NJ: Humanities Press.

Moseley, Fred and Martha Campbell (ed.) 1997. *New Investigations of Marx's Method.* Atlantic Highlands, NJ: Humanities Press.

Mosse,George L. 1975. *The Nationalization of the Masses.* New York: New American Library.

Murray, (John) Patrick. 2002. "Reply to Geert Reuten." *Historical Materialism* 10(1): 155–176.

Murray, (John) Patrick. 2000a. "Marx's 'Truly Social' Labour Theory of Value: Part I, Abstract Labour in Marxian Value Theory." *Historical Materialism* 6: 27–66.

Murray, (John) Patrick. 2000b. "Marx's 'Truly Social' Labour Theory of Value: Part II, How Is Labor that Is Under the Sway of Capital *Actually* Abstract?" *Historical Materialism* 7: 99–136.

Murray, (John) Patrick. 1988. *Marx's Theory of Scientific Knowledge*. Atlantic Highlands, NJ: Humanities Press International.

Myerson, Roger B. 1991. *Game Theory: Analysis of Conflict*. Cambridge, MA: Harvard University Press.

Nash, John Forbes. 1997 [1953]. *Essays on Game Theory*. Northampton, MA: Edward Elgar Publishing.

Negri, Antonio. 1991. *Marx Beyond Marx: Lessons on the Grundrisse*. trans. Harry Cleaver, et al. Brooklyn, NY: Autonomedia/Pluto.

Nelson, Timothy. 1996. "Sacrifice of Praise: Emotion and Collective Participation in an African American Worship Service." *Sociology of Religion* 57(4): 379–396.

Neuhaus, Gerd. 1993. *Theodizee – Abbruch oder Anstoss des Glaubens*. Freiburg: Herder.

Nicol, Donald M. 1993 [1972]. *The Last Centuries of Byzantium, 1261–1453*. Cambridge: Cambridge University Press.

Nietzsche, Friedrich. 1995. *Unpublished Writings from the Period of Unfashionable Observations*. Stanford: Stanford University Press.

Nietzsche, Friedrich. 1969. *On the Genealogy of Morals*. trans. Walter Kaufmann and R. J. Hollingdale. New York: Vintage Books.

Nietzsche, Friedrich. 1968. *Twilight of the Idols/The Anti-Christ*. London: Penguin Books.

Nietzsche, Friedrich. 1967. *On the Genealogy of Morals and Ecce Homo*. New York: Vintage Books.

Nigosian, Solomon A. 1993. *The Zoroastrian Faith*. Montreal: McGill Queen's University Press.

Norwich, John Julius. 1995. *Byzantium, Vol. 3: The Decline and Fall*. New York: Alfred A. Knopf.

Norwich, John Julius. 1989. *Byzantium, Vol. 1: The Early Centuries*. New York: Alfred A. Knopf.

Nowak, Leszek. 1980. *The Structure of Idealization: Towards a Systematic Interpretation of the Marxian Idea of Science*. Dordrecht, Boston & London: D. Reidel Publishing Co.

O'Dea, Thomas, F. 1966. *The Sociology of Religion*. Englewood Cliffs, NJ: Prentice Hall, Inc.

O'Toole, Roger. 1984. *Religion: Classical Sociological Approaches*. Toronto: McGraw-Hill Ryerson.

Oelmüller, Willi. 1990. *Theodizee-Gott vor Gericht*. München: Wilhelm Fink Verlag.

Oishi, Takahisa. 2001. *The Unknown Marx: Reconstructing a Unified Perspective*. London: Pluto Press.

Olson, Mancur. 1971 [1964]. *Logic of Collective Action: Public Goods and the Theory of Groups*. Cambridge, MA: Harvard University Press.

Olson, Richard. 1988. *The Largest Congregations in the United States: An Empirical Study of Church Growth and Decline.* Ann Arbor, MI: University Microfilms.

Ostrom, Elinor and James Walker. 2003. *Trust and Reciprocity: Interdisciplinary Lessons for Experimental Research.* Washington, DC: Russell Sage Foundation.

Ott, Michael. 2001. *Max Horkheimer's Critical Theory of Religion: The Meaning of Religion in the Struggle for Human Emancipation.* Lanham/New York/Oxford: University Press of America.

Paassen, Pierre and Wise, James Waterman. 1934. *Nazism: An Assault on Civilization.* New York: Harrison Smith and Robert Haas.

Pagels, Elaine. 2004 [1979]. *The Gnostic Gospels.* New York: Random House.

Pagels, Elaine. 1989. *Adam, Eve, and the Serpent.* New York: Vintage Books.

Papes, Richard. 2005. *Dying to Win: The Strategic Logic of Suicide Terrorism.* New York: Random House.

Parkes, C. M., P. Laungani, and B. Young. 1997. "Culture and Religion." Pp. 10–23 in *Death and Bereavement Across Cultures*, edited by C. M. Parkes, P. Laungani, B. Young. New York: Routledge.

Parsons, Talcott. 1991 [1951]. *The Social System.* New York: Routledge.

Parsons, Talcott. 1965. *Societies: Evolutionary and Comparative Perspectives.* Englewood Cliffs, NJ: Prentice Hall, Inc.

Parsons, Talcott. 1964. *The System of Modern Societies.* Englewood Cliffs, NJ: Prentice Hall, Inc.

Petras, James and Henry Veltmeyer. 2005. "Foreign Aid, Neoliberalism and U.S. Imperialism." Pp. 120–126 in *Neoliberalism: A Critical Reader,* edited by Alfredo Saad-Filho and Deborah Johnston. Ann Arbor, MI: Pluto Press.

Petras, James and Henry Veltmeyer. 2001. *Globalization Unmasked: Imperialism in the 21st. Century.* Halifax, Nova Scotia: Fernwood Publishing Ltd.

Popper, Karl. R. 1967. *The Open Society.* New York: Harper Publishers.

Popper, Karl. R. 1961. *The Poverty of Historicism.* New York: Harper Publishers.

Postone, Moishe. 1993. *Time, Labor, and Social Domination: A Reinterpretation of Marx's Critical Theory.* Cambridge, UK: Cambridge University Press.

Prawer, S. S. 1976. *Karl Marx and World Literature.* Oxford: Clarendon Press.

Preus, James S. 1987. *Explaining Religion.* New Haven, CT: Yale University Press.

Prinz, A. M. 1969. "Background and Ulterior Motives of Marx's 'Preface' of 1859." *Journal of the History of Ideas* 30(3): 437–450.

Radice, Hugo. 2005. "Neoliberal Globalisation: Imperialism without Empires?" Pp. 91–98 in *Neoliberalism: A Critical Reader,* edited by Alfredo Saad-Filho and Deborah Johnston. Ann Arbor, MI: Pluto Press.

Raphael, Freddy. 1981. "Die Juden als Gastvolk im Werk Max Webers." Pp. 224–262 in *Max Weber's Studie über das Antike Judentum*, edited by Wolfgang Schluchter. Frankfurt am Main: Suhrkamp Verlag.

Rauschning, Hermann. 1940. *Gespräch mit Hitler.* New York: Europa Verlag.

Rawls, Anne Warfield. 2005. *Epistemology and Practice: Durkheim's Elementary Forms.* Cambridge, MA: Cambridge University Press.

Rawls, Anne Warfield. 2003a. "Orders of Interaction and Intelligibility: Intersections Between Goffman and Garfinkel by Way of Durkheim," in *Goffman's Legacy*, edited by Javier Trevino. Boulder, CO: Rowman and Littlefield.

Rawls, Anne Warfield. 2003b. "Conflict as a Foundation for Consensus: Contradictions of Industrial Capitalism in Book III of Durkheim's Division of Labor." *Critical Sociology* 29(3): 295–335.

Rawls, Anne Warfield. 2002. "Editor's Introduction." *Ethnomethodology's Program: Working Out Durkheim's Aphorism*. Boulder: Rowman and Littlefield.

Rawls, Anne Warfield. 2001. "Durkheim's Treatment of Practice." *Journal of Classical Sociology* 1(1): 33–68.

Rawls, Anne Warfield. 1987. "The Interaction Order Sui Generis: Goffman's Contradiction to Social Theory." *Sociological Theory* 5(2): 136–149.

Regnault, Felix. 1933. "Les Maladies de Karl Marx." *Revue Anthropologique* 43.

Reinhardt, Mark. 1997. *The Art of Being Free: Taking Liberties with Tocqueville, Marx, and Arendt*. Ithaca, NY & London: Cornell University Press.

Reuten, Geert. 2000. "The Interconnection of Systematic Dialectics and Historical Materialism." *Historical Materialism* 7: 137–166.

Riker, William. 1990. "Political Science and Rational Choice." in *Perspectives on Positive Political Economy*, edited by James Alt & Kenneth Shepsle. Cambridge: Cambridge University Press.

Riley, Gregory J. 2001. *The River of God: A New History of Christian Origins*. New York: HarperCollins.

Rissmann, Michael. 2001. *Hitler's Gott: Vorsehungsglaube und Sendungsbewusstsein eines Diktators*. Zürich/München: Piper Verlag.

Roberts, William Clare. 2003. "Marx Contra the Democrats: The Force of *The Eighteenth Brumaire*." *Strategies: Journal of Theory, Culture & Politics* 16:1: 51–64.

Rodinson, Maxime. 1974. *Islam and Capitalism*. London: Allen Lane.

Rojo, Sergio Vuscovic. 1988. "La religion, opium du peuple et protestation contre la misère réele: Les positions de Marx et de Lénine." *Social Compass* 35(2–3): 197–230.

Roof, Wade Clark and William McKinney. 1987. *American Mainline Religion: Its Changing Shape and Future*. New Brunswick, NJ: Rutgers University Press.

Rosenbaum, R. 1999. *Die Hitler Debatte: Explaining Hitler*. München/Wien: Europa Verlag.

Roy, Oliver. 1994. *The Failure of Political Islam*. Cambridge: Harvard University Press.

Runciman, Steven. 1990. *The Fall of Constantinople, 1453*. Cambridge: Cambridge University Press.

Runciman, Steven. 1987. *A History of the Crusades: Volume 1: The First Crusade and the Foundation of the Kingdom of Jerusalem*. Cambridge: Cambridge University Press.

Ryan, W. F. 1999. *The Bathhouse at Midnight: Magic in Russia*. University Park, PA: Pennsylvania State University Press.

Scatamburlo, Valerie and Lauren Langman. 2001. "Fanon Speaks to Subaltern" *Current Perspectives in Social Theory* 20: 253–286.

Scheff, Thomas J. 1994. *Bloody Revenge: Emotions, Nationalism, and War*. Boulder: Westview Press.

Scheible, Hartmut. 1989. *Theodor W. Adorno*. Reinbeck bei Hamburg: Rowohlt Verlag.

Schiper, I. 1959. "Max Weber on the Sociological Basis of the Jewish Religion." *Jewish Journal of Sociology* 1: 250–260.

Schluchter, Wolfgang. 1999. "Hindrances to Modernity, Max Weber and Islam." Pp. 53–138 in *Max Weber and Islam*, edited by Toby Huff and Wolfgang Schluchter. New Brunswick, N.J.: Transaction.

Schluchter, Wolfgang. 1989. *Rationalism, Religion, and Domination: A Weberian Perspective*. trans. Neil Solomon. Berkeley: University of California Press.

Schluchter, Wolfgang. 1985. "Einleitung: Max Webers Analyse des antiken Christentum Grundzüge eines unvollendeten Projekts." Pp. 11–71 in *Max Webers Sicht des antiken Christentums*, edited by Wolfgang Schluchter. Frankfurt am Main: Suhrkamp Verlag.

Schluchter, Wolfgang. 1981. "Altisraelistische religiöse Ethik und okzidentaler Rationalismus." Pp. 11–77 in *Max Webers Studie über das Antike Judentum*, edited by Wolfgang Schluchter. Frankfurt am Main: Suhrkamp Verlag.

Schmidt, Alfred. 1981. *Kritische Theorie: Humanismus. Aufklarung*. Stuttgart: Philipp reclam.

Schmidt, Alfred. 1981a. *History and Structure: An Essay on Hegelian-Marxist and Structuralist Theories of History*. trans. Jeffrey Herf. Cambridge, MA: MIT Press.

Schmidt, Alfred and Norbert Altwicker. 1986. *Max Horkheimer heute: Werk und Wirkung*. Frankfurt am Main: Fischer Verlag.

Scholem, Gershom. 1989. *The Correspondence of Walter Benjamin and Gershom Scholem. 1932–1940*. New York: Schocken Books.

Scholem, Gershom. 1977. *Von Berlin nach Jerusalem*. Frankfurt am Main: Suhrkamp Verlag.

Scholem, Gershom. 1973. *Zur Kabbala und ihrer Symbolik*. Frankfurt am Main: Suhrkamp Verlag.

Scholem, Gershom. 1957. *Die jüdische Mystik in ihren Hauptströmungen*. Zürich: Rhein Verlag AG.

Schopenhauer, Arthur. 1989. *Parerga und Paralipomena II: Sämtliche Werke*. Frankfurt am Main: Suhrkamp Verlag.

Schornick, Andrew. 1996. *The Anti-Semitism of Father Coughlin and the End of his Radio Career* (unpublished research paper, Detroit).

Schuster, Ekkehard and Reinhold Boschert-Kimmig. 1993. *Trotzdem hoffen: Mit Johann Baptist Metz und Elie Wiesel im Gespräch*. Mainz: Matthias Grünewald Verlag.

Schweppenhäuser, Gerhard. 1996. *Theodor W. Adorno zur Einführung*. Hamburg: Junius Verlag.

Seery, John Evan. 1990. *Political Returns: Irony in Politics and Theory from Plato to the Antinuclear Movement*. Boulder, CO: Westview Press.

Seligman, Adam. 2000. *The Problem of Trust*. Princeton: Princeton University Press.

Sen, Amartya K. 1977. "Rational Fools: A Critique of the Behavioral Foundations of Economic Theory." *Philosophy & Public Affairs* 6(4): 317–344.

Seznec, Jean. 1995 [1953]. *The Survival of the Pagan Gods: The Mythological Tradition and Its Place in Renaissance Humanism and Art*. Princeton: Princeton University Press.

Shakespeare, William. 1963 [c. 1601]. *The Tragedy of Hamlet Prince of Denmark*. New York: Signet Classics.

Sharot, Stephen. 2002. "Beyond Christianity: A Critique of the Rational Choice Theory of Religion from a Weberian and Comparative Religions Perspective." *Sociology of Religion*, 36(4): 427–454.

Shmueli, Efraim. 1968. "The Pariah People and its Charismatic Leadership: A reevaluation of Max Weber's Ancient Judaism" in *Proceedings – American Academy for Jewish Research* 36: 167–247.

Siebert, J. Rudolf. 2005. "The Critical Theory of Society: The Longing for the Totally Other" *Critical Sociology* 31(1–2): 57–113.

Siebert, J. Rudolf. 2002. *From Critical Theory to Communicative Political Theology: Personal Autonomy and Universal Solidarity*. New York/Bern/Frankfurt am Main/Paris: Peter Lang.

Siebert, J. Rudolf. 2001. *The Critical Theory of Religion: The Frankfurt School*. Lanham/Maryland/London: The Scarecrow Press, Inc.

Siebert, J. Rudolf. 1995. "There is a World beyond Kalamazoo. Biographical Story. From Frankfurt through Kalamazoo to Dubrovnik and Yalta," in *Grass Roots Review* 5 (Spring).

Siebert, J. Rudolf. 1993. *Recht, Macht und Liebe. Georg W. Rudolphi's Prophetische Politische Theologie*. Frankfurt am Main: Haag-Herchen Verlag.

Siebert, J. Rudolf. 1987. *Horkheimer's Critical Sociology of Religion: The Relative and the Transcendent*. Washington D.C.: University Press of America.

Sklair, Leslie. 2001. *The Transnational Capitalist Class*. Oxford: Blackwell.

Smellie, William, ed. 1771. *Encyclopædia Britannica, or, A dictionary of arts and sciences, compiled upon a new plan: in which the different sciences and arts are digested into distinct treatises or systems, and the various technical terms, &c. are explained as they occur in the order of the alphabet*. Edinburgh: Printed for A. Bell and C. Macfarquhar and sold by Colin Macfarquhar.

Smith, Jonathan Z. 1998. "Religion, religions, religious." in *Critical Terms for Religious Studies*, edited by Mark C. Taylor. Chicago: University of Chicago Press.

Smith, Jonathan Z. 1990. *Drudgery Divine: On the Comparisons of Early Christianities and the Religions of Late Antiquity*. Chicago: University of Chicago Press.

Smith, Wilfred Cantwell. 1978. *The Meaning and End of Religion*. New York: Harper & Row.

Smith, Wilfred Cantwell. 1963. *The Meaning and End of Religion*. San Francisco: Harper & Row.

Sölle, Dorothee. 1989. *Leiden*. Marburg: Kreuz Verlag.

Solomon, N. 1996. *Judaism: A Very Short Introduction*. Oxford: University Press.

Soucek, Priscilla. 1997. "Byzantium and the Islamic East." *The Glory of Byzantium*, edited by Helen C. Evans and William D. Wixom. New York: The New York Metropolitan Museum of Art/Harry N. Abrams, Inc.

Spickard, James V. 1998. "Rethinking Religious Social Action: What is 'Rational' About Rational-Choice Theory?" *Sociology of Religion* 59(2): 99–115.

Spiro, Melford E. 1966. "Religion: Problems of definition and explanation." *Anthropological Approaches to the Study of Religion*, edited by M. Banton. London: Tavistock.

Stark, Rodney. 2001. *One True God: Historical Consequences of Monotheism*. Princeton, NJ: Princeton University Press.

Stark, Rodney. 1997. *The Rise of Christianity: How the Obscure, Marginal Jesus Movement Became the Dominant Religious Force in the Western World in a Few Centuries*. San Francisco: HarperSanFrancisco.

Stark, Rodney. 1997a. "Bringing Theory Back In." Pp. 3–23 in *Rational Choice Theory and Religion: Summary and Assessment*, edited by Lawrence A. Young. New York and London: Routledge.

Stark, Rodney. 1997b. "German and German-American Religiousness." *Journal for the Scientific Study of Religion* 36(2): 182–193.

Stark, Rodney. 1996. *The Rise of Christianity: A Sociologist Reconsiders History*. Princeton, NJ: Princeton University Press.

Stark, Rodney and William Sims Bainbridge. 1997. *The Rise of Christianity*. San Francisco: HarperCollins.

Stark, Rodney and William Sims Bainbridge. 1987. *A Theory of Religion*. New York and Bern: Peter Lang.

Stark, Rodney and William Sims Bainbridge. 1985. *The Future of Religion*. Berkeley: University of California Press.

Stark, Rodney and Roger Finke. 2000. *Acts of Faith: Explaining the Human Side of Religion*. Berkeley: University of California Press.

Stark, Rodney and Laurence R. Iannaccone. 1994. "A Supply-Side Reinterpretation of the 'Secularization' of Europe." *Journal for the Scientific Study of Religion* 33(3): 230–252.

Steinert, Heinz. 1989. *Adorno in Wien*. Frankfurt am Main: Fischer Verlag.

Stoddard, Lothrop. 1940. *Into the Darkness*. New York: Duell, Sloan and Pearce.

Stoker, Bram. 2003. *Dracula*. Revised Edition. New York: Penguin Books.

Stone, Ronald H. and Weaver, Mathew Lon. 1998. *Against the Third Reich*. Louisville, Kentucky: Westminster John Knox Press.

Stoyanov, Yuri. 2000. *The Other God: Dualistic Religions from Antiquity to the Cathar Heresy*. New Haven and London: Yale University Press.

Sutcliffe, Bob. 2002. "How Many Capitalisms? Historical Materialism in the Debates about Imperialism and Globalization." Pp. 40–58 in *Historical Materialism and Globalization*, edited by Mark Rupert and Hazel Smith. New York: Routledge.

Tabbaa, Yasser. 1986. "Bronze Shapes in Iranian Ceramics of the Twelfth and Thirteenth Centuries." *Muquarnas* 4: 98–113.

Taubes, Jacob. 1966. "Die Entstehung des jüdischen Pariavolkes: Ideologiekritische Noten zu Max Webers 'Gesammelte Aufsätze zur Religionsoziologie,' Bd. III, 'Das antike Judentum'." In *Max Weber: Gedächtnisschrift der Ludwig-Maximilian-Universität München zur 100. Wiederkehr seines Geburtstages 1964*. hrsg. v. Karl Engisch, Bernhard Pfister and Johannes Winckelmann. Berlin: Duncker & Humblot.

Taylor, Charles. 1989. *Sources of the Self: The Making of the Modern Identity*. Cambridge, Mass.: Harvard University Press.

Taylor, F. 1983. *The Goebbels Diaries 1939–1941*. New York: G. P. Putnam's Sons.

Taylor, Telforf. 1986. *Hitler's Secret Book*. New York: Bramhall House.

Theunissen, Michael. 1983. "Negativität bei Adorno." *Adorno-Konferenz*, edited by Ludwig von Friedeburg & Jürgen Habermas.

Theweleit, Klaus. 1987. *Male Fantasies.* Minneapolis: University of Minnesota Press.

Thomas, Thelma K. 1997. "Christians in the Islamic East." *The Glory of Byzantium,* edited by Helen C. Evans and William D. Wixom. New York: The New York Metropolitan Museum of Art/Harry N. Abrams, Inc.

Thomson, F. J. 1978. "The Nature of the Reception of Christian Byzantine Culture in Russia in the Tenth to Thirteenth Centuries and its Implication for Russian Culture." *Slavica Gandensia* 5: 107–139.

Tilton, Jeff Todd. 1978. "Some Recent Pentecostal Revivals: A Report in Words and Photographs." *Georgia Review* 32(3): 579–603.

Titus Livius (Livy). 1966 [c. 12 AD]. "History of Rome, I. i–vii, LCL." *Roman Civilization, Sourcebook I: The Republic,* edited by Naphtali Lewis and Meyer Reinhold. New York: Harper and Row.

Todenhofer, Juergen. 2003. *Wer weint schon um Abdul and Tanya? Die Irrtümer des Kreuzzugs gegen den Terrror.* Freiburg/Basel/Wien: Herder.

Trevor-Roper, Hugh. 1969. "The European Witch Craze of the Sixteenth and Seventeenth Centuries." *Essays.* Oxford: Oxford University Press.

Tucker, Robert C. 1978. *Marx-Engels Reader.* New York/London: W. W. Norton and Company.

Turcan, Robert. 1996. *The Cults of the Roman Empire.* Malden, MA: Blackwell Publishers.

Turner, Bryan. 1974. *Weber and Islam.* London: Henley and Boston.

Turner, Denys. 1991. "Religion: Illusion and Liberation." In *The Cambridge Companion to Marx,* edited by Terell Carver. New York: Cambridge University Press.

The United Nations Development Program and the Arab Fund for Economic and Social Development. 2002. *Human Development Report 2002.* New York: United Nations Publications.

Valentin, Hugo. 1936. *Antisemitism: Historically and Critically Examined.* New York: The Viking Press.

Vaughn, John. 1993. *Megachurches and American Cities: How Megachurches Grow.* Grand Rapids, MI: Baker Books.

Vryonis, Speros P. 1997. "Byzantine Society and Civilization." *The Glory of Byzantium,* edited by Helen C. Evans and William D. Wixom. New York: The New York Metropolitan Museum of Art/Harry N. Abrams, Inc.

Vryonis, Speros P. 1985. "The Impact of Hellenism: Greek Culture in the Moslem and Slav Worlds." *The Greek World: Classical, Byzantine, and Modern,* edited by Robert Browning. London: Verso Press.

Waite, Gary K. 2003. *Heresy, Magic, and Witchcraft in Early Modern Europe.* New York: Palgrave MacMillan.

Walter, Tony. 1997. "Secularization." Pp. 166–187 in *Death and Bereavement Across Cultures,* edited by C. M. Parkes, P. Laungani, & B. Young. New York: Routledge.

Walter, Tony. 1994. *The Revival of Death.* New York: Routledge.

Walter, Tony. 1991. "Modern Death – taboo or not taboo?" *Sociology* 25(2): 293–310.

Warner, R. Stephen. 1993. "Work in Progress Toward a New Paradigm for the Sociological Study of Religion in the United States." *American Journal of Sociology* 98: 1044–1093.

Warren, Donald. 1996. *Radio Priest Charles Coughlin, the Father of Hate Radio.* New York/London: The Free Press.

Watson, James L. 1988. "The Structure of Chinese Funerary Rites: Elementary Forms, Ritual Sequence, and the Primacy of Performance." Pp. 3–19 in *Death Ritual in Late Imperial and Modern China*, edited by James L. Watson and Evelyn S. Rawski. Berkeley: University of California Press.

Weber, Bernd. 1979. "'Hitlerwelle' und historisch-polotischer Unterricht." In *Frankfurter Hefte* 34/3/März.

Weber, Max. 2001 [1920]. *The Protestant Ethic and the Spirit of Capitalism*. Boston: Roxbury Publishing.

Weber, Max. 1978. *Economy and Society*. 2 Vols. edited by Guenther Roth and Claus Wittich. Berkeley: University of California Press.

Weber, Max. 1985. *Wirtschaft und Gesellschaft*. Tübingen: J. C. B. Mohr (Paul Siebeck).

Weber, Max. 1963. *The Sociology of Religion*. trans. Ephraim Fischoff. Boston: Beacon Press.

Weber, Max. 1952. *Ancient Judaism*. trans. Hans H. Gerth and Don Martindale. New York: The Free Press.

Weber, Max. 1921. *Gesammelte Aufsätze zur Religionssoziologie III*. Tübingen: J. C. B. Mohr (Paul Siebeck).

West, Thomas H. 1991. *Ultimate Hope without God: The Atheistic Eschatology of Ernst Bloch*. New York: Peter Lang.

White, James D. 1994. "Marx: From 'The Critique of Political Economy' to *Capital*." *Studies in Marxism* 1: 89–105.

Wiebe, Donald. 1998. *The Politics of Religious Studies: The Continuing Conflict with Theology in the Academy*. New York: St. Martin's Press.

Wilson, John and Harvey Clow. 1981. "Themes of Power and Control in a Pentecostal Assembly." *Journal for the Scientific Study of Religion* 20(3): 241–250.

Wilson, William Julius. 1987. *The Truly Disadvantaged: The Inner City, the Underclass, and Public Policy*. Chicago: The University of Chicago Press.

Witte, Bernd. 1985. *Walter Benjamin mit Selbstzeugnissen und Bilddokumenten*. Reinbeck bei Hamburg: Rowohlt Verlag.

Wolfart, Johannes. 2000. "Postmodernism." Pp. 380–395 in *Guide to the Study of Religion*, edited by Willi Braun and Russell T. McCutcheon. New York: Cassell.

Wolff, Robert Paul. 1988. *Moneybags Must Be So Lucky: On the Literary Structure of Capital*. Amherst, MA: University of Massachusetts Press.

Wood, Ellen Meiksins. 2002. "Global Capital, National States." Pp. 17–39 in *Historical Materialism and Globalization*, edited by Mark Rupert and Hazel Smith. New York: Routledge.

The Works of Josephus: Complete and Unabridged. 1987. New Updated Edition. trans. William Whiston. Peabody, MA: Hendrickson Publishers.

Wright, Bonnie. 2005 "'Discerning the Spirit' in the Context of Racial Integration and Conflict in Two Assemblies of God Churches." *Journal for the Theory of Social Behavior* 35(4): 413–435.

Wuthnow, Robert. 1988. *The Restructuring of American Religion*. Princeton: Princeton University Press.

Zerin, Eduard. 1998. "Karl Popper on God: The Lost Interview." *Skeptic* 6: 2.

Index